Ryan Ye

HOLT McDOUGAL

Discovering FRENCH Today!

FRENCH 1B
Deuxième partie

Jean-Paul Valette
Rebecca M. Valette

HOLT McDOUGAL

 HOUGHTON MIFFLIN HARCOURT

Teacher Reviewers

Paul Giles
Forsyth Central High School, Georgia

Thierry Gustave
Lincoln School, Rhode Island

David Miller
Davis High School, Utah

Teacher Panel

Linda Davisson
Wilbur Middle School, Kansas

Korey Dugger
Austin-East Magnet High School, Tennessee

Carolyn Fletcher
Bonita High School, California

Paul Giles
Forsyth Central High School, Georgia

Carole Lapointe-Prospère
West Roxbury High School, Massachusetts

Paul J. Maher
West Seneca East Senior High School, New York

Ann Minor
St. Andrew's Episcopal School, Mississippi

Dr. Mary Schense
Manzano High School, New Mexico

Martha Schillerstrom
Glenbard East High School, Illinois

Jennifer Schoenfeld
Lawton Community Schools, Michigan

Student Reviewers

Rebecca Lange
Washington

Donald Medor
Massachusetts

Teacher Review Board

Sue Arandjelovic
Dobson High School, Arizona

Kay Dagg
Washburn Rural High School, Kansas

Olga Davis
G.H. Englesby Junior High School, Massachusetts

Tina Dietrich
Washington Junior High School, Ohio

Rosine Gardner
Newcomb Central School, New York

Bill Price
Day Junior High School, Massachusetts

T. Jeffrey Richards
Roosevelt High School, South Dakota

Margie Ricks
Dulles High School, Texas

Valerie Sacks
Britton Middle School, California

Cover photography

Front Cover ©Patrice Coppee/Workbook Stock/Getty Images
Back Cover Level 1a: ©David Noble/Travel Pictures; Level 1b: ©Patrice Coppee/Workbook Stock/Getty Images; Level 1: ©Travelpix Ltd/Stone/Getty Images; Level 2: ©David Sanger/The Image Bank/Getty Images; Level 3: ©Shaen Adey/Gallo Images/Getty Images

Printed in the U.S.A.

ISBN 978-0-547-87277-3

8 9 10 0868 20 19 18 17 16

4500624034 A B C D E F G

Reprise

Bonjour 2

THÈME Getting reacquainted

DIGITAL FRENCH
my.hrw.com

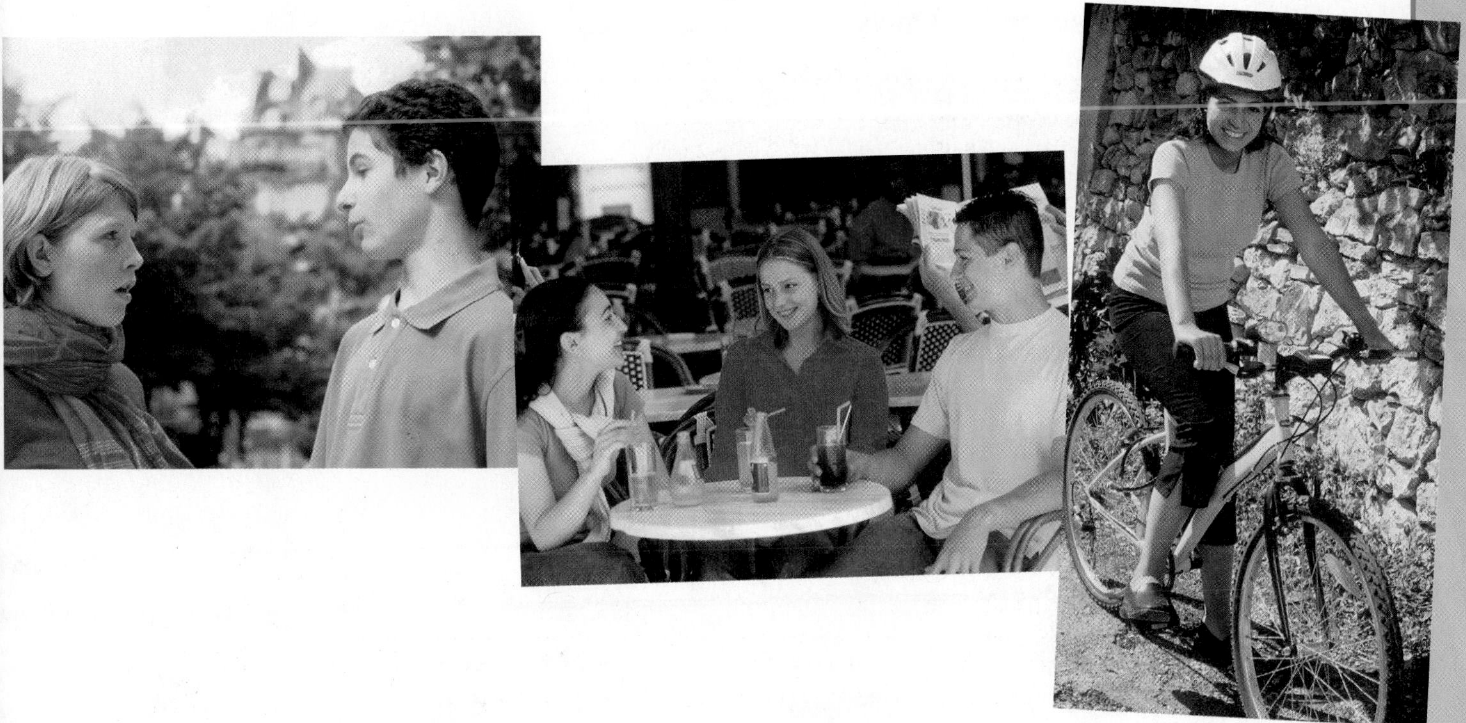

Unité 5

En ville

THÈME Visiting a French City

DIGITAL FRENCH
my.hrw.com

Unité 6

Le shopping 254

THÈME Buying clothes

DIGITAL FRENCH
my.hrw.com

Unité 7

Le temps libre 306

THÈME Leisure time activities

DIGITAL FRENCH
my.hrw.com

librairie
DIGITAL FRENCH
my.hrw.com

Unité 8

THÈME Food and meals

DIGITAL FRENCH
my.hrw.com

Reference Section

DIGITAL FRENCH
my.hrw.com

Bonjour, la France!

CONNAISSEZ-VOUS LA FRANCE? *(Do you know France?)*

- In area, France is the second-largest country in Western Europe. It is smaller than Texas, but bigger than California.
- Geographically, France is a very diversified country, with the highest mountains in Europe (**les Alpes** and **les Pyrénées**) and an extensive coastline along the Atlantic (**l'océan Atlantique**) and the Mediterranean (**la Méditerranée**).
- France consists of many different regions which have maintained their traditions, their culture, and — in some cases — their own language. Some of the traditional provinces are Normandy and Brittany (**la Normandie** and **la Bretagne**) in the west, Alsace (**l'Alsace**) in the east, Touraine (**la Touraine**) in the center, and Provence (**la Provence**) in the south.

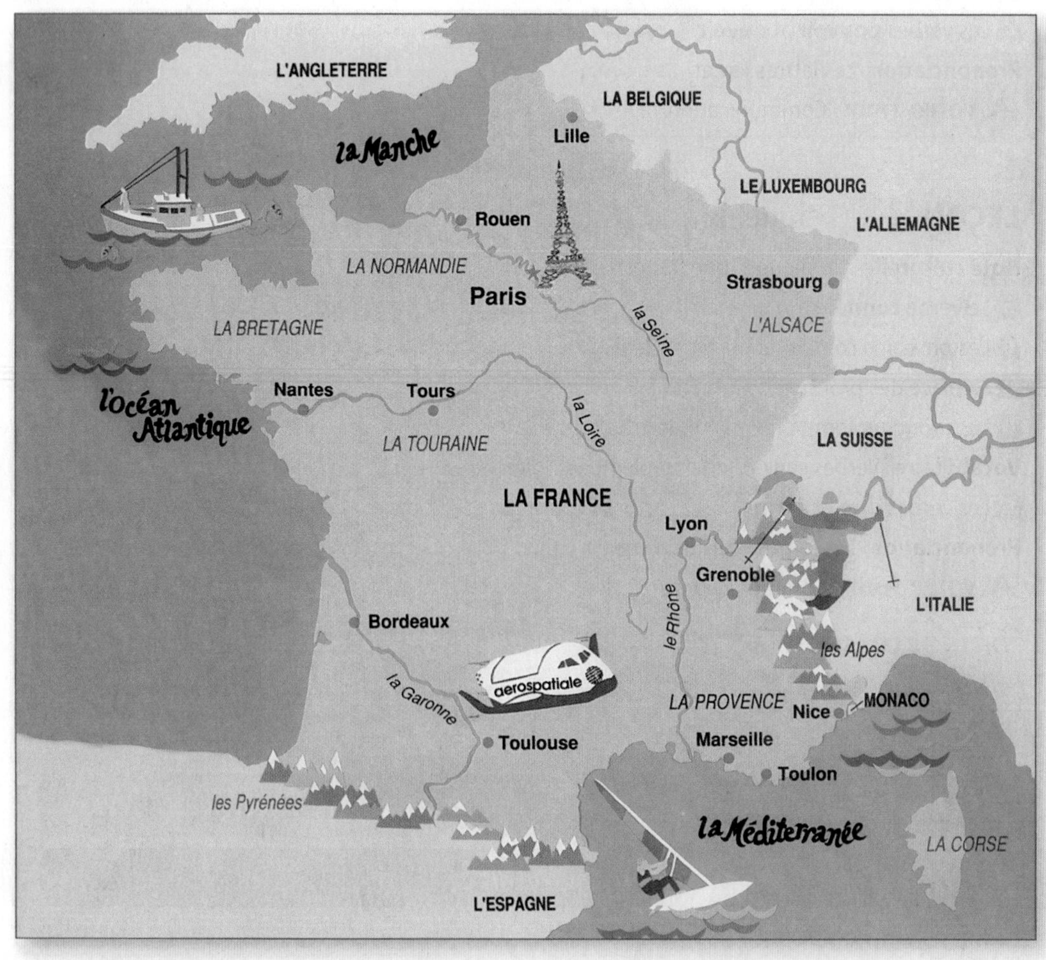

Paris: Montmartre
Paris, the capital of France, is also its economic, intellectual, and artistic center. For many people, Paris is the most beautiful city in the world.

Snowboarding in the Alps
During winter vacation, many French young people enjoy snowboarding or skiing. The most popular destinations are the Alps and the Pyrenees.

Château de Chenonceau
The long history of France is evident in its many castles and monuments. This chateau, built in the 16th century, attracts nearly one million visitors a year.

Home in Provence
The French love flowers and take pride in making their homes beautiful. This house is built in the traditional style of Provence, a region in southern France.

Bonjour, le monde francophone!

CANADA
About one-third of the population speaks French. These French speakers live mainly in the province of Quebec (**le Québec**). They are descendants of French settlers who came to Canada in the 17th and 18th centuries.

HAITI
Haïti is the first Black Republic. Its people speak Creole and French.

MARTINIQUE AND GUADELOUPE
These two Caribbean islands (**la Martinique** and **la Guadeloupe**) are part of France. Their inhabitants, primarily of African ancestry, are French citizens.

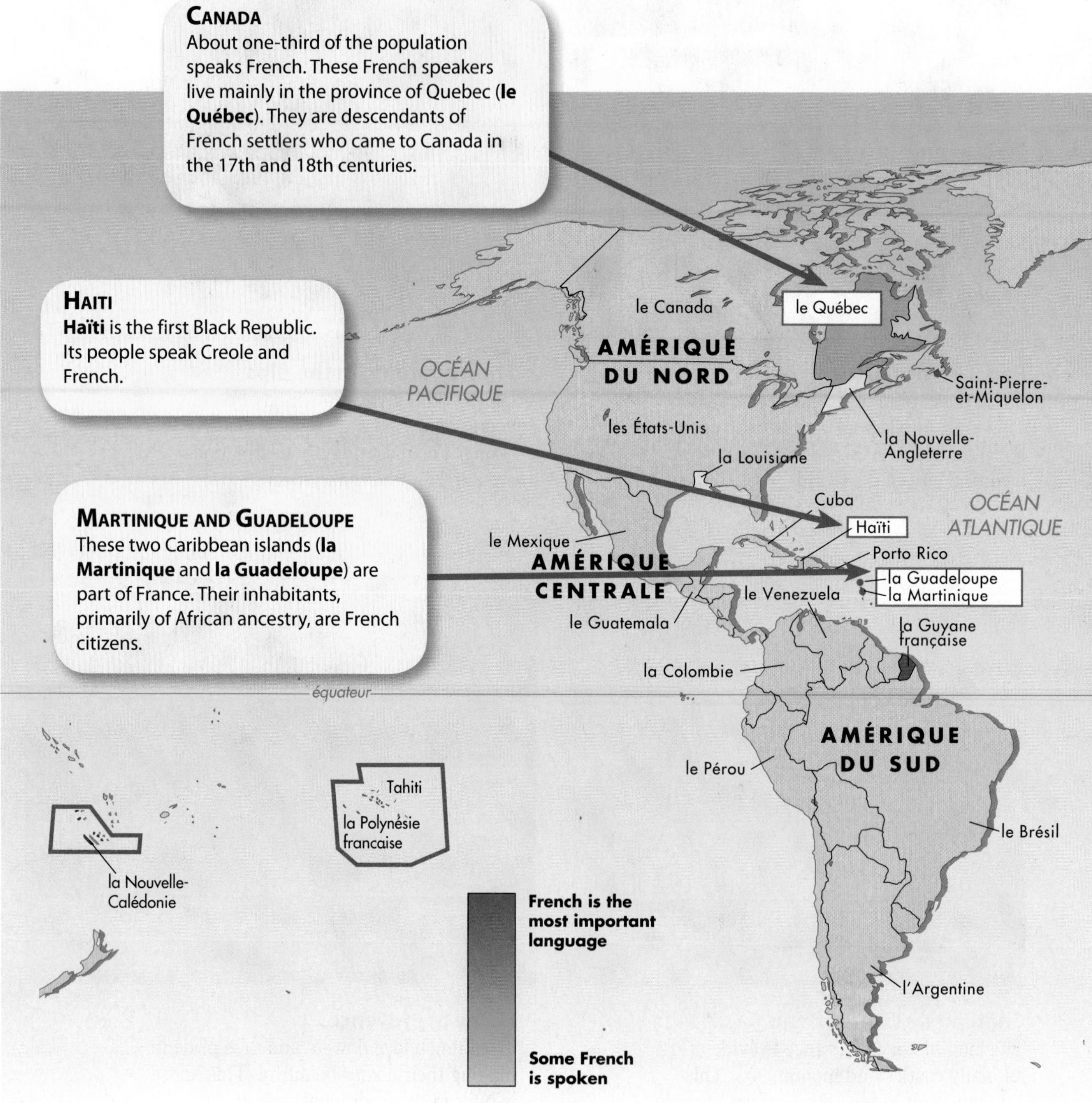

EUROPE
French is spoken in parts of Belgium (**la Belgique**), Switzerland (**la Suisse**), and Luxembourg (**le Luxembourg**).

NORTH AFRICA
French is understood and spoken by many people of Algeria (**l'Algérie**), Morocco (**le Maroc**), and Tunisia (**la Tunisie**). More than two million people from these countries have emigrated to France and have become French citizens.

WESTERN AND CENTRAL AFRICA
About twenty African countries have adopted French as their official language. These countries include Senegal (**le Sénégal**), the Ivory Coast (**la Côte d'Ivoire**), and the Democratic Republic of Congo (**la République démocratique du Congo**). French is also spoken on the large island of Madagascar (**Madagascar**).

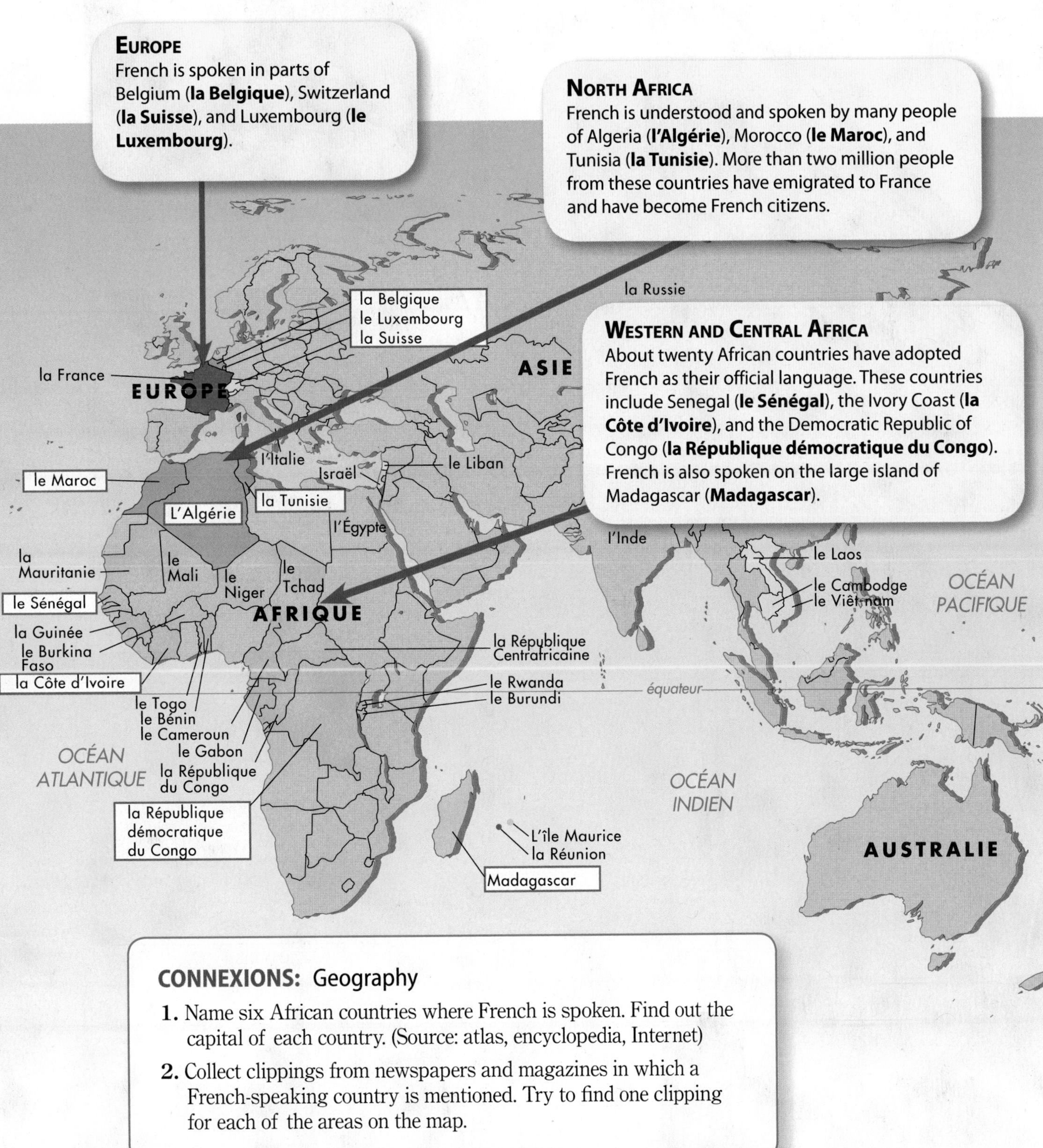

CONNEXIONS: Geography

1. Name six African countries where French is spoken. Find out the capital of each country. (Source: atlas, encyclopedia, Internet)
2. Collect clippings from newspapers and magazines in which a French-speaking country is mentioned. Try to find one clipping for each of the areas on the map.

Bonjour!

We hope that you had a relaxing summer vacation and we would like to welcome you back to ***Discovering French Today!*** This year you will learn how to carry out longer conversations in French: talking about your family and discussing things you plan to do. You will learn how to go shopping for clothes and discuss fashions, how to go shopping for food and order in a restaurant. You will also learn how to talk about things you did yesterday or last week or last month.

First, however, you will probably want to review what you learned last year. The opening section, which we call *Reprise,* gives you the opportunity to get to know your classmates and refresh your French. You may also want to familiarize yourself with the review charts and summaries in Appendix A on pages R1–R8. Finally, the *Le savez-vous?* section lets you see how much you remember about French and francophone culture around the world.

Once you feel comfortable hearing and speaking French again, you will continue with the new lessons, each accompanied by video segments which introduce you to French young people and how they live their daily lives.

We trust that as the year progresses you will find it both fun and exciting to communicate more effectively in French and to learn more about the French-speaking world.

Bonne chance!

Jean-Paul Valette Rebecca M. Valette

Reprise

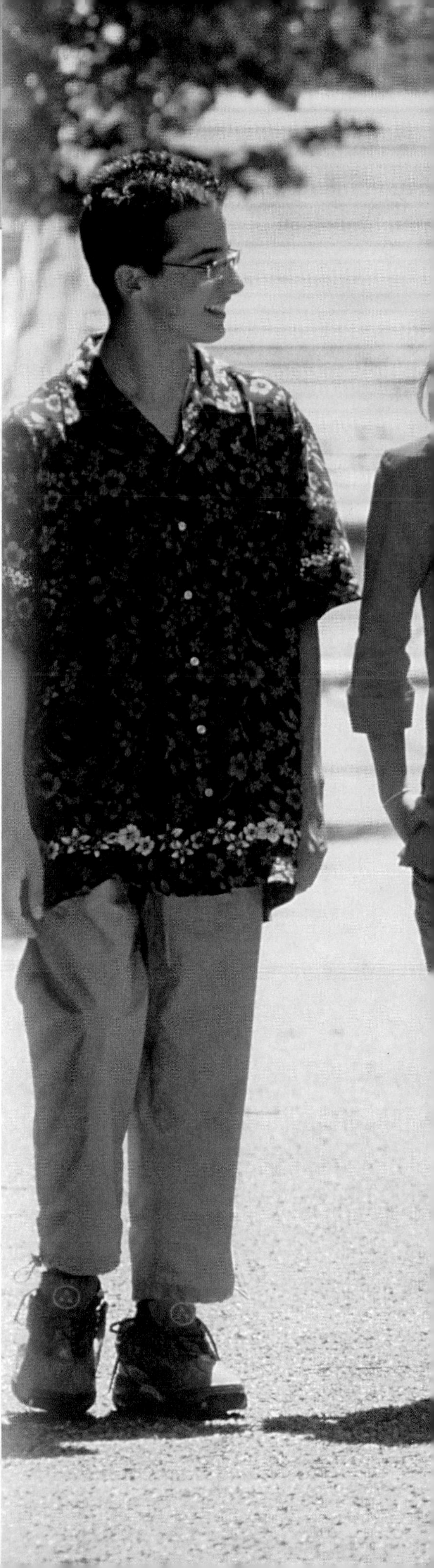

Bonjour!

RAPPEL 1 Les personnes

RAPPEL 2 Les choses de la vie courante

RAPPEL 3 Les activités

RAPPEL 4 Expressions de tous les jours

LE SAVEZ-VOUS?

THÈME ET OBJECTIFS

Getting Reacquainted

In **Reprise**, you will become reacquainted with the French-speaking world: its people, its culture, its language.

In this opening unit, you will have the opportunity to brush up on your French skills. In particular, you will practice . . .

- describing yourself and others
- talking about your possessions and your room
- asking and answering questions about what people are doing
- expressing your preferences
- extending and accepting (or turning down) invitations
- ordering food in a café

In addition, you will review . . .

- how to count
- how to give the date and tell time
- how to talk about the weather

DIGITAL FRENCH my.hrw.com
ONLINE STUDENT EDITION with...

performance space
News Networking
@HOMETUTOR

- Audio Resources
- Video Resources
- Interactive Flashcards
- WebQuest

PRACTICE FRENCH WITH HOLT MCDOUGAL APPS!

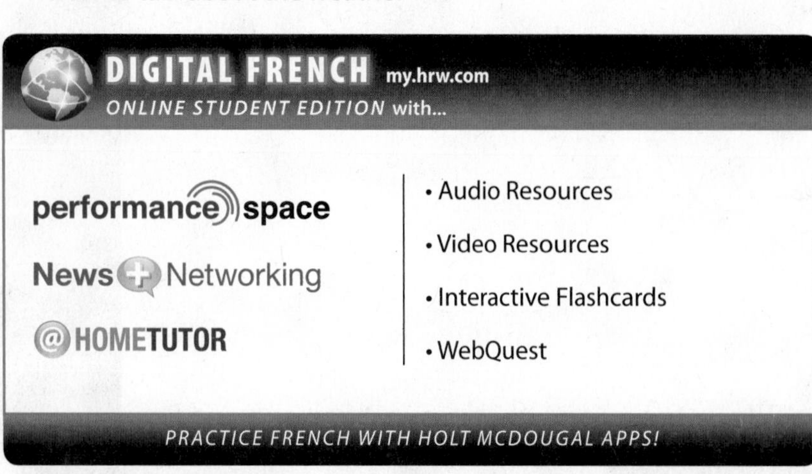

Bonjour!

Bonjour!

Je m'appelle Amélie Blanchard et j'ai quinze ans. J'habite avec ma famille à Orléans, une ville° située à 100 (cent) kilomètres de Paris. J'ai un frère, mais je n'ai pas de soeur. Mon frère s'appelle Jean-Marc. Il a neuf ans et il est très pénible!

J'aime beaucoup les animaux. J'ai un canari, un chat et un chien. Mon chien s'appelle Attila, mais il est très gentil. (Il est beaucoup plus gentil que° mon petit frère.)

J'aime beaucoup la musique, en particulier le rock et le rap.

Je suis sportive. Mes sports préférés sont le snowboard et le tennis. Je joue bien (mais je ne suis pas une championne!).

En classe, je suis une assez bonne élève, excepté en maths où ça ne va pas très bien. Mes matières préférées sont l'anglais et l'espagnol. Je parle assez bien ces° deux langues. (Aujourd'hui, il est important de parler plusieurs° langues si on° veut avoir un bon travail.°)

J'adore voyager. Un jour, je voudrais visiter les États-Unis et aussi le Mexique.

Salut!

Je m'appelle Jean-Philippe Jamin. J'ai seize ans et j'habite à la Guadeloupe avec ma famille. J'ai une petite soeur et un grand frère. Ma petite soeur a six ans. Elle s'appelle Claudine et elle est très mignonne. Mon frère s'appelle Thomas. Il n'habite pas avec nous. Il habite à Paris où il est étudiant en médecine.

Moi, je suis élève au lycée Baimbridge à Pointe-à-Pitre. Mes matières préférées sont les maths et l'informatique. Je voudrais être ingénieur.

J'aime les sports, en particulier le foot. Je joue dans un club amateur. J'aime aussi nager. Je nage très souvent parce qu'ici, à la Guadeloupe, il fait toujours beau.

ville *city* **plus gentil que** *nicer than* **ces** *those* **plusieurs** *several* **on** *one* **travail** *job*

Ça va?

Je m'appelle Martine Nguyen et j'ai quinze ans. Ma famille est d'origine vietnamienne, mais maintenant nous habitons en France, dans la région de Lyon.

J'ai un grand frère. Il s'appelle Guillaume et il est très sympa.° J'ai beaucoup d'amis. J'ai une bonne copine (c'est une voisine), mais je n'ai pas de copain.

J'aime la danse et la musique classique. J'aime aussi la nature. Le week-end, quand il fait beau, je fais des promenades en scooter dans la campagne° avec ma copine. Parfois,° je travaille dans le restaurant de mes parents. (C'est un restaurant vietnamien, bien sûr!) Et vous, qu'est-ce que vous faites le week-end?

sympa = sympathique **campagne** *countryside* **Parfois** *Sometimes*

À votre tour!

Of the three French teenagers who have introduced themselves, which one would you choose as a penpal? In a short paragraph, explain ...

- what you have in common with that person
- why you find him/her interesting.

Je voudrais correspondre avec Amélie. Elle a un petit frère. Moi, aussi, j'ai un petit frère. Il a 9 ans et ...

NOTE Culturelle

1 La France multi-culturelle

Although of different origins, Amélie, Jean-Philippe and Martine are typical French teenagers. France, like many modern countries, has a very diverse population which includes people of a great variety of cultural and ethnic backgrounds. Since France is located in Western Europe, the great majority of its citizens are of European, but not necessarily of French, origin. As a matter of fact, many French people claim Spanish, Italian or Polish ancestry. Because of various historical circumstances, France also has an ever-growing non-European population. These new French immigrants come primarily from North Africa (Algeria, Morocco, Tunisia), West Africa (Senegal, Mali, Ivory Coast, Chad), and Southeast Asia (Vietnam and Cambodia). And we should not forget the people of the Caribbean islands of Martinique and Guadeloupe, who are French citizens of African origin, and the people of Tahiti, also French citizens, who are Polynesian.

France is truly multi-ethnic and multi-cultural. The growing cultural diversity of its population makes it a richer and more interesting country. As the French people say: "Vive la différence!"

Pierre - un jeune de la Guadeloupe

2 La Guadeloupe

Like Martinique, Guadeloupe is a Caribbean island which is part of the French national territory. Its inhabitants, who are mostly of African ancestry, are therefore French citizens.

Et vous?

Maintenant, parlez de vous. Pour cela, complétez les phrases avec l'une des expressions suggérées ou une expression de votre choix.

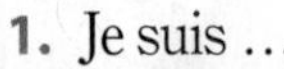

1. Je suis …
   - américain(e)
   - canadien(ne)
   - français(e)
   - ?

2. J'ai …
   - 13 ans
   - 14 ans
   - 15 ans
   - ?

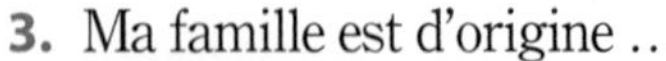

3. Ma famille est d'origine …
   - européenne
   - africaine
   - hispanique
   - asiatique
   - amérindienne *(native American)*
   - mixte
   - ?

4. J'ai …
   - un frère
   - une soeur
   - un frère, mais pas de soeur
   - ?

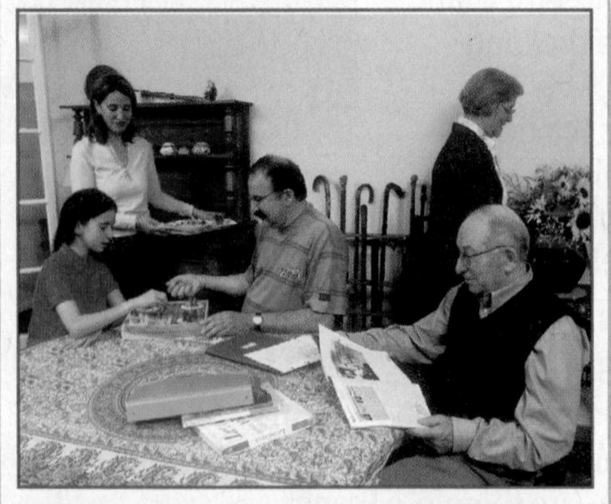

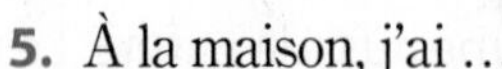

5. À la maison, j'ai …
   - un chien
   - un chat
   - un canari
   - un hamster
   - un poisson rouge
   - *(goldfish)*
   - un lapin *(rabbit)*
   - ?

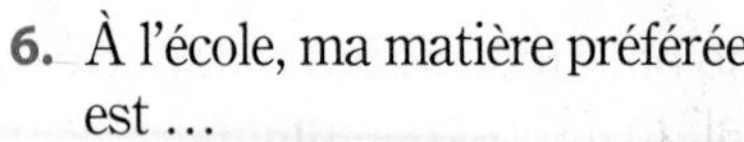

6. À l'école, ma matière préférée est …
   - l'histoire
   - l'anglais
   - le français
   - les maths
   - les sciences
   - ?

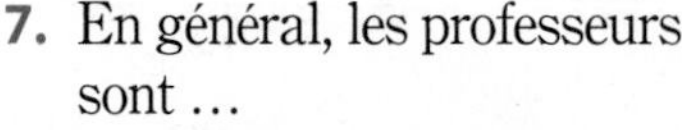

7. En général, les professeurs sont …
   - sympathiques
   - intéressants
   - stricts
   - justes *(fair)*
   - ?

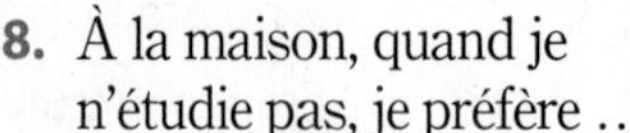

8. À la maison, quand je n'étudie pas, je préfère …
   - regarder la télé
   - jouer aux jeux vidéo
   - téléphoner à mes copains
   - aider *(help)* mes parents
   - ?

9. Quand je suis dans ma chambre, je préfère …
   - étudier
   - écouter la radio
   - lire *(read)* un livre
   - lire un magazine
   - ?

10. Ma musique préférée est …
    - le rock
    - le rap
    - la musique classique
    - ?

11. Pour mon anniversaire, je voudrais avoir …
    - un vélo
    - un portable
    - des vêtements
    - 2 billets pour
    - un concert
    - ?

12. Le week-end, je préfère dîner ...
    - à la maison
    - au restaurant avec ma famille
    - au restaurant avec mes copains
    - ?

13. Quand je suis au restaurant, je préfère manger ...
    - un hamburger
    - une pizza
    - une salade
    - ?

14. Mon sport préféré est ...
    - le basket
    - le baseball
    - le foot
    - le football américain
    - ?

15. Ma saison préférée est ...
    - l'automne
    - l'hiver
    - le printemps
    - l'été

16. Quand il fait beau, je préfère ...
    - nager
    - faire une promenade à vélo
    - faire du sport
    - rester *(stay)* à la maison
    - ?

17. En été, quand je suis en vacances, je préfère ...
    - travailler
    - étudier
    - rester *(stay)* à
    - la maison
    - voyager
    - ?

18. Un jour *(one day)*, je voudrais visiter ...
    - la France
    - le Mexique
    - le Canada
    - l'Afrique
    - ?

19. Pour moi, la chose la plus *(most)* importante dans la vie *(life)*, est de (d')...
    - avoir des amis sympathiques
    - faire des choses intéressantes
    - avoir un bon job
    - voyager beaucoup
    - ?

Rappel

1

Les personnes

 **RAPPEL**

In French, all nouns are MASCULINE or FEMININE, SINGULAR or PLURAL.

un frère **une** soeur **des** copains

Révision

If you need to review the forms of other words that introduce nouns, go to Appendix A, p. R1.

Révision

If you need to review the names of family members and other people, go to Appendix A, p. R2.

1 La famille de Véronique

PARLER/ÉCRIRE This picture was taken at a gathering of Véronique's family. Choose a member of the family (or a pet) and give his/her name. If you wish, you may describe the person (approximate age, other characteristics).

▶ **Le frère de Véronique s'appelle Thomas. Il a dix ans. Il est petit.**

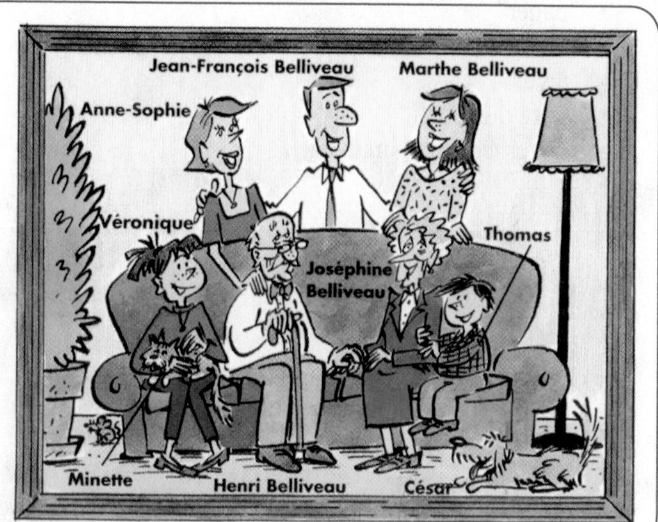

RAPPEL

ADJECTIVES agree with the NOUNS they describe.

Philippe est **grand.** Pauline est **grande.**

Révision

If you need to review the forms of descriptive adjectives, go to Appendix A, p. R1.

Révision

If you need to review adjectives describing common nationalities and physical traits, go to Appendix A, p. R2.

2 Le congrès des jeunes

PARLER/ÉCRIRE The following young people are representing their countries at an international youth conference. Choose one of the delegates. Give his/her nationality and a brief physical description.

▶ **Bob est américain. Il est blond. Il n'est pas très grand.**

3 Nationalités

PARLER/ÉCRIRE The following people live in the cities indicated in parentheses. Give each one's nationality.

▶ **(Acapulco) Teresa est mexicaine.**

1. (Rome) Mario et Silvia …
2. (Hong Kong) Madame Li …
3. (Genève) Nous …
4. (Madrid) Toi et José, vous …
5. (Zurich) Tu …
6. (Barcelone) Mes cousins …
7. (Liverpool) Ma tante …
8. (Beijing) Vous …

Révision

If you need to review the forms of **être**, go to Appendix A, p. R5.

RAPPEL

In French, adjectives usually come after the noun.

un garçon **sympathique** une fille **sportive**

Révision

If you want to review adjectives describing personality traits, go to Appendix A, p. R2.

4 Opinion personnelle

PARLER/ÉCRIRE Choose one of the following people and express your opinion about that person by using the suggested nouns and adjectives.

▶ **Whoopi Goldberg est une actrice amusante.**

mon copain	un garçon
ma copine	une fille
le/la prof	un homme
Matt Damon	une femme
Oprah Winfrey	une personne
Whoopi Goldberg	un acteur
Britney Spears	une actrice
Albert Einstein	
Harry Potter	
??	

▶ *How to ask someone's name and age:*

Comment t'appelles-tu? **Je m'appelle ...**	*What's your name?* *My name is ...*	**Je m'appelle Frédéric.**
Comment s'appelle ...?	*What's the name of ...*	**Comment s'appelle ta copine?**
[Comment s'appelle-t-il/elle?] **Il/elle s'appelle ...**	*What's his/her name?* *His/her name is ...*	**Elle s'appelle Sophie.**
Quel âge as-tu? **J'ai ... ans.**	*How old are you?* *I'm ... (years old).*	**J'ai seize ans.**
Quel âge a ...	*How old is ...?*	**Quel âge a ton frère?**
[Quel âge a-t-il/elle?] **Il/elle a ... ans.**	*How old is he/she?* *He/she is ... (years old).*	**Il a quinze ans.**

5 À votre avis *(In your opinion)*

PARLER Point to the pictures and ask your partner the name and age of each person.

Titi

Monsieur Lecourbe

Zoé

Madame Martin

Cédric

Révision

If you need to review numbers, go to Appendix A, p. R7.

À votre tour!

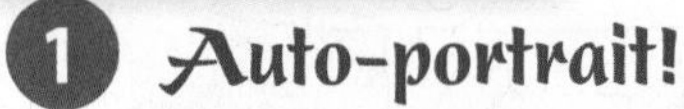

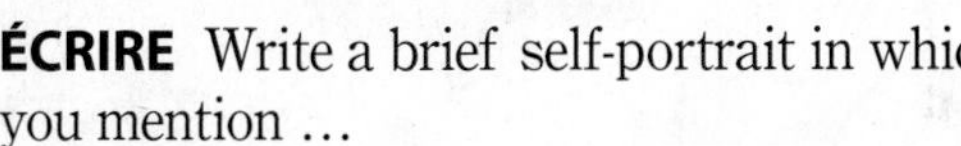

1 Auto-portrait!

ÉCRIRE Write a brief self-portrait in which you mention …

- your name
- your nationality
- your age
- 2 physical traits
- 2 personality traits that you have
- 1 personality trait that you do not have

2 Les amis parfaits

PARLER/ÉCRIRE Describe the perfect friends — one male and one female. List 5 traits for each friend, ranking them in order of importance. Compare your lists with those of your partner. Are you in agreement?

3 Famille

ÉCRIRE In a letter to your French penpal, describe your brothers and sisters (or cousins, if you prefer). You may also write about your pets.

- Say how many brothers and sisters (or cousins) you have.
- Write a short description of each one: age, physical and personality traits.
- Mention what pets you have (if any) and describe them.

4 Situations

PARLER Find a partner and imagine that the two of you are in the following situations. Prepare and act out the conversations.

1. At a party organized by the International Students' Club, you meet a teenager who speaks French. Ask this new person …
   - his/her name
   - how old he/she is
   - if he/she is French or Canadian
2. Your French friend is showing you photos of his/her family. You want to know more about his/her younger brother. Ask your friend …
   - the name of his/her brother
   - his age
   - if he is nice
3. You are looking for people to form a basketball team. Your friend mentions his/her neighbor as a possible candidate. Ask your friend …
   - how old his/her neighbor is
   - if he/she is tall or short
   - if he/she is athletic
4. During vacation, your cousin has met an interesting French teenager at the beach. Ask your cousin …
   - the name of his/her friend
   - if he/she is cute
   - if he/she is an interesting boy/girl

Rappel 2

Les choses de la vie courante

RAPPEL

In French, objects are MASCULINE or FEMININE.

They are introduced by **un, une** in the singular, or **des** in the plural.

un vélo **une** voiture **des** livres

Révision

If you need to review the names of common objects, go to Appendix A, p. R3.

RAPPEL

In NEGATIVE sentences, **un, une, des → de (d')**

J'ai un vélo. Je n'ai **pas de** moto. Je n'ai **pas d'**auto.

Révision

If you need to review colors, go to Appendix A, p. R4.

1 Mes possessions 

PARLER Ask if your partner has the following objects. (If the answer is yes, your partner may want to describe the object: its color, size, or other characteristics.)

▶ — **Tu as un appareil-photo?**
— **Oui, j'ai un appareil-photo. Il est noir. Il est japonais. Il marche assez bien. (Non, je n'ai pas d'appareil-photo.)**

▶     

2 Qu'est-ce qu'ils ont?

LIRE Read what the people below are doing, and say which objects they have. Be logical!

▶ Pauline fait un problème de maths.
Elle a une calculatrice.

1. Nous jouons au tennis.
2. Vous écoutez de la musique.
3. Philippe écrit *(is writing)* une lettre à une copine.
4. Mes parents font un voyage au Canada.
5. J'étudie la leçon.
6. Tu regardes une comédie.

Révision

If you need to review the forms of **avoir**, go to Appendix A, p. R6.

Quel objet?

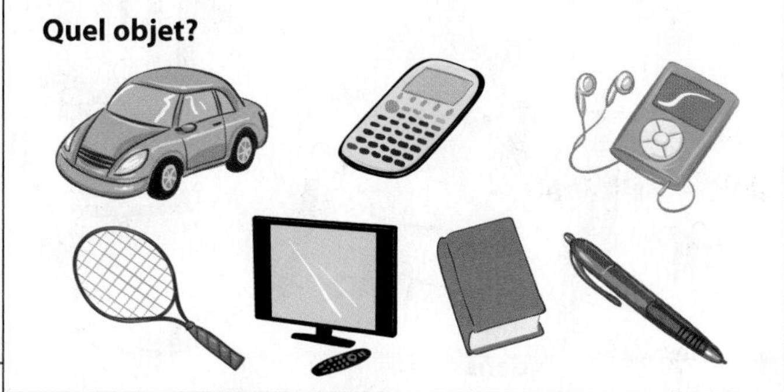

▶ *How to ask or say where things are:*

Qu'est-ce qu'il y a ...?	*What is there ...?*	**Qu'est-ce qu'il y a dans le garage?**
Il y a ...		**Il y a une voiture.**
Il n'y a pas ...		**Il n'y a pas de vélos.**
Est-ce qu'il y a ...?		**Est-ce qu'il y a une mobylette?**

3 Qu'est-ce qu'il y a ...?

PARLER/ÉCRIRE Identify at least four objects in each of the following illustrations.

Sur le bureau, il y a ...

Sur la table, ...

Dans la chambre, ...

Dans le sac, ...

▶ How to say where things are located:

4 La chambre d'Éric

PARLER Éric is not too orderly. Whenever he is looking for something, it is his sister Stéphanie who tells him where it is. With a partner, choose an object in the room and play the roles of Éric and Stéphanie.

ÉRIC: **Dis, Stéphanie, tu sais où est ma raquette?**
Stéphanie: **Ta raquette? Elle est dans le sac.**

À votre tour!

Digital performance space

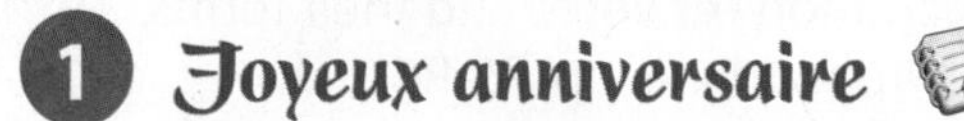

1 Joyeux anniversaire

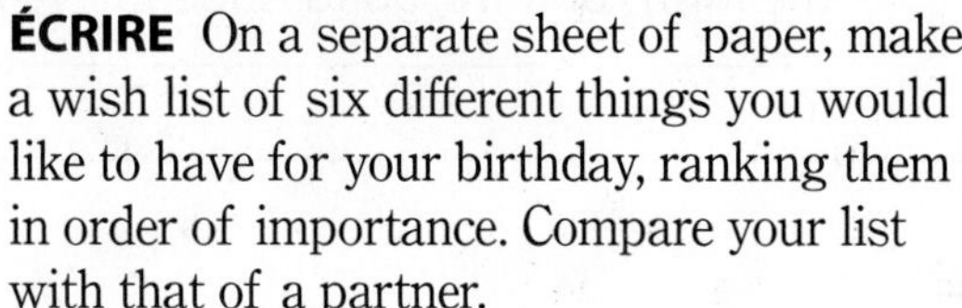

ÉCRIRE On a separate sheet of paper, make a wish list of six different things you would like to have for your birthday, ranking them in order of importance. Compare your list with that of a partner.

2 Ma chambre

ÉCRIRE Write a letter to a French penpal describing your room. You may want to mention …

- the size and color of your room
- the various items of furniture
- various objects that you have in your room and where they are located

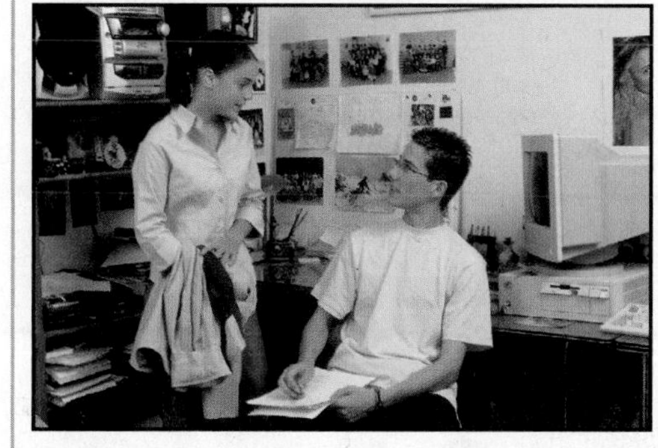

3 Situations

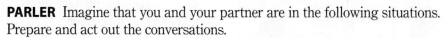

PARLER Imagine that you and your partner are in the following situations. Prepare and act out the conversations.

1. You are spending two weeks in France with a host family. A classmate has invited you to play tennis, but you don't have a racket. Ask Pierre, your "French brother," …

- if he has a racket
- if it is a good racket
- where the racket is (in his room? on his bed?)

2. You are with a host family in France and would like to listen to some music. Ask Sylvie, your "French sister," …

- if she has a MP3 player
- if it works well
- if she likes American music

Rappel 3

Les activités

 **RAPPEL**

To describe what people do, we use VERBS.

- Many French verbs end in **-er.**
- **Faire** *(to do, to make)* is an important verb to know.

Révision

If you need to review ...

- the common **-er** verbs and their forms, go to Appendix A, pp. R5-R6.
- the forms of **faire**, go to Appendix A, p. R5.

1 Qu'est-ce qu'ils font? PARLER

1. Est-ce qu'ils habitent à Paris ou à Québec?
2. Est-ce qu'ils dînent à la maison ou au restaurant?
3. Est-ce qu'ils mangent un steak-frites ou une omelette?

4. Est-ce que Catherine étudie l'anglais ou l'espagnol?
5. Est-ce qu'elle écoute la radio ou un lecteur MP3?
6. Est-ce qu'elle regarde la télé?

7. Est-ce qu'ils font un match de volley ou un match de tennis?
8. Est-ce que la fille joue bien ou mal?
9. Est-ce que le garçon fait attention?

RAPPEL

The most common way to ask a YES/NO QUESTION is to begin the sentence with **est-ce que.**

Est-ce que tu joues au foot?

RAPPEL

To make a sentence NEGATIVE, use the following pattern:

ne + VERB + **pas**	Je **ne** parle **pas** chinois.	Vous **ne** travaillez **pas.**
↓		
n' (+ VOWEL SOUND)	Je **n'**habite **pas** en France.	Nous **n'**étudions **pas.**

2 Conversation 

PARLER Ask your partner if he/she does the following activities. If your partner answers yes, ask a second question using the expression in parentheses.

▶ —Est-ce que tu joues au tennis?
—Oui, je joue au tennis!
—Est-ce que tu joues bien?
—Non, je ne joue pas bien.

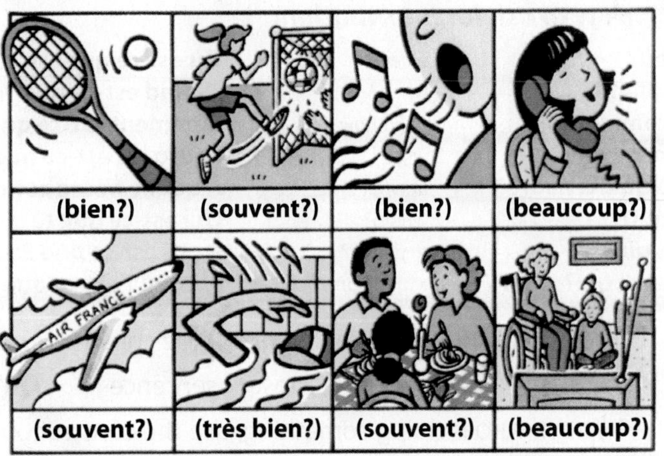

3 Oui ou non?

PARLER Say whether or not the people below are engaged in the following activities.

1. À la maison, **je ...**
- étudier beaucoup?
- téléphoner souvent?
- regarder la télé?

2. En classe, **nous ...**
- parler toujours français?
- écouter le prof?
- faire attention?

3. Le week-end, mes copains et moi, **nous ...**
- travailler?
- faire des promenades en ville?
- organiser des boums?

4. Mon copain/ma copine ...
- parler français?
- étudier l'espagnol?
- jouer au basket?

5. Quand je suis en vacances, **je ...**
- travailler?
- nager souvent?
- voyager?

6. En général, **les jeunes Américains ...**
- étudier beaucoup?
- aimer la musique classique?
- faire beaucoup de sport?

RAPPEL

To ask for SPECIFIC INFORMATION, you can use the following construction:
QUESTION WORD + **est-ce que** + rest of sentence
Où est-ce que tu habites? *Where do you live?*

▶ How to ask for information:

où?	*where?*	**Où est-ce que** ton copain habite?
quand?	*when?*	**Quand est-ce que** vous voyagez?
comment?	*how? how well?*	**Comment est-ce que** vous jouez au foot? bien ou mal?
pourquoi?	*why?*	**Pourquoi est-ce que** tu étudies le français?
à quelle heure?	*at what time?*	**À quelle heure est-ce que** nous dînons?
qui?	*whom?*	**Qui est-ce que** tu invites à la boum?
à qui?	*to whom?*	**À qui est-ce que** Pauline téléphone?
avec qui?	*with whom?*	**Avec qui est-ce que** vous jouez aux jeux vidéo?

→ to ask WHAT people are doing, use the construction:

qu'est-ce que + rest of sentence **Qu'est-ce que** tu fais demain?

→ To ask WHO is doing something, use the construction:

qui + verb **Qui** habite ici?

4 Faisons connaissance *(Let's get to know each other)*

PARLER Find out more about your classmates by asking them a few questions. Use the suggested cues.

- où? / habiter
- à quelle heure? / dîner
- quand? / regarder la télé
- à qui? / téléphoner souvent
- comment? / chanter
- avec qui? / parler français
- pourquoi? / étudier le français
- avec qui? / dîner au restaurant
- où? / jouer au basket
- où ?/ nager en été

▶ How to express what you like, want, can and must do:

Est-ce que tu aimes ...?		**Est-ce que tu peux ...?**	
J'aime ...	*I like ...*	**Je peux ...**	*I can, I am able to ...*
Je n'aime pas ...		**Je ne peux pas ...**	
Je préfère ...			
Est-ce que tu veux ...?		**Est-ce que tu dois ...?**	
Je veux ...	*I want ...*	**Je dois ...**	*I have to, I must ...*
Je ne veux pas ...			
Je voudrais ...	*I would like ...*	**Je ne dois pas ...**	

→ Note the use of **je veux bien** to answer an invitation.

—Est-ce que tu veux faire une promenade avec moi?

—Oui, **je veux bien.**

5 Et toi?

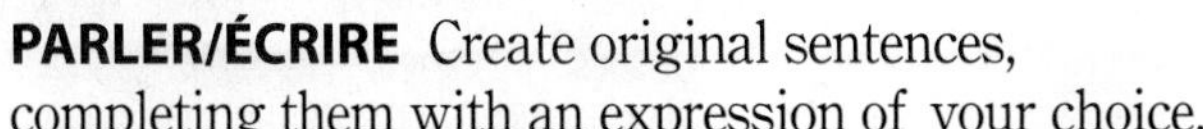

PARLER/ÉCRIRE Create original sentences, completing them with an expression of your choice.

En général, À la maison, En classe, Quand je suis avec mes amis, Quand je suis en vacances,	j'aime ... je n'aime pas ... je préfère ... je peux ... je ne peux pas ... je dois ...

6 Invitations

PARLER Invite your partner to do one of the following activities with you. If your partner accepts, he/she may ask for more details **(où? quand? à quelle heure?)**. If he/she does not accept, ask why and your partner will give you an excuse.

▶ **—Est-ce que tu veux jouer au tennis avec moi?**
—Oui, je veux bien! Quand?
—Samedi après-midi.

[Non, je ne peux pas.
—Pourquoi?
—Je dois étudier.]

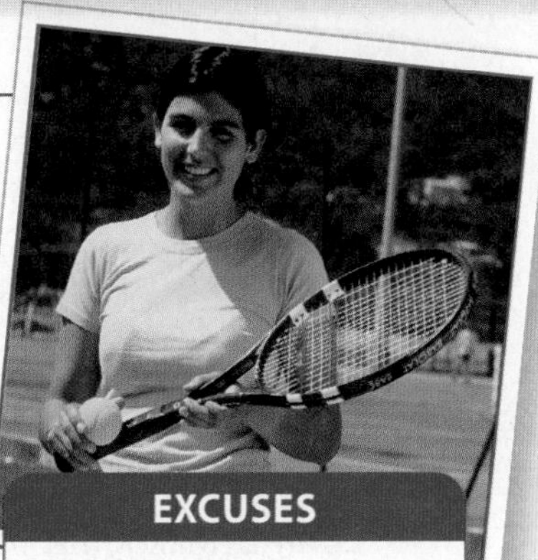

INVITATIONS

- jouer au foot
- jouer au basket
- dîner en ville
- faire une promenade
- regarder la télé
- écouter de la musique
- organiser une boum
- ??

EXCUSES

- étudier
- travailler
- téléphoner à mon cousin
- aider *(to help)* ma mère
- aider mon petit frère
- ??

À votre tour!

Digital performance space

1 Vive la différence! 

ÉCRIRE On a sheet of paper, write in order of preference the five activities you like best. (Mention only those you can name in French). Also write two activities that you do not like to do. Get together with a partner and compare your lists.

- What are the activities that you both like?
- What are the activities that neither of you like?

2 Correspondance 

ÉCRIRE Write an e-mail to your new French penpal Véronique.

In your e-mail, mention ...

- your name
- where you live
- what language(s) you study
- if you speak them well
- what things you like to do at home
- what sports you play
- what other things you like to do

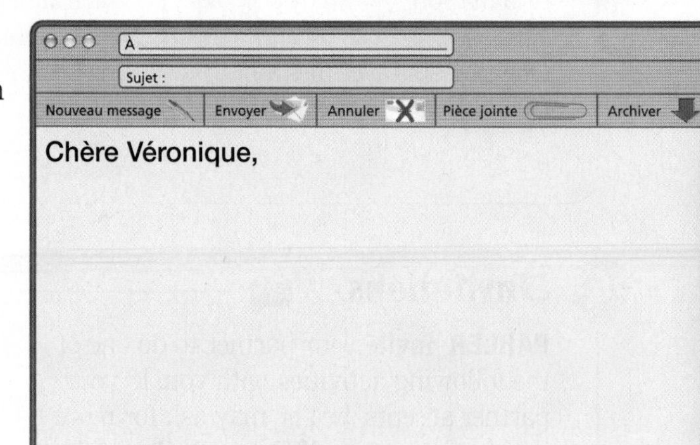

3 Week-end 

ÉCRIRE Make a list of three activities that you would like to do this weekend, and ask your partner if he/she likes these activities.

When you have found an activity you both like, ask your partner if he/she would like to join you in that activity.

Determine the place **(où?)**, the date **(quand?)** and the time **(à quelle heure?)**.

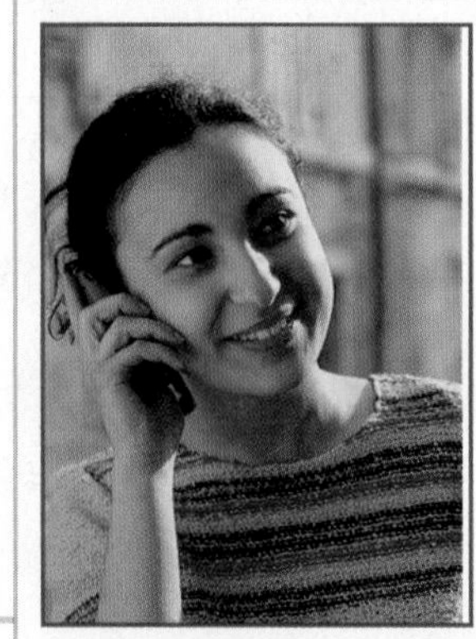

À votre tour!

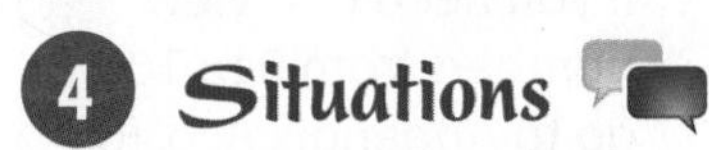

4 Situations

PARLER Imagine that you and your partner are in the following situations. Prepare and act out the conversations below.

You meet a Canadian teenager on the bus.

Ask him/her …
- where he/she lives
- if he/she prefers to speak English or French
- if he/she travels a lot

You meet a French teenager at the beach.

Ask your new friend …
- if he/she likes to swim
- if he/she wants to play soccer
- what he/she wants to do after that **(après)**

Your partner has invited two French friends, Philippe and Olivier, to a party. You are going to the same party.

Ask your partner …
- if Philippe and Olivier speak English
- if they like to dance
- what they like to do

Your friend has a cousin named Valérie who is French. You want to know more about Valérie.

Ask your friend …
- where his/her cousin lives
- if she studies English in class
- how well she speaks English

It is Saturday afternoon. You and your French friend have decided to have dinner downtown.

Ask your friend …
- at what time he/she wants to have dinner
- where he/she wants to have dinner
- what he/she wants to eat

You are at a summer tennis camp. There you have met a young Haitian who speaks French.

Ask your Haitian friend …
- if he/she has a tennis racket
- how well he/she plays tennis
- if he/she wants to play a game with you
- at what time?

You are in a café in Paris with a friend.

Ask your friend …
- what he/she wants to eat
- what he/she wants to drink **(boire)**
- if he/she wants to go for a walk afterwards **(après)**

Rappel

Expressions de tous les jours

1 Ariane 

PARLER Ariane is the French rocket that launches European space satellites. With your partners, start the countdown for liftoff. You may start from 100, or any other number of your choice. You may stop the countdown when you wish.

Révision

If you need to review numbers from 0 to 100, go to Appendix A, p. R7.

2 Loto

ÉCOUTER Your teacher will call out certain numbers. Raise your hand when you hear a number on your card.

3	12		36		50	61	71		90
7	16	27		42		65		84	95
	18	28		49	56		78	89	97

3 Dis-moi ... PARLER

1. Quelle heure est-il?
2. À quelle heure finit la classe de français?
3. À quelle heure est-ce que tu dînes en général?
4. Quelle heure est-il maintenant à Paris? et à Québec?
5. Quel jour est-ce aujourd'hui? et demain?
6. Quel est ton jour préféré?
7. Quel est ton mois préféré?
8. Quelle est la date d'aujourd'hui?
9. Quand est-ce, ton anniversaire?

Révision

If you need to review time, dates and the days of the week, go to Appendix A, pp. R7-R8.

4 Joyeux anniversaire! 

PARLER Ask 5 different classmates when their birthdays are and find out who has a birthday closest to your own.

5 Quel temps fait-il?

PARLER/ÉCRIRE You are the weather reporter at a French TV station. Give the weather for each of the following French-speaking cities.

6 Les quatre saisons 

ÉCRIRE Write a note to your French penpal describing the weather in your region for each season of the year.

Révision

If you need to review weather and seasons, go to Appendix A, p. R8.

▶ To order in a café:

— **Vous désirez, monsieur, mademoiselle?**

— **Je voudrais** | **un jus de pomme.**
une crêpe.

— **Ça fait combien?**
C'est combien?
— **C'est 9 euros.**

Révision

If you need to review names of foods and beverages, go to Appendix A, p. R4.

 Au Rallye 

PARLER You are at a French café called **Le Rallye**. The server (your partner) is taking your order. Order something to drink and something to eat from the menu. Then ask the server for the bill.

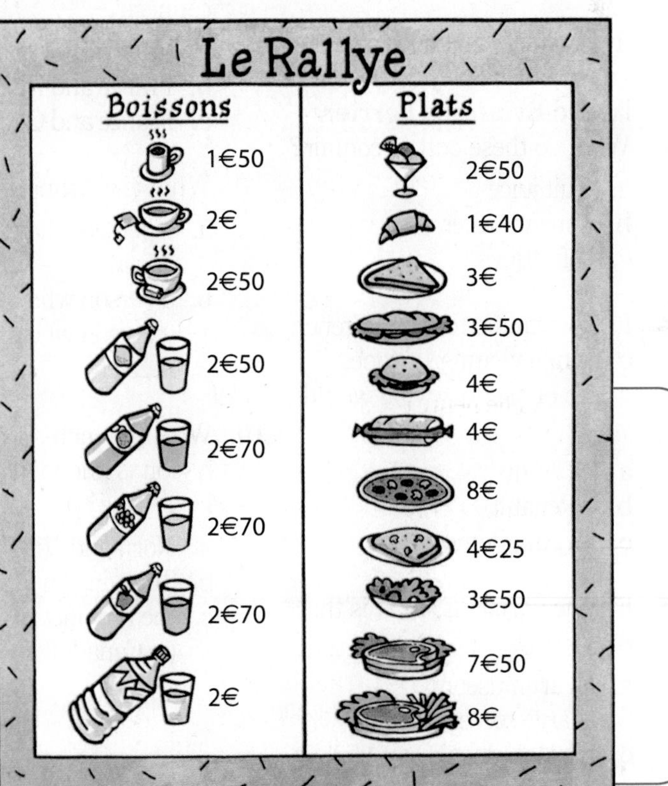

Le savez-vous?

What do you know about France and the French-speaking world? Maybe more than you think! Read the following questions and try to answer them, guessing when necessary. How many questions did you answer correctly? (The answers are at the end of the self-test.)

1. If you were in France, where would you go to buy **croissants?**
   a. a bakery
   b. a dairy shop
   c. a vegetable stand

2. Which of the following popular cheeses is *not* of French origin?
   a. brie
   b. camembert
   c. parmesan

3. In an American supermarket you can often find bottles labeled **Évian** and **Perrier.** What do these bottles contain?
   a. fruit juice
   b. mineral water
   c. soft drinks

4. If you wanted to rent a French car while visiting Europe, which of the following would you choose?
   a. an Audi
   b. a Renault
   c. an Alfa-Roméo

5. For the Parisians, what is the **métro?**
   a. an art museum
   b. a large soccer stadium
   c. the local subway system

6. The **Tour de France** is the most-watched sporting event in France. What is it?
   a. a soccer championship
   b. a tennis tournament
   c. a bicycle race

7. France is considered a pioneer in transportation technology. What is **le Concorde?**
   a. a high-speed train
   b. a supersonic passenger plane
   c. an automated subway system

8. The **Eurotunnel** is a 30-mile tunnel beneath the sea. Which countries does it connect?
   a. France and Spain
   b. France and England
   c. France and Germany

9. What is a "francophone"?
   a. a person who enjoys French cuisine
   b. a person who likes France
   c. a person who speaks French natively

10. Which French-speaking region is known as **la Belle Province?**
    a. Normandy (in France)
    b. Touraine (in France)
    c. the Province of Quebec (in Canada)

11. If you were going to Africa, in which of the following countries would you be able to use your French?
    a. Senegal
    b. Kenya
    c. South Africa

12. Which of the following Caribbean islands are part of France?
    a. Jamaica and Bermuda
    b. Martinique and Guadeloupe
    c. Aruba and Bonaire

13. Jacques-Yves Cousteau was a famous French scientist. If you were to become a member of the **Société Cousteau**, which cause would you promote?
    a. the anti-smoking campaign
    b. the protection of the oceans
    c. the anti-nuclear movement

14. Claude Monet (1840-1926) is one of the best-known French painters. With which artistic movement is he associated?
    a. Cubism
    b. Impressionism
    c. Surrealism

15. Since its inception, the Nobel Prize has been awarded to many French citizens. In which of the following categories do the French have the highest percentage of winners?
    a. physics
    b. literature
    c. medicine

Les relations franco-américaines

Ever since the French came to help the American patriots during the American Revolution (1775-1783), France and the United States have maintained a strong friendship. What do you know about this "French-American connection"?

16. Which of the following American cities is named after a French king?
- a. Saint Louis
- b. Georgetown
- c. Williamsburg

17. Which American state was formerly a French territory?
- a. Virginia
- b. Florida
- c. Louisiana

18. LaFayette is a hero to both the French and the Americans. In which aspect of United States history did he play an important role?
- a. the American Revolution
- b. the Civil War
- c. the exploration of the West

19. Which famous American statesman was ambassador to France?
- a. Benjamin Franklin
- b. George Washington
- c. Andrew Jackson

20. Which American city was designed by the French architect Pierre L'Enfant?
- a. Boston
- b. Chicago
- c. Washington, DC

21. Which large American company was founded by a French industrialist?
- a. Exxon
- b. DuPont
- c. General Motors

22. Which famous monument is a gift of the people of France to the people of the United States?
- a. the Statue of Liberty
- b. the Lincoln Memorial
- c. the Liberty Bell

23. Which future American president commanded the Allied forces which liberated France in 1944?
- a. Harry Truman
- b. Dwight Eisenhower
- c. John F. Kennedy

24. Approximately how many Americans are of French origin?
- a. 100,000
- b. 1,000,000
- c. 3,500,000

25. Which state in the United States has the highest proportion of native speakers of French?
- a. Nevada
- b. New Hampshire
- c. New Mexico

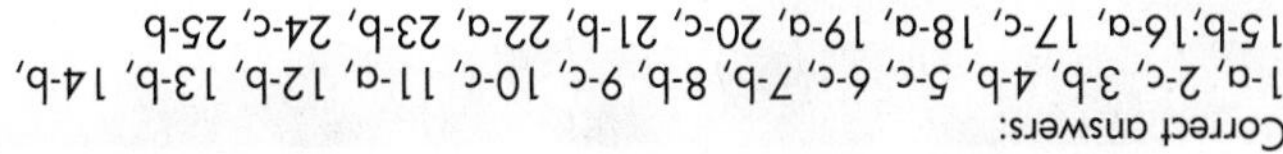

Correct answers:
1-a, 2-c, 3-b, 4-b, 5-c, 6-c, 7-b, 8-b, 9-c, 10-c, 11-a, 12-b, 13-b, 14-b,
15-b; 16-a, 17-c, 18-a, 19-a, 20-c, 21-b, 22-a, 23-b, 24-c, 25-b

Unité 5

En ville

THÈME ET OBJECTIFS

Visiting a French city

There are many things to do in a city: places to visit, concerts to attend, sports to play.

In this unit, you will learn ...

- to describe your city, its public buildings, and places of interest
- to ask for and give directions
- to talk about the various places you go to during the week and on weekends
- to describe your house or apartment

You will also be able ...

- to discuss your future plans and say what you are going to do
- to talk about your friends and their families

DIGITAL FRENCH my.hrw.com

ONLINE STUDENT EDITION with...

- Audio Resources
- Video Resources
- Interactive Flashcards
- WebQuest

PRACTICE FRENCH WITH HOLT MCDOUGAL APPS!

Leçon

13

LE FRANÇAIS PRATIQUE

Vocabulaire et Culture

La ville et la maison

Accent sur ... les villes françaises

- Today 80% of the French population lives in cities and their surrounding suburbs.
- French cities have a long history. Paris, Lyon, Marseille, and Nice were founded well over two thousand years ago!
- Cities in France differ in urban design from cities in the United States.
  - —The downtown area **(le centre-ville)** is the historical district with buildings and monuments dating back several centuries. Usually no buildings are taller than six stories. With the many cafés, restaurants, stores, and movie houses, it is a very animated area that attracts many young people.
  - —The suburbs **(la banlieue)** is where the tall apartment buildings and office buildings are located. Young people who live in the Parisian suburbs often get together in the local shopping mall **(le centre commercial)** which offers shops, cafés, and cinemas.

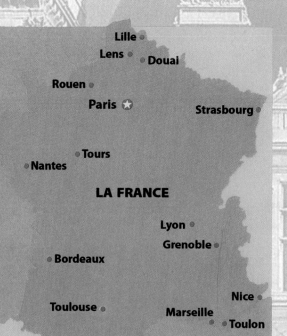

The largest French cities:

	POPULATION (URBAN AREA)
Paris	11 000 000
Marseille	1 600 000
Lyon	1 500 000
Lille	1 000 000
Nice	950 000
Toulouse	900 000
Bordeaux	850 000
Nantes	600 000
Toulon	550 000
Douai-Lens	500 000
Grenoble	500 000
Rouen	450 000
Strasbourg	450 000

Lille
Lens
Douai
Rouen
Paris
Strasbourg
Tours
Nantes
LA FRANCE
Lyon
Grenoble
Bordeaux
Nice
Toulouse
Marseille
Toulon

@HOMETUTOR
my.hrw.com

Ici, à Tours

Tours est une ville de 150 000 (cent cinquante mille) habitants située à 200 kilomètres au sud-ouest de Paris. C'est une ville française typique.

L'Hôtel de Ville

Au centre, il y a l'hôtel de ville qui est le bâtiment administratif principal. C'est ici que les gens viennent se marier.

bâtiment: building; viennent: come; se marier: to get married

La place Plumereau

La place Plumereau est située dans un quartier très ancien. Il y a beaucoup de maisons historiques, et aussi beaucoup de cafés où viennent les jeunes de Tours. C'est un endroit très animé.

quartier: district; endroit: place

Le Château de Tours

Comme beaucoup de villes françaises, Tours a un château historique. Ce château est une ancienne forteresse royale. Aujourd'hui, c'est un bâtiment administratif.

ancienne: former

Une maison près de Tours

Les Français qui n'habitent pas dans le centre-ville préfèrent habiter dans une maison individuelle. Cette maison de la région de Tours a deux étages.

étages: floors

A VOCABULAIRE Où habites-tu?

▶How to talk about where one lives:

Où habites-tu?

J'habite
- à Tours.
- à Villeneuve
- dans **une grande ville** *(city, town)*
- dans **un petit village**
- dans **un joli quartier** *(neighborhood)*
- dans **une rue** *(street)* intéressante

Quelle est **ton adresse?**

J'habite
- 32, **avenue** Victor Hugo.
- 14, **rue** La Fayette
- 50, **boulevard** Wilson

NOTE Culturelle

Le nom des rues

En France, les rues ont très souvent le nom de personnes célèbres,° en particulier écrivains,° artistes et personnalités politiques.

- **Victor Hugo** (1802-1885) est un très grand poète. Il a aussi écrit° *Les Misérables* qui° a inspiré une comédie musicale moderne.
- **La Fayette** (1757-1834) est un aristocrate français. Ami de Georges Washington, il a joué un rôle important pendant la Révolution américaine.

célèbres *famous* **écrivains** *writers* **a écrit** *wrote* **qui** *which*

1 Expression personnelle

PARLER/ÉCRIRE Describe where you live by completing the following sentences.

1. J'habite à …
2. Ma ville est (n'est pas) …
   (grande? petite? moderne? jolie?)
   Mon village est (n'est pas) …
   (grand? petit? joli?)
3. Mon quartier est (n'est pas) …
   (intéressant? joli? moderne?)
4. Mon adresse est …
5. Ma ville favorite est …
6. Un jour, je voudrais visiter … *(name of city)*

2 Interview 

PARLER/ÉCRIRE You are a French journalist writing an article about living conditions in the United States. Interview a classmate and find out the following information.

1. Where does he/she live?
2. Is his/her city large or small?
3. Is his/her city pretty?
4. What is his/her address?

B VOCABULAIRE Ma ville

▶ *How to talk about one's hometown:*

Dans ma rue, il y a ...

HÔTEL
CAFÉ
Restaurant
SUPERMARCHÉ
Lucie magasin de mode

un hôtel **un café** **un restaurant** **un supermarché** **un magasin**

Dans mon quartier, il y a ...

CINÉMA
ÉCOLE
ÉGLISE
CENTRE COMMERCIAL

un cinéma **une école** **une église** **un centre commercial**

Dans ma ville, il y a ...

BIBLIOTHÈQUE
THÉÂTRE
MUSÉE
HÔPITAL

une bibliothèque **un théâtre** **un musée** **un hôpital**

Il y a aussi ...

une piscine **un parc** **un stade** **une plage**

3 Mon quartier

PARLER Say whether the following places are located in the area where you live. If so, you may want to give the name of the place.

▶ école **Il y a une école. Elle s'appelle «Washington School».**
(Il n'y a pas d'école.)

1. restaurant
2. cinéma
3. église
4. centre commercial
5. bibliothèque
6. café
7. plage
8. supermarché
9. hôpital
10. parc
11. stade
12. musée
13. hôtel
14. piscine
15. théâtre

4 À Montréal

PARLER You are visiting your friend Pauline in Montreal. For each of the situations below, decide where you would like to go. Ask Pauline if there is such a place in her neighborhood.

▶ You are hungry.

Pauline, est-ce qu'il y a un restaurant dans ton quartier?

1. You want to have a soft drink.
2. You want to see a movie.
3. You want to swim a few laps.
4. You want to run on a track.
5. You want to read a book about Canada.
6. You want to see a French play.
7. You want to buy some fruit and crackers.
8. You want to see an art exhibit.
9. You want to play frisbee on the grass.
10. You slipped and you're afraid you sprained your ankle.

COMMUNAUTÉS

Do French-speaking visitors sometimes come to your community? As a class project, prepare a map of your city on which you label key places and buildings in French. Maybe your local chamber of commerce would like to make such a map available for tourists.

C VOCABULAIRE Pour demander un renseignement *(information)*

▶ *How to ask for directions:*

Pardon, | monsieur. Où est l'hôtel Normandie?
Excusez-moi, | madame
| mademoiselle

Il est dans la rue Jean Moulin.

Pardon, monsieur. Où est l'hôtel Normandie?

Il est dans la rue Jean Moulin.

Où est-ce qu'il y a un café?

Il y a un café | **rue** Saint Paul.
| **boulevard** Masséna
| **avenue** de Lyon

une rue
un boulevard
une avenue

Où est-ce? *(Where is it?)*
Est-ce que c'est **loin** *(far)*?

Non, ce n'est pas loin.
C'est **près** *(nearby)*.

Où est-ce? Est-ce que c'est loin?

Non, ce n'est pas loin. C'est près.

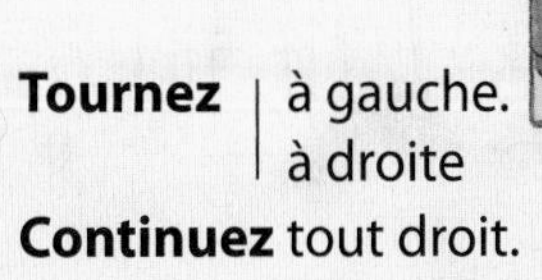

C'est | **à gauche** *(to the left)*.
| **à droite** *(to the right)*
| **tout droit** *(straight ahead)*

Tournez | à gauche.
| à droite

Continuez tout droit.

Merci beaucoup!

5 En ville

PARLER A tourist who is visiting a French city asks a local resident how to get to the following places. Act out the dialogues.

▶ —Pardon, mademoiselle (monsieur).
Où est le Café de la Poste?
—Le Café de la Poste? Il est dans la rue Pascal.
—Où est-ce?
—Continuez tout droit!
—Merci, mademoiselle (monsieur).

▶ 

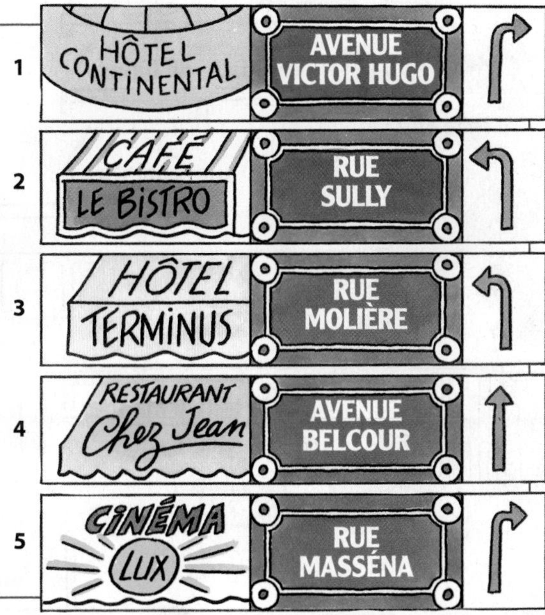

D VOCABULAIRE Ma maison

J'habite dans une maison.

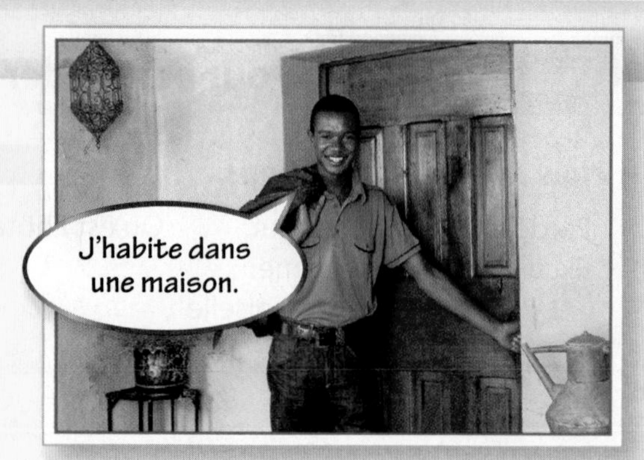

▶ *How to describe one's home:*

J'habite dans | **une maison** *(house)*.
un appartement
un immeuble *(apartment building)*

Ma maison/mon appartement est | **moderne.**
confortable

Ma chambre est | **en haut** *(upstairs)*.
en bas *(downstairs)*

La maison

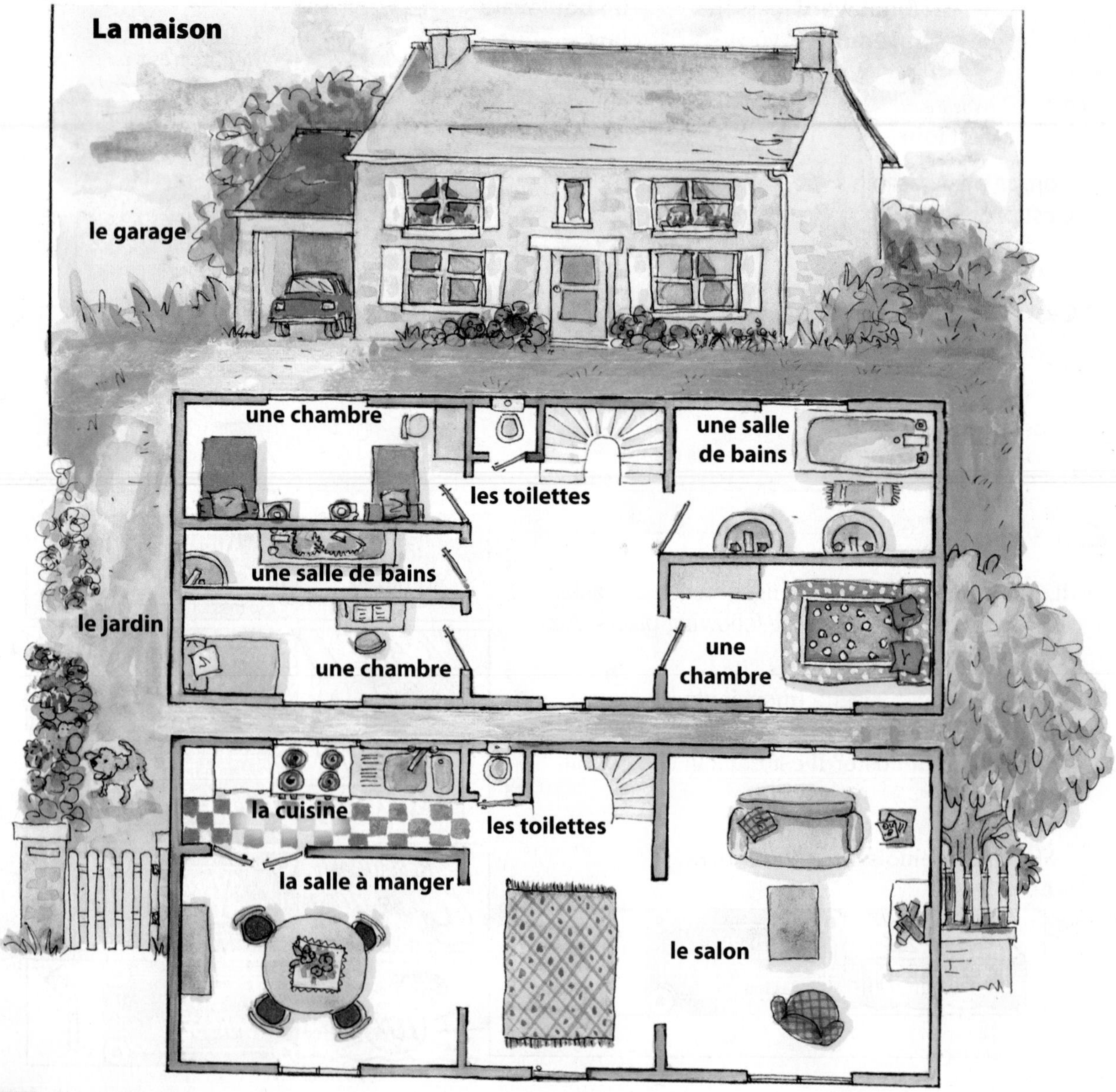

le garage
une chambre
les toilettes
une salle de bains
une salle de bains
le jardin
une chambre
une chambre
la cuisine
les toilettes
la salle à manger
le salon

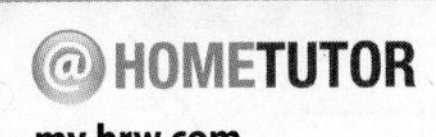

6 Ma maison

PARLER/ÉCRIRE Describe your home by completing the following sentences.

1. J'habite dans ... (une maison? un appartement?)
2. Mon appartement est ... (grand? petit? confortable? joli?)
   Ma maison est ... (grande? petite? confortable? jolie?)
3. La cuisine est ... (grande? petite? moderne?)
4. La cuisine est peinte *(painted)* en ... (jaune? vert? gris? blanc? ??)
5. Ma chambre est peinte en ... (bleu? rose? ??)
6. Dans le salon, il y a ... (une télé? un sofa? des plantes vertes? ??)
7. En général, nous dînons dans ... (la cuisine? la salle à manger?)
8. Ma maison/mon appartement a ... (un jardin? un garage? ??)

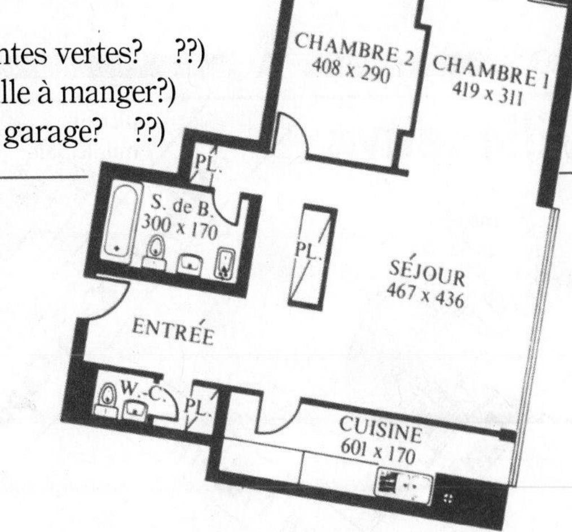

7 En haut ou en bas?

PARLER Imagine that you live in a two-story house. Indicate where the following rooms are located.

▶ ma chambre

1. la cuisine
2. la salle à manger
3. les toilettes
4. la salle de bains
5. la chambre de mes *(my)* parents
6. le salon

COMPARAISON CULTURELLE

In traditional French homes, the toilet **(WC)** is in a small room separate from the main bathroom.

8 Où sont-ils?

PARLER/ÉCRIRE From what the following people are doing, guess where they are — in or around the house.

▶ Madame Martin répare *(is repairing)* la voiture.
Elle est dans le garage.

1. Nous dînons.
2. Tu regardes la télé.
3. Antoine et Juliette jouent au frisbee.
4. J'étudie le français.
5. Monsieur Martin prépare le dîner.
6. Henri se lave *(is washing up)*.
7. Ma soeur téléphone à son copain.

À votre tour!

Digital performance space

OBJECTIFS

Now you can . . .
- describe your town and your neighborhood
- ask and give directions

Écoutez bien! 

ÉCOUTER Look at the map of Villeneuve. You will hear where certain people are. If they are somewhere on the left side of the map, mark A. If they are on the right side of the map, mark B.

A								
B								
	1	2	3	4	5	6	7	8

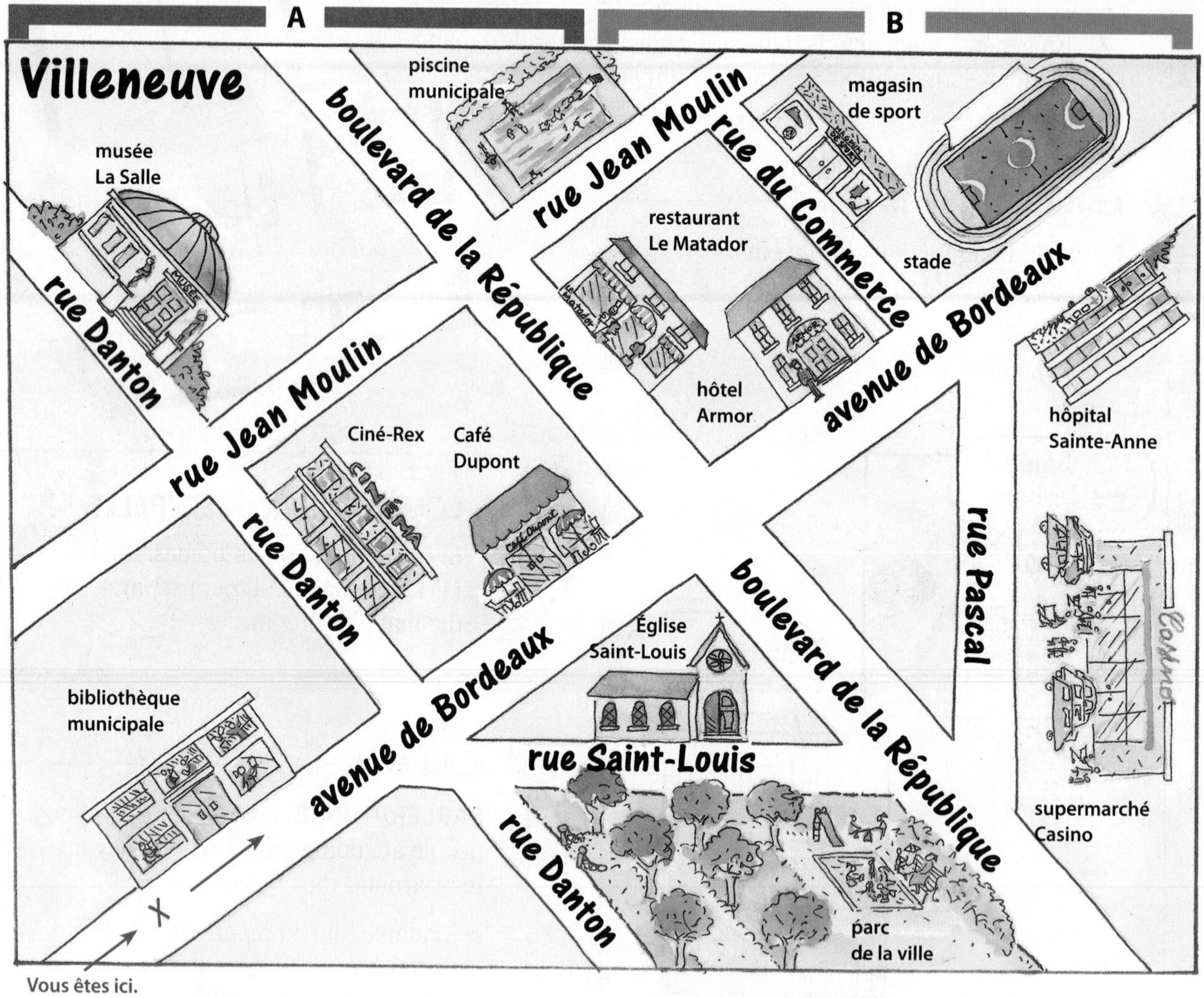

Mon quartier 

ÉCRIRE Describe your neighborhood, listing five places and giving their names.

▶ **Dans mon quartier, il y a un supermarché. C'est le supermarché Casino.**

3 Créa-dialogue 

PARLER You have just arrived in Villeneuve, where you will spend the summer. Ask a pedestrian where you can find the places represented by the symbols. He (She) will give you the location of each place, according to the map.

▶ —Pardon, monsieur (madame). Où est-ce qu'il y a un hôtel?
—Il y a un hôtel avenue de Bordeaux.
—Est-ce que c'est loin?
—Non, c'est près.
—Merci beaucoup!

4 Où est-ce?  

PARLER Now you have been in Villeneuve for several weeks and are familiar with the city. You meet a tourist on the **avenue de Bordeaux** at the place indicated by an X on the map. The tourist asks you where certain places are and you indicate how to get there.

Pardon, monsieur. Où est l'hôpital Sainte-Anne?
C'est tout droit, mademoiselle.
Merci bien, monsieur.

▶ l'hôpital Sainte-Anne

1. le musée La Salle
2. le supermarché Casino
3. l'hôtel Armor
4. le restaurant Le Matador
5. l'église Saint-Louis

5 Composition: La maison idéale 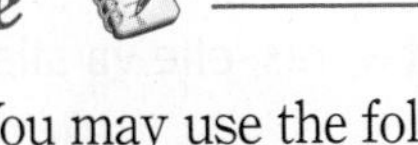

ÉCRIRE Briefly describe your dream house. You may use the following adjectives to describe the various rooms: **grand, petit, moderne, confortable, joli,** as well as colors. If you wish, sketch and label a floor plan.

▶ **La maison idéale est grande et moderne. Le salon est . . .**

Week-end à Paris

AUDIO

Aujourd'hui c'est samedi.
Les élèves ne vont pas en classe. *are not going*
Où est-ce qu'ils vont alors?
Ça dépend!

Thomas va au café. *is going*
Il a un rendez-vous avec une copine. *date*

Florence et Karine vont aux Champs-Élysées.
Elles vont regarder les vêtements dans les magasins. *clothes*
Après, elles vont aller au cinéma. *Afterward / to go*

Daniel va chez son copain Laurent. *to the house of / his*
Les garçons vont jouer aux jeux vidéo.
Après, ils vont aller au musée des sciences de la Villette.
Ils vont jouer avec les machines électroniques.

Béatrice a un grand sac et des lunettes de soleil. *sunglasses*
Est-ce qu'elle va à un rendez-vous secret?
Non! Elle va au Centre Pompidou.
Elle va regarder les acrobates.
Et après, elle va aller à un concert.

Et Jean-François? Qu'est-ce qu'il va faire aujourd'hui?
Est-ce qu'il va visiter le Centre Pompidou?
Est-ce qu'il va regarder les acrobates?
Est-ce qu'il va aller à un concert?
Hélas, non! *Alas (Unfortunately)*
Il va rester à la maison. *to stay*
Pourquoi? Parce qu'il est malade. *sick*
Pauvre Jean-François! *Poor*
Il fait si beau dehors! *so / outside*

@HOMETUTOR my.hrw.com

Compréhension

1. Quel jour est-ce aujourd'hui?
2. Pourquoi est-ce que Thomas va au café?
3. Avec qui est-ce que Florence va au cinéma?
4. Où va Daniel? Qu'est-ce qu'il fait avec Laurent?
5. Où va Béatrice?
6. Pourquoi est-ce que Jean-François ne va pas en ville?
7. Quel temps fait-il aujourd'hui?

À Paris

Paris offre beaucoup d'attractions diverses pour les jeunes.

Les Champs-Élysées

Les Champs-Élysées sont une très longue et très large° avenue avec beaucoup de cafés, de restaurants, de cinémas et de boutiques élégantes.

Le Centre Pompidou

Le Centre Pompidou est un grand musée d'art moderne. C'est aussi un centre culturel avec un grand nombre de salles° multimédia pour les jeunes. Devant le musée, il y a une place où les acrobates, les mimes, les jongleurs° et les musiciens démontrent leurs° talents. Ici, le spectacle est permanent.

Le Parc de la Villette

Le Parc de la Villette est un musée scientifique pour les jeunes. À la Géode, ils peuvent voir° des films sur un grand écran panoramique Omni. Au Zénith, ils peuvent assister à° des concerts de rock et de musique techno.

large *wide* **salles** *large rooms* **jongleurs** *jugglers* **leurs** *their* **peuvent voir** *can see* **assister à** *attend*

A Le verbe *aller*

Aller *(to go)* is the only IRREGULAR verb that ends in **-er.** Note the forms of **aller** in the present tense.

aller	*to go*	J'aime **aller** au cinéma.
je **vais**	*I go, I am going*	Je **vais** à un concert.
tu **vas**	*you go, you are going*	**Vas**-tu à la boum?
il/elle **va**	*he/she goes, he/she is going*	Paul **va** à l'école.
nous **allons**	*we go, we are going*	Nous **allons** au café.
vous **allez**	*you go, you are going*	Est-ce que vous **allez** là-bas?
ils/elles **vont**	*they go, they are going*	Ils ne **vont** pas en classe.

→ Remember that **aller** is used in asking people how they feel.

Ça **va?**	Oui, ça **va.**
Comment **vas**-tu?	Je **vais** bien, merci.
Comment **allez**-vous?	Très bien.

→ **Aller** is used in many common expressions.

- To encourage someone to do something:
  Vas-y! *Come on! Go ahead! Do it!*

- To tell someone to go away:
  Va-t'en! *Go away!*

- To tell friends to start doing something:
  Allons-y! *Let's go!*

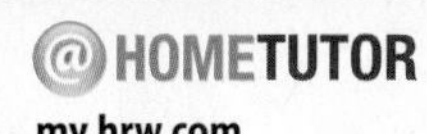

1 Les vacances

PARLER/ÉCRIRE The following students at a boarding school in Nice are going home for vacation. Indicate to which of the cities they are going, according to the luggage tags shown below.

▶ Jean-Michel est canadien.

1. Je suis suisse.
2. Charlotte est américaine.
3. Nous sommes italiens.
4. Tu es français.
5. Vous êtes espagnols.
6. Michiko est japonaise.
7. Mike et Shelley sont anglais.
8. Ana et Carlos sont mexicains.

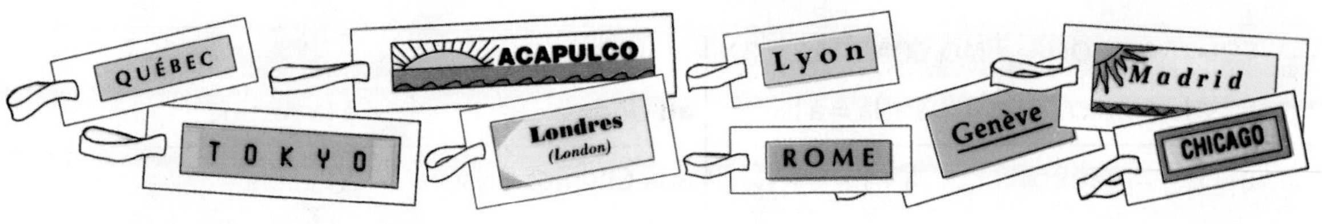

2 Jamais le dimanche! *(Never on Sunday!)*

PARLER/ÉCRIRE On Sundays, French students do not go to class. They all go somewhere else. Express this according to the model.

▶ nous / en ville
Le dimanche, nous n'allons pas en classe.
Nous allons en ville.

1. Philippe / au café
2. vous / au cinéma
3. Céline et Michèle / à un concert
4. Jérôme / au restaurant
5. je / à un match de foot
6. tu / à la piscine
7. Éric et Léa / à la plage
8. Mes copains / au stade
9. Hélène / au centre commercial
10. Vous / dans les magasins

B La préposition *à; à* + l'article défini

The preposition **à** has several meanings:

in	Patrick habite **à** Paris.	*Patrick lives **in** Paris.*
at	Nous sommes **à** la piscine.	*We are **at** the pool.*
to	Est-ce que tu vas **à** Toulouse?	*Are you going **to** Toulouse?*

CONTRACTIONS

Note the forms of **à** + DEFINITE ARTICLE in the sentences below.

Voici **le** café.	Marc est **au** café.	Corinne va **au** café.
Voici **les** Champs-Élysées.	Tu es **aux** Champs-Élysées.	Je vais **aux** Champs-Élysées.
Voici **la** piscine.	Anne est **à la** piscine.	Éric va **à la** piscine.
Voici **l'**hôtel.	Je suis **à l'**hôtel.	Vous allez **à l'**hôtel.

The preposition **à** contracts with **le** and **les,** but not with **la** and **l'.**

CONTRACTION	NO CONTRACTION		
à + le → **au**	à + la = **à la**	**au** cinéma	**à la** piscine
à + les → **aux**	à + l' = **à l'**	**aux** Champs-Élysées	**à l'**école

→ There is liaison after **aux** when the next word begins with a vowel sound.

Le professeur parle **aux‿élèves.** (z) Je téléphone **aux‿amis** de Claire. (z)

3 Dans la rue

PARLER Two friends meet in the street and talk about where they are going. ▶

4 Préférences

PARLER Ask your classmates about their preferences. Be sure to use contractions when needed.

▶ aller à (le concert ou le théâtre?)

1. dîner à (la maison ou le restaurant)?
2. étudier à (la bibliothèque ou la maison)?
3. nager à (la piscine ou la plage)?
4. regarder un match de foot à (la télé ou le stade)?
5. aller à (le cinéma ou le musée)?

Tu préfères aller au concert ou au théâtre?
Je préfère aller au concert.
(Je préfère aller au théâtre.)

5 À Paris

PARLER You are living in Paris. A friend asks you where you are going and why. Act out the dialogues with a classmate.

▶ **—Où vas-tu?**
—Je vais à l'Opéra.
—Pourquoi?
—Parce que j'aime la danse classique.

	OÙ?	POURQUOI?
▶	l'Opéra	J'aime la danse classique.
1.	l'Alliance Française	J'ai une classe de français.
2.	le Centre Pompidou	J'aime l'art moderne.
3.	le musée d'Orsay	C'est un musée intéressant.
4.	les Champs-Élysées	J'ai un rendez-vous là-bas.
5.	la tour Eiffel	Il y a une belle vue *(view)* sur Paris.
6.	le Zénith	Il y a un concert de rock.
7.	la Villette	Il y a une exposition *(exhibit)* intéressante.
8.	le stade de France	Il y a un match de foot.

6 Où vont-ils?

PARLER/ÉCRIRE Say where the following people are going, according to what they like to do.

▶ Daniel aime danser.
Il va à la discothèque.

1. Corinne aime l'art moderne.
2. Jean-François aime manger.
3. Delphine aime les westerns.
4. Marina aime nager.
5. Éric aime regarder les magazines.
6. Denise aime faire des promenades.
7. Philippe aime la musique.
8. Alice aime le football.
9. Cécile aime le shopping.

le stade
la bibliothèque
le cinéma
le centre commercial
le musée
le parc
le restaurant
la piscine
le concert

VOCABULAIRE En ville

▶ Quelques endroits et quelques événements où aller

un endroit	*place*	**un match**	*game*	**une boum**	*party*
un événement	*event*	**un pique-nique**	*picnic*	**une fête**	*party*
un concert	*concert*	**un rendez-vous**	*appointment, date*	**une soirée**	*evening party*
un film	*movie*				

Verbes

arriver	*to arrive, come*	**J'arrive** à l'école à 9 heures.
rentrer	*to go back, come back*	À quelle heure **rentres**-tu à la maison?
rester	*to stay*	Les touristes **restent** à l'hôtel.

Expressions

à pied	*on foot*	**en voiture**	*by car*	**en métro**	*by subway*
à vélo	*by bicycle*	**en bus**	*by bus*	**en taxi**	*by taxi*
		en train	*by train*		

faire une promenade à pied	*to go for a walk*
faire une promenade à vélo	*to go for a ride (by bike)*
faire une promenade en voiture	*to go for a drive*

7 Questions personnelles PARLER/ÉCRIRE

1. En général, à quelle heure est-ce que tu arrives à l'école?
2. À quelle heure est-ce que tu rentres à la maison? Qu'est-ce que tu fais quand tu rentres à la maison?
3. Comment vas-tu à l'école? à pied, à vélo, en voiture ou en bus?
4. Le week-end, est-ce que tu restes à la maison? Où vas-tu?
5. Comment vas-tu à la piscine? à la plage? au cinéma?
6. Est-ce que tu aimes faire des promenades à pied? Où vas-tu? avec qui?
7. Est-ce que tu aimes faire des promenades à vélo? Où vas-tu?
8. En général, est-ce que tu aimes regarder les films à la télé? Quels films est-ce que tu préfères? (les films d'action? les films de science-fiction? les comédies?)
9. Quand tu as un rendez-vous avec un copain ou une copine, où allez-vous?
10. À quels événements aimes-tu aller? Pourquoi?

@HOMETUTOR
my.hrw.com

C La préposition *chez*

Note the use of **chez** in the following sentences.

Paul est **chez Céline.**	*Paul is* ***at Céline's (house).***
Je dîne **chez un copain.**	*I am having dinner* ***at a friend's (home).***
Nathalie va **chez Juliette.**	*Nathalie is going* ***to Juliette's (apartment).***
Tu vas **chez ta cousine.**	*You are going* ***to your cousin's (place).***

The French equivalent of *to* or *at someone's (house, home)* is the construction:

chez + PERSON	**chez** Béatrice **chez** ma cousine

→ Note the interrogative expression: **chez qui?**
Chez qui vas-tu? ***To whose house*** *are you going?*

Chez Carla
Spécialités italiennes
MENU

Pizza 4 fromages	€ 8,00
Pizza margarita	€ 10,00
Pizza napolitana	€ 11,00
Spaghetti bolognaise	€ 7,50
Tortellini alla carbonara	€ 9,00
Salade verte	€ 4,00
Salade caprese	€ 5,00
Dessert du jour	€ 4,00

Réservation 01-46-77-52-51

8 En vacances

PARLER/ÉCRIRE When we are on vacation, we often like to visit friends and relatives. Say where the following people are going.

▶ Claire / Marc
Claire va chez Marc.

1. Hélène / Jérôme
2. Jean-Paul / Lucie
3. tu / un copain
4. Corinne / une cousine
5. vous / des copines à Québec
6. nous / un cousin à Paris

9 Week-end

PARLER On weekends, we often like to visit friends and do things together. Say how the following people are spending Sunday afternoon.

▶ Cécile / jouer au ping-pong / Robert

1. Julie / aller / Béatrice
2. Claire / dîner / des cousins
3. Antoine / jouer au croquet / Sylvie
4. Marc / écouter de la musique / un copain
5. Mathieu / regarder la télé / une copine
6. Élodie / jouer aux jeux vidéo / Thomas
7. Nous / manger une pizza / Léa
8. Vous / regarder un DVD / Éric
9. Tu / jouer au basket / Alice

Cécile joue au ping-pong chez Robert.

D La construction *aller* + l'infinitif

The following sentences describe what people are *going to do*.
Note how the verb **aller** is used to describe these FUTURE events.

Nathalie **va nager.**	*Nathalie* ***is going to swim.***
Paul et Marc **vont jouer** au tennis.	*Paul and Marc* ***are going to play*** *tennis.*
Nous **allons rester** à la maison.	*We* ***are going to stay*** *home.*
Je **vais aller** en ville.	***I am going to go*** *downtown.*

To express the NEAR FUTURE, the French use the construction:

PRESENT of **aller** + INFINITIVE

→ In negative sentences, the construction is:

SUBJECT +	**ne** +	PRESENT of **aller** +	**pas** +	INFINITIVE ...
Sylvie	**ne**	va	**pas**	écouter le concert avec nous.

→ Note the interrogative forms:

Qu'est-ce que tu vas faire?	***What are you going*** *to do?*
Quand est-ce que vous allez rentrer?	***When are you going*** *to come back?*

Language Comparison
To talk about FUTURE plans and intentions, French and English frequently use similar verbs: **aller** *(to be going to)*.

10 Tourisme

PARLER/ÉCRIRE Say where the following people are going this summer and what they are going to visit.

▶ Monique (à Paris / le Louvre)
Monique va à Paris. Elle va visiter le Louvre.

1. Alice (à New York / la statue de la Liberté)
2. nous (en Égypte / les pyramides)
3. vous (à Rome / le Colisée)
4. tu (à La Nouvelle Orléans / le Vieux Carré)
5. je (à San Francisco / Chinatown)
6. les élèves (à San Antonio / l'Alamo)
7. Madame Lambert (à Beijing / la Cité interdite *[Forbidden City]*)
8. les touristes (à Kyoto / les temples)

11 Qu'est-ce que tu vas faire? 

PARLER Ask your classmates if they are going to do the following things this weekend.

▶ étudier

1. travailler
2. surfer sur le Net
3. regarder la télé
4. aller au cinéma
5. inviter des amis
6. aller à une boum
7. jouer aux jeux vidéo
8. rester à la maison
9. faire une promenade à vélo

Est-ce que tu vas étudier?
Oui, je vais étudier.
(Non, je ne vais pas étudier.)

12 Un jeu: Descriptions

PARLER/ÉCRIRE Choose a person from Column A and say where the person is, what he or she has, and what he or she is going to do. Use the verbs **être, avoir,** and **aller** with the phrases in columns B, C, and D. How many logical descriptions can you make?

▶ **Monique est en ville. Elle a un vélo. Elle va faire une promenade.**

A	B	C	D
tu	sur le court	des livres	aller dans les magasins
Monique	à la bibliothèque	un vélo	étudier
je	au salon	20 euros	faire une promenade
les amis	en ville	une télé	regarder un film
nous	à la maison	un MP3	faire un match
vous	au café	une raquette	écouter de la musique

Prononciation 

Les semi-voyelles /w/ et /j/

In French, the semi-vowels /w/ and /j/ are pronounced very quickly, almost like consonants.

/w/  /j/

oui

très bien

Répétez:

/w/ **oui chouette Louise**

/wa/, /wɛ̃/ **moi toi pourquoi voiture loin**
Chouette! La voiture de Louise n'est pas loin.

/j/ **bien chien radio piano Pierre Daniel violon pied étudiant**
Pierre écoute la radio avec Daniel.

À votre tour!

OBJECTIFS

Now you can . . .
- talk about places you go to
- discuss what you are going to do in the future

 Allô!  

PARLER Anne is calling Jérôme. Match Jérôme's answers with Anne's questions. Then act out the dialogue with a friend.

a À dix heures.

b Peut-être! Il y a un très bon film au Rex.

c Nous allons faire une promenade en ville.

d Non, j'ai un rendez-vous avec Christine.

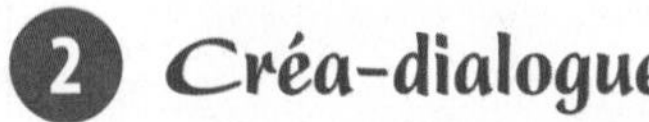  

PARLER As you are going for a walk in town, you meet several friends. Ask them where they are going and what they are going to do there.

▶

OÙ?	ACTIVITÉ
	dîner avec un copain

▶ —Salut, <u>Alison</u>. Ça va?
—Oui, ça va!
—Où vas-tu?
—Je vais au <u>restaurant</u>.
—Ah bon? Qu'est-ce que tu vas faire là-bas?
—Je vais <u>dîner avec un copain</u>.
—Avec qui?
—Avec <u>Chris</u>.

OÙ?	ACTIVITÉ
1 CAFÉ	manger une pizza
2	faire une promenade
3	jouer au foot
4	nager
5	jouer au volley
6	travailler
7	??

3 Conversation libre 

PARLER Have a conversation with a classmate. Ask your classmate questions about what he/she plans to do on the weekend. Try to find out as much as possible, using yes/no questions.

4 Qu'est-ce que vous allez faire? 

ÉCRIRE Leave a note for your friend Jean-Marc, telling him three things that you and your friends are going to do tonight and three things that you are going to do this weekend.

Jean-Marc
Ce soir (Tonight)
1. Nous allons ...
2.
3.

5 Bonnes résolutions 

ÉCRIRE Imagine that it is January 1 and you are making up New Year's resolutions. On a separate sheet of paper, describe six of your resolutions by saying what you are going to do and what you are not going to do in the coming year.

1er JANVIER
1. Je vais toujours parler français en classe.
2. Je ne vais pas être pénible avec mes copains...

LESSON REVIEW
my.hrw.com

Leçon

15

Conversation et Culture

Au Café de l'Univers

AUDIO

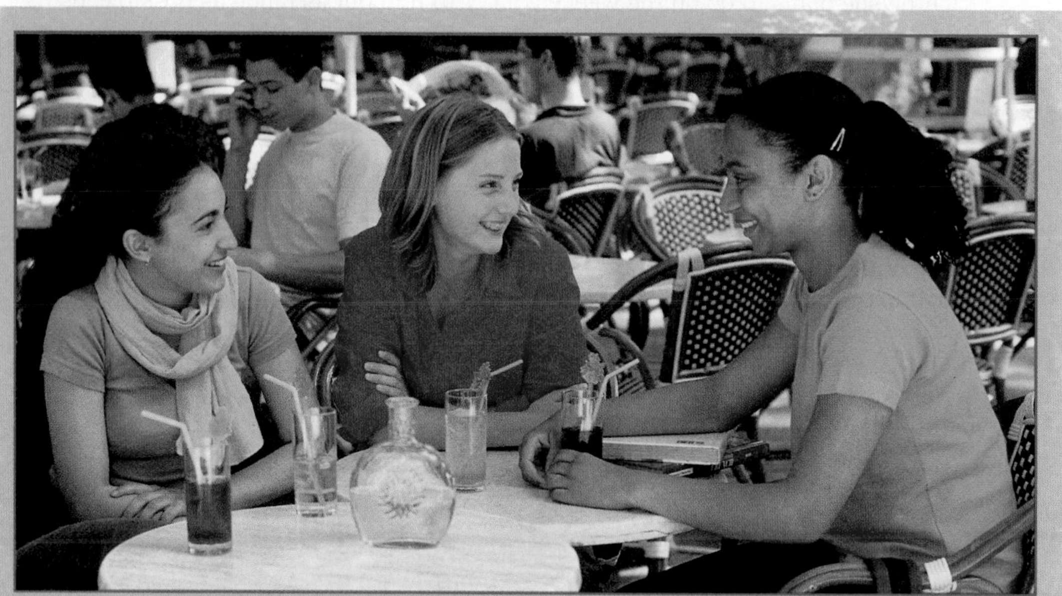

Où vas-tu après les cours? — *after school*
Est-ce que tu vas directement chez toi? — *straight/home*
Valérie, elle, ne va pas directement chez elle. — *to her house*
Elle va au Café de l'Univers avec ses copines Fatima et Zaïna.
Elle vient souvent ici avec elles. — *comes*

À la table de Valérie, la conversation est toujours très animée. — *lively*
De quoi parlent les filles aujourd'hui? — *About what*

Est-ce qu'elles parlent | de l'examen d'histoire? — *history test*
du problème de maths?
de la classe de sciences?

Non!

Est-ce qu'elles parlent | du week-end prochain? — *next*
des vacances?

Non plus! — *Not that either!*

Est-ce qu'elles parlent | du nouveau copain de Marie-Claire? — *new*
de la cousine de Pauline?
des amis de Véronique?

Pas du tout! — *Not at all!*

Aujourd'hui, les filles parlent d'un sujet beaucoup plus important! — *subject/more*
Elles parlent du nouveau prof d'anglais! (C'est un jeune professeur américain. Il est très intéressant, très amusant, très sympathique ... et surtout il est très mignon!) — *above all*

@HOMETUTOR
my.hrw.com

Compréhension

1. Où va Valérie après les cours?
2. Avec qui est-ce qu'elle va au café?
3. Qu'est-ce que les filles font au café?
4. Est-ce qu'elles parlent de l'école?
5. Est-ce qu'elles parlent des activités du week-end?
6. De quelle *(which)* personne parlent-elles aujourd'hui?
7. De quelle nationalité est le professeur d'anglais?
8. Comment est-il?

Et toi?

Describe what you do by completing the following sentences.

1. En général, après les cours,
   je vais …
   je ne vais pas …

   - à la bibliothèque
   - chez mes *(my)* copains
   - au café
   - directement chez moi

2. Avec mes copains,
   je parle …
   je ne parle pas …

   - de la classe de français
   - du prof de français
   - des examens
   - du week-end

3. Avec mes parents,
   je parle …
   je ne parle pas …

   - de l'école
   - de la classe de français
   - de mes notes *(grades)*
   - de mes copains

4. Avec mon frère ou ma soeur,
   je parle …
   je ne parle pas …

   - de mes copains
   - du week-end
   - de mes problèmes
   - des vacances

NOTE Culturelle

Au café

On peut° faire beaucoup de choses différentes dans un café français. On peut manger un sandwich. On peut commander° un jus de fruits. On peut étudier. On peut jouer aux jeux électroniques. Dans les cybercafés, on peut aussi surfer sur l'Internet. Les jeunes Français vont au café principalement pour retrouver° leurs° copains et passer° un bon moment avec eux.°

Un café français est divisé en deux parties: l'intérieur et la terrasse.° Au printemps et en été, les Français préfèrent s'asseoir° à la terrasse. Là, ils peuvent° profiter du soleil° et regarder les gens qui passent dans la rue.

On peut *One can* **commander** *order* **retrouver** *meet* **leurs** *their* **passer** *spend* **eux** *them*
la terrasse *terrace (outdoor section of a café)* **s'asseoir** *to sit* **peuvent** *can* **profiter du soleil** *enjoy the sun*

A Le verbe *venir*

The verb **venir** *(to come)* is irregular. Note the forms of **venir** in the present tense.

venir		Nous allons **venir** avec des amis.
je	**viens**	Je **viens** avec toi.
tu	**viens**	Est-ce que tu **viens** au cinéma?
il/elle	**vient**	Monique ne **vient** pas avec nous.
nous	**venons**	Nous **venons** à cinq heures.
vous	**venez**	À quelle heure **venez**-vous à la boum?
ils/elles	**viennent**	Ils **viennent** de Paris, n'est-ce pas?

→ **Revenir** *(to come back)* is conjugated like **venir.**

—À quelle heure **revenez**-vous?
—Nous **revenons** à dix heures.

→ Note the interrogative expression: **d'où?** *(from where?)*

D'où viens-tu? *__Where__ do you come __from__?*

1 Tu viens?

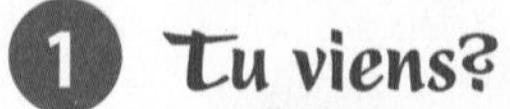

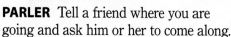

PARLER Tell a friend where you are going and ask him or her to come along.

▸ à la pizzeria

1. au café
2. à la bibliothèque
3. à la piscine
4. au cybercafé
5. au centre commercial
6. au magasin
7. au stade
8. en classe

Je vais à la pizzeria. Tu viens avec moi?
D'accord, je viens.
(Non, je ne viens pas.)

2 Le pique-nique du Club français

PARLER/ÉCRIRE The French Club has organized a picnic. Say who is coming and who is not.

▸ Philippe (non)
Philippe ne vient pas.

1. Alice (oui)
2. Jean-Pierre (non)
3. Paul et Caroline (oui)
4. vous (non)
5. je (oui)
6. nous (non)
7. tu (non)
8. le prof de français (oui)
9. le prof d'anglais (oui)

@HOMETUTOR
my.hrw.com

B La préposition *de; de* + l'article défini

The preposition **de** has several meanings:

from	Nous venons **de** la bibliothèque.	*We are coming **from** the library.*
of	Quelle est l'adresse **de** l'école?	*What is the address **of** the school?*
about	Je parle **de** mon copain.	*I am talking **about** my friend.*

CONTRACTIONS

Note the forms of **de** + DEFINITE ARTICLE in the sentences below.

Voici **le** café.	Marc vient **du** café.
Voici **les** Champs-Élysées.	Nous venons **des** Champs-Élysées.
Voici **la** piscine.	Tu reviens **de la** piscine.
Voici **l'**hôtel.	Les touristes arrivent **de l'**hôtel.

The preposition **de** contracts with **le** and **les,** but not with **la** and **l'.**

CONTRACTION	NO CONTRACTION		
de + le → **du**	de + la = **de la**	**du** café	**de la** plage
de + les → **des**	de + l' = **de l'**	**des** magasins	**de l'**école

→ There is liaison after **des** when the next word begins with a vowel sound.
Où sont les livres **des** ‿ **étudiants?** (z)

3 Rendez-vous

PARLER The following students live in Paris. On a Saturday afternoon they are meeting in a café. Say where each one is coming from.

▶ Jacques: le musée d'Orsay

1. Sylvie: le Louvre
2. Isabelle: le parc de la Villette
3. Jean-Paul: le Centre Pompidou
4. François: le Quartier latin
5. Cécile: l'avenue de l'Opéra
6. Nicole: la tour Eiffel
7. Marc: le jardin du Luxembourg
8. André: les Champs-Élysées
9. Pierre: les Galeries Lafayette
10. Corinne: la rue Bonaparte

Jacques vient du musée d'Orsay.

4 D'où viens-tu? 

PARLER During vacation, Olivier goes out every day. When he gets home, his sister Sophie asks him where he is coming from.

▶ mardi

D'où viens-tu?
Je viens du centre commercial.

1. lundi
2. mercredi
3. vendredi
4. dimanche
5. samedi
6. jeudi

LUNDI	le restaurant
▶ MARDI	le centre commercial
MERCREDI	la bibliothèque
JEUDI	l'opéra
VENDREDI	le concert de rock
SAMEDI	le pique-nique de Monique
DIMANCHE	la boum de Christine

VOCABULAIRE Les sports, les jeux et la musique

▶ *Les sports*

le foot(ball)
le basket(ball)
le ping-pong
le volley(ball)
le tennis
le baseball

▶ *Les jeux* *(games)*

les échecs *(chess)*
les jeux vidéo
les jeux d'ordinateur
les dames *(checkers)*
les cartes *(cards)*

▶ *Les instruments de musique*

le piano
le violon
le saxo(phone)
le clavier *(keyboard)*
la flûte
la guitare
la clarinette
la batterie *(drums)*

jouer à + **le, la, les** + SPORT or GAME	*to play*	Nous **jouons au** tennis.
jouer de + **le, la, les** + INSTRUMENT	*to play*	Alice **joue du** piano.

5 Activités 

PARLER Ask your classmates if they play the following instruments and games.

▶ —Est-ce que tu joues au ping-pong?
—Oui, je joue au ping-pong.
(Non, je ne joue pas au ping-pong.)

▶ —Est-ce que tu joues du piano?
—Oui, je joue du piano.
(Non, je ne joue pas du piano.)

@HOMETUTOR my.hrw.com

C Les pronoms accentués

In the answers to the questions below, the nouns in heavy print are replaced by pronouns. These pronouns are called STRESS PRONOUNS. Note their forms.

—François dîne avec **Florence?** *Is François having dinner with* ***Florence?***
—Oui, il dîne avec **elle.** *Yes, he is having dinner with* ***her.***

—Tu parles de **Jean-Paul?** *Are you talking about* ***Jean-Paul?***
—Non, je ne parle pas de **lui.** *No, I'm not talking about* ***him.***

FORMS

(SUBJECT PRONOUNS)	STRESS PRONOUNS	(SUBJECT PRONOUNS)	STRESS PRONOUNS
(je)	**moi**	(nous)	**nous**
(tu)	**toi**	(vous)	**vous**
(il)	**lui**	(ils)	**eux**
(elle)	**elle**	(elles)	**elles**

USES

Stress pronouns are used:

- to reinforce a subject pronoun
  Moi, je parle français. ***I*** *speak French.*
  Vous, vous parlez anglais. ***You*** *speak English.*
- after **c'est** and **ce n'est pas**
  —C'est Paul là-bas?
  —Non, ce n'est pas **lui.** *No, it's not* ***him.***
- in short sentences where there is no verb
  —Qui parle français ici?
  —**Moi!** ***I do!***
- before and after **et** and **ou**
  Lui et moi, nous sommes copains. ***He and I,*** *(we) are friends.*
- After prepositions such as **de, avec, pour, chez**
  Voici Marc et Paul. Je parle souvent **d'eux.** *I often talk* ***about them.***
  Voici Isabelle. Je vais au cinéma **avec elle.** *I go to the movies* ***with her.***
  Voici M. Mercier. Nous travaillons **pour lui.** *We work* ***for him.***

➔ Note the meaning of **chez** + STRESS PRONOUN:
Je vais **chez moi.** *I am going* ***home.***
Paul étudie **chez lui.** *Paul is studying* ***at home.***

Tu viens **chez nous?** *Are you coming* ***to our house?***
Je suis chez Alice. Je dîne **chez elle.** *I am having dinner* ***at her place.***

6 Samedi soir *(Saturday night)*

PARLER/ÉCRIRE On Saturday night, some people stay home and others do not. Read what the following people are doing and say whether or not they are at home.

▶ Alice étudie.
Elle est chez elle.

▶ Paul va au cinéma.
Il n'est pas chez lui.

1. François regarde la télé.
2. Mélanie va au cinéma.
3. Marc et Pierre dînent en ville.
4. Léa et Pauline écoutent de la musique.
5. Les voisins font une promenade.
6. Je travaille avec mon père.
7. Tu vas au théâtre.
8. Nous allons à la bibliothèque.
9. Tu prépares le dîner.

7 Questions personnelles

PARLER/ÉCRIRE Use stress pronouns in your answers.

1. Tu étudies souvent avec tes *(your)* copains?
2. Tu vas souvent chez ta cousine?
3. Tu travailles pour les voisins?
4. Tu parles français avec ton père?
5. Tu vas souvent au cinéma avec tes copines?
6. Tu restes chez toi le week-end?
7. Tu restes chez toi pendant *(during)* les vacances?
8. Tu voyages avec tes parents?
9. Tu joues aux jeux vidéo avec ton copain?
10. Tu vas souvent chez tes voisins?

VOCABULAIRE Expressions pour la conversation

▶ ***How to express surprise:***

Vraiment?! *Really?!*
—Je parle chinois.
—Vraiment?!

▶ ***How to contradict someone:***

Pas du tout! *Not at all! Definitely not!*
—Tu es anglais?
—Pas du tout! Je suis français!

8 Commérage *(Gossip)* 

PARLER Élodie likes to gossip. Act out the dialogues between her and her friend Thomas.

▶ Marina dîne avec Jean-Pierre.

1. Éric dîne avec Alice.
2. Thérèse va chez Paul.
3. Jérôme est au cinéma avec Delphine.
4. Monsieur Mercier travaille pour Mademoiselle Duval.
5. Philippe travaille pour le voisin.
6. Marc et Vincent dansent avec Mélanie et Juliette.

@HOMETUTOR
my.hrw.com

D La construction: nom + *de* + nom

Compare the word order in French and English.

J'ai une raquette.	C'est une **raquette de tennis.**	*It's a* ***tennis racket.***
Paul a une voiture.	C'est une **voiture de sport.**	*It's a* ***sports car.***

When one noun is used to modify another noun, the French construction is:

MAIN NOUN + **de** + MODIFYING NOUN	**une classe de français.**
↓ **d'** (+ VOWEL SOUND)	**une classe d'espagnol.**

→ There is no article after **de.**

LANGUAGE COMPARISON

In French, when one noun modifies another, the main noun comes FIRST.

In English, the main noun comes SECOND.

un **jeu** d'ordinateur *a computer* ***game***

9 Précisions

PARLER Complete the following sentences with an expression consisting of de + underlined noun.

▶ J'aime le sport. J'ai une voiture …

J'ai une voiture de sport!

1. Claire aime le ping-pong. Elle a une raquette …
2. Nous adorons le rock. Nous écoutons un concert …
3. Jacques aime le jazz. Il écoute un programme …
4. Vous étudiez l'anglais. Vous avez un livre …
5. Tu étudies le piano. Aujourd'hui, tu as une leçon …
6. Léa étudie l'espagnol. Elle a un bon prof …
7. Je regarde mes photos. J'ai un album …
8. Pierre joue au baseball. Il a une batte …
9. J'aime la musique africaine. J'ai des CD …
10. Paul est bon en maths. Il fait un problème …

Prononciation 

Les voyelles /ø/ **et** /œ/

The letters "**eu**" and "**oeu**" represent vowel sounds that do not exist in English but that are not very hard to pronounce.

/ø/

deux

/œ/

neuf

Répétez:

/ø/ **deux eux je veux je peux un peu jeux il pleut un euro**
Tu peux aller chez eux.

/œ/ **neuf soeur heure professeur jeune**
Ma soeur arrive à neuf heures.

À votre tour!

OBJECTIFS

Now you can …
- let people know if you are coming with them or not
- talk about the musical instruments, sports, and games that you play

1 Conversation

PARLER Saturday afternoon, Henri meets Stéphanie downtown. Match Henri's questions with Stéphanie's answers. Then act out the conversation with a classmate.

1 Salut, Stéphanie! D'où viens-tu?
2 Et où vas-tu maintenant?
3 Tu ne veux pas venir au cinéma avec moi?
4 Ah bon? Pourquoi?
a J'ai un examen d'anglais lundi.
b Du supermarché.
c Je rentre chez moi.
d Je ne peux pas. Je dois étudier.

2 Créa-dialogue

PARLER Ask your classmates whom they are going to visit and what they are going to do. Then decide if you are going to come along.

▶ —Où vas-tu?
—Je vais chez Jean-Claude. Tu viens?
—Ça dépend! Qu'est-ce que tu vas faire chez lui?
—Nous allons jouer au ping-pong.
—D'accord, je viens!
(Non, je ne viens pas.)

▶ Jean-Claude

CHEZ QUI?	1. Françoise	2. Corinne et Claire	3. Nicolas et Patrick	4. mon cousin	5. ma cousine	6. des copains
ACTIVITÉ						

3 Retour à la maison

PARLER This afternoon, the following people went downtown. Say which places they are coming from.

▶ Nous venons de l'école.

▶ nous

1	2	3
tu	vous	Madame Simon
4	**5**	**6**
Monsieur Dupont	Claire et Diane	Daniel et Philippe

4 Message illustré

ÉCRIRE Frédéric likes to use illustrations in his diary. Transcribe what he has written about himself and others, replacing the pictures with the corresponding missing words.

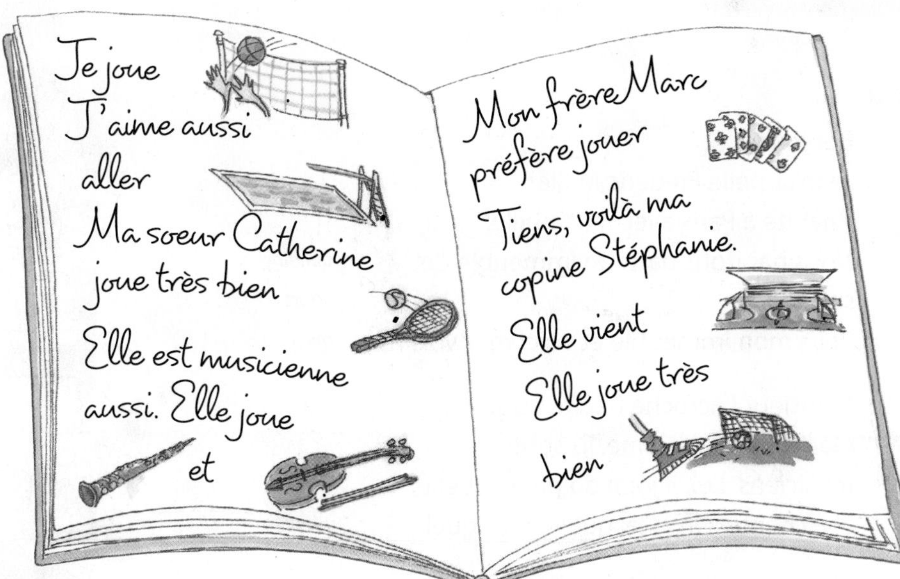

Je joue
J'aime aussi
aller
Ma soeur Catherine
joue très bien
Elle est musicienne
aussi. Elle joue
et
Mon frère Marc
préfère jouer
Tiens, voilà ma
copine Stéphanie.
Elle vient
Elle joue très
bien

5 Un mail à Sandrine 

ÉCRIRE In a recent e-mail, Sandrine, your French pen pal, mentioned various hobbies she enjoys. In a short e-mail, tell her . . .

- which sports you play
- which musical instruments you play
- which games you play

▶ **Chère Sandrine,**
J'aime beaucoup les sports. Je joue au . . .

parc	supermarché	stade
école	bibliothèque	piscine

Leçon 16

Conversation et Culture

Mes voisins

AUDIO

Bonjour!	
Je m'appelle Frédéric Mallet.	
J'habite à Paris avec ma famille.	
Nous habitons dans un immeuble de	*building*
six étages.	*floors*
Voici mon immeuble et voici mes voisins.	*my*
Monsieur Lacroche habite au sixième	*sixth*
étage avec sa femme. Ils sont	
musiciens. Lui, il joue du piano et elle,	
elle chante. Oh là là, quelle musique!	*what*
Mademoiselle Jolivet habite au	
cinquième étage avec son oncle et	*fifth / her*
sa tante.	*her*
Paul, mon meilleur ami, habite au	*best*
quatrième étage avec sa soeur et	*fourth / his*
ses parents.	*his*
Mademoiselle Ménard habite au	
troisième étage avec son chien	*third*
Pomme, ses deux chats Fritz et Arthur,	
son perroquet Coco et son canari	*parrot*
Froufrou. (Je pense que c'est une	*think / that*
personne très intéressante, mais mon	
père pense qu'elle est un peu bizarre.)	
Monsieur et Madame Boutin habitent	
au deuxième étage avec leur	*second / their*
fils et leurs deux filles.	*son / daughters*
Et qui habite au premier étage?	
C'est un garçon super-intelligent,	
super-cool et très sympathique!	
Et ce garçon … c'est moi!	

@HOMETUTOR
my.hrw.com

Compréhension

1. Où habite Frédéric Mallet?
2. Combien (*How many*) d'étages a son immeuble?
3. Qui habite à chaque (*each*) étage?
4. Quelle est la profession des Lacroche?
5. Selon toi (*In your opinion*), est-ce que Mademoiselle Ménard est une personne bizarre ou intéressante? Pourquoi?

COMPARAISONS *Culturelles*

The floors of buildings are numbered differently in France and in the United States. Compare:

- **rez-de-chaussée** — *ground floor or first floor*
- **premier étage (1er étage)** — *second floor*
- **deuxième étage (2ème étage)** — *third floor*

NOTE: In the older downtown areas of French cities, apartment houses have a maximum of six stories. This is because until the twentieth century there were no elevators and people had to use the stairs.

NOTE *Culturelle*

Les animaux domestiques en France

La France a une population de 60 millions d'habitants et de 42 millions d'animaux domestiques.° Les Français adorent les animaux. Une famille sur deux° a un animal domestique. Par ordre de préférence, les principaux animaux domestiques sont les chiens (39%: trente-neuf pour cent), les chats (35%), les poissons (12%), les oiseaux (5%) et les hamsters (4%). Il y a aussi un certain nombre de serpents, de tortues et de lapins.

un hamster

un lapin

une tortue

un oiseau

un poisson

un poisson rouge

animaux domestiques *pets* **une ... sur deux** *one out of two*

A La possession avec *de*

Note the words in heavy print:

Voici une moto.	C'est la moto **de Frédéric.**	*It's **Frédéric's** motorcycle.*
Voici un vélo.	C'est le vélo **de Sophie.**	*It's **Sophie's** bike.*

To express POSSESSION, French speakers use the construction:

le/la/les + NOUN + **de** + OWNER ↓ **d'**(+ VOWEL SOUND)	la radio **de** Thomas les livres **de** Claire la maison **d'**Émilie

→ The same construction is used to express RELATIONSHIP:

C'est **le copain de Daniel.** *That's **Daniel's friend.***
C'est **la mère de Paul.** *That's **Paul's mother.***

→ Remember that **de** contracts with **le** and **les:**

Où est le chat **du voisin?** *Where is the **neighbor's** cat?*
C'est la chambre **des enfants.** *This is the **children's** room.*

→ While English often indicates possession with **'s,** French always uses **de.**

la copine **de Monique** ***Monique's** friend (the friend **of Monique**)*

1 Présentations *(Introductions)*

PARLER Imagine that you are hosting a party in France. Introduce the following people.

▶ Jean-Marc (cousin/Sylvie)

Jean-Marc est le cousin de Sylvie.

1. Carole (cousine / Jacques)
2. Michel (copain / Caroline)
3. Philippe (camarade / Charles)
4. Robert (frère / Guillaume)
5. Marina (copine / Paul)
6. Pauline (amie / Éric)
7. Alice (soeur / Karine)

2 Échanges

PARLER/ÉCRIRE The following friends have decided to trade a few of their possessions. On a separate sheet of paper, write out what each person has, once the exchange has been completed.

ÉCHANGE

Marc Alice Éric Laure

@HOMETUTOR
my.hrw.com

VOCABULAIRE La famille 

la famille *(family)*
les grands-parents
- **le grand-père** — **la grand-mère**

les parents *(parents)*
- **le père** — **la mère**
- **le mari** *(husband)* — **la femme** *(wife)*

les enfants *(children)*
- **un enfant** — **une enfant**
- **le frère** — **la soeur**
- **le fils** *(son)* — **la fille** *(daughter)*

les parents *(relatives)*
- **l'oncle** — **la tante** *(aunt)*
- **le cousin** — **la cousine**

3 La famille de Frédéric

PARLER/ÉCRIRE Frédéric has drawn his family tree. Study it and explain the relationships between the people below.

▶ Éric / Alice Vidal
Éric est le fils d'Alice Vidal.

1. Léa / Frédéric
2. Martine Mallet / Léa
3. Albert et Julie Mallet / Éric
4. Alice Vidal / Frédéric
5. Jean Mallet / Martine Mallet
6. Alice Vidal / Maurice Vidal
7. Julie Mallet / Éric
8. Élodie / Maurice Vidal
9. Léa / Éric
10. Frédéric / Élodie

▶ **Marc a la guitare d'Alice et ...**

▶

B Les adjectifs possessifs: *mon, ton, son*

LEARNING ABOUT LANGUAGE

French, like English, shows possession and relationship with POSSESSIVE ADJECTIVES:

ma voiture (***my** car*), **mon** père (***my** father*)

In French, possessive adjectives AGREE with the nouns they introduce.

Note the forms of the possessive adjectives in the chart below:

(POSSESSOR)		SINGULAR MASCULINE	SINGULAR FEMININE	PLURAL			
(je)	*my*	**mon**	**ma**	**mes**	**mon** frère	**ma** soeur	**mes** copains
(tu)	*your*	**ton**	**ta**	**tes**	**ton** oncle	**ta** tante	**tes** cousins
(il)	*his*	**son**	**sa**	**ses**	**son** père	**sa** mère	**ses** parents
(elle)	*her*	**son**	**sa**	**ses**	**son** père	**sa** mère	**ses** parents

→ The feminine singular forms **ma, ta, sa** become **mon, ton, son** before a vowel sound.

une amie	**mon** amie	**ton** amie	**son** amie
une auto	**mon** auto	**ton** auto	**son** auto

→ There is liaison after **mon, ton, son, mes, tes, ses** before a vowel sound.

mon oncle   **mes** amis

→ The choice between **son, sa,** and **ses** depends on the gender (masculine or feminine) and the number (singular or plural) of the noun that *follows*.

It does NOT depend on the gender of the possessor (that is, whether the owner is male or female). Compare:

PERSONNALISE TON PORTABLE

	un vélo	une radio	des livres
Voici Frédéric	Voici son vélo. (his bike)	Voici sa radio. (his radio)	Voici ses livres. (his books)
Voici Sophie	Voici son vélo. (her bike)	Voici sa radio. (her radio)	Voici ses livres. (her books)

@HOMETUTOR
my.hrw.com

4 Marc et Hélène 

PARLER Marc never knows where his things are, but Hélène does. Play both roles.

▶ le vélo/dans le garage
—Où est mon vélo?
—Ton vélo? Il est dans le garage.

1. les DVD/ici
2. la raquette/là-bas
3. la montre/sur toi
4. les livres/dans le sac
5. le portable/sur le bureau
6. le chat/derrière la porte
7. l'appareil-photo/dans la chambre
8. la tablette/sur la table

5 Invitations

PARLER/ÉCRIRE Say whom each person is inviting to the school party, using the appropriate possessive adjectives.

▶ **Michel/la copine**
Michel invite sa copine.

1. André/la cousine
2. Jean-Claude/la soeur
3. Marie-Noëlle/les frères
4. Pascal/l'amie Sophie
5. Monique/les cousins
6. Nathalie/l'ami Marc
7. Georges/l'amie Cécile
8. Paul/l'amie Thérèse

6 Chez Marie et Christophe Boutin

PARLER/ÉCRIRE Items 1 to 8 belong to Marie. Items 9 to 16 belong to Christophe. Point these things out.

Marie

▶ le vélo **C'est son vélo.**

1. la tablette
2. le sac
3. le chien
4. l'album
5. l'ordinateur
6. la guitare
7. les DVD
8. les magazines

Christophe

▶ les CD **Ce sont ses CD.**

9. la guitare
10. la radio
11. le chat
12. le scooter
13. les livres
14. la montre
15. les photos
16. les skis

VOCABULAIRE Expression pour la conversation

▶ ***How to question a statement or express a doubt:***

Tu es sûr(e)? *Are you sure?* —C'est mon pantalon *(pants)!*
—Tu es sûr?

 Après la soirée 

PARLER Last night Frédéric and Paul gave a party. They realize that their friends left certain things behind. Frédéric thinks he knows what belongs to whom.

▶ le sac/Claire
FRÉDÉRIC: **Voici le sac de Claire.**
PAUL: **Tu es sûr?**
FRÉDÉRIC: **Mais oui, c'est son sac!**

1. le sac/Jean-Pierre
2. la guitare/Antoine
3. l'appareil-photo/Cécile
4. le MP3/Stéphanie
5. les DVD/Léa
6. le portable/Thomas

C Les adjectifs possessifs: *notre, votre, leur*

Note the forms of the possessive adjectives in the chart below:

(POSSESSOR)		SINGULAR	PLURAL		
(nous)	*our*	**notre**	**nos**	**notre** prof	**nos** livres
(vous)	*your*	**votre**	**vos**	**votre** ami	**vos** copains
(ils/elles)	*their*	**leur**	**leurs**	**leur** radio	**leurs** amies

→ There is liaison after **nos, vos, leurs** when the next word begins with a vowel sound.

nos amis **vos** amies **leurs** ordinateurs

C'est son vélo.

C'est leur vélo.

8 Au centre commercial

PARLER At the mall, a customer is looking for various things. The person at the information desk indicates where they can be found. Play both roles.

▶ les jeux vidéo/là-bas

S'il vous plaît, où sont vos jeux vidéo?
INFORMATION
Nos jeux vidéo sont là-bas.

1. les livres/à gauche
2. les affiches/à droite
3. le restaurant/en haut
4. le garage/en bas
5. les ordinateurs/ici
6. la cafétéria/tout droit

9 Les millionnaires

PARLER/ÉCRIRE Imagine you are showing a millionaire's estate to French visitors.

▶ la maison
Voici leur maison.

1. la piscine
2. la Rolls Royce
3. les chiens
4. le parc
5. l'hélicoptère
6. les courts de tennis

10 En famille

PARLER/ÉCRIRE We often do things with our family. Complete each sentence with a possessive adjective: **son, sa, ses, leur,** or **leurs.**

▶ **Pascal joue au tennis avec sa cousine.**
▶ **Éric et Paul jouent aux cartes avec leurs cousins.**

1. Frédéric dîne chez … oncle.
2. André dîne chez … grands-parents.
3. Caroline et Paul vont chez … grand-mère.
4. Mlle Vénard fait une promenade avec … chien.
5. Antoine va à la piscine avec … soeur.
6. Stéphanie et Céline vont au cinéma avec … parents.
7. M. et Mme Boutin voyagent avec … fille.
8. Mme Denis visite Paris avec … fils, Marc et Frédéric.

@HOMETUTOR
my.hrw.com

D Les nombres ordinaux

Compare the following regular numbers and the ordinal numbers in French:

(2)	deux	**deuxième**	Février est le **deuxième** mois de l'année.
(3)	trois	**troisième**	Mercredi est le **troisième** jour de la semaine.
(4)	quatre	**quatrième**	J'habite au **quatrième** étage *(floor)*.

To form ordinal numbers, French speakers use the following pattern:

NUMBER (minus final **-e**, if any) + **-ième**

(6)	six	:	**six**	+	**-ième**	→	**sixième**
(11)	onze	:	**onz-**	+	**-ième**	→	**onzième**

→ EXCEPTIONS: (1) un (une) → **premier (première)**
(5) cinq → **cinquième**
(9) neuf → **neuvième**

→ Ordinal numbers are adjectives and come BEFORE the noun.

LEARNING ABOUT LANGUAGE

Numbers like *first, second, third, fourth, fifth* are used to rank persons or things—to put them in a given order.

They are called ORDINAL NUMBERS.

In English, most ordinal numbers end in *-th*.

11 La course *(The race)*

PARLER/ÉCRIRE Frédéric and his friends are participating in a five-kilometer race. Announce the order of arrival of the following runners.

▶ Paul (6)

1. Frédéric (4)
2. Jérôme (7)
3. Christophe (8)
4. Sophie (2)
5. Christine (1)
6. Claire (10)
7. Karine (11)
8. Olivier (12)

Prononciation 

Les voyelles /o/ et /ɔ/

The French vowel /o/ is pronounced with more tension than in English. It is usually the last sound in a word.

/o/

vélo

/ɔ/

téléphone

Répétez: /o/ **vélo radio nos vos eau château chaud**
Nos vélos sont au château.

The French vowel /ɔ/ occurs in the middle of a word. Imitate the model carefully.

Répétez: /ɔ/ **téléphone école Nicole notre votre copain prof dommage**
Comment s'appelle votre prof?

À votre tour!

OBJECTIFS

Now you can . . .
- talk about your family and your relatives
- identify things as belonging to you or to someone else
- talk about your pets

1 Allô!

PARLER Émilie is on the phone with Bernard. Match Émilie's questions with Bernard's answers. Then act out the dialogue with a classmate.

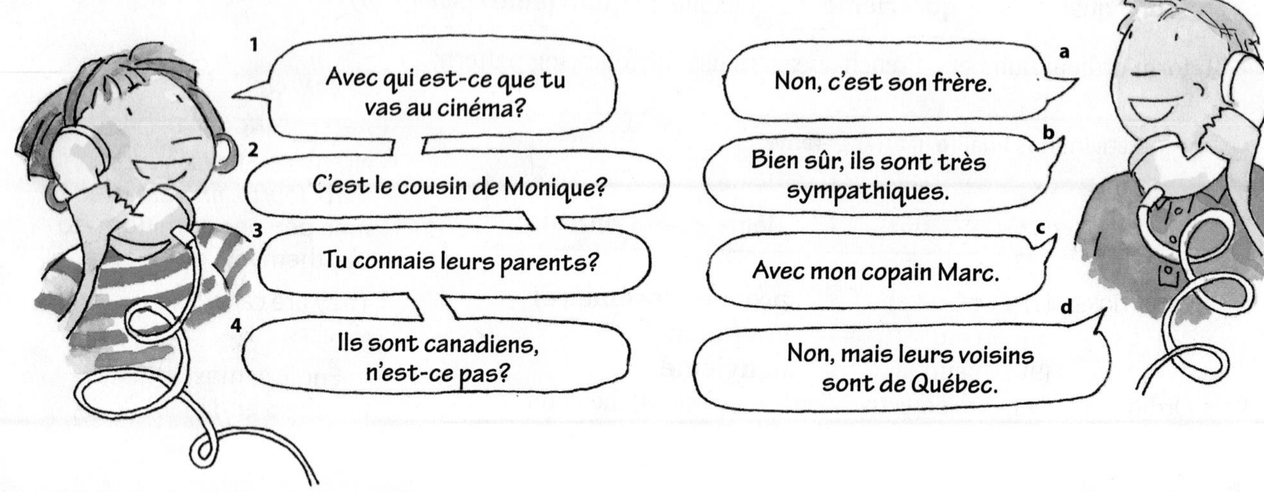

1 Avec qui est-ce que tu vas au cinéma?
2 C'est le cousin de Monique?
3 Tu connais leurs parents?
4 Ils sont canadiens, n'est-ce pas?
a Non, c'est son frère.
b Bien sûr, ils sont très sympathiques.
c Avec mon copain Marc.
d Non, mais leurs voisins sont de Québec.

2 Créa-dialogue

PARLER We often identify objects by their color. Create conversations with your classmates according to the model.

le vélo / Paul?

1. la guitare / Alice?
2. le scooter / Paul et Anne?
3. le chien / tes cousins?
4. la mobylette / Isabelle?
5. la maison / M. et Mme Lavoie?
6. la voiture / ton oncle?

▶ —C'est le vélo de Paul?
—Non, ce n'est pas son vélo.
—Tu es sûr?
—Mais oui. Son vélo est bleu.

3 Composition: un animal domestique 

ÉCRIRE Write a short composition about a pet: either your own pet, a pet belonging to a friend, or an imaginary pet. You may mention …

- the type of animal
- its name
- its age
- its size
- its eating habits
- some physical and personality traits

4 Composition: Ma famille 

ÉCRIRE Select five people in your family and write one to three sentences about each person.

Mon cousin s'appelle John. Il habite à San Francisco. Il a seize ans.

5 Arbre généalogique *(Family tree)*

ÉCRIRE On a separate sheet of paper, draw your own (real or imaginary) family tree. Label the people and indicate their relationships to you.

Tests de contrôle

By taking the following tests, you can check your progress in French and also prepare for the unit test. Write your answers on a separate sheet of paper.

1 The right place

Review...
- places and rooms of the house: pp. 197 and 200

Complete each of the following sentences by filling in the blank with one of the places in the box. Be logical and do not use the same word more than once.

bibliothèque chambre cuisine école église immeuble
jardin magasin piscine plage salle de bains salle à manger

1. Le réfrigérateur est dans la —.
2. Quand il y a des invités *(guests)*, nous dînons dans la —.
3. Dans le —, il y a un lilas *(lilac tree)*.
4. Dans le complexe sportif où nous allons, il y a une — olympique.
5. Il y a beaucoup de livres à la — de la ville.
6. Dans ma —, il y a une table et un grand lit.
7. En été, nous allons en vacances sur une — de l'Atlantique.
8. Il y a une — catholique dans notre quartier.
9. Le samedi, les élèves américains ne vont pas à l'—.
10. Le shampooing *(shampoo)* est dans la —.
11. Mes cousins habitent dans un grand — moderne.
12. Je vais acheter un ordinateur dans un — d'équipement électronique.

2 The right choice

Review...
- use of **à**, **de**, and **chez** pp. 208, 210, 211, 219, 220, and 223

Choose the word or expression in parentheses which logically completes each of the following sentences.

1. Marc dîne — restaurant. **(à, au)**
2. Thomas nage — piscine. **(la, à la)**
3. Le professeur parle — élèves. **(aux, les)**
4. Les élèves vont — école en bus. **(à la, à l')**
5. Nous faisons une promenade — pied. **(à, au)**
6. Pauline va — sa copine Isabelle. **(à, chez)**
7. Nous revenons — école à trois heures. **(à l', de l')**
8. Les touristes arrivent — musée. **(du, de l')**
9. J'aime jouer — football. **(au, du)**
10. Est-ce que tu joues — clarinette? **(à la, de la)**
11. Comment s'appelle la copine — Monique? **(de, à)**
12. Voici la maison — voisins. **(des, de)**

3 The right owner

Review...
- possessive adjectives: pp. 230 and 232

Complete each of the following sentences with the possessive adjective that corresponds to the underlined subject.

▶ Jean-Paul regarde **ses** photos.

1. Tu téléphones à — copine.
2. Je vais souvent au cinéma avec — amis.
3. Marc dîne chez — tante.
4. Alice invite — voisins à la boum.
5. Isabelle n'a pas — appareil-photo avec elle.
6. Thomas et Charlotte sont en vacances chez — oncle.
7. Les élèves respectent — professeurs.
8. Vous parlez avec — amie Mélanie.
9. Nous allons visiter Paris avec — professeur de français.
10. Est-ce que vous écoutez toujours — parents?

4 Aller and venir

Review...
- **aller and venir:** pp. 206, 212, and 218

Complete the following sentences with the appropriate forms of **aller** or **venir.**

1. Attendez-moi *(Wait for me)*! Je —.
2. Thomas et Céline — très souvent au cinéma.
3. Qu'est-ce que tu — faire samedi?
4. Nous — aller à une boum.
5. Le professeur est canadien. Il — de Montréal.
6. Je — souvent à la piscine parce que j'aime nager.
7. Nicolas n'a pas faim. Il — du restaurant.
8. D'où est-ce que vous —?

5 Composition: La maison idéale

Digital performance space

Write a short paragraph of five or six sentences describing your ideal house and its rooms. Does it have a garden? Where is it located? What do you especially like about it?

STRATEGY Writing

a	b	c
Sketch out a floor plan of your ideal house, labelling the rooms.	Organize your paragraph, concluding with why you like this house.	Reread your composition to be sure you have spelled all the names of the rooms correctly.

Vocabulaire

POUR COMMUNIQUER

Asking where people are going

Où vas-tu?		*Where are you going?*
Je vais à + PLACE, EVENT	**Je vais au concert.**	*I am going to the concert.*
Je vais chez + PERSON	**Je vais chez Pierre.**	*I am going to Pierre's house.*
Je vais chez + STRESS PRONOUN	**Je vais chez moi.**	*I am going to my house.*

Asking where people are coming from

D'où est-ce que tu viens?		*Where are you coming from?*
Je viens de + PLACE	**Je viens de la piscine.**	*I am coming from the pool.*

Asking for directions

Excusez-moi, où est [le théâtre]? *Excuse me, where is [the theater]?*	**Est-ce que c'est loin? / près?**	*Is it far? / nearby / close?*
	Tournez à gauche. / à droite.	*Turn to the left. / to the right.*
	Continuez tout droit.	*Continue straight ahead.*
Pardon, où sont [les toilettes]? *Excuse me, where are [the toilets]?*	**Elles sont en haut. / en bas.**	*They are upstairs. / downstairs.*

Talking about future plans

Qu'est-ce que tu vas faire?	*What are you going to do?*
Je vais [travailler].	*I am going [to work].*

Expressing possession

C'est mon (ton, son ...) livre.	*That's my (your, his/her, ...) book.*

MOTS ET EXPRESSIONS

Moyens de transport *(means of transportation)*

à pied	*on foot*	**en bus**	*by bus*	**en train**	*by train*
à vélo	*by bicycle*	**en métro**	*by subway*	**en voiture**	*by car*
		en taxi	*by taxi*		

La ville

un boulevard	*boulevard*	**une adresse**	*address*
un café	*café*	**une avenue**	*avenue*
un centre commercial	*mall, shopping center*	**une bibliothèque**	*library*
un cinéma	*movie theater*	**une école**	*school*
un hôpital	*hospital*	**une église**	*church*
un hôtel	*hotel*	**une piscine**	*(swimming) pool*
un magasin	*store*	**une plage**	*beach*
un musée	*museum*	**une rue**	*street*
un parc	*park*	**une ville**	*city, town*
un quartier	*neighborhood*		
un restaurant	*restaurant*		
un stade	*stadium*		
un supermarché	*supermarket*		
un théâtre	*theater*		
un village	*town, village*		

Interactive Flashcards
@HOMETUTOR
my.hrw.com

La maison

un appartement	*apartment*	**une chambre**	*bedroom*
un garage	*garage*	**une cuisine**	*kitchen*
un immeuble	*apartment building*	**une maison**	*house*
un jardin	*garden, yard*	**une salle à manger**	*dining room*
un salon	*living room*	**une salle de bains**	*bathroom*
		les toilettes	*bathroom, toilet*

Quelques endroits où aller

un concert	*concert*	**un film**	*movie*	**une boum**	*party (casual)*
un endroit	*place*	**un pique-nique**	*picnic*	**une fête**	*party*
un événement	*event*	**un rendez-vous**	*date, appointment*	**une soirée**	*party (evening)*

La famille

les parents	*parents; relatives*	**la famille**	*family*
les grands-parents	*grandparents*		
le grand-père	*grandfather*	**la grand-mère**	*grandmother*
le père	*father*	**la mère**	*mother*
le mari	*husband*	**la femme**	*wife*
un enfant	*child*	**une enfant**	*child*
le fils	*son*	**la fille**	*daughter*
le frère	*brother*	**la soeur**	*sister*
l'oncle	*uncle*	**la tante**	*aunt*
le cousin	*cousin*	**la cousine**	*cousin*

Verbes en *-er*

arriver	*to arrive, to come*
rentrer	*to go back, come back*
rester	*to stay*
jouer à + SPORT, GAME	*to play (a sport, game)*
jouer de + INSTRUMENT	*to play (an instrument)*

Verbes irréguliers

aller	*to go*
faire une promenade à pied	*to go for a walk*
faire une promenade à vélo	*to go for a bike ride*
faire une promenade en voiture	*to go for a drive*
venir	*to come*
revenir	*to come back*

Les sports

le baseball	*baseball*
le basket(ball)	*basketball*
le foot(ball)	*soccer*
le ping-pong	*ping-pong*
le tennis	*tennis*
le volley(ball)	*volleyball*

Les jeux

les échecs	*chess*	**les cartes**	*cards*
les jeux d'ordinateur	*computer games*	**les dames**	*checkers*
les jeux vidéo	*video games*		

Les instruments de musique

le clavier	*keyboard*	**la batterie**	*drums*
le piano	*piano*	**la clarinette**	*clarinet*
le saxo(phone)	*saxophone*	**la flûte**	*flute*
le violon	*violin*	**la guitare**	*guitar*

Les nombres ordinaux

premier (première)	*first*	**septième**	*seventh*
deuxième	*second*	**huitième**	*eighth*
troisième	*third*	**neuvième**	*ninth*
quatrième	*fourth*	**dixième**	*tenth*
cinquième	*fifth*	**onzième**	*eleventh*
sixième	*sixth*	**douzième**	*twelfth*

Expressions utiles

Pas du tout!	*Not at all! Definitely not!*
Vraiment?!	*Really?!*
Tu es sûr(e)?	*Are you sure?*
Vas-y!	*Go on!*
Va-t'en!	*Go away!*

LES JEUNES FRANÇAIS ET le cinéma

Le samedi, les jeunes Français adorent aller au cinéma. C'est pour eux l'occasion de voir° un bon film et aussi d'être avec leurs copains. Quand ils sont en ville, ils peuvent° aller dans les cinémas de quartier. Mais en général, ils préfèrent les «multiplexes». Là, ils ont le choix entre 6 et 12 films différents. Dans les grands multiplexes, il y a aussi des restaurants, des boutiques et des salles de jeux vidéo où ils peuvent aller avant° et après le film. Les jeunes qui vont souvent au cinéma peuvent acheter° une carte de multiplexe.° Avec cette° carte qui coûte vingt euros par mois, ils peuvent voir un nombre illimité de films dans leur multiplexe favori.

Les jeunes Français vont au cinéma pour voir les films français récents. Ils aiment aussi les films américains, en particulier les films d'action, les films de science-fiction et les comédies. Les jeunes qui parlent bien anglais peuvent voir ces films en «version originale» — avec, bien sûr, des sous-titres° en français.

voir *to see* **peuvent** *can* **avant** *before* **acheter** *buy*
carte de multiplexe *movie pass* **cette** *that* **ces** *these* **sous-titres** *subtitles*

COMPARAISONS *Culturelles*

Compare the movie-going preferences of French and American teenagers by filling in the following chart:

Les préférences	Les jeunes Français	Moi	Différence ou similarité?
• Quel jour?	________	________	________
• Dans quelle sorte de cinéma?	________	________	________
• Quels films?	________	________	________

Additional readings @ my.hrw.com
FRENCH InterActive Reader

Films américains, public français

Voici une liste de films américains qui ont eu° beaucoup de succès en France. Est-ce que vous pouvez° identifier ces films? Lisez° le titre° français de chaque° film. Faites correspondre° le titre de ce film avec le titre américain.

ont eu *have had* **pouvez** *can* **Lisez** *Read* **titre** *title* **chaque** *each* **Faites correspondre** *Match*

TITRES FRANÇAIS	TITRES AMÉRICAINS
1. Blanche-Neige et les sept nains (1937)	A. The Lion King
2. Le Magicien d'Oz (1939)	B. The Godfather
3. Le Parrain (1972)	C. Midnight in Paris
4. Les Aventuriers de l'arche perdue (1981)	D. Saving Private Ryan
5. Retour vers le futur (1985)	E. The Pianist
6. La Liste de Schindler (1993)	F. Snow White and the Seven Dwarves
7. Le Roi Lion (1994)	G. The Wizard of Oz
8. Il faut sauver le soldat Ryan (1998)	H. Raiders of the Lost Ark
9. Le Pianiste (2002)	I. Schindler's List
10. Minuit à Paris (2011)	J. Back to the Future

CONNEXIONS

Use the Internet to find out which American films are currently playing in Paris. As you read the French titles, can you guess the original English titles?

Tintin et ses amis

Tintin et Milou

Tous° les jeunes Français connaissent° Tintin. Tintin n'est pas une personne réelle. C'est le héros d'une bande dessinée° très populaire en France et dans le monde° entier. «Les Aventures de Tintin» ont été publiées en français, mais aussi en anglais, en espagnol, en italien, en chinois, en japonais ... au total dans 80 langues° différentes.

Tintin a dix-sept ans et il est belge.° C'est un journaliste-détective. Il est intelligent et courageux et il adore voyager. Il va en Égypte, au Congo, en Chine, au Tibet, au Mexique et en Amérique. Il va même° sur° la lune, bien avant° les astronautes américains. Dans ses voyages, il connaît° des aventures extraordinaires. Tintin est l'ami de la justice et l'ennemi du mal.° Il protège ses amis et il s'attaque aux dictateurs, aux trafiquants de drogue° et aux marchands d'armes.° Il est souvent en danger, mais il triomphe toujours.

EN BREF: LA BELGIQUE

Capitale: Bruxelles
Population: 10 600 000
Langues officielles: français, flamand° et allemand°

La Belgique est une monarchie constitutionnelle avec un roi,° le roi Albert II. Sa capitale, Bruxelles, est le siège° de la Commission Européenne.

flamand *Flemish* **allemand** *German* **roi** *king* **siège** *seat*

Dans ses aventures, Tintin est toujours accompagné de son chien, Milou. Milou est un petit fox terrier blanc intuitif et courageux qui protège son maître quand il est attaqué. Il accompagne Tintin dans toutes ses aventures. Quand il va avec lui sur la lune, il est équipé d'une combinaison spatiale° pour chiens.

Tous *All* **connaissent** *know* **bande dessinée** *comic strip* **monde** *world* **langues** *languages* **belge** *Belgian* **même** *even* **sur** *on* **avant** *before* **connaît** *experiences* **mal** *evil* **trafiquants de drogue** *drug dealers* **armes** *weapons* **combinaison spatiale** *space suit*

Additional readings @ **my.hrw.com**
FRENCH InterActive Reader

Tintin a d'autres compagnons d'aventures, très sympathiques, mais un peu bizarres.

le capitaine Haddock

Le capitaine Haddock habite au château° de Moulinsart en Belgique. C'est un ancien° officier de la marine marchande. Il est brave et courageux ... mais il est aussi très irritable.

Garnements! *Rascals!*
Iconoclastes! *Iconoclasts! (people who attack and seek to overthrow traditional ideas)* **château** *castle* **ancien** *former*

Dupont et Dupond

Dupont et Dupond sont presque° identiques, mais ils ne sont pas frères. Ce sont des policiers méthodiques ... mais incompétents.

presque *almost*

le professeur Tournesol

Le professeur Tournesol est un génie scientifique. Il est modeste et réservé et comme° beaucoup de professeurs, il est très distrait.°

comme *like* **distrait** *absent-minded*

STRATEGY Reading

Recognizing Cognate Patterns Recognizing French-English cognate patterns will help you increase your reading vocabulary and improve your reading comprehension. Here are some common patterns:

FRENCH	ENGLISH	FRENCH	ENGLISH
-aire	*-ar, -ary*	**extraordinaire**	*extraordinary*
-eux, -euse	*-ous*	**courageux**	*courageous*
-ique	*-ic, -ical*	**identique**	*identical*
-iste	*-ist, -istic*	**journaliste**	*journalist*
-é	*-ed*	**réservé**	*reserved*

COMMUNAUTÉS

Organize a **fête Tintin** for the language classes in your school. You may display Tintin books in French and other languages and show a video or DVD of some of Tintin's adventures. Encourage your classmates to come dressed as Tintin characters.

Et vous?

Quelle est ta bande dessinée favorite? Qui sont les héros? Pourquoi est-ce que tu aimes cette bande dessinée?

Bonjour, Ousmane!

Bonjour! Je m'appelle Ousmane. J'adore la musique. J'aime surtout le rap et le rock. Mon chanteur° préféré est MC Solaar. Il chante très bien. J'ai beaucoup de CD de lui. Ma soeur, elle, préfère le blues et le jazz.

Je suis un peu musicien. Je joue de la guitare. Et je ne joue pas trop mal. J'ai organisé° un petit orchestre° de rock avec des copains. Nous répétons° le mercredi après-midi. Nous ne répétons pas chez moi, parce que ma mère déteste ça.° Parfois,° le week-end, nous jouons à des boums pour nos amis.

chanteur *singer* **ai organisé** *organized* **orchestre** *band*
répétons *rehearse* **ça** *that* **Parfois** *Sometimes*

Compréhension

1. Quelle est la musique préférée d'Ousmane?
2. De quel instrument est-ce qu'il joue?
3. Quand est-ce qu'il répète avec ses copains?
4. Pourquoi est-ce qu'il ne répète pas à la maison?

Activité écrite

Write a short note to Ousmane in which you describe your musical preferences. Use the following suggestions:

- J'aime … (quelles musiques?)
- Je déteste … (quelles musiques?)
- Mon groupe préféré est … (qui?)
- Ils/Elles chantent … (comment?)

Additional readings @ my.hrw.com
FRENCH
InterActive Reader

MC Solaar

le «Monsieur Rap» français

MC Solaar est né° à Dakar au Sénégal. Il s'appelle en réalité Claude M'Barali. Ses parents émigrent en France quand il a six mois. Il fait ses études dans la région parisienne. Après° le bac, il s'intéresse à° la musique. Il compose des chansons° françaises sur des rythmes de rap américain. Ses chansons ont beaucoup de succès. MC Solaar donne° des concerts en France, mais aussi en Angleterre,° en Allemagne,° en Russie et dans les pays° d'Afrique.

Aujourd'hui, MC Solaar est le «Monsieur Rap» français! Dans ses chansons, il exprime° des messages positifs contre° la violence et pour la paix.° Voilà pourquoi il est très populaire en France et dans le monde° francophone.

est né *was born* **Après** *After* **s'intéresse à** *becomes interested in* **chansons** *songs* **donne** *gives* **Angleterre** *England* **Allemagne** *Germany* **pays** *countries* **exprime** *expresses* **contre** *against* **la paix** *peace* **monde** *world*

CONNEXIONS

With 2 or 3 classmates, select a French singer, such as MC Solaar. Go on the Internet and obtain as much information as you can about the person you have chosen. If possible, get samples of his or her music. Share your findings with the rest of the class.

COMMUNAUTÉ

Prepare a short program about music from the French-speaking world. You may want to include pictures of the performers, selections of their recordings, and perhaps a world map showing their countries of origin. Present your program to another class at school or at a local senior center.

À Paris

Bonjour, Paris!

Quelques faits

- Paris est la capitale de la France.
- Paris est une très grande ville. La ville de Paris a deux millions d'habitants. La région parisienne a onze millions d'habitants. Vingt pour cent (20%) des Français habitent dans la région parisienne.
- Paris est situé° sur la Seine. Ce fleuve° divise° la ville en deux parties: la rive° droite (au nord) et la rive gauche (au sud).
- Administrativement, Paris est divisé en vingt arrondissements.°
- Paris est une ville très ancienne.° Elle a plus de° deux mille° ans.
- Paris est aussi une ville moderne et dynamique. C'est le centre économique, industriel et commercial de la France.
- Avec ses musées, ses théâtres, ses bibliothèques et ses écoles d'art, Paris est un centre culturel et artistique très important.
- Avec ses nombreux° monuments et ses larges avenues, Paris est une très belle ville. Pour beaucoup de gens, c'est la plus° belle ville du monde.° Chaque année,° des millions de touristes visitent Paris.

---

situé *located* **fleuve** *river* **divise** *divides*
rive *(river)bank* **arrondissements** *districts*
ancienne *old* **plus de** *more than* **mille** *thousand*
nombreux *many* **la plus** *the most* **monde** *world*
Chaque année *Each year*

IMAGES

GARE DE LYON
BASTILLE
RÉPUBLIQUE
Mairie du XIème
LA DÉFENSE
Seine
BUTTE MONTMARTRE
ARC DE TRIOMPHE
OPÉRA
MADELEINE
RIVE DROITE
GRAND PALAIS
PLACE DE LA CONCORDE
TOUR EIFFEL
INVALIDES
RIVE GAUCHE
TOUR MONTPARNASSE
SORBONNE
QUARTIER LATIN
OPÉRA DE LA BASTILLE
PALAIS OMNISPORTS
PASTA
METROPOLITAIN
PALAIS ROYAL MUSEE DU LOUVRE
PHARAON

Le Paris TRADITIONNEL

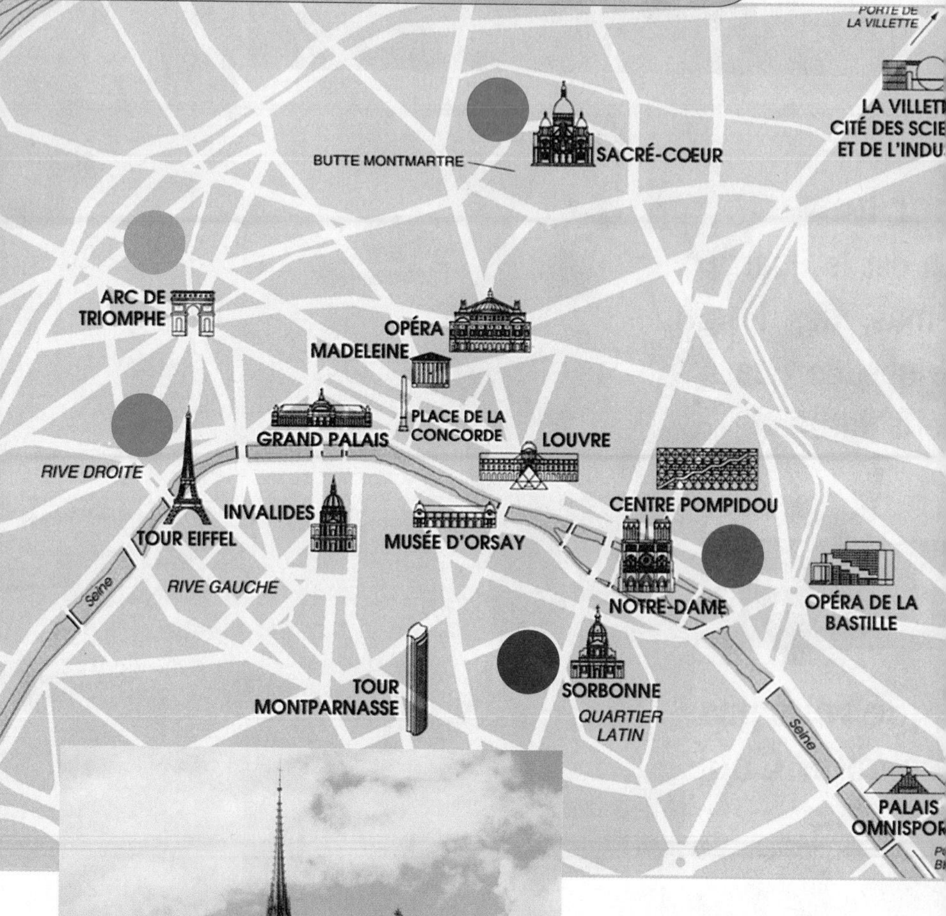

La tour Eiffel

Pour beaucoup de gens, **la tour Eiffel** est le symbole de Paris. Cette° immense tour de fer° a trois cent mètres de haut.° Elle a été inaugurée en 1889 (dix-huit cent quatre-vingt-neuf) par l'ingénieur Gustave Eiffel. Du sommet de la tour Eiffel, on° a une très belle vue sur Paris.

Notre-Dame

Notre-Dame est la cathédrale de Paris. Elle est située au centre de Paris sur une île,° l'île de la Cité. Notre-Dame a été construite° aux douzième et treizième siècles.°

Cette *This* **fer** *iron* **a trois cent mètres de haut** *is 300 meters high* **on** *one* **île** *island* **a été construite** *was built* **siècles** *centuries*

Le Sacré-Coeur

Le Sacré-Coeur est une église de pierre° blanche qui domine Paris. Cette église est située sur la butte° Montmartre. Montmartre est un quartier pittoresque. Les artistes viennent ici pour peindre° et les touristes viennent pour regarder les artistes. Si vous voulez° avoir un souvenir personnel de Paris, allez à Montmartre et demandez à° un artiste de faire votre portrait.

Le Quartier latin

Le Quartier latin est le quartier des étudiants. C'est un quartier très animé avec des cafés, des cinémas, des librairies° et des restaurants exotiques et bon marché.° Pourquoi est-ce que ce quartier s'appelle «Quartier latin»? Parce qu'autrefois° les étudiants parlaient° latin ici.

L'Arc de Triomphe et les Champs-Élysées

L'Arc de Triomphe est un monument qui° commémore les victoires de Napoléon (1769–1821). Ce monument est situé en haut° des Champs-Élysées.

Les Champs-Élysées sont une très grande et très belle avenue. Pour les Parisiens, c'est la plus° belle avenue du monde.

Activité Culturelle

Imaginez que vous passez une journée° à Paris. Où allez-vous aller le matin? Où allez-vous aller l'après-midi? Choisissez deux endroits à visiter et expliquez° votre choix.°

pierre *stone* **butte** *hill* **peindre** *to paint* **voulez** *want* **demandez à** *ask* **librairies** *bookstores*
bon marché *inexpensive* **autrefois** *in the past* **parlaient** *used to speak* **qui** *which* **en haut** *at the top*
la plus *the most* **passez une journée** *are spending a day* **expliquez** *explain* **choix** *choice*

IMAGES

Le nouveau Paris

Le Louvre et la pyramide du Louvre

Le Louvre est une ancienne° résidence royale transformée en musée. C'est dans ce° musée que se trouve° la fameuse «Mona Lisa». On entre dans le Louvre par° une pyramide de verre.° Cette pyramide moderne a été construite° par l'architecte américain I.M. Pei. Avec sa pyramide, le Louvre est le symbole du nouveau° Paris, à la fois° moderne et traditionnel.

Le Centre Pompidou

Le Centre Pompidou est le monument le plus° visité de Paris. C'est un musée d'art moderne. C'est aussi une bibliothèque, une cinémathèque et un centre audio-visuel. À l'extérieur,° sur l'esplanade, il y a des musiciens, des mimes, des acrobates, des jongleurs° … Un peu plus loin,° il y a une place° avec des fontaines, un bassin° et des sculptures mobiles.

Le musée d'Orsay

Autrefois,° c'était° une gare.° Aujourd'hui, c'est un musée. On vient ici admirer les chefs-d'oeuvre° des grands peintres° et sculpteurs français du dix-neuvième siècle.° On peut,° par exemple, admirer les oeuvres° de Monet, de Claudel, de Renoir, de Morisot et de Toulouse-Lautrec. À l'extérieur, il y a des sculptures qui représentent les cinq continents.

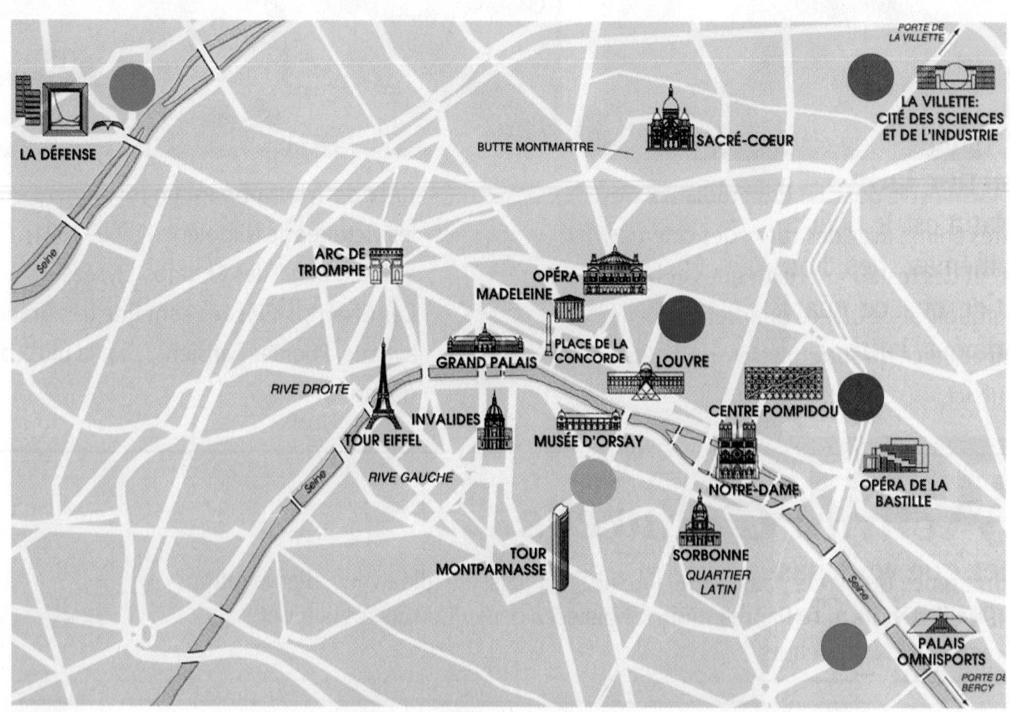

ancienne *former* **ce** *this* **se trouve** *is located* **par** *by* **verre** *glass* **a été construite** *was built* **nouveau** *new* **à la fois** *at the same time* **le plus** *the most* **À l'extérieur** *Outside* **jongleurs** *jugglers* **plus loin** *farther away* **place** *square* **bassin** *ornamental pool* **Autrefois** *Formerly* **c'était** *it used to be* **gare** *train station* **chefs-d'oeuvre** *masterpieces* **peintres** *painters* **siècle** *century* **peut** *can* **oeuvres** *works*

LE PALAIS OMNISPORTS DE BERCY

Sport ou musique? **Bercy** est un stade couvert° pour tous les sports. C'est aussi une immense salle° de concert. On vient ici écouter et applaudir les vedettes° de la chanson° française ... et de la chanson américaine.

LE PARC DE LA VILLETTE

Le parc de la Villette est un lieu° de récréation pour les jeunes de tout âge.° On trouve ici des parcs pour enfants,° des terrains de jeu° et différentes° constructions ultra-modernes.

- Le Zénith est une salle de concert où viennent les vedettes du monde° entier.
- La Géode est un cinéma omnimax avec un écran° circulaire géant.
- La Cité des sciences et de l'industrie est un grand musée scientifique où les jeunes peuvent° faire leurs propres° expériences° et jouer avec toutes sortes de gadgets électroniques.

LA DÉFENSE ET SON ARCHE

La Défense est le nouveau centre d'affaires° situé à l'ouest de Paris. Chaque° jour, des milliers° de Parisiens viennent travailler dans ses gratte-ciel° de verre. Il y a aussi des magasins, des cinémas, des restaurants et une patinoire.° La Grande Arche a été construite pour commémorer le deux centième anniversaire de la Révolution française.

Activité Culturelle

Vous êtes à Paris pour une semaine. Pendant votre séjour, vous voulez faire les choses suivantes. Dites où vous allez pour cela.

▶ **Lundi, je veux voir une exposition d'art moderne. Je vais au Centre Pompidou.**

	Quand?	Pourquoi?	Où?
▶	lundi	voir *(to see)* une exposition d'art moderne	??
	mardi	voir une exposition sur les lasers	??
	mercredi	voir la «Mona Lisa»	??
	jeudi	voir un match de basket	??
	vendredi	voir une exposition sur Toulouse-Lautrec	??
	samedi	aller dans les magasins et faire du shopping	??

couvert *covered* **salle** *hall* **vedettes** *stars* **chanson** *song* **lieu** *place* **de tout âge** *of all ages* **parcs pour enfants** *playgrounds* **terrains de jeu** *playing fields* **différentes** *several* **monde** *world* **écran** *screen* **peuvent** *can* **propres** *own* **expériences** *experiments* **affaires** *business* **Chaque** *Each* **des milliers** *thousands* **gratte-ciel** *skyscrapers* **patinoire** *skating rink*

Précédente
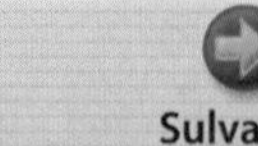
Sulvante

Recharger

Accueil

Rechercher
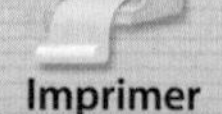
Imprimer

Sécurité

Adresse

Salut, les amis!

Je m'appelle Jean-Marc Lacoste. Je suis parisien. J'habite rue Racine. C'est une petite rue du Quartier latin. Notre appartement est situé au quatrième étage° d'un vieil° immeuble. L'immeuble est très ancien (il n'y a pas d'ascenseur°), mais notre appartement est moderne et confortable.

Je vais à l'École Alsacienne où je suis élève de seconde. En général, je vais là-bas en bus. Quand il fait beau, je prends° mon scooter, ou bien° je vais à pied. C'est assez loin, mais j'adore marcher.

En semaine, j'ai beaucoup de travail et je n'ai pas le temps° de sortir.° Le week-end, c'est différent. Qu'est-ce que je fais? Ça dépend! Quand j'ai de l'argent,° je vais au concert. Le week-end prochain,° j'espère aller à Bercy écouter le groupe U2. Quand je n'ai pas d'argent, je vais au Centre Pompidou. Là, au moins,° le spectacle° est gratuit.°

J'aime aussi me promener° dans mon quartier avec mes copains. Il y a toujours quelque chose° à faire au Quartier latin. On° va au cinéma. On va dans les magasins de musique pour écouter les nouveaux albums. On va dans les librairies° pour regarder les vieux livres et les bandes dessinées.° On va au café. Là, on regarde les gens qui passent dans la rue. Parfois,° on rencontre° des filles …

Et vous, quand est-ce que vous allez venir à Paris? Bientôt,° j'espère. Je vous attends!°

Amitiés,°

Jean-Marc

étage *floor* **vieil** *old* **ascenseur** *elevator* **prends** *take* **ou bien** *or else* **temps** *time* **sortir** *go out* **argent** *money* **prochain** *next* **au moins** *at least* **spectacle** *show* **gratuit** *free* **me promener** *to go for walks* **quelque chose** *something* **On** *We* **librairies** *bookstores* **bandes dessinées** *comics* **Parfois** *Sometimes* **rencontre** *meet* **Bientôt** *Soon* **Je vous attends!** *I'm expecting you!* **Amitiés** *In friendship*

PARIS en BATEAU-MOUCHE

Comment visiter Paris? On peut° visiter Paris en taxi, mais c'est cher.° On peut prendre° le bus. C'est amusant, mais la circulation° à Paris est souvent difficile. On peut prendre le métro. C'est pratique, rapide et bon marché,° mais on ne voit rien.°

Pourquoi ne pas faire une promenade° en bateau-mouche?° Les bateaux-mouches sont des bateaux modernes et confortables qui circulent sur la Seine. Pendant° la promenade, on peut prendre des photos et admirer les monuments le long de° la Seine. Le soir, on peut voir les monuments illuminés!

Activité Culturelle

Vous faites une promenade en bateau-mouche. Quels° monuments est-ce que vous pouvez° voir?

On peut *One can* **cher** *expensive* **prendre** *take* **circulation** *traffic* **bon marché** *inexpensive* **ne voit rien** *sees nothing*
Pourquoi ne pas faire une promenade *Why not take a ride* **bateau-mouche** *sight-seeing boat* **Pendant** *During* **le long de** *along*
Quels *Which* **pouvez** *can*

Unité 6

Le shopping

THÈME ET OBJECTIFS

Buying clothes

Are you interested in clothes? When you visit France, you will enjoy going window shopping. In fact, you will probably want to try on a few items and buy something special to bring home.

In this unit, you will learn ...

- to name and describe the clothes you wear
- to discuss style
- to shop for clothes and other items
- to talk about money

You will also be able ...

- to make comparisons
- to point out certain people or objects to your friends

SALAMANDER
TRUFFAUT

Leçon 17

Vocabulaire et Culture

LE FRANÇAIS PRATIQUE

DVD AUDIO

L'achat des vêtements

Accent sur ... l'élégance française

France is a leader in high fashion. French fashion design houses, such as Dior, Chanel, Yves Saint Laurent and Pierre Cardin, are known all over the world for the style and quality of their creations.

French young people like to be in style, even if their clothes are casual and not too expensive. Depending on their budgets, they buy their clothes at ...

- **une grande surface** *(low-cost chain store)*
- **un grand magasin** *(department store)*
- **une boutique de vêtements** *(clothing store)*
- **une boutique de soldes** *(discount clothing shop)*
- **le marché aux puces** *(flea market)*

Mélanie cherche une robe pour aller au mariage de sa cousine. Quelle robe est-ce qu'elle va acheter?

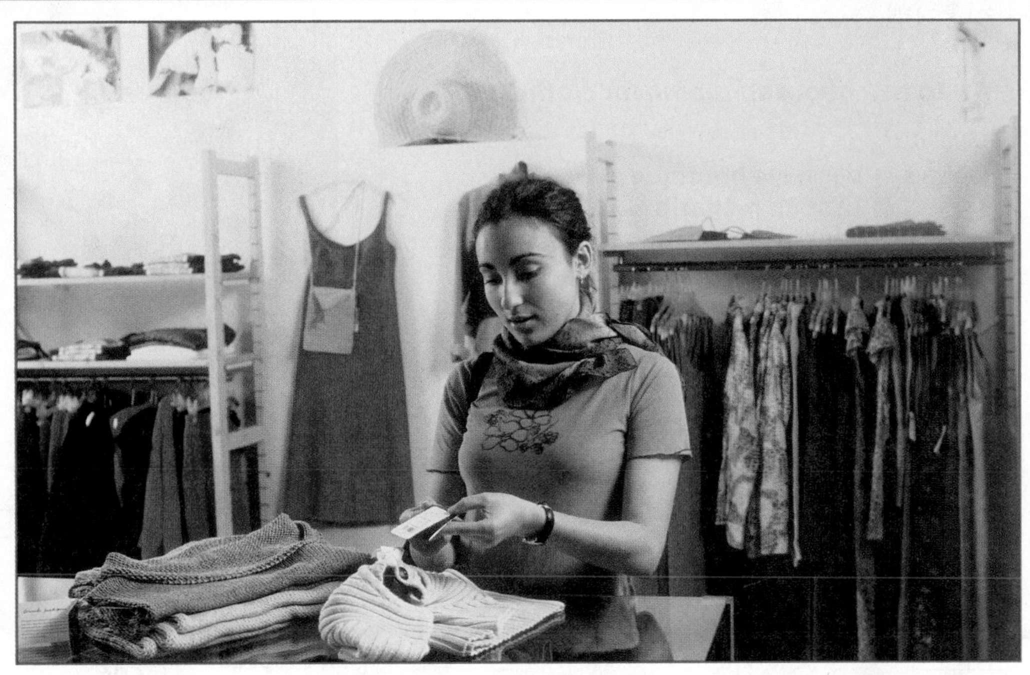

Fatima est dans une boutique de vêtements. Ici les vêtements sont très élégants … et très chers aussi.

Patrick et Béatrice achètent leurs vêtements dans une grande surface. Ici les vêtements sont de bonne qualité et ils ne sont pas trop chers.

Michel est dans un magasin de chaussures. Quelles chaussures est-ce qu'il va acheter? Des baskets ou des chaussures de sport?

Leçon 17

Vocabulaire et Communication

A VOCABULAIRE Les vêtements

▶ How to talk about shopping for clothes:

Où vas-tu?

Je vais | dans **une boutique** *(shop)*.
dans **un magasin** *(store)*
dans **un grand magasin** *(department store)*

Qu'est-ce que tu vas **acheter** *(to buy)*?

Je vais acheter **des vêtements** *(clothes)*.

Les vêtements

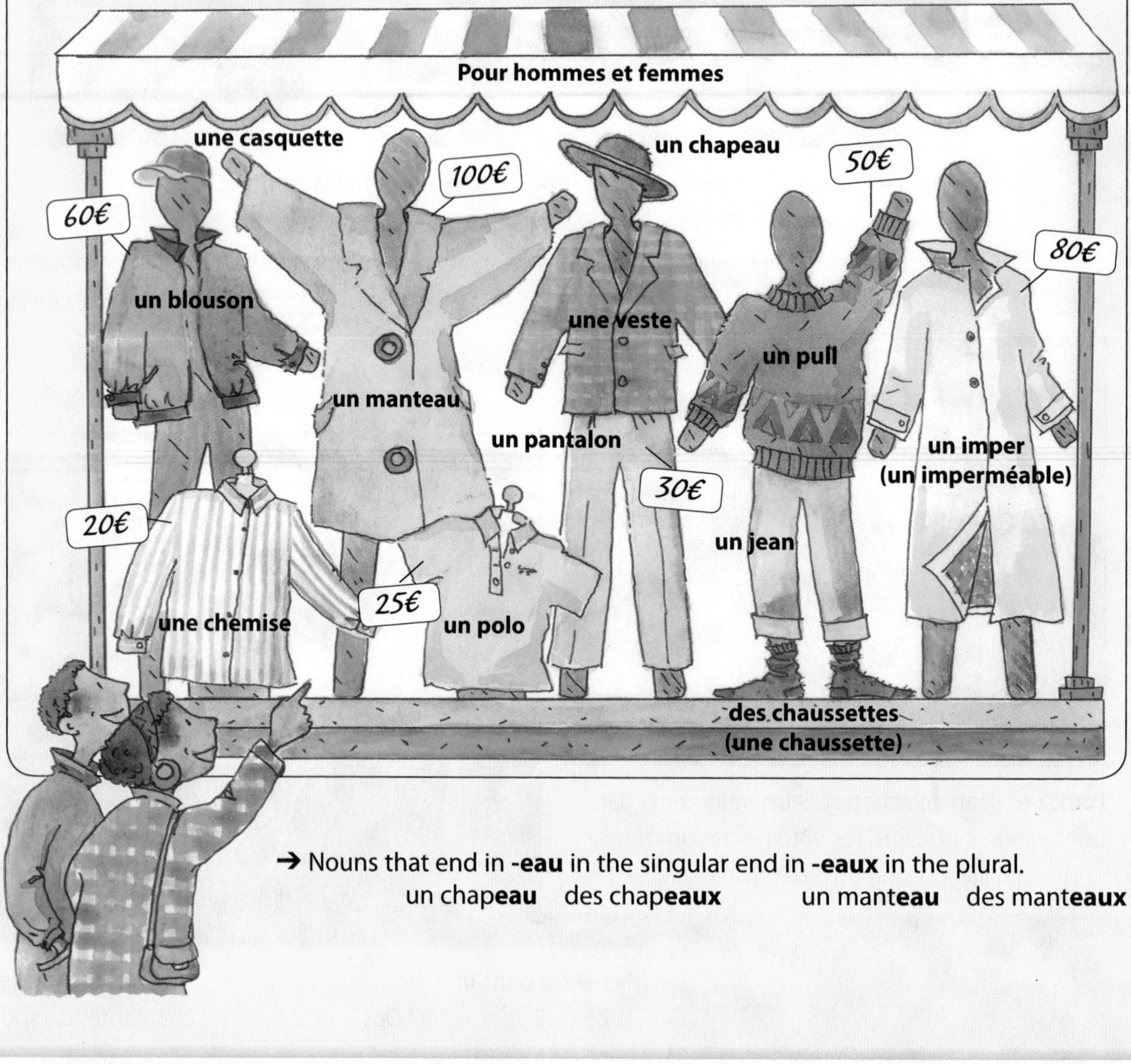

Pour hommes et femmes

une casquette
un chapeau
60€
100€
50€
80€
un blouson
une veste
un pull
un manteau
un pantalon
30€
un imper (un imperméable)
20€
un jean
25€
une chemise
un polo
des chaussettes (une chaussette)

→ Nouns that end in **-eau** in the singular end in **-eaux** in the plural.

un chap**eau** des chap**eaux** un mant**eau** des mant**eaux**

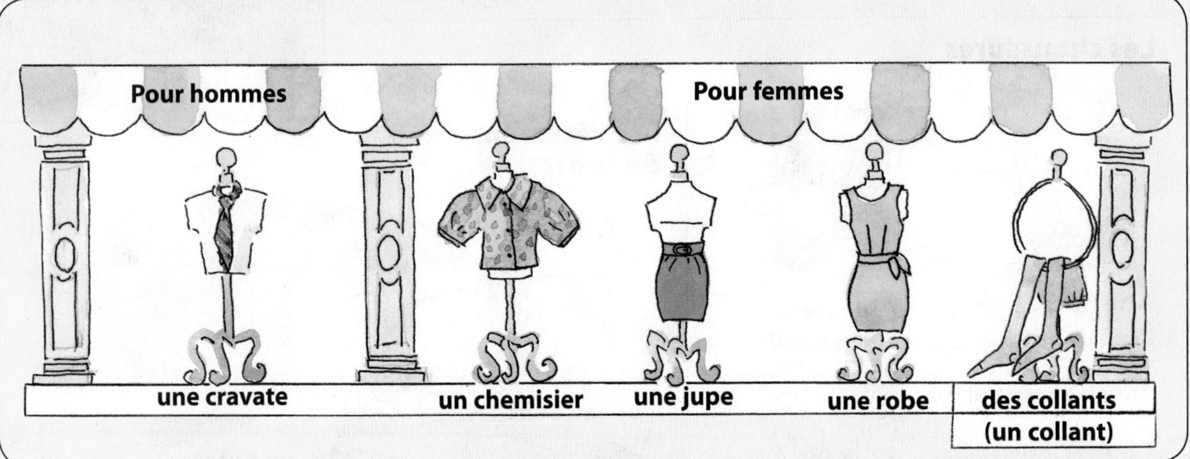

acheter	*to buy*	Je vais **acheter** une cravate.
porter	*to wear*	Qu'est-ce que tu vas **porter** demain?
mettre	*to put on, wear*	Oh là là, il fait froid. Je vais **mettre** un pull.

→ **Mettre** is irregular. *(Its forms are presented in Leçon 18.)*

1 Shopping

PARLER Below are the names of several Paris stores. Using the illustrations as a guide, talk to a classmate about where you are going shopping and what you plan to buy.

▶ —Où vas-tu?
—Je vais au Monoprix.
—Qu'est-ce que tu vas acheter?
—Je vais acheter une chemise.

2 Quels vêtements?

PARLER/ÉCRIRE What we wear often depends on the circumstances: where we are, what we will be doing, what the weather is like. Complete the following sentences with the appropriate items of clothing.

1. Aujourd'hui, je porte …
2. Le professeur porte …
3. L'élève à ma gauche porte …
4. L'élève à ma droite porte …
5. Quand je vais à une boum, je porte …
6. Quand je vais dans un restaurant élégant, je porte …
7. S'il pleut *(If it rains)* demain, je vais mettre …
8. S'il fait chaud demain, je vais mettre …
9. Si *(If)* je vais en ville samedi, je vais mettre …
10. Si je vais à un concert dimanche, je vais mettre …

Je vais mettre des lunettes de soleil.

B VOCABULAIRE D'autres vêtements et accessoires

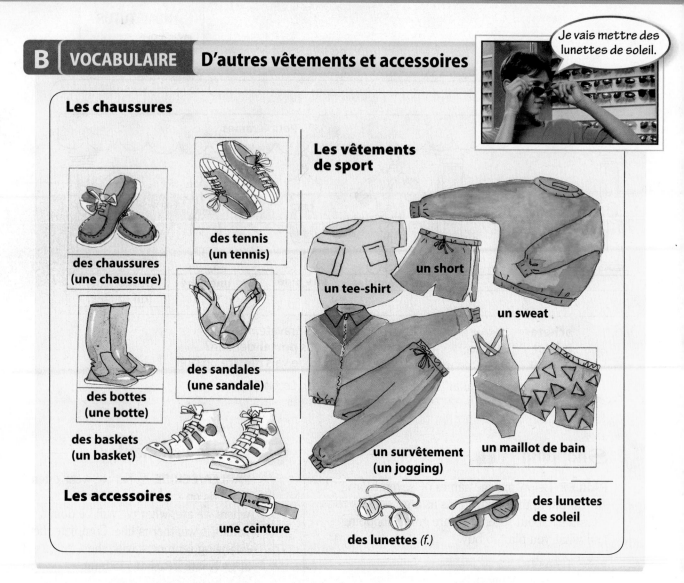

Les chaussures

- des chaussures (une chaussure)
- des tennis (un tennis) 
- des bottes (une botte) 
- des sandales (une sandale) 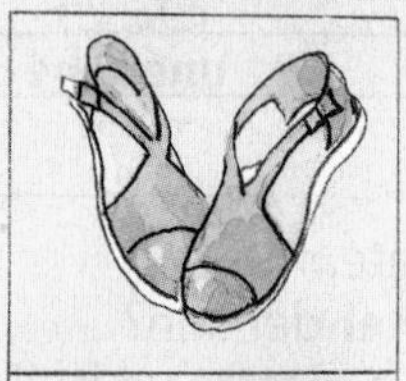
- des baskets (un basket) 

Les vêtements de sport

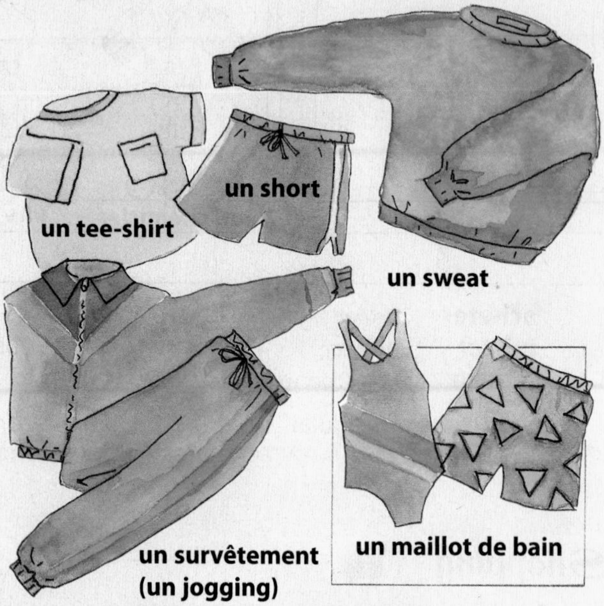

- un tee-shirt
- un short
- un sweat
- un survêtement (un jogging)
- un maillot de bain

Les accessoires

- une ceinture
- des lunettes (*f.*) 
- des lunettes de soleil 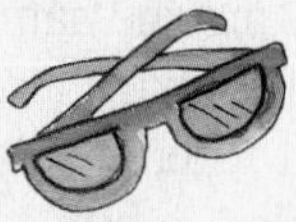

3 À la plage de Deauville

PARLER/ÉCRIRE You are spending the summer vacation in Deauville, a popular seaside resort in Normandy. Describe what you and your friends are wearing.

▶ Paul porte un maillot de bain …

▶ Paul 1. Anne 2. Sophie 3. Michel 4. Catherine 5. moi

4 Qu'est-ce que tu portes?

PARLER Ask your classmates what they wear in the following circumstances. Let them use their imagination.

▶ jouer au tennis

1. aller à la piscine
2. aller à la plage
3. jouer au basket
4. travailler dans le jardin
5. aller au gymnase *(gym)*
6. faire une promenade dans la forêt *(forest)*
7. faire une promenade dans la neige *(snow)*

5 Un jeu

PARLER/ÉCRIRE When you see what people are wearing, you can often tell what they are going to do. How many different logical sentences can you make in five minutes using the elements of A, B, and C? Follow the model below.

A	B	C
André	un maillot de bain	nager
Sylvie	des lunettes de soleil	aller à la plage
Paul et Éric	un short	aller à un concert
Michèle et Anne	des chaussettes blanches	jouer au tennis
	un sweat	jouer au volley
	un pantalon très chic	jouer au foot
	des chaussures noires	aller à la campagne *(country)*
	des bottes	faire du jogging *(to jog)*
	un costume *(suit)*	dîner en ville
	une robe	
	une casquette	

Sylvie porte un short. Elle va jouer au foot.

6 Joyeux anniversaire!

PARLER/ÉCRIRE The following people are celebrating their birthdays. Find a present for each person by choosing an item of clothing from pages 258, 259, or 260.

1. Pour mon père (ma mère), je vais acheter …
2. Pour ma grand-mère (mon grand-père), …
3. Pour ma petite cousine Élodie (10 ans), …
4. Pour mon grand frère Guillaume (18 ans), …
5. Pour le professeur, …
6. Pour mon meilleur *(best)* ami, …
7. Pour ma meilleure amie, …

C VOCABULAIRE Dans un magasin

Pardon, madame.
Vous désirez, mademoiselle?
Je cherche un pantalon.

▶ How to get help from a salesperson:

Pardon, monsieur (madame).
Vous désirez *(May I help you),* | **monsieur? madame mademoiselle**

Je cherche *(I'm looking for)* ...
un pantalon.
Quel est le prix *(What is the price)* du pantalon?
Combien *(How much)* **coûte** le pantalon?
Combien est-ce qu'il coûte?
Il coûte 40 euros.

Je cherche ...
une veste.
Quel est le prix de la veste?
Combien coûte la veste?
Combien est-ce qu'elle coûte?
Elle coûte 65 euros.

▶ How to discuss clothes with a friend:

Qu'est-ce que tu penses du pantalon vert?
(What do you think of ...?)
Comment trouves-tu le pantalon vert?
(What do you think of ...?)

Qu'est-ce que tu penses de la veste verte?
Comment trouves-tu la veste verte?

Comment trouves-tu le pantalon vert?
Il est trop petit.

Il est | **joli.** **élégant** **génial** *(terrific)* **chouette** *(neat)* **à la mode** *(in style)*
Il est | **moche** *(plain, ugly).* **démodé** *(out of style)*
Il est **trop** *(too)* | **petit.** **grand** *(big)* **court** *(short)* **long** *(long)*
Il est | **cher** *(expensive).* **bon marché** *(cheap)*

Elle est | **jolie.** **élégante** **géniale** **chouette** **à la mode**
Elle est | **moche.** **démodée**
Elle est **trop** | **petite.** **grande** **courte** **longue**
Elle est | **chère.** **bon marché**

➔ The expression **bon marché** is INVARIABLE. It does not take adjective endings.
Les chaussures blanches sont **bon marché.**

VERBES

chercher	*to look for*	Je **cherche** un jean.
coûter	*to cost*	Les chaussures **coûtent** 60 euros.
penser	*to think*	Qu'est-ce que tu **penses** de cette *(this)* robe?
penser que	*to think (that)*	Je **pense qu'**elle est géniale!
trouver	*to find*	Je ne **trouve** pas ma veste.
	to think of	Comment **trouves**-tu mes lunettes de soleil?

➔ The verb **penser** is often used alone.
Tu **penses?** *Do you think so?* Je **ne pense pas.** *I don't think so.*

@HOMETUTOR
my.hrw.com

Les nombres de 100 à 1000

100	**cent**	200	**deux cents**	500	**cinq cents**	800	**huit cents**
101	**cent un**	300	**trois cents**	600	**six cents**	900	**neuf cents**
102	**cent deux**	400	**quatre cents**	700	**sept cents**	1000	**mille**

7 Au marché aux puces

PARLER You are at the Paris flea market looking for clothes with a French friend. Explain why you are not buying the following items. Use your imagination … and expressions from the **Vocabulaire.**

▶ **—Tu vas acheter le blouson?**
—Non, je ne pense pas.
—Pourquoi pas?
—Il est trop grand.

▶ 

8 C'est combien?

PARLER Ask your friends how much the following items cost.

▶ **—Combien coûte la veste?**
—Elle coûte cent vingt euros.

▶ 

1 

2 

3 

4 

5 

6 

7 

8 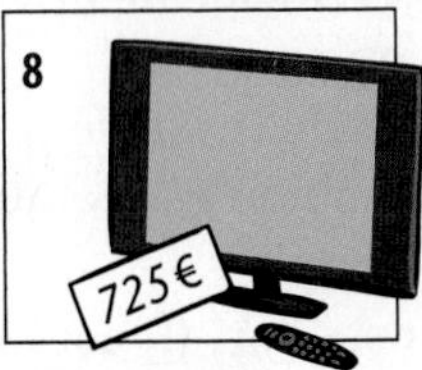

9 

À votre tour!

OBJECTIFS

Now you can . . .
- name and describe the clothes you wear
- discuss their style and their fit
- count to 1000

1 Écoutez bien!

ÉCOUTER Thomas and Frédéric are both getting ready to leave on vacation. Listen to the following sentences which mention items that they are packing. If the item belongs to Thomas, mark A. If the item belongs to Frédéric, mark B.

	1	2	3	4	5	6
A: Thomas						
B: Frédéric						

A. Thomas

B. Frédéric

2 Créa-dialogue

PARLER You are at Place Bonaventure in Montreal looking at clothes in various shops. You like what the salesperson shows you and ask how much each item costs. React to the price.

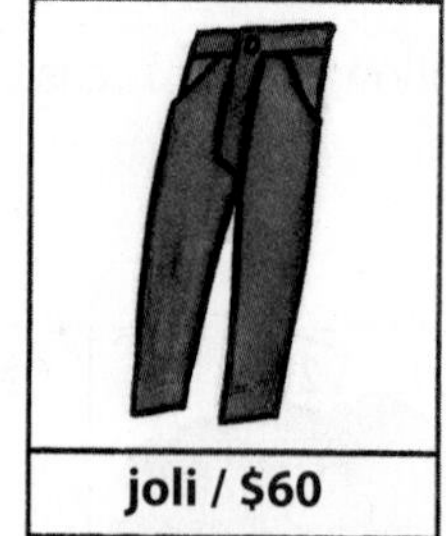

▶ joli / $60

1. élégant / $30

2. joli / $350

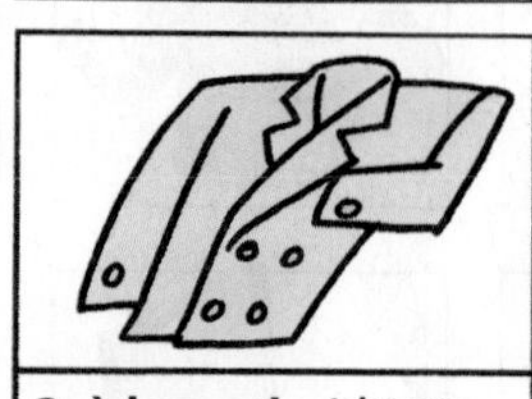

3. à la mode / $250

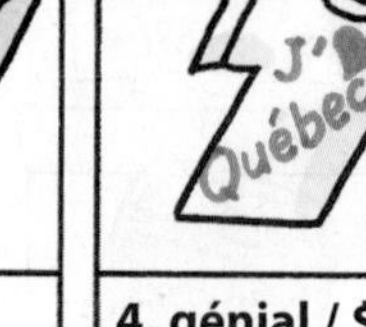

4. génial / $15

▶ —Vous désirez, monsieur (mademoiselle)?
—Je cherche <u>un pantalon</u>.
—Comment trouvez-vous <u>le pantalon gris</u>?
—Il est <u>joli</u>. Combien est-ce qu'il coûte?
—<u>Soixante</u> dollars.
—Oh là là, <u>il</u> est cher! (<u>Il</u> est bon marché.)

3 Conversation dirigée  

PARLER Sophie and Christophe are shopping in a department store. Act out their conversation in French.

Sophie		Christophe
asks Christophe what he is looking for	→	answers that he is looking for a baseball cap
asks him what he thinks of the yellow cap	← →	says that it is terrific but adds that he is going to buy the blue cap
asks how much it costs	← →	answers 5 euros
says that it is inexpensive but adds that it is too small	←	

4 Qu'est-ce qui ne va pas? *(What's wrong?)*

PARLER Explain what is wrong with the clothes that these people just bought at a sale.

▶ **Le chapeau de Monsieur Dupont est trop grand.**

Monsieur Dupont **Édouard**

5 Les valises 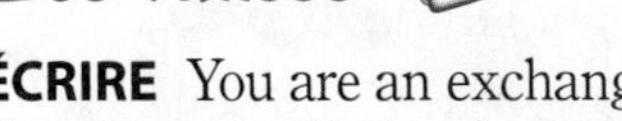

ÉCRIRE You are an exchange student in Paris. Your host family has invited you to spend:

- one weekend in Nice to go sailing
- one weekend in Chamonix to go skiing

Make a list of the different clothes you will take on each trip.

6 À l'aéroport

ÉCRIRE You are flying to Paris tomorrow on an exchange program. Your hosts plan to meet you at the airport, but don't have your picture. Write them an e-mail explaining what you look like and what you will be wearing.

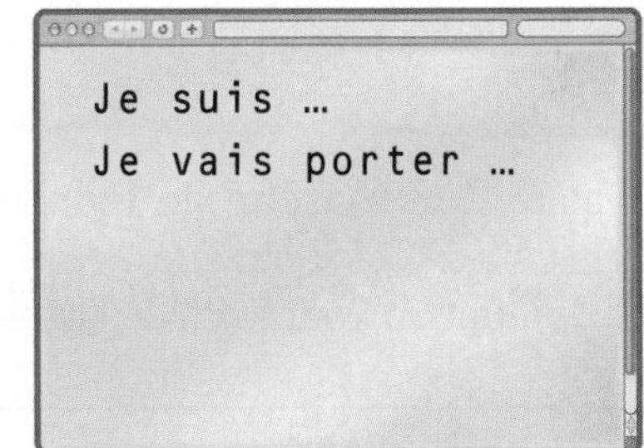

Leçon 18

Conversation et Culture

Rien n'est parfait!

DVD AUDIO

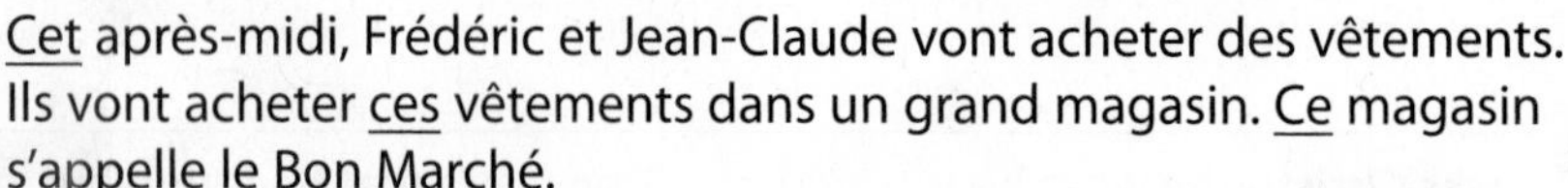

Cet après-midi, Frédéric et Jean-Claude vont acheter des vêtements. Ils vont acheter ces vêtements dans un grand magasin. Ce magasin s'appelle le Bon Marché.

This
these/This

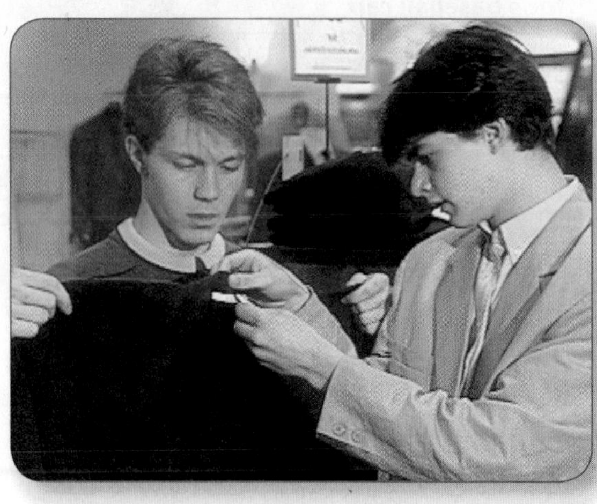

Scène 1.

Frédéric et Jean-Claude regardent les pulls.

Frédéric: Regarde! Comment trouves-tu ce pull?

Jean-Claude: Quel pull? — *Which*

Frédéric: Ce pull bleu.

Jean-Claude: Il est chouette.

Frédéric: C'est vrai, il est très chouette.

Jean-Claude: *(qui regarde le prix)* Il est aussi très cher.

Frédéric: Combien est-ce qu'il coûte?

Jean-Claude: Deux cents euros.

Frédéric: Deux cents euros! Quelle horreur! — *What a scandal!*

NOTE Culturelle

Le grand magasin

Le grand magasin est un magasin de 4 ou 5 étages où on peut° acheter toutes° sortes de produits différents: vêtements, parfums, meubles,° alimentation° générale, etc. ... Le grand magasin est une idée française. Le premier grand magasin a été créé° en 1852 par Aristide Boucicaut (1810–1877). Ce magasin existe toujours° et s'appelle «le Bon Marché». L'idée de Monsieur Boucicaut était° d'offrir à sa clientèle une marchandise de bonne qualité à des prix bon marché ... d'où° le nom «Bon Marché». Son idée a été vite° copiée dans toutes les villes.

on peut *one can* **toutes** *all* **meubles** *furniture* **alimentation** *food*
a été créé *was created* **toujours** *still* **était** *was* **d'où** *hence* **vite** *quickly*

COMPARAISONS Culturelles

French department stores, such as **le Bon Marché, le Printemps,** and **les Galeries Lafayette** have Internet sites. Check out one of these stores. How do its products compare to what you find in your local department stores?

SCÈNE 2.
Maintenant Frédéric et Jean-Claude regardent les vestes.

Frédéric: Quelle veste est-ce que tu préfères?
Jean-Claude: Je préfère cette veste jaune. Elle est très élégante et elle n'est pas très chère.
Frédéric: Oui, mais elle est trop grande pour toi!
Jean-Claude: Dommage!

SCÈNE 3.
Frédéric est au rayon des chaussures. Quelles chaussures est-ce qu'il va acheter? — *department*

Jean-Claude: Alors, quelles chaussures est-ce que tu achètes?
Frédéric: J'achète ces chaussures noires. Elles sont très confortables … et elles ne sont pas chères. Regarde, elles sont en solde. — *on sale*
Jean-Claude: C'est vrai, elles sont en solde … mais elles ne sont plus à la mode. — *are no longer*
Frédéric: Hélas, rien n'est parfait! — *Too bad/nothing is perfect*

Compréhension

1. Où vont Frédéric et Jean-Claude cet après-midi?
2. Qu'est-ce qu'ils vont faire?
3. Qu'est-ce qu'ils regardent d'abord (*first*)?
4. Combien coûte le pull bleu?
5. Quelle est la réaction de Frédéric?
6. Qu'est-ce que Jean-Claude pense de la veste jaune?
7. Pourquoi est-ce qu'il n'achète pas la veste?
8. Qu'est-ce que Frédéric pense des chaussures noires?
9. Pourquoi est-ce qu'il n'achète pas les chaussures?

A Les verbes *acheter* et *préférer*

Verbs like **acheter** (*to buy*) end in: **e** + CONSONANT + **-er.**
Verbs like **préférer** (*to prefer*) end in: **é** + CONSONANT + **-er.**

Note the forms of these two verbs in the chart, paying attention to:

- the **e** of the stem of **ach<u>e</u>ter**
- the **é** of the stem of **préf<u>é</u>rer**

INFINITIVE	acheter	préférer
PRESENT	J' **achète** une veste.	Je **préfère** la veste bleue.
	Tu **achètes** une cravate.	Tu **préfères** la cravate jaune.
	Il/Elle **achète** un imper.	Il/Elle **préfère** l'imper gris.
	Nous **achetons** un jean.	Nous **préférons** le jean noir.
	Vous **achetez** un short.	Vous **préférez** le short blanc.
	Ils/Elles **achètent** un pull.	Ils/Elles **préfèrent** le pull rouge.

➔ Verbs like **acheter** and **préférer** take regular endings and have the following changes in the stem:

ach<u>e</u>ter	**e → è**	in the **je, tu, il,** and **ils** forms of the present
préf<u>é</u>rer	**é → è**	

1 Achats *(Purchases)*

PARLER/ÉCRIRE What we buy depends on how much money we have. Complete the sentences below with **acheter** and one or more of the items from the list.

1. Avec dix dollars, tu …
2. Avec quinze dollars, j' …
3. Avec trente dollars, nous …
4. Avec cinquante dollars, Jean-Claude …
5. Avec cent dollars, vous …
6. Avec quinze mille dollars, mes parents …
7. Avec ?? dollars, mon cousin …
8. Avec ?? dollars, j' …

une voiture

des chaussures

une cravate

un survêtement

des lunettes de soleil

un polo

une veste

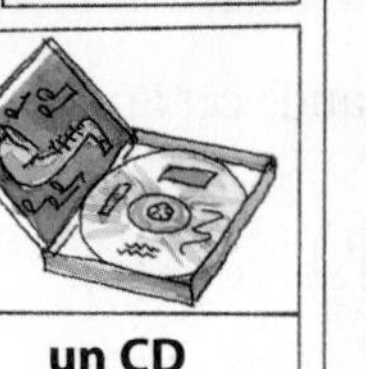
un CD

un jean

??

@HOMETUTOR
my.hrw.com

VOCABULAIRE Verbes comme (*like*) *acheter* et *préférer*

acheter	*to buy*	Qu'est-ce que tu **achètes?**
amener	*to bring (a person)*	François **amène** sa copine à la boum.
préférer	*to prefer*	**Préfères**-tu le manteau ou l'imper?
espérer	*to hope*	J'**espère** visiter Paris en été.

→ In French, there are two verbs that correspond to the English to *bring:*

amener + PEOPLE	J'**amène** une copine au pique-nique.
apporter + THINGS	J'**apporte** des sandwichs au pique-nique.

2 Pique-nique

PARLER/ÉCRIRE Everyone is bringing someone or something to the picnic. Complete the sentences below with the appropriate forms of **amener** or **apporter.**

▶ **Nous amenons un copain.** **Marc apporte des sandwichs.**

1. Tu … ta guitare.
2. Philippe … sa soeur.
3. Nous … nos voisins.
4. Vous … un dessert.
5. Michèle … des sodas.
6. Antoine et Vincent … leur cousine.
7. Raphaël … ses CD.
8. Mon cousin … sa copine.
9. J' … mon MP3.
10. Léa et Émilie … leurs portables.

3 Expression personnelle

Quand je vais à une fête, j'apporte mon portable.
Et moi, j'apporte ma guitare.

PARLER/ÉCRIRE Complete the sentences below with one of the suggested options or an expression of your choice. Note: You may wish to make some of the sentences negative.

1. Quand je vais à une fête, j'amène … (des copains, une copine, ma grand-mère, ??)
   J'apporte … (des sandwichs, ma guitare, mes CD, mon portable, ??)
2. Quand je vais à un pique-nique, j'amène … (ma soeur, une copine, mon chien, ??)
   J'apporte … (mon MP3, mon livre de français, des sandwichs, ??)
3. Le week-end, je préfère … (étudier, aller au cinéma, rester à la maison, ??)
   Ce *(This)* week-end, j'espère … (avoir un rendez-vous avec un copain ou une copine, travailler, jouer au volley, ??)
4. Pendant *(During)* les vacances, j'espère … (rester à la maison, trouver un job, voyager, ??)
5. Un jour, j'espère … (visiter la France, parler français, aller à l'université, être millionnaire, ??)

B L'adjectif démonstratif *ce*

LEARNING ABOUT LANGUAGE

DEMONSTRATIVE ADJECTIVES *(this, that)* are used to point out specific people or things.

In French, the demonstrative adjective **ce** always agrees with the noun it introduces.

Note the forms of the demonstrative adjective **ce** in the chart below.

	SINGULAR *(this, that)*	PLURAL *(these, those)*		
MASCULINE	**ce** → **cet** (+ VOWEL SOUND)	**ces**	**ce** blouson **cet** homme	**ces** blousons **ces** hommes
FEMININE	**cette**	**ces**	**cette** veste **cette** amie	**ces** vestes **ces** amies

→ There is liaison after **cet** and **ces** when the next word begins with a vowel sound.

→ To distinguish between a person or an object that is close by and one that is further away, the French sometimes use **-ci** or **-là** after the noun.

Philippe achète **cette chemise-ci.** — *Philippe is buying **this shirt** (over here).*
François achète **cette chemise-là.** — *François is buying **that shirt** (over there).*

4 Aux Galeries Lafayette

PARLER Marc and Nathalie are at the Galeries Lafayette department store. Marc likes everything that Nathalie shows him. Play both roles.

▶ une robe (jolie) — NATHALIE: **Regarde cette robe!**
MARC: **Elle est jolie!**

1. un imper (élégant)
2. des bottes (à la mode)
3. une casquette (géniale)
4. un survêtement (chouette)
5. des livres (amusants)
6. un ordinateur (génial)
7. une télé (moderne)
8. une ceinture (jolie)
9. des sandales (jolies)

5 Différences d'opinion

PARLER Whenever they go shopping together, Éric and Brigitte cannot agree on what they like. Play both roles.

▶ un short

J'aime ce short-ci.
Eh bien, moi, je préfère ce short-là.

1. une chemise
2. un blouson
3. des chaussures
4. des lunettes
5. une casquette
6. une affiche
7. un stylo
8. un ordinateur

@HOMETUTOR
my.hrw.com

C L'adjectif interrogatif *quel?*

The interrogative adjective **quel** *(what? which?)* is used in questions. It agrees with the noun it introduces and has the following forms:

	SINGULAR	PLURAL		
MASCULINE	**quel**	**quels**	**Quel** garçon?	**Quels** cousins?
FEMININE	**quelle**	**quelles**	**Quelle** fille?	**Quelles** copines?

→ Note the liaison after **quels** and **quelles** when the next word begins with a vowel sound.
Quelles affiches est-ce que tu préfères?

6 Vêtements d'été

J'achète un pantalon.
Quel pantalon est-ce que tu achètes?
Ce pantalon noir.

PARLER You are shopping for the following items before going on a summer trip to France. A friend is asking you which ones you are buying. Identify each item by color.

▶ **un pantalon/noir**

1. un maillot de bain/bleu

2. des chaussettes/vertes

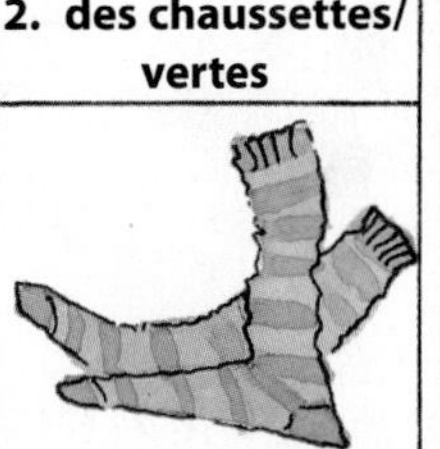

3. une jupe/jaune

4. une veste/bleue

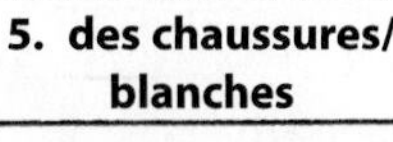

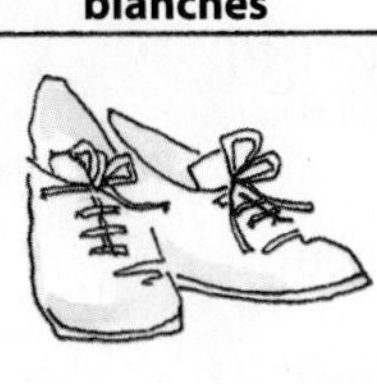

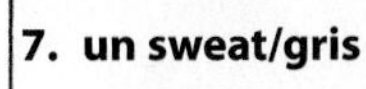

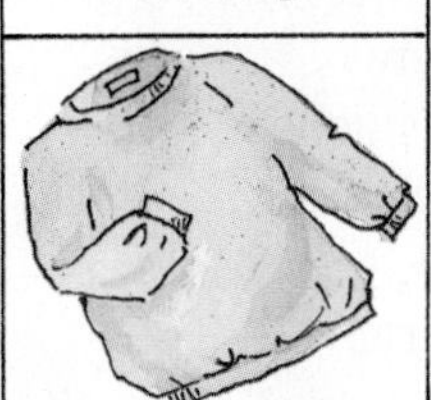

8. une chemise /orange

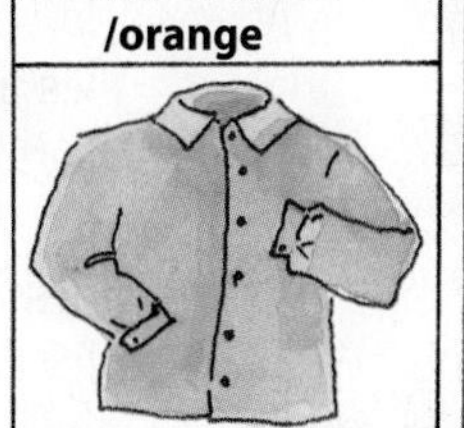

7 Questions personnelles PARLER/ÉCRIRE

1. À quelle école vas-tu?
2. Dans quel magasin achètes-tu tes vêtements?
3. Dans quel magasin achètes-tu tes chaussures?
4. Quelle est ta couleur préférée?
5. Quels programmes aimes-tu regarder à la télé?
6. Quel est ton restaurant préféré?
7. Quelle est ta classe préférée?

D Le verbe *mettre*

The verb **mettre** (*to put, place*) is irregular. Note its forms in the chart below.

INFINITIVE	mettre	
PRESENT	je **mets**	nous **mettons**
	tu **mets**	vous **mettez**
	il/elle **met**	ils/elles **mettent**

→ In the singular forms, the "**t**" of the stem is silent. The "**t**" is pronounced in the plural forms.

→ The verb **mettre** has several English equivalents:

to put, place	Je **mets** mes livres sur la table.
to put on, wear	Caroline **met** une robe rouge.
to turn on	Nous **mettons** la télé.

8 Où?

PARLER/ÉCRIRE Say where the people of Column A put the objects of Column B, by choosing a place from Column C. Be logical!

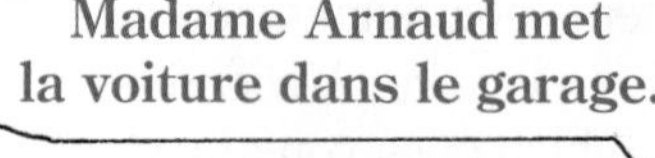

Madame Arnaud met la voiture dans le garage.

A	B	C
moi	la glace	dans le salon
nous	la voiture	sur la table
toi	les livres	dans le placard (*closet*)
vous	le téléphone	dans le garage
Christine	les vêtements	sur le bureau
le professeur	des plantes vertes	dans le réfrigérateur
Marc et Philippe	les cartes	sous le lit

@HOMETUTOR
my.hrw.com

9 Questions personnelles PARLER/ÉCRIRE

1. Est-ce que tu mets la radio quand tu étudies?
2. Chez vous, est-ce que vous mettez la télé quand vous dînez?
3. Est-ce que tu mets des lunettes de soleil quand tu vas à la plage?
4. Où est-ce que tes parents mettent leur voiture? (dans le garage? dans la rue?)
5. Quels programmes de télé est-ce que tu mets le dimanche? le samedi?
6. Quels CD est-ce que tu mets quand tu vas à une boum?
7. Quels vêtements est-ce que tu mets quand il fait froid?
8. Quels vêtements est-ce que tu mets quand tu joues au basket?

Prononciation

e = /ə/ e = /ɛ/ è = /ɛ/

Les lettres «e» et «è»

chemise **chaussette** **chère**

Practice pronouncing "**e**" within a word:

- /ə/ (as in **je**) [… "**e**" + *one* CONSONANT + VOWEL]

Répétez: **chemise regarder Denise Renée petit venir**

Note that in the middle of a word the /ə/ is sometimes silent.

Répétez: **acheter achetons amener samedi rarement avenue**

- /ɛ/ (as in **elle**) [… "**e**" + *two* CONSONANTS + VOWEL]

Répétez: **chaussette veste quelle cette rester professeur raquette**

Now practice pronouncing "**è**" within a word:

- /ɛ/ (as in **elle**) [… "**è**" + *one* CONSONANT + VOWEL]

Répétez: **chère père mère achète amènent espère deuxième**

À votre tour!

OBJECTIFS

Now you can . . .
- talk about what you plan to buy
- discuss your preferences
- point out certain people or objects

1 La bonne réponse

PARLER Alice is talking to her cousin Jérôme. Match Alice's questions with Jérôme's answers. Act out the dialogue with a classmate.

Alice
1 Je vais à la soirée de Delphine. Et toi?
2 Tu amènes une copine?
3 Qu'est-ce que vous allez apporter?
4 Qu'est-ce que tu vas mettre?

Jérôme
a Oui, Christine.
b Mon pull jaune et mon blouson marron.
c Nous allons acheter des pizzas.
d Moi aussi.

2 Créa-dialogue

PARLER Ask your classmates what they think about the following. They will answer affirmatively or negatively.

▶ —Comment trouves-tu cette fille?
—Quelle fille?
—Cette fille-là!
—Eh bien, je pense qu'elle est jolie.
(Elle n'est pas jolie.)

▶ jolie?

1. intéressants?

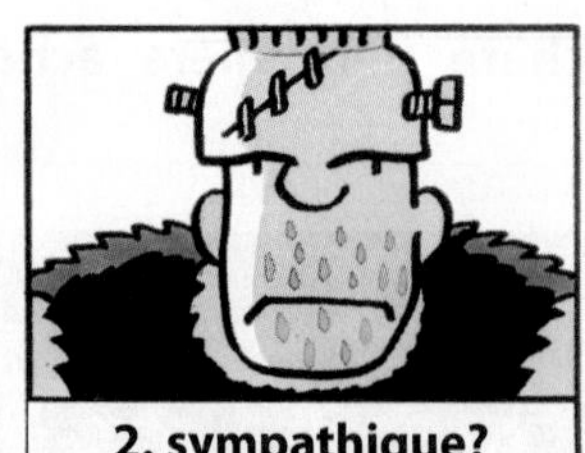

2. sympathique?

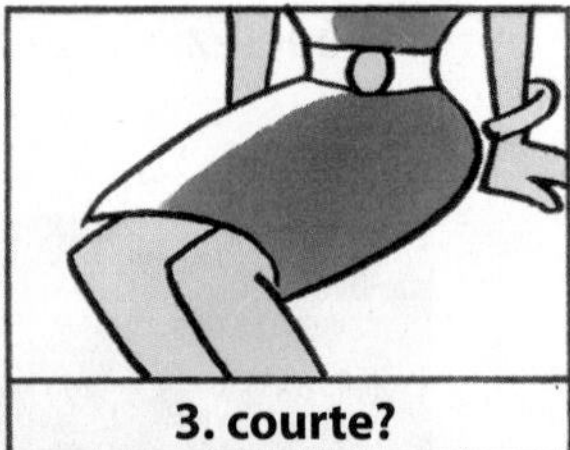

3. courte?

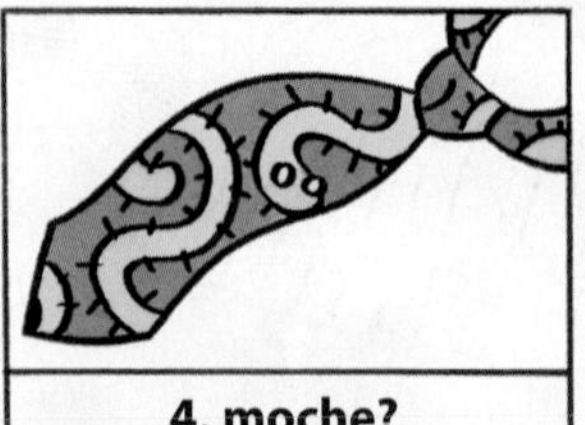

4. moche?

5. bon marché?

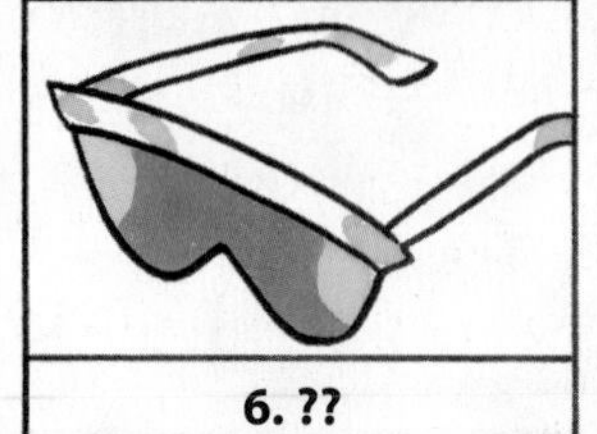

6. ??

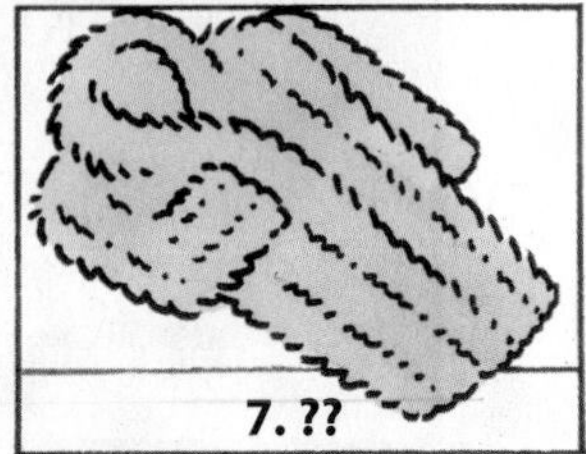

7. ??

3 Shopping 

PARLER You and a friend are shopping by catalog. Choose an object and tell your friend what you are buying. Identify it by color and explain why you like it.

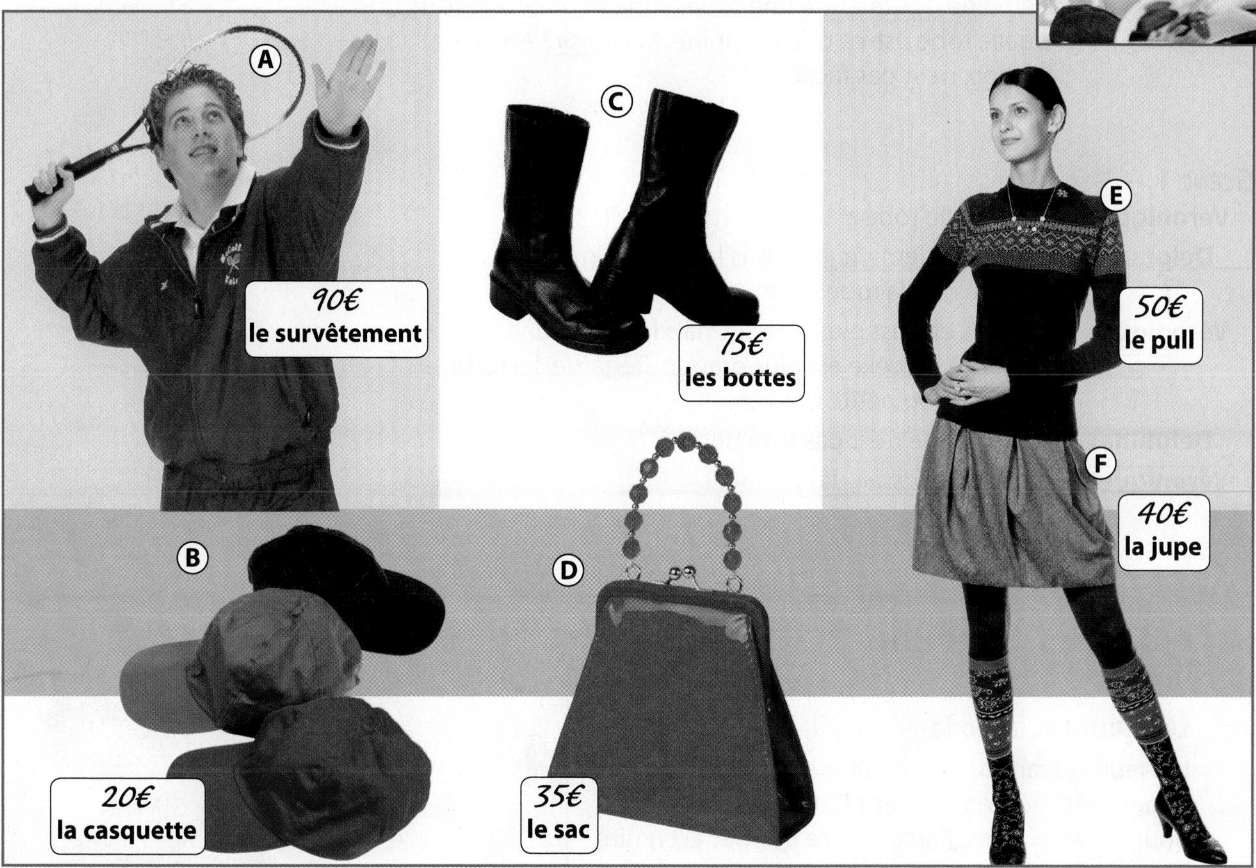

▶ —Je vais acheter un sac.
—Quel sac?
—Ce sac rose.
—Pourquoi?
—Parce qu'il est joli.

4 Composition: La soirée

ÉCRIRE You have been invited to a party by a French friend. In a short paragraph, describe …

- what clothes you are going to wear
- whom you are going to bring along
- what things you are going to bring (food? music? camera?)

Leçon 19

Conversation et Culture

Un choix difficile

DVD  AUDIO 

Dans un mois, Delphine va aller au mariage de sa cousine. Elle va acheter une nouvelle robe pour cette occasion. Pour cela, elle va dans un magasin de vêtements avec sa copine Véronique. Il y a beaucoup de jolies robes dans ce magasin. — *new*

Delphine hésite entre une robe jaune et une robe rouge. Quelle robe est-ce que Delphine va choisir? Ah là là, le choix n'est pas facile. — *is hesitating/between*, *to choose*, *choice*

Scène 1.

Véronique: Alors, quelle robe est-ce que tu choisis?

Delphine: Eh bien, finalement je choisis la robe rouge. Elle est plus jolie que la robe jaune. — *finally*, *prettier than*

Véronique: C'est vrai, elle est plus jolie … mais la robe jaune est moins chère et elle est plus grande. Regarde. La robe rouge est trop petite pour toi. — *less/larger*

Delphine: Mais non, elle n'est pas trop petite.

Véronique: Bon, écoute, essaie-la! — *try it!*

NOTE Culturelle

Les jeunes et la mode

Les jeunes Français aiment être à la mode. Ils dépensent° trente pour cent (30%) de leur budget pour les vêtements. Parce que ce budget est limité, ils font très attention quand ils choisissent leurs vêtements. Heureusement,° il y a des boutiques spécialisées dans la mode des jeunes, comme Zara, Mango et Etam, où les vêtements ne sont pas trop° chers.

Certains jeunes préfèrent la «mode rétro». Ils achètent leurs vêtements au marché aux puces.°

dépensent *spend* **Heureusement** *Fortunately* **trop** *too* **marché aux puces** *flea market*

@HOMETUTOR
my.hrw.com

SCÈNE 2.

Delphine sort de la cabine d'essayage. — *comes out/fitting room*

Delphine: C'est vrai, la robe rouge est plus petite mais ce n'est pas un problème — *smaller*

Véronique: Pourquoi?

Delphine: Parce que j'ai un mois pour maigrir. — *to lose weight*

Véronique: Et si tu grossis? — *if/gain weight*

Delphine: Toi, tais-toi! — *be quiet*

Compréhension

1. Où vont Delphine et Véronique?
2. Qu'est-ce que Delphine va acheter?
3. Pourquoi?
4. Delphine hésite entre deux robes. De quelle couleur sont-elles?
5. Quelle robe est-ce qu'elle choisit?
6. Pourquoi est-ce qu'elle préfère la robe rouge?
7. Selon *(According to)* Véronique, quel est le problème avec la robe rouge?
8. Qu'est-ce que Delphine doit *(must)* faire pour porter la robe?

A Les verbes réguliers en *-ir*

Many French verbs end in **-ir.** Most of these verbs are conjugated like **finir** (*to finish*). Note the forms of this verb in the present tense, paying special attention to the endings.

INFINITIVE	finir	STEM (infinitive minus -ir)	ENDINGS
PRESENT	Je **finis** à deux heures.	fin-	**-is**
	Tu **finis** à une heure.		**-is**
	Il/Elle **finit** à cinq heures.		**-it**
	Nous **finissons** à midi.		**-issons**
	Vous **finissez** à une heure.		**-issez**
	Ils/Elles **finissent** à minuit.		**-issent**

1 Le marathon de Paris

PARLER/ÉCRIRE Not all runners finish the Paris marathon. Say who does and who does not.

▶ Philippe (non) — **Philippe ne finit pas.**

1. moi (oui)
2. toi (non)
3. nous (oui)
4. vous (non)
5. Éric (oui)
6. Stéphanie (non)
7. Frédéric et Marc (non)
8. Anne et Cécile (oui)

VOCABULAIRE Verbes réguliers en *-ir*

choisir	*to choose*	Quelle veste **choisis**-tu?
finir	*to finish*	Les classes **finissent** à midi.
grossir	*to gain weight, get fat*	Marc **grossit** parce qu'il mange beaucoup.
maigrir	*to lose weight, get thin*	Je **maigris** parce que je mange peu.
réussir	*to succeed*	Tu vas **réussir** parce que tu travailles!
réussir à un examen	*to pass an exam*	Nous **réussissons à nos examens.**

2 Le régime (Diet)

PARLER/ÉCRIRE Read about the following people. Say if they are gaining or losing weight.

▶ Philippe mange beaucoup de pizzas.
Il grossit. Il ne maigrit pas.

1. Vous faites des exercices.
2. Nous allons souvent au gymnase.
3. Vous êtes inactifs.
4. Je mange des carottes.
5. Monsieur Moreau adore la bonne cuisine.
6. Vous n'êtes pas très sportifs.
7. Ces personnes mangent trop (*too much*).
8. Je nage, je joue au volley et je fais des promenades.

@HOMETUTOR
my.hrw.com

3 Questions personnelles PARLER/ÉCRIRE

1. À quelle heure finissent les classes?
2. À quelle heure finit la classe de français?
3. Quand finit l'école cette année *(year)?*
4. Tu es invité(e) au restaurant ou au cinéma. Où choisis-tu d'aller?
5. Quand tu vas au cinéma avec ta famille, qui choisit le film?
6. En général, est-ce que tu réussis à tes examens? Est-ce que tu vas réussir à l'examen de français? Et tes copains?

B Les adjectifs *beau, nouveau* et *vieux*

The adjectives **beau** *(beautiful, good-looking)*, **nouveau** *(new)*, and **vieux** *(old)* are irregular.

		beau	nouveau	vieux
SINGULAR	MASC	le **beau** manteau (le **bel** imper)	le **nouveau** manteau (le **nouvel** imper)	le **vieux** manteau (le **vieil** imper)
	FEM.	la **belle** veste	la **nouvelle** veste	la **vieille** veste
PLURAL	MASC.	les **beaux** manteaux	les **nouveaux** manteaux	les **vieux** manteaux
	FEM.	les **belles** vestes	les **nouvelles** vestes	les **vieilles** vestes

→ The adjectives **beau**, **nouveau**, and **vieux** usually come BEFORE the noun. If the noun begins with a vowel sound, there is liaison between the adjective and the noun.

les **nouveaux** ordinateurs les **belles** affiches les **vieux** impers

→ In the masculine singular, the liaison forms **bel, nouvel,** and **vieil** are used before a vowel sound. Note that **vieil** is pronounced like **vieille:**

un **vieil** imper une **vieille** robe

4 La collection de printemps

PARLER Mod Boutique is presenting its spring collection. Point out all the items you like to a French friend, using the appropriate forms of **beau.**

▶ une chemise
Regarde la belle chemise!

1. une robe
2. un pantalon
3. des jeans
4. des blousons
5. une veste
6. un imper
7. des sandales
8. un manteau
9. un chapeau
10. des tee-shirts

5 Différences d'opinion

PARLER François is showing the new things he bought to his sister Valérie. She prefers his old things.

▶ des chaussures

1. un polo
2. des lunettes de soleil
3. un imper
4. des affiches
5. une casquette
6. une montre
7. un ordinateur
8. des baskets
9. un survêtement

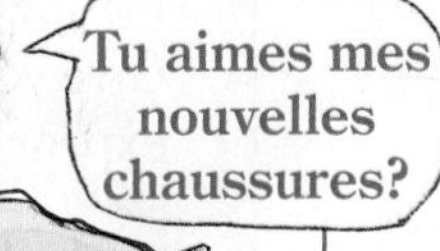

Tu aimes mes nouvelles chaussures?

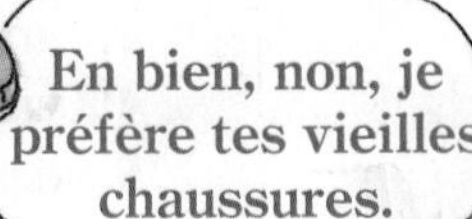

En bien, non, je préfère tes vieilles chaussures.

C La comparaison avec les adjectifs

Note how COMPARISONS are expressed in French.

Cet imper est **plus cher que** ce manteau. ... *more expensive than ...*
Cette jupe est **plus jolie que** cette robe. ... *prettier than ...*

Paul est **moins sportif que** Patrick. ... *less athletic than ...*
Il est **moins amusant que** lui. ... *less amusing than ...*

Je suis **aussi grand que** toi. ... *as tall as ...*
Tu n'es **pas aussi timide que** moi. ... *not as timid as ...*

To make comparisons with adjectives, French speakers use the following constructions:

+ plus		**plus cher (que)**	*more expensive (than)*
– moins	+ ADJECTIVE (+ **que** ...)	**moins cher (que)**	*less expensive (than)*
= aussi		**aussi cher (que)**	*as expensive (as)*

→ Note the irregular **plus** form of **bon** *(good)*:

plus + bon(ne) → meilleur(e) *(better)*

Ta pizza est **bonne**, mais mon sandwich est **meilleur**.

→ There is liaison after **plus** and **moins** when the next word begins with a vowel sound.

Cette robe-ci est **plus élégante**. Ce livre-là est **moins intéressant**.

→ In comparisons, the adjective always agrees with the noun (or pronoun) it describes.

La jupe est plus **chère** que le chemisier.

Les vestes sont moins **chères** que les manteaux.

→ In comparisons with people, STRESS PRONOUNS are used after **que**.

Paul est plus petit **que moi**. Je suis plus grand **que lui**.

6 Comparaisons

PARLER/ÉCRIRE How much do you think the following pairs of items cost? Give your opinion, saying whether the first one is more expensive, less expensive, or as expensive as the second one.

▶ une guitare/une raquette — **Une guitare est plus (moins, aussi) chère qu'une raquette.**

1. un vélo/un scooter
2. une mobylette/une moto
3. une pizza/un sandwich
4. une télé/un ordinateur
5. des chaussures/des sandales
6. une casquette/des lunettes de soleil
7. des bottes/des tennis
8. un short/un maillot de bain
9. un MP3/une montre
10. un portable/une tablette

@HOMETUTOR
my.hrw.com

VOCABULAIRE Expression pour la conversation

▶ ***How to introduce a personal opinion:***

à mon avis ... — *in my opinion ...* — **À mon avis,** le français est facile.

7 Expression personnelle

À mon avis, le tennis est plus (moins, aussi) intéressant que le ping-pong.

PARLER Compare the following by using the adjectives suggested. Give your personal opinion.

▶ le tennis/intéressant/le ping-pong

1. le basket/intéressant/le foot
2. l'anglais/facile/le français
3. la classe de français/amusant/la classe d'anglais
4. la Floride/beau/la Californie
5. les Yankees/bon/les Red Sox
6. la cuisine américaine/bon/la cuisine française
7. les filles/intelligent/les garçons
8. l'argent *(money)*/important/l'amitié *(friendship)*

8 Et toi?

PARLER Use the appropriate stress pronouns in answering the questions below.

▶ **—Es-tu plus grand(e) que ton copain?**
—Oui, je suis plus grand(e) que lui.
(Non, je suis moins grand(e) que lui.)
(Je suis aussi grand(e) que lui.)

1. Es-tu plus grand(e) que ta mère?
2. Es-tu aussi riche que Bill Gates?
3. Es-tu plus sportif (sportive) que tes copains?
4. Es-tu plus intelligent(e) qu'Einstein?

Prononciation

Les lettres «ill»

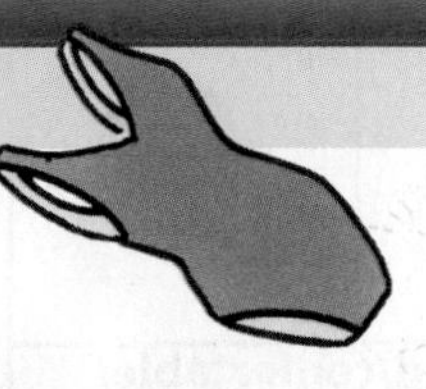

maillot

In the middle of a word, the letters "**ill**" usually represent the sound /j/ like the "**y**" of *yes*.

Répétez: **maillot travaillez oreille vieille fille famille juillet**
En juillet, Mireille va travailler pour sa vieille tante.

At the end of a word, the sound /j/ is sometimes spelled **il.**

Répétez: **appareil-photo vieil travail** *(job)*
Mon oncle a un vieil appareil-photo.

EXCEPTION: The letters **ill** are pronounced /il/ in the following words:

Répétez: **ville village mille Lille**

À votre tour!

OBJECTIFS

Now you can . . .
- make comparisons
- discuss your choices

Digital performance space

1 La bonne réponse

PARLER François and Stéphanie are shopping. Match François's questions with Stéphanie's answers. Act out the dialogue with a classmate.

François
1 Tu aimes cette veste verte?
2 Combien est-ce qu'elle coûte?
3 Et qu'est-ce que tu penses de cette veste rouge?
4 Alors, qu'est-ce que tu vas choisir?
Stéphanie
a 300 euros.
b À mon avis, elle est moins jolie.
c La veste bleue. Elle est meilleur marché et elle est aussi élégante.
d Oui, mais elle est très chère.

2 Créa-dialogue

PARLER With a classmate, prepare a dialogue comparing the items in one of the following pictures. Use the suggested verb and some of the suggested adjectives.

▶ —Tu choisis la voiture rouge ou la voiture noire?
—Je choisis la voiture rouge.
—Pourquoi?
—Parce qu'elle est plus petite et moins chère.

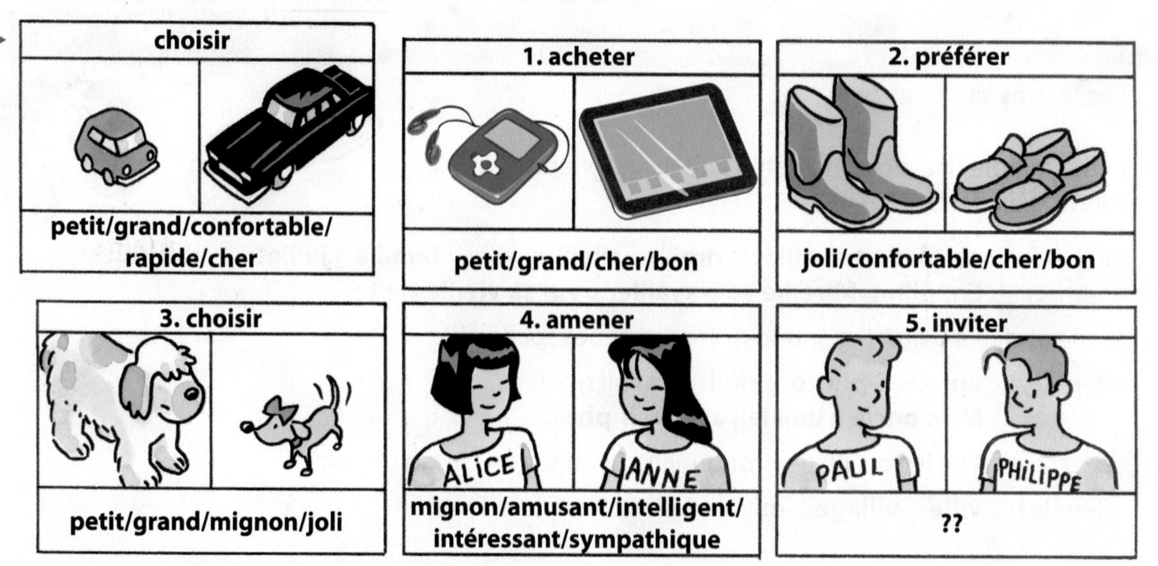

3 Choix personnels 

PARLER Select two people or two items in each of the following categories and ask a classmate to indicate which one he/she prefers. You may ask your classmate to explain why.

▶ 2 actors

Tu préfères Tom Hanks ou Brad Pitt?
Je préfère Brad Pitt.
Pourquoi?
Parce que Brad Pitt est plus mignon que Tom Hanks.
(plus beau, plus jeune ...)

CATEGORIES:

- ▶ 2 actors
- 2 actresses
- 2 singers (male)
- 2 singers (female)
- 2 baseball teams
- 2 cities
- 2 restaurants in your town
- 2 stores in your town

4 Composition: Portrait comparatif 

ÉCRIRE Write a description of yourself, comparing yourself to six other people (your friends, your family, well-known personalities, etc.) You may use some of the following adjectives:

▶ Je suis moins sportif (sportive) que Sammy Sosa (Venus Williams).

grand petit jeune vieux amusant intelligent bête
sportif sympathique timide gentil génial optimiste

5 Composition: Comparaisons personnelles 

ÉCRIRE Choose a friend or relative about your age. Give this person's name and age. Then, in a short paragraph, compare yourself to that person in terms of physical appearance and personality traits.

▶ **Mon cousin s'appelle Patrick. Il a quinze ans. Je suis plus jeune que lui, mais il est moins grand que moi ...**

Leçon 20

Conversation et Culture

Alice a un job

DVD AUDIO

Alice a un nouveau job. Elle travaille dans un magasin de matériel audio-visuel. Dans ce magasin, on vend toutes sortes de choses. *one, they / sell(s) / all*

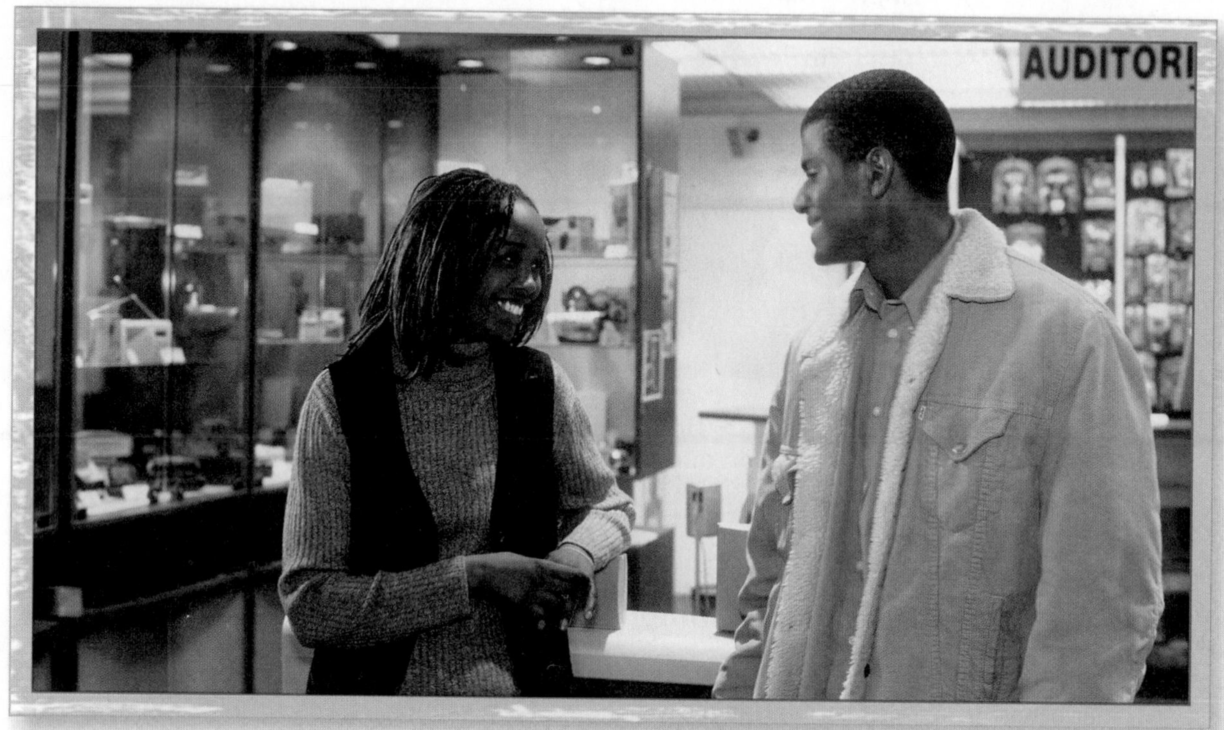

Un jour, son cousin Jérôme lui rend visite. *comes to visit her*

Jérôme: Salut, ça va?

Alice: Oui, ça va.

Jérôme: Et ce nouveau job?

Alice: C'est super.

Jérôme: Qu'est-ce qu'on vend dans ton magasin?

Alice: Eh bien, tu vois, on vend toutes sortes de matériel audio-visuel … Moi, je vends des mini-chaînes. *see*

Jérôme: Tu es bien payée? *paid*

Alice: Non, on n'est pas très bien payé, mais on a des réductions sur l'équipement stéréo et sur les CD et les DVD.

Jérôme: Qu'est-ce que tu vas faire avec ton argent? *money*

Alice: Je ne sais pas … J'ai envie de voyager cet été. *feel like*

Jérôme: Tu as de la chance. Moi aussi, j'ai envie de voyager, mais je n'ai pas d'argent. *are lucky*

Alice: Écoute, Jérôme, si tu as besoin d'argent, fais comme moi. *need / do as I do*

Jérôme: Comment? *What?*

Alice: Cherche un job! *Find*

@HOMETUTOR
my.hrw.com

Compréhension

1. Où travaille Alice?
2. Qu'est-ce qu'elle vend?
3. Qu'est-ce qu'elle espère faire cet été?
4. Pourquoi est-ce que Jérôme ne va pas voyager?
5. Qu'est-ce que Jérôme doit *(must)* faire pour avoir de l'argent?

NOTE Culturelle

L'argent° des jeunes

Contrairement à beaucoup de jeunes Américains, les jeunes Français n'ont pas de travail° régulier. Par exemple, ils ne travaillent pas dans les supermarchés, les boutiques ou les stations-service. Occasionnellement, ils font des petits jobs pour leurs voisins: baby-sitting, promenade de chiens,° lavage° de voitures, etc.

En général, ils dépendent de la générosité de leurs parents pour leur argent. Le montant° qu'ils reçoivent varie avec l'âge, les résultats scolaires,° et la situation économique de la famille. Ils reçoivent aussi de l'argent de leur famille et de leurs parrains° et marraines° pour des occasions spéciales: Noël, jour de l'An° et anniversaire.

Voici combien d'argent les jeunes Français ont en moyenne: °

ÂGE	MONTANT PAR MOIS
7-11 ans	12 euros
12-13 ans	20 euros
14-17 ans	50 euros

argent *money* **travail** *work*
promenade de chiens *dog walking* **lavage** *washing*
montant *amount* **résultats scolaires** *report cards*
parrains *godfathers* **marraines** *godmothers*
jour de l'An *New Year's Day* **en moyenne** *on the average*

COMPARAISONS Culturelles

- Compare how teenagers in France and in the United States get their spending money.
- Why do you think French teenagers do not have regular jobs?

VOCABULAIRE L'argent

NOMS

l'argent *(m.)*	*money*	**une pièce** *coin*
un billet	*bill, paper money*	

ADJECTIFS

riche ≠ pauvre	*rich ≠ poor*

VERBES

dépenser	*to spend*	Je n'aime pas **dépenser** mon argent.
gagner	*to earn,*	Je **gagne** 10 dollars par *(per)* jour.
	to win	Tu joues bien. Tu vas **gagner** le match.
payer	*to pay, pay for*	Qui va **payer** aujourd'hui?

EXPRESSIONS

combien + VERB	*how much*	**Combien** coûte cette montre?
combien de + NOUN	*how much*	**Combien d'**argent as-tu?
	how many	**Combien de** CD as-tu?
avoir besoin de + NOUN	*to need*	**J'ai besoin de** 5 dollars.
+ INFINITIVE	*to need to, have to*	**J'ai besoin de** travailler.
avoir envie de + NOUN	*to want*	**J'ai envie d'**une pizza.
+ INFINITIVE	*to feel like, want to*	**J'ai envie de** manger.

➔ Verbs like **payer** that end in **-yer**, have the following stem change:
y → i in the **je, tu, il, ils** forms of the verb

je **paie** tu **paies** il/elle **paie** ils/elles **paient**
but: nous **payons** vous **payez**

Money does not buy happiness.

PARLER Ask your classmates how many of the following they have.

▶ **des CD** —**Combien de CD as-tu?**
—**J'ai vingt CD.**
(Je n'ai pas de CD.)

1. des frères
2. des soeurs
3. des casquettes
4. des affiches
5. des tee-shirts
6. des jeans
7. des billets d'un dollar
8. des pièces de dix cents

@HOMETUTOR
my.hrw.com

2 Qu'est-ce que tu as envie de faire?

PARLER Ask your classmates if they feel like doing the following things.

▶ **aller au cinéma**

1. aller au restaurant
2. manger une pizza
3. aller à la piscine
4. parler français
5. écouter de la musique
6. visiter Paris
7. jouer au Frisbee
8. acheter une moto
9. faire une promenade
10. surfer sur l'Internet

3 Au restaurant

PARLER/ÉCRIRE The following students are in a restaurant in Quebec. Say what they feel like buying and estimate how much money they need.

▶ **Hélène/une pizza**
Hélène a envie d'une pizza.
Elle a besoin de cinq dollars.

1. Marc/un sandwich
2. nous/une glace
3. moi/un soda
4. toi/un jus d'orange
5. vous/une salade
6. mes copains/un steak

4 Questions personnelles PARLER/ÉCRIRE

1. Est-ce que tu as un job? Où est-ce que tu travailles? Combien est-ce que tu gagnes par *(per)* heure? par semaine?
2. Quand tu vas au cinéma, qui paie? toi ou ton copain (ta copine)?
3. Combien est-ce que tu paies quand tu achètes un hamburger? une pizza? une glace?
4. Est-ce que tu as des pièces dans ta poche *(pocket)*? quelles pièces?
5. Qui est représenté sur le billet d'un dollar? sur le billet de cinq dollars? sur le billet de dix dollars?
6. Est-ce que tu préfères dépenser ou économiser *(to save)* ton argent? Pourquoi?
7. Est-ce que tu espères être riche un jour? Pourquoi?

Le Vendôme
36, Côte de la Montagne
Québec
tél 692.0557

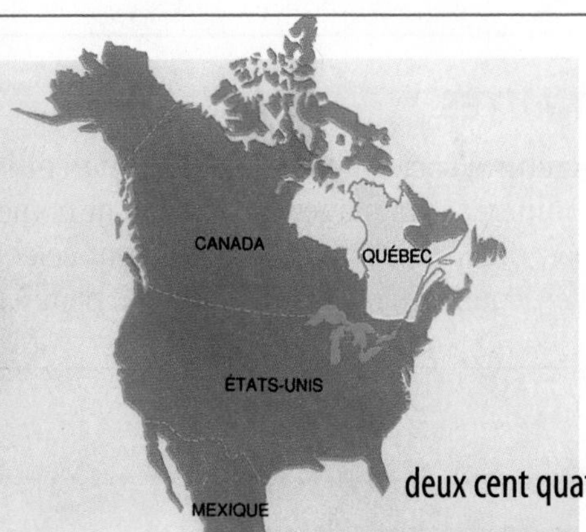

A Le pronom *on*

Note the use of the subject pronoun **on** in the sentences below.

Qu'est-ce qu'**on** vend ici?	*What do **they** (do **you**) sell here?*
Où est-ce qu'**on** achète ce CD?	*Where does **one** (do **people**) buy that CD?*
En France, **on** parle français.	*In France, **people (you, they)** speak French.*

The pronoun **on** is used in general statements, according to the construction:

on + il/elle - form of verb	**On** travaille beaucoup.	***One** works a lot.* ***They** work a lot.* ***You** work a lot.* ***People** work a lot.*

→ There is liaison after **on** when the next word begins with a vowel sound.
Est-ce qu'**on** invite Stéphanie à la boum?

→ In conversation, **on** is often used instead of **nous:**

—Est-ce qu'**on** dîne à la maison?	*Are **we** having dinner at home?*
—Non, **on** va au restaurant.	*No, **we** are going to the restaurant.*

5 Ici on parle ...

PARLER/ÉCRIRE Imagine that you have won a grand prize of a world tour. Say which of the following languages is spoken in each of the cities that you will be visiting.

▶ Acapulco

À Acapulco, on parle espagnol.

1. Québec
2. Boston
3. Madrid
4. Bruxelles
5. Genève
6. Tokyo
7. Buenos Aires
8. Londres *(London)*
9. Rome
10. Beijing

anglais	espagnol	français
japonais	italien	chinois

COMMUNAUTÉS

In a multi-cultural society, people speak different languages and have different customs. How many different languages are spoken at home by classmates in your school? What are some of their different customs and different celebrations? As a class project, put up a wall map showing their countries of origin. Do some come from French-speaking areas?

@HOMETUTOR
my.hrw.com

VOCABULAIRE Expression pour la conversation

How to indicate approval:

C'est une bonne idée! *That's a good idea!*

6 Projets de week-end

PARLER Suggest possible weekend activities to your classmates. They will let you know whether they think each idea is a good one or not.

▶ aller au café

1. jouer aux jeux vidéo?
2. aller à la bibliothèque?
3. aller à la plage?
4. téléphoner au professeur?
5. faire une promenade à vélo?
6. aller dans les magasins?
7. acheter des vêtements?
8. écouter de la musique?

On va au café?
Oui, c'est une bonne idée!
Non, ce n'est pas une bonne idée.

7 En Amérique et en France

PARLER An American student and a French student are comparing certain aspects of life in their own countries. Play both roles.

▶ jouer au baseball (au foot)

En Amérique, on joue au baseball.
En France, on joue au foot.

1. parler anglais (français)
2. étudier le français (l'anglais)
3. dîner à six heures (à huit heures)
4. manger des hamburgers (des omelettes)
5. voyager souvent en avion *(by plane)* (en train)
6. skier dans le Colorado (dans les Alpes)
7. aller à l'école le mercredi après-midi (le samedi matin)
8. chanter «la Bannière étoilée» *("The Star-Spangled Banner")* («la Marseillaise»)

8 Expression personnelle

PARLER/ÉCRIRE Describe what you, your friends, and your relatives generally do. Complete the following sentences according to your personal routine.

1. À la maison, on dîne … (à quelle heure?)
2. À la télé, on regarde … (quel programme?)
3. À la cafétéria de l'école, on mange … (quoi?)
4. En été, on va … (où?)
5. Le week-end, avec mes copains, on va … (où?)
6. Avec mes copains, on joue … (à quel sport? à quel jeu?)
7. On a une classe de français … (quels jours?)
8. On a un examen de français … (quel jour?)

B Les verbes réguliers en *-re*

Many French verbs end in **-re.** Most of these are conjugated like **vendre** *(to sell).* Note the forms of this verb in the present tense, paying special attention to the endings.

INFINITIVE	vendre		STEM (infinitive minus **-re**)	ENDINGS
PRESENT	Je	**vends** ma raquette.	vend-	-s
	Tu	**vends** ton scooter.		-s
	Il/Elle/On	**vend** son ordinateur.		—
	Nous	**vendons** nos livres.		-ons
	Vous	**vendez** vos CD.		-ez
	Ils/Elles	**vendent** leur voiture.		-ent

→ The "**d**" of the stem is silent in the singular forms, but it is pronounced in the plural forms.

VOCABULAIRE Verbes réguliers en *-re*

attendre	*to wait, wait for*	Pierre **attend** Michèle au café.
entendre	*to hear*	Est-ce que tu **entends** la radio?
perdre	*to lose, waste*	Jean-Claude **perd** le match.
rendre visite à	*to visit (a person)*	Je **rends visite à** mon oncle.
répondre à	*to answer*	Nous **répondons à** la question du prof.
vendre	*to sell*	À qui **vends**-tu ton vélo?

→ There are two French verbs that correspond to the English verb *to visit.*

visiter (+ PLACES)	Nous **visitons** Québec.
rendre visite à (+ PEOPLE)	Nous **rendons visite à** nos cousins canadiens.

9 Rendez-vous

PARLER/ÉCRIRE The following people have been shopping and are now waiting for their friends at a café. Express this, using the appropriate forms of the verb **attendre.**

▶ Jérôme (Michèle) **Jérôme attend Michèle.**

1. nous (nos copains)
2. vous (vos cousines)
3. moi (Antoine)
4. toi (Julie)
5. Olivier et Éric (Élodie et Sophie)
6. les étudiants (les étudiantes)
7. Julien et moi, nous (Pauline et Mélanie)
8. Annette et toi, vous (Jean-Marc)
9. on (notre copine)
10. Stéphanie (Léa)

10 Qui?

PARLER/ÉCRIRE Who is doing what? Answer the following questions, using the suggested subjects.

1. Qui perd le match?
   (toi, vous, Alice)
2. Qui rend visite à Pierre?
   (Paul, Léa et Hélène, toi)
3. Qui entend l'avion *(plane)?*
   (moi, vous, les voisins)
4. Qui vend des CD?
   (on, ce magasin, ces boutiques)
5. Qui attend le bus?
   (les élèves, le professeur, on, vous)
6. Qui répond au professeur?
   (toi, nous, les élèves)

11 Qu'est-ce qu'ils font?

PARLER/ÉCRIRE Say what the following people do by completing each sentence with the appropriate form of one of the verbs from the list. Be logical!

1. Guillaume est patient. Il … ses amis.
2. Vous êtes à Paris. Vous … à vos cousins français.
3. Tu joues mal. Tu … le match.
4. Je suis chez moi. J' … un bruit *(noise)* curieux.
5. Nous sommes en classe. Nous … aux questions du professeur.
6. Julie travaille dans une boutique. Elle … des robes.
7. On est au café. On … nos copains.

attendre	entendre	rendre visite
vendre	perdre	répondre

C L'impératif

LEARNING ABOUT LANGUAGE

The IMPERATIVE is used to make suggestions and to give orders and advice. The commands or suggestions may be affirmative or negative.

Compare the French and English forms of the imperative.

Écoute ce CD!	***Listen*** *to this CD!*
Ne vendez pas votre voiture!	***Don't sell*** *your car!*
Allons au cinéma!	***Let's go*** *to the movies!*

Note the forms of the imperative in the chart below.

INFINITIVE	parler	finir	vendre	aller
IMPERATIVE				
(tu)	**parle**	**finis**	**vends**	**va**
(vous)	**parlez**	**finissez**	**vendez**	**allez**
(nous)	**parlons**	**finissons**	**vendons**	**allons**

For regular verbs and most irregular verbs, the forms of the imperative are the same as the corresponding forms of the present tense.

→ NOTE: For all **-er** verbs, including **aller,** the **-s** of the **tu** form is dropped. Compare:

Tu **parles** anglais.	**Parle** français, s'il te plaît!
Tu **vas** au café.	**Va** à la bibliothèque!

→ The negative imperative is formed as follows:

ne + VERB + **pas …**   **Ne choisis pas** ce blouson.

12 Mais oui! 

PARLER You have organized a party at your home. Valérie offers to do the following. You accept.

▶ apporter une pizza?

1. faire une salade?
2. inviter nos copains?
3. acheter des sodas?
4. apporter des CD?
5. choisir la musique de danse?
6. venir à huit heures?
7. téléphoner aux voisins?
8. faire des sandwichs?

13 L'ange et le démon *(The angel and the devil)* 

PARLER Véronique is wondering whether she should do certain things. The angel gives her good advice. The devil gives her bad advice. Play both roles.

▶ étudier les verbes
Étudie les verbes.
N'étudie pas les verbes.

1. téléphoner à ta tante
2. attendre tes copains
3. faire attention en classe
4. aller à l'école
5. finir la leçon
6. écouter tes professeurs
7. mettre *(set)* la table
8. aider tes amis
9. rendre visite à ta grand-mère
10. choisir des copains sympathiques
11. faire tes devoirs *(homework)*
12. réussir à l'examen

14 Oui ou non?

PARLER For each of the following situations, give your classmates advice as to what to do and what not to do. Be logical.

▶ Nous sommes en vacances. (étudier? voyager?)
N'étudiez pas! Voyagez!

1. Nous sommes à Paris. (parler anglais? parler français?)
2. C'est dimanche. (aller à la bibliothèque? aller au cinéma?)
3. Il fait beau. (rester à la maison? faire une promenade?)
4. Il fait froid. (mettre un pull? mettre un tee-shirt?)
5. Il est onze heures du soir. (rester au café? rentrer à la maison?)
6. Il fait très chaud. (aller à la piscine? regarder la télé?)

@HOMETUTOR
my.hrw.com

15 L'esprit de contradiction *(Disagreement)* 

PARLER Make suggestions to your friends about things to do. Your friends will not agree and will suggest something else.

▶ aller au cinéma (à la plage)

Allons au cinéma!
Non, n'allons pas au cinéma! Allons à la plage!

1. jouer au tennis (aux jeux vidéo)
2. écouter la radio (un MP3)
3. regarder la télé (un film vidéo)
4. dîner au restaurant (à la maison)
5. inviter Michèle (Sophie)
6. organiser un barbecue (une boum)
7. faire des sandwichs (une pizza)
8. aller au musée (à la bibliothèque)
9. faire une promenade à pied (en voiture)
10. rendre visite à nos voisins (à nos copains)

Prononciation  an, en /ɑ̃/

Les lettres «an» **et** «en»

The letters "**an**" and "**en**" represent the nasal vowel /ɑ̃/.
Be sure not to pronounce the sound "**n**" after the vowel.

enfant

Répétez:

/ɑ̃/ **enfant an manteau collants grand élégant**

André mange un grand sandwich.

/ɑ̃/ **enfant en argent dépenser attends entend vend envie**

Vincent dépense rarement son argent.

À votre tour!

OBJECTIFS

Now you can ...
- make suggestions
- tell others what to do

1 La bonne réponse 

PARLER Anne is talking to Jean-François. Match Anne's questions with Jean-François's answers. You may act out the conversation with a classmate.

Anne
1 Est-ce que tu rends visite à tes cousins ce week-end?
2 Tu veux aller dans les boutiques avec moi?
3 Est-ce que tu as envie d'aller au cinéma?
4 Et après (*afterwards*) qu'est-ce qu'on fait?

Jean-François
a Eh bien, allons au restaurant!
b Bonne idée! Il y a un nouveau film au «Majestic».
c Écoute! Je n'ai pas besoin de vêtements.
d Non, je reste ici.

2 Créa-dialogue  

PARLER When we are with our friends, it is not always easy to agree on what to do. With your classmates, discuss the following possibilities.

Quand?	Première suggestion	Deuxième suggestion
▶ samedi	aller au cinéma	rendre visite à nos amis
1. ce soir (*tonight*)	étudier	regarder la télé
2. dimanche	aller en ville	dîner au restaurant
3. après (*after*) les classes	jouer au basket	faire une promenade
4. cet été	chercher un job	voyager
5. ce week-end	faire un pique-nique	??
6. demain	aller à la bibliothèque	??

3 Conseils 

PARLER Your friends tell you what they would like to do. Give them appropriate advice, either positive or negative. Use your imagination.

▶ Je voudrais maigrir. **Alors, mange moins. (Alors, ne mange pas de pizza.)**

1. Je voudrais avoir un «A» en français.
2. Je voudrais gagner beaucoup d'argent.
3. Je voudrais organiser une boum.
4. Je voudrais préparer un barbecue.

4 Que faire? 

PARLER Give a classmate advice about what to do or not to do in the following circumstances.

Pendant (*During*) la classe	Ce soir	Ce week-end	Pendant les vacances
écouter le prof parler à tes copains regarder les bandes dessinées (*comics*) manger un sandwich répondre en français ??	étudier aller au cinéma préparer tes leçons aider (*help*) ta mère surfer sur l'Internet ??	rester à la maison aller en ville dépenser ton argent organiser une boum faire une promenade à pied ??	voyager travailler grossir oublier (*forget*) ton français ??

▶ Pendant la classe, écoute le prof. Ne parle pas à tes copains.

5 Bon voyage! 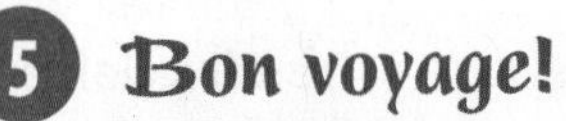

ÉCRIRE Your French friend Ariane is going to visit the United States next summer with her cousin. They are traveling on a low budget and are asking you for advice as to how to save money. Make a list of suggestions, including five things they could do and five things they should not do. You may want to use some of the following ideas:

▶ Voyagez en bus. Ne voyagez pas en train.

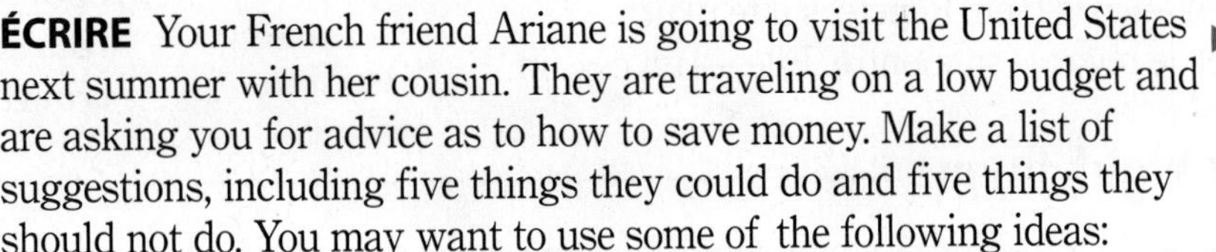

- voyager (comment?)
- rester (dans quels hôtels?)
- dîner (dans quels restaurants?)
- visiter (quelles villes?)
- aller (où?)
- acheter (quelles choses?)
- apporter (quelles choses?)

Tests de contrôle

By taking the following tests, you can check your progress in French and also prepare for the unit test. Write your answers on a separate sheet of paper.

Review...
- items of clothing: pp. 258, 259, and 260

1 The right item

Give the names of the following items of clothing, using the appropriate article: **un, une,** or **des.**

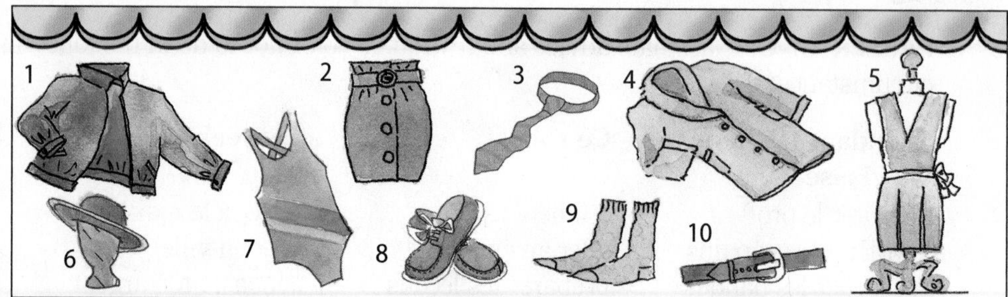

Dans ce magasin, il y a ...

1. __	**3.** __	**5.** __	**7.** __	**9.** __
2. __	**4.** __	**6.** __	**8.** __	**10.** __

Review...
- new verbs: pp. 259, 262, 269, 278, and 290

2 The right activity

Complete each of the following sentences with the appropriate forms of the verbs in the box. Be logical in your choice of verbs and do not use the same word more than once.

1. Philippe — des sandwichs à la boum.
2. Caroline — sa nouvelle robe.
3. Thomas — parce qu'il mange trop *(too much)*.
4. Léa — un copain au pique-nique.
5. Céline — aux examens parce qu'elle étudie beaucoup.
6. Mélanie ne — pas son stylo. Où est-il?
7. Charlotte est en vacances. Elle — à son oncle.
8. Pierre — à un mail.
9. Je n' — pas bien. Répète, s'il te plaît.
10. Cécile regarde sa montre. Elle — un copain.

amener
apporter
attendre
entendre
grossir
porter
rendre visite
répondre
réussir
trouver

Review...
- **beau, nouveau,** and **vieux:** p. 279

3 The right form

Complete the following sentences with the appropriate forms of **beau, nouveau,** and **vieux.** Be logical in your choices.

1. Dans ce quartier moderne, il y a beaucoup de — immeubles.
2. Ma grand-mère a 82 ans. Elle est —.
3. Catherine est très jolie. C'est une — fille, n'est-ce pas?
4. Mon ordinateur ne marche pas. J'ai besoin d'un — ordinateur.
5. Nicolas va nettoyer *(to clean)* le garage. Il met ses — vêtements.

4 The right comparison

Make logical comparisons using the adjectives in parentheses.

(grand) **1.** La France est — les États-Unis *(United States)*.
(élégant) **2.** Une belle chemise est — un vieux tee-shirt.
(rapide) **3.** Les voitures de sport sont — les limousines.
(bon) **4.** À l'examen, un «A» est — un «C».

Review...
- comparisons: p. 280

5 Ce or quel?

Complete the following sentences with the appropriate forms of **ce** or **quel.**

1. — blouson préfères-tu?
2. J'aime — lunettes!
3. — veste est chère!
4. — casquette achetez-vous?
5. — copains invites-tu?
6. — chaussures mets-tu?
7. Comment s'appelle — garçon?
8. Qui est — homme?

Review...
- ce and **quel** pp. 270 and 271

6 The right verb

Complete the following sentences with the appropriate forms of the verbs in parentheses.

1. (acheter)
J'— une chemise. Nous — une montre. Qu'est-ce que tu —?
2. (mettre)
Marc — un tee-shirt. Je — un short. Qu'est-ce que vous —?
3. (choisir)
Vous — des vêtements. Ils — des tennis. Éric — un polo.
4. (finir)
Nous — les devoirs. Je — un livre. Pauline — la pizza.
5. (vendre)
Ils — leur maison. Je — mon vélo. Claire — sa voiture.
6. (attendre)
Les touristes — le train. J'— le bus. Nous — un copain.

Review...
- verb forms: pp. 268, 272, 278 and 290

7 Composition: Un mariage

Digital performance space

Imagine that you are a reporter for the society column of your local newspaper. You are attending an elegant wedding. Describe what the following people are wearing: **la mariée** *(the bride)*, **le marié** *(the groom)*, and **les demoiselles d'honneur** *(the bridesmaids)*. Be imaginative but use only vocabulary and expressions that you know in French.

STRATEGY Writing

a For each of the following, list the clothes and their colors.

la mariée	le marié	les demoiselles d'honneur

b Write three short paragraphs describing what each person is wearing.

c Reread your composition and be sure you have spelled all the items of clothing correctly and have used the correct forms of the color adjectives.

Vocabulaire

POUR COMMUNIQUER

Shopping for clothes

Pardon…	*Excuse me …*	**Quel est le prix de …?**	*What is the price of …?*
Vous désirez, (monsieur)?	*May I help you, (Sir)?*	**Combien coûte …**	*How much does … cost?*
Je cherche …	*I'm looking for …*		

Expressing opinions and making comparisons

Qu'est-ce que tu penses de [la robe rose]?	*What do you think of [the pink dress]?*
Comment tu trouves [la robe noire]?	*What do you think of [the black dress]?*

La robe rose est	**plus belle que** **moins belle que** **aussi belle que**	**la robe noire.**	*The pink dress is*	*more beautiful than* *less beautiful than* *as beautiful as*	*the black dress.*

MOTS ET EXPRESSIONS

Les magasins

un magasin	*store*	**une boutique**	*shop*
un grand magasin	*department store*		

L'argent

l'argent	*money*	**une pièce**	*coin*
un billet	*bill, paper money*		

Les vêtements et les accessoires

des baskets	*(hightop) sneakers*	**des bottes**	*boots*
un blouson	*jacket*	**une casquette**	*baseball cap*
un chapeau	*hat*	**une ceinture**	*belt*
un chemisier	*blouse*	**des chaussettes**	*socks*
des collants	*tights*	**des chaussures**	*shoes*
un imper(méable)	*raincoat*	**une chemise**	*shirt*
un jean	*jeans*	**une cravate**	*tie*
un jogging	*jogging suit*	**une jupe**	*skirt*
un maillot de bain	*bathing suit*	**des lunettes**	*glasses*
un manteau	*overcoat*	**des lunettes de soleil**	*sunglasses*
un pantalon	*pants*	**une robe**	*dress*
un polo	*polo shirt*	**des sandales**	*sandals*
un pull	*sweater*	**une veste**	*jacket*
un short	*shorts*		
un survêtement	*track suit*		
un sweat	*sweatshirt*		
un tee-shirt	*t-shirt*		
des tennis	*sneakers*		

Interactive Flashcards
@HOMETUTOR
my.hrw.com

La description

à la mode	*in style*	**joli(e)**	*pretty*
beau (belle)	*beautiful*	**long(ue)**	*long*
bon marché	*cheap*	**meilleur(e)**	*better*
cher (chère)	*expensive*	**moche**	*ugly*
chouette	*neat*	**nouveau (nouvelle)**	*new*
court(e)	*short*	**pauvre**	*poor*
démodé(e)	*out of style*	**petit(e)**	*small*
élégant(e)	*elegant*	**riche**	*rich*
génial(e)	*terrific*	**vieux (vieille)**	*old*
grand(e)	*big*		

Verbes réguliers en *-er*

chercher	*to look for*
coûter	*to cost*
dépenser	*to spend*
gagner	*to earn; to win*
penser (que)	*to think (that)*
porter	*to wear*
trouver	*to find; to think of*

Verbes avec changements orthographiques

acheter	*to buy*
amener	*to bring (a person)*
espérer	*to hope*
préférer	*to prefer*
payer	*to pay, to pay for*

Verbes réguliers en *-ir*

choisir	*to choose*
finir	*to finish*
grossir	*to gain weight*
maigrir	*to lose weight*
réussir	*to succeed*
réussir à un examen	*to pass an exam*

Verbes réguliers en *-re*

attendre	*to wait, to wait for*
entendre	*to hear*
perdre	*to lose, to waste*
rendre visite à	*to visit (a person)*
répondre à	*to answer*
vendre	*to sell*

Verbes irréguliers

avoir besoin de + *noun*	*to need*	**avoir envie de + *noun***	*to want*
avoir besoin de + *infinitive*	*to need to, to have to*	**avoir envie de + *infinitive***	*to feel like, to want to*
		mettre	*to put, to put on*

Les nombres de 100 à 1000

100	**cent**	**200**	**deux cents**	**500**	**cinq cents**	**800**	**huit cents**
101	**cent un**	**300**	**trois cents**	**600**	**six cents**	**900**	**neuf cents**
102	**cent deux**	**400**	**quatre cents**	**700**	**sept cents**	**1000**	**mille**

Expressions utiles

à mon avis	*in my opinion*	**combien + *verb***	*how much*
Eh bien!	*Well!*	**combien de + *noun***	*how much, how many*
C'est une bonne idée!	*That's a good idea!*	**trop + *adjective***	*too*
ce, cet, cette, ces	*this, that, these, those*		
quel, quelle, quels, quelles	*what, which*		

Achats° par INTERNET

En France, comme° aux États-Unis,° on peut faire beaucoup d'achats par Internet. Ces vêtements figurent° sur un catalogue en ligne d'une compagnie française spécialisée dans la vente° de vêtements par correspondance.°

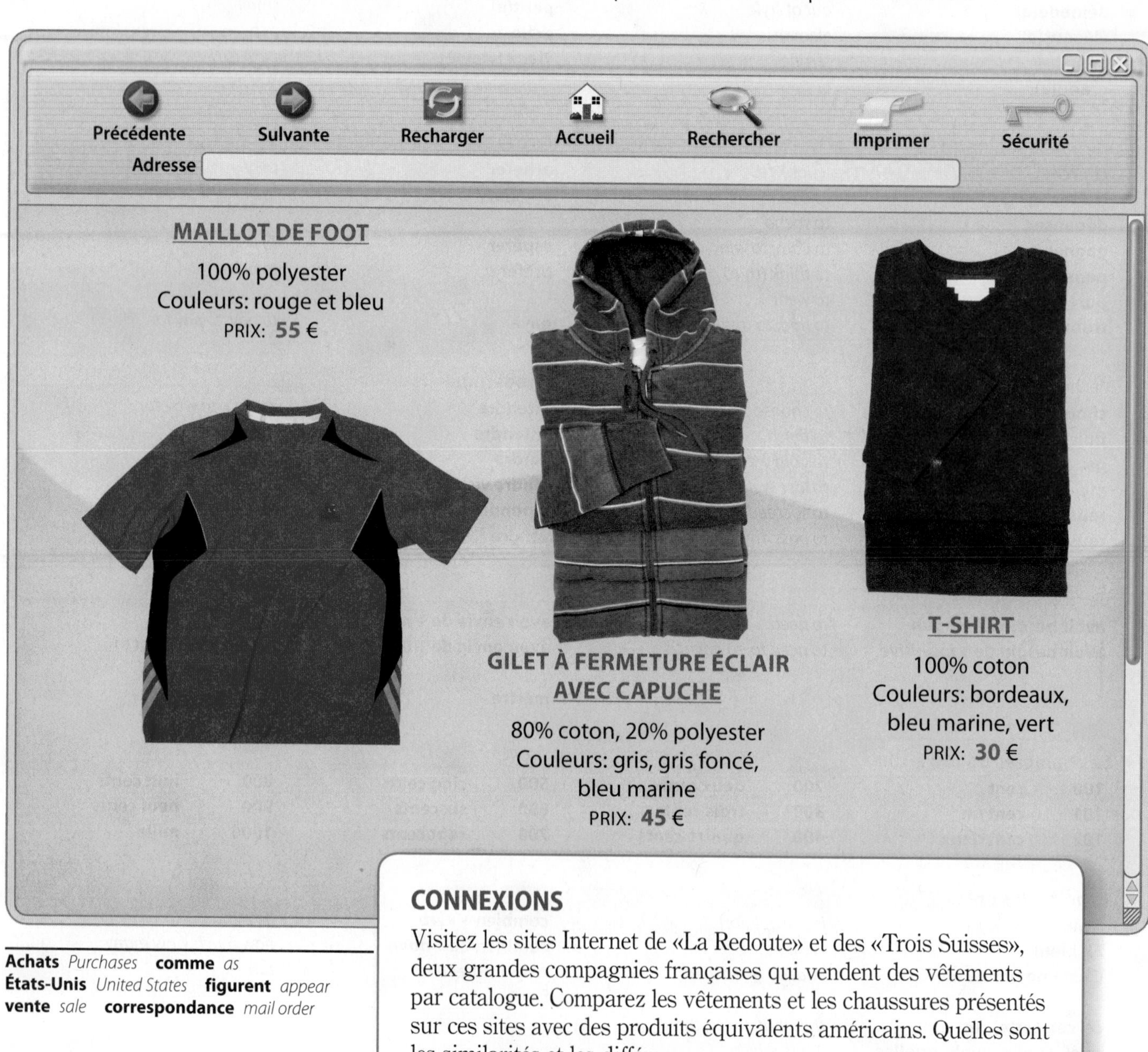

Achats *Purchases* **comme** *as*
États-Unis *United States* **figurent** *appear*
vente *sale* **correspondance** *mail order*

CONNEXIONS

Visitez les sites Internet de «La Redoute» et des «Trois Suisses», deux grandes compagnies françaises qui vendent des vêtements par catalogue. Comparez les vêtements et les chaussures présentés sur ces sites avec des produits équivalents américains. Quelles sont les similarités et les différences …

- en type de produits?
- en style?
- en prix?

Additional readings @ my.hrw.com
FRENCH InterActive Reader

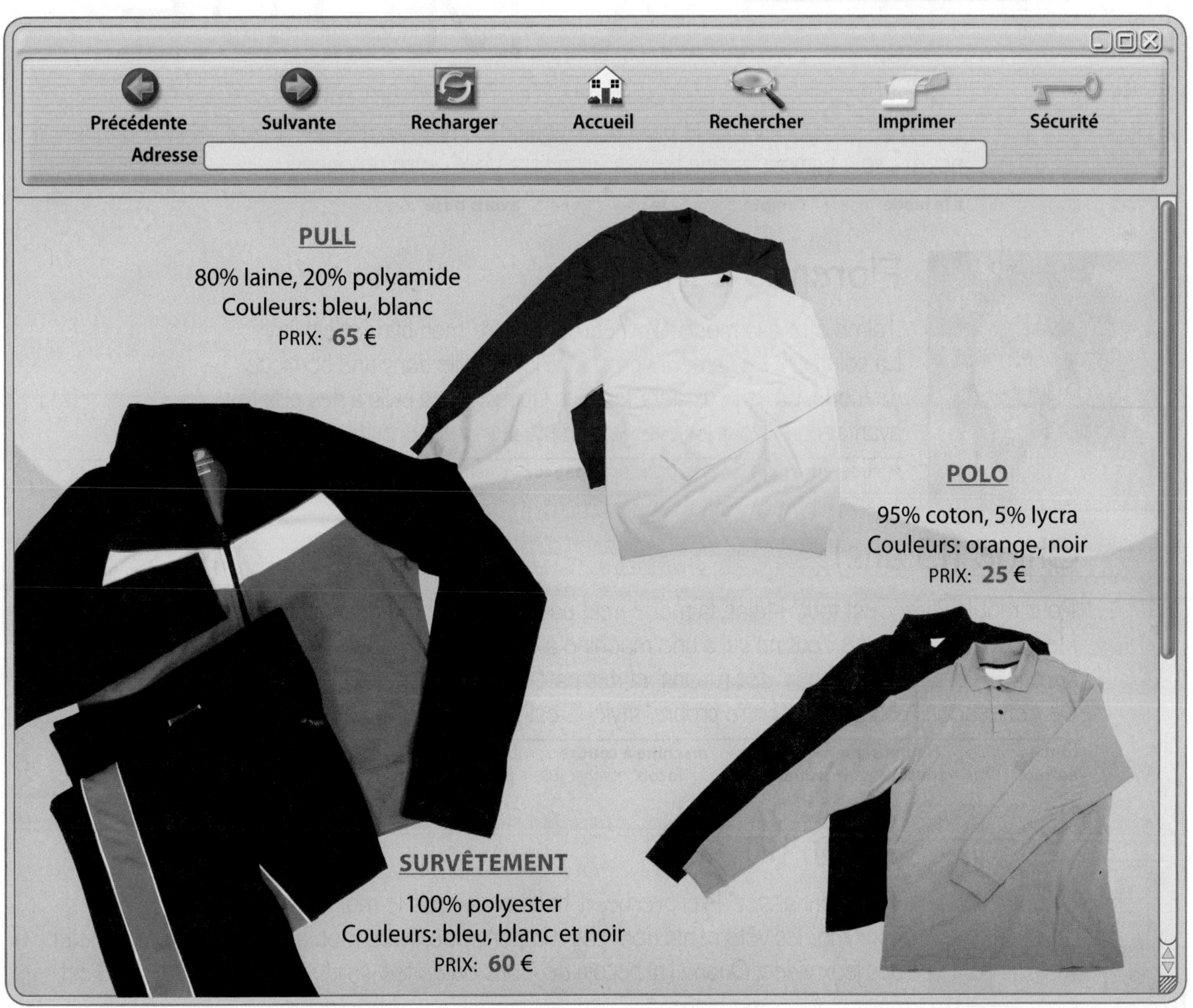

Et vous?

Vous êtes en France et vous voulez acheter deux vêtements différents comme cadeaux (*presents*) pour des amis aux États-Unis. Votre budget est limité à un total de 100 euros. Faites votre sélection.

	Pour qui?	Vêtement	Textile	Couleur	Prix
1.					
2.					

Prix total:

Les jeunes Français et LA MODE

Est-ce que vous aimez être à la mode?° Où est-ce que vous achetez vos vêtements? Et qu'est-ce qui compte° le plus° pour vous? le style? la qualité? le prix? Nous avons posé° ces questions à cinq jeunes Français. Voilà leurs réponses.

à la mode *in style* **compte** *counts* **le plus** *the most* **avons posé** *asked*

Florence (16 ans)

J'aime être à la mode. Malheureusement,° mon budget est limité. La solution? Le samedi après-midi je travaille dans une boutique de mode. Là, je peux acheter mes jupes et mes pulls à des prix très avantageux.° Pour le reste, je compte sur la générosité de mes parents.

Malheureusement *Unfortunately* **avantageux** *reasonable*

Chloé (15 ans)

Pour moi, le style, c'est tout.° Hélas, la mode n'est pas bon marché. Heureusement,° j'ai une cousine qui a une machine à coudre° et qui est très adroite.° Alors, nous cousons° des rubans° et des patchs sur nos vêtements. De cette façon,° nous créons notre propre° style. C'est génial, non?

tout *everything* **Heureusement** *Fortunately* **machine à coudre** *sewing machine*
adroite *skillful* **cousons** *sew* **rubans** *ribbons* **façon** *manner, way* **propre** *own*

Julien (14 ans)

Vous connaissez° le proverbe: «L'habit ne fait pas le moine*.» Eh bien, pour moi, les vêtements n'ont pas d'importance. Avec mon argent, je préfère acheter des jeux vidéo. Quand j'ai besoin de jeans ou de tee-shirts, je vais aux puces.° C'est pas cher et c'est marrant!

connaissez *know* **[marché] aux puces** *flea market* **marrant** *fun*

**Clothes don't make the man. (The habit doesn't make the monk.)*

Robert (15 ans)

Aujourd'hui la présentation extérieure est très importante. Mais il n'est pas nécessaire d'être à la mode pour être bien habillé.° Pour moi, la qualité des vêtements est aussi importante que leur style. En général, j'attends les soldes. J'achète peu de vêtements mais je fais attention à la qualité.

habillé *dressed*

Additional readings @ **my.hrw.com**
FRENCH InterActive Reader

Éric (12 ans)

Moi, je n'ai pas le choix!° C'est ma mère qui choisit mes vêtements. En ce qui concerne° la mode, elle n'est pas dans le coup.° Elle achète tout sur catalogue et elle choisit ce qui est le moins cher.° C'est pas drôle.

choix *choice* **En ce qui concerne** *As for* **dans le coup** *with it*
le moins cher *the cheapest (the least expensive)*

STRATEGY Reading

Understanding casual French speech

The interviews you read were conducted orally. Notice how casual French speech is different from standard written language.

- Spoken language often contains slang expressions.
  Elle n'est pas dans le coup! C'est marrant! C'est génial!
- Spoken French sometimes drops the **ne** in **ne … pas.**
  C'est pas cher. = Ce n'est pas cher.

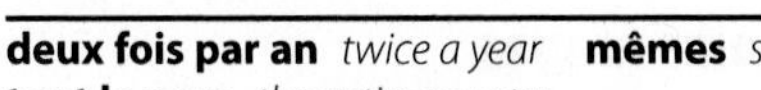

NOTE Culturelle

Les soldes

En France, les boutiques de vêtements ont des soldes deux fois par an.° Les dates de ces soldes sont déterminées par le gouvernement et sont les mêmes° dans tout le pays.° Au moment des soldes, on peut acheter des vêtements de bonne qualité à des prix avantageux.

deux fois par an *twice a year* **mêmes** *same*
tout le pays *the entire country*

Et vous?

Voici ce que disent les jeunes Français. Est-ce que c'est vrai pour vous aussi?

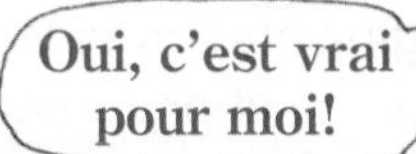

Oui, c'est vrai pour moi!

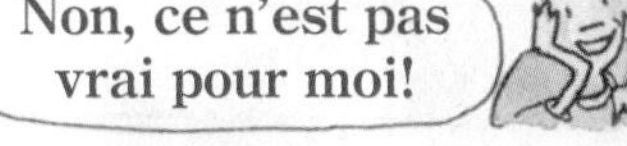

Non, ce n'est pas vrai pour moi!

OUI OU NON?

1. J'aime être à la mode.
2. Mon budget est limité.
3. J'attends les soldes.
4. Je fais attention à la qualité.
5. Je couds des patchs sur mes jeans.
6. Ma mère choisit mes vêtements.
7. Je préfère acheter des jeux vidéo.
8. J'achète mes vêtements aux puces.

Bonjour, Fatima!

Je m'appelle Fatima et j'ai quinze ans. J'habite dans la banlieue° de Paris. Mes parents sont généreux mais ils ne sont pas très riches. Alors, je n'ai pas beaucoup d'argent de poche: cinquante euros par mois. Ce n'est pas une fortune! Heureusement,° je fais du baby-sitting pour les voisins quand ils vont au cinéma le week-end. Je gagne cinq euros par heure.

J'adore les vêtements. Avec ma copine Djemila, on achète des magazines de mode et on va dans les magasins. Quand on entre dans une boutique, c'est généralement plus pour regarder que pour acheter. J'achète mes nouveaux pulls pendant la période des soldes. Par contre,° j'achète assez souvent des bracelets et des boucles d'oreille.° On trouve des choses géniales dans les petites boutiques de mon quartier. Quand je veux changer de «look», je change de boucles d'oreille et je change de vernis à ongles° et de rouge à lèvres.° C'est facile et ça ne coûte pas cher!

banlieue *suburbs* **Heureusement** *Fortunately* **Par contre** *On the other hand* **boucles d'oreille** *earrings*
vernis à ongles *nail polish* **rouge à lèvres** *lipstick*

NOTE Culturelle

Prénoms arabes

Fatima et **Djemila** sont des jeunes filles d'origine «maghrébine». Elles portent° des noms typiquement arabes.

Le Maghreb est une région géographique constituée par **le Maroc**,° **l'Algérie** et **la Tunisie**. Quatre millions de Français (sur une population totale de soixante millions) sont d'origine maghrébine. Beaucoup parlent arabe et pratiquent la religion musulmane.°

portent = ont **Maroc** *Morocco*
musulmane *Moslem*

Additional readings @ **my.hrw.com**
FRENCH InterActive Reader

Compréhension

1. Comment est-ce que Fatima gagne son argent?
2. Qu'est-ce qu'elle fait avec sa copine?
3. Qu'est-ce qu'elle achète avec son argent?
4. Qu'est-ce qu'elle fait pour changer de look?

Et vous?

Quelles ressemblances (*similarities*) et quelles différences est-ce que vous trouvez entre Fatima et vous? Faites une liste de ces ressemblances et de ces différences.

- âge
- parents
- argent de poche
- achats de vêtements
- achats d'accessoires
- comment changer de look

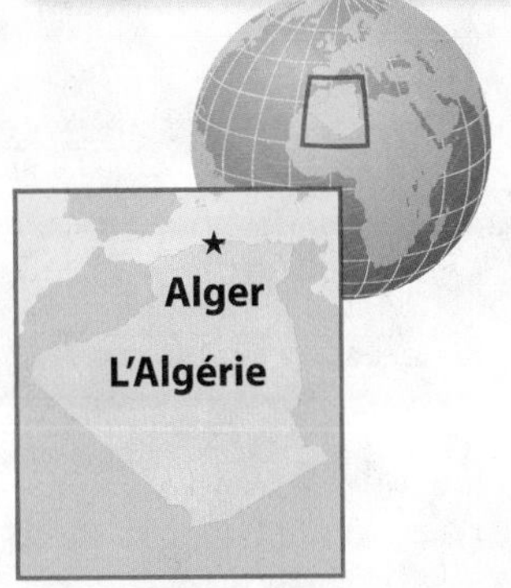

EN BREF:
L'ALGÉRIE

Population: 36 millions
Capitale: Alger
Langues: arabe, berbère, français

L'Algérie est un pays° d'Afrique du Nord. Colonie française pendant plus de 100 ans, l'Algérie est devenue indépendante en 1962. La majorité des Algériens sont arabes et pratiquent la religion musulmane. Des millions d'Algériens ont immigré en France et sont devenus Français. Pour cette raison,° la France est maintenant le pays avec la plus grande population musulmane d'Europe.

La présence algérienne influence la vie° ordinaire des Français. Par exemple, les Français mangent du couscous* qui est une spécialité d'Afrique du Nord, et beaucoup de jeunes écoutent le raï qui est une musique d'origine algérienne.

pays *country* **raison** *reason* **vie** *life*
* **Couscous** *is a type of semolina (white gritty wheat) which is usually cooked with meat and vegetables as a main dish, but which can also be steamed and served cold in salads.*

COMMUNAUTÉS

Explore Internet sources to find out more about the Muslim religion. Or perhaps there is a Muslim person in your school or in your community whom you could invite to talk to your class. Use the information you gather to make a bulletin board display explaining the basic tenets of the Muslim faith.

Unité 7

Le temps libre

THÈME ET OBJECTIFS

Leisure-time activities

We work hard during the week, but we also need time to relax.

In this unit, you will learn ...

- to discuss your weekend activities
- to talk about individual summer and winter sports
- to describe your vacation and travel plans

You will also be able ...

- to describe what you did and where you went yesterday, last week, or last summer
- more generally, to narrate what happened at any time in the past

Leçon 21

LE FRANÇAIS PRATIQUE

DVD AUDIO

Vocabulaire et Culture

Le week-end et les vacances

Accent sur ... les loisirs

When given the choice, French people would rather have more free time than more money. For them, leisure time is an essential component of what they call **la qualité de la vie** *(quality of life)*. By law, they work only thirty-five hours per week and they have a minimum of five weeks of vacation per year.

Like their parents, French teenagers value their leisure time and try to make the most of it. What are their favorite activities? Here is what they do when they have a free evening.

Qu'est-ce que tu aimes faire le soir?	GARÇONS	FILLES
Je regarde la télé.	24%	18%
Je sors° avec mes copains.	20%	18%
Je vais au cinéma.	16%	14%
Je lis.°	14%	20%
Je vais au concert ou au théâtre.	10%	12%
Je vais danser.	8%	12%
Je fais du sport.	6%	4%
Je bricole.°	2%	2%

sors *go out* **lis** *read* **bricole** *do things around the house*

Michèle est très sportive. Elle fait souvent du jogging dans le parc de la ville.

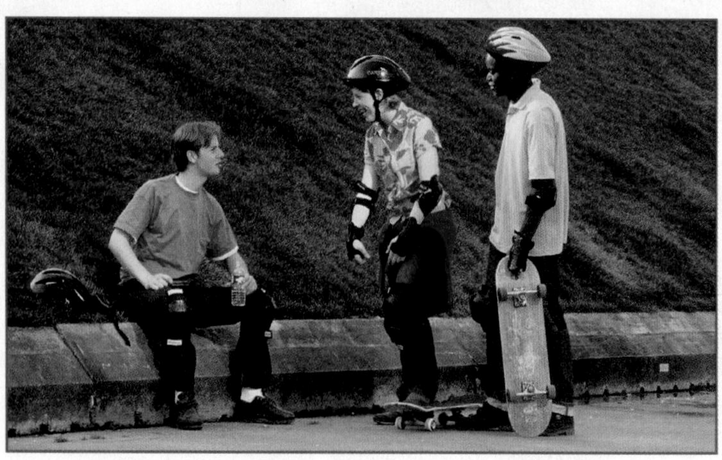

Thomas adore faire du skate. Le samedi, il va au skatepark avec ses copains.

@HOMETUTOR
my.hrw.com

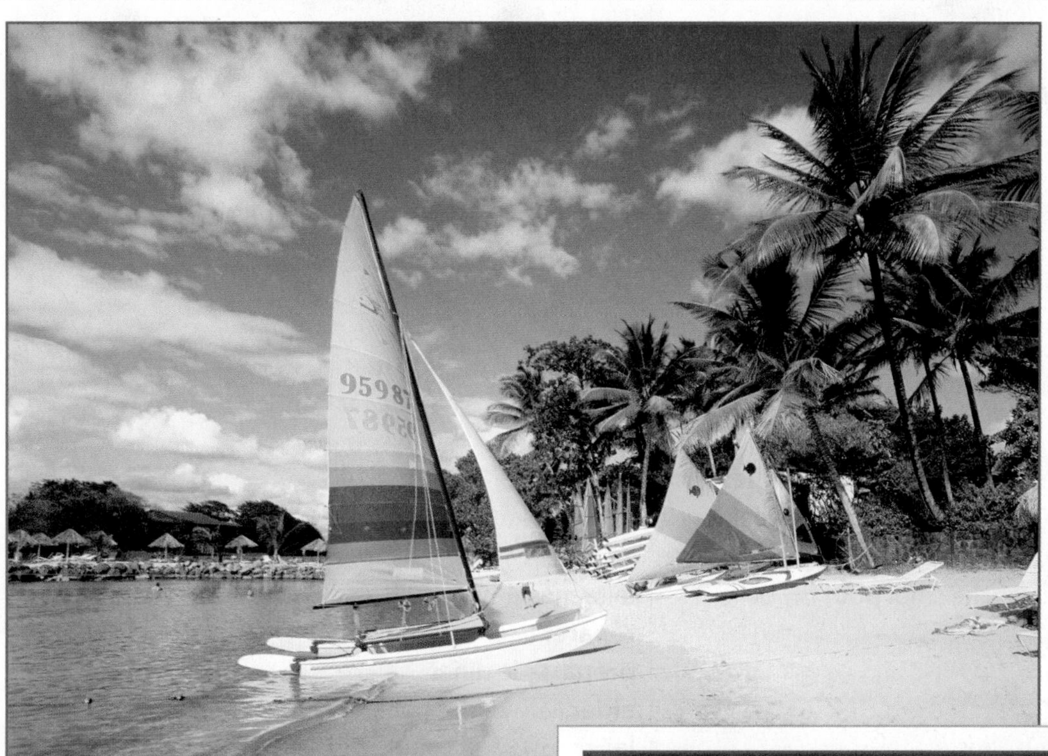

À la Martinique il fait beau tout le temps. À la plage, on fait du surf ou de la planche à voile.

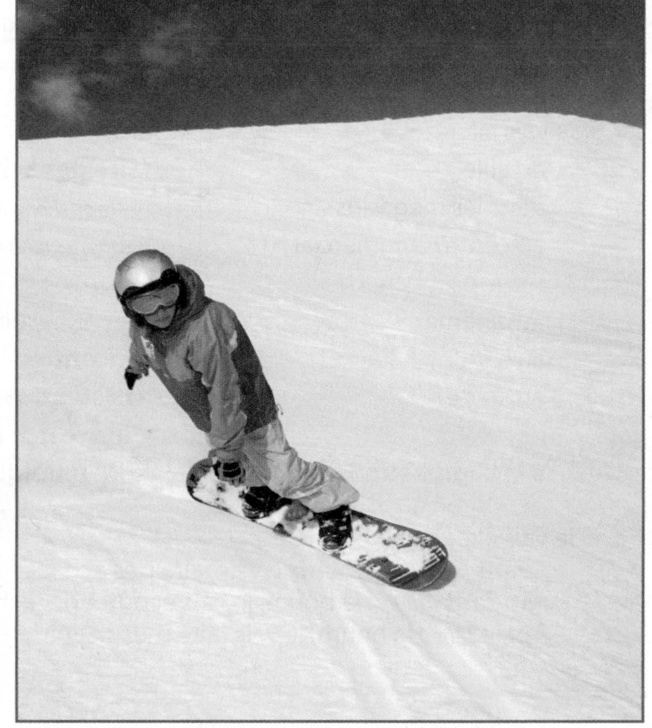

En hiver, beaucoup de jeunes Français vont à la montagne avec leur famille ou leur école. Le snowboard — ou le surf — est un sport très populaire.

A VOCABULAIRE Le week-end

▶ How to plan your weekend activities:

METROPOLITAIN
Qu'est-ce que tu vas faire samedi?
Je vais rester chez moi pour réparer mon vélo.

Qu'est-ce que tu vas faire | samedi?
samedi **matin**
dimanche **après-midi**
demain **soir**
ce **week-end**
le week-end **prochain** *(next)*

le matin *morning*
l'après-midi *(m.) afternoon*
le soir *evening*

Je vais rester chez moi **pour** *(in order to)* | faire mes **devoirs** *(homework).*
réparer *(to fix)* mon vélo
préparer le dîner
aider *(to help)* mes parents
laver *(to wash)* la voiture
nettoyer *(to clean)* le garage
ranger *(to pick up)* ma chambre

Je vais aller … | pour …
en ville
dans les magasins
au centre commercial | **faire des achats** *(to go shopping).*
louer *(to rent)* un film

au cinéma
au café
au stade | **voir** *(to see)* un film
rencontrer *(to meet)* des copains
assister à *(to go to, attend)* un match de foot

à la campagne *(countryside)* | **faire un pique-nique** *(to have a picnic)*

Moi, je vais aller en ville pour faire des achats.
PRINTEMPS

Je vais aller à une boum.
Avant *(Before)* la boum, je vais faire des achats.
Pendant *(During)* la boum, je vais écouter de la musique.
Après *(After)* la boum, je vais faire mes devoirs.

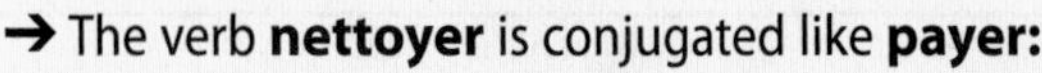

➔ The verb **nettoyer** is conjugated like **payer:**

je **nettoie** tu **nettoies** il/elle/on **nettoie** ils/elles **nettoient**
but: nous **nettoyons** vous **nettoyez**

@HOMETUTOR
my.hrw.com

1 Et toi?

PARLER/ÉCRIRE Décris tes activités. Pour cela, complète les phrases suivantes.

1. En général, je vais au cinéma …	• le vendredi soir • le samedi soir	• le dimanche après-midi • … ?
2. En général, je fais mes devoirs …	• avant le dîner • après le dîner	• pendant la classe • … ?
3. Je préfère assister à …	• un match de foot • un match de baseball	• un concert de rock • … ?
4. En général, quand je rentre chez moi après les classes, …	• je fais mes devoirs • je regarde la télé	• j'aide ma mère ou mon père • … ?
5. J'aime aller en ville pour …	• voir un film • rencontrer mes copains	• faire des achats • … ?
6. En général, je préfère faire mes achats …	• seul(e) *(by myself)* • avec mes copains	• avec mes frères et mes soeurs • … ?
7. En été, je préfère faire un pique-nique …	• dans mon jardin • à la campagne	• à la plage • … ?
8. Pour aider mes parents à la maison, je préfère …	• ranger le salon • laver la voiture	• nettoyer le garage • … ?

2 Qu'est-ce qu'ils font?

PARLER/ÉCRIRE Informez-vous sur les personnes suivantes. Décrivez ce qu'elles font ou ce qu'elles vont faire. Pour cela, complétez les phrases avec une expression du **Vocabulaire** à la page 310.

▶ Sandrine est au garage.
Elle répare son vélo (sa mobylette).

1. Mme Jolivet est dans la cuisine. Elle …
2. Vincent Jolivet est aussi dans la cuisine. Il …
3. Anne et Sylvie sont au Bon Marché. Elles …
4. Je suis dans ma chambre et je regarde mon livre de français. Je …
5. Olivier et ses copains achètent des billets *(tickets)* de cinéma. Ils vont …
6. Mes amis vont à Yankee Stadium. Ils vont …
7. Tu vas au café. Tu vas …
8. Vous faites des sandwichs. Vous allez … à la campagne.

3 Mon calendrier personnel

PARLER/ÉCRIRE Décrivez ce que vous allez faire.

MERCREDI

1. Après la classe, je vais …
2. Avant le dîner, …
3. Après le dîner, …
4. Demain soir, …
5. Vendredi soir, …
6. Samedi après-midi, …
7. Samedi soir, …
8. Dimanche après-midi, …
9. Pendant les vacances, …

B VOCABULAIRE Les vacances

Qu'est-ce que tu vas faire cet été?
Je vais aller à la mer.

▶ *How to plan your vacation activities:*

Qu'est-ce que tu vas faire | à **Noël?**
à **Pâques**
pendant *(during)* **les vacances** de printemps
pendant **les grandes vacances**
cet été

Noël *Christmas*
Pâques *Easter*
les vacances *vacation*
les grandes vacances *summer vacation*

Je vais aller | à **la mer** *(ocean, shore).*
à **la montagne** *(mountains)*

Je vais voyager | en avion. | **un avion** *plane*
en train | **un train** *train*
en autocar | **un autocar, un car** *touring bus*
en bateau | **un bateau** *boat, ship*
en voiture

Je vais voyager en avion.

Je vais voyager | **seul(e)** *(alone).*
avec ma famille

Je vais **passer** *(to spend)* | dix jours / six semaines / deux mois | là-bas.

un jour *day*
une semaine *week*
un mois *month*

J'aime | **le ski** *(skiing).*
le ski nautique *(water-skiing)*

En hiver, je vais à la montagne pour **faire du ski** *(to ski).*
En été, je vais à la mer pour **faire du ski nautique** *(to water-ski).*

J'aime le ski!

Mont Ste-Anne
Le ski à votre porte . . .

@HOMETUTOR
my.hrw.com

VOCABULAIRE Activités sportives

le sport	*sport(s)*	Je **fais du sport.**	*I practice sports.*
le jogging	*jogging*	Nous **faisons du jogging.**	*We jog.*
la natation	*swimming*	Tu **fais de la natation?**	*Do you go swimming?*
l'escalade *(f.)*	*rock climbing*	J'aime **faire de l'escalade.**	*I like to go rock climbing.*
le ski	*skiing*	Tu **fais du ski?**	*Do you ski?*
le ski nautique	*water-skiing*	Anne **fait du ski nautique.**	*Anne water-skis.*
la voile	*sailing*	Paul **fait de la voile.**	*Paul sails.*
la planche à voile	*windsurfing*	Vous **faites de la planche à voile?**	*Do you windsurf?*

le roller	*in-line skating*	**des rollers**	*in-line skates*
le skate	*skateboarding*	**un skate**	*skateboard*
le snowboard	*snowboarding*	**un snowboard**	*snowboard*
le VTT	*mountain biking*	**un VTT**	*mountain bike*

➔ To describe participation in individual sports or other activities, the French use the construction:

faire { **du** / **de la** / **de l'** } + *SPORT OR ACTIVITY*

le roller → **faire du roller**
la voile → **faire de la voile**
l'escalade → **faire de l'escalade**

NOTE Culturelle

Les sports d'hiver

À Noël et pendant les vacances de février, beaucoup de jeunes Français vont à la montagne avec leur famille pour faire des sports d'hiver. Certaines écoles organisent des «classes de neige». Les élèves étudient le matin et font du sport l'après-midi.

Le ski est un sport très populaire. Mais beaucoup de jeunes préfèrent faire du snowboard, une spécialité dans laquelle° plusieurs° Françaises ont été° championnes olympiques.

laquelle *which* **plusieurs** *several* **ont été** *have been*

4 Et toi?

PARLER/ÉCRIRE Indique tes préférences personnelles en complétant les phrases suivantes.

1. Mes vacances préférées sont …
   - les vacances de Noël
   - les vacances de printemps
   - les grandes vacances
   - … ?
2. Pendant les grandes vacances, je préfère …
   - aller à la mer
   - aller à la montagne
   - aller à la campagne
   - … ?
3. En été, je vais à la plage spécialement *(especially)* pour …
   - nager
   - faire du ski nautique
   - bronzer *(to get a tan)*
   - … ?
4. Je voudrais aller dans le Colorado pour …
   - faire du ski
   - faire de l'escalade
   - faire du VTT
   - … ?
5. Je voudrais aller à la Martinique principalement *(mainly)* pour …
   - parler français
   - faire de la planche à voile
   - faire de la plongée *(scuba diving)*
   - … ?

5 Leurs activités favorites

PARLER/ÉCRIRE Les personnes suivantes ont certaines activités favorites. Lisez où elles sont et dites ce qu'elles font. Pour cela choisissez une activité appropriée de la liste à droite.

▶ Anne est dans un studio de danse.
Elle fait de la danse moderne.

1. Jean-Pierre est au stade.
2. Je suis à la plage.
3. En juillet, nous allons dans le Colorado.
4. Tu passes les vacances de Noël en Suisse.
5. Mes copains passent les vacances à la campagne.
6. Pauline et Marie sont à la salle *(room)* de gymnastique.
7. Vous êtes à la mer.
8. Nous sommes à Tahiti.
9. Avant le dîner, nous allons au parc municipal.
10. Je suis à la Martinique.

la gymnastique
la danse moderne
le sport
le jogging
le camping
la voile
la planche à voile
le ski
le ski nautique
l'escalade

@HOMETUTOR
my.hrw.com

6. Mon sport préféré est …	• la natation • le snowboard	• le roller • … ?
7. Pour mon anniversaire, je préfère avoir …	• un skate • des rollers	• un VTT • … ?
8. Avec mes copains, je préfère …	• faire du roller • faire du skate	• faire du jogging • … ?
9. Quand je voyage pendant les vacances, je préfère voyager …	• seul(e) • avec mes copains	• avec ma famille • … ?
10. Je voudrais aller à Paris et rester là-bas pendant *(for)* …	• dix jours • trois semaines	• six mois • … ?

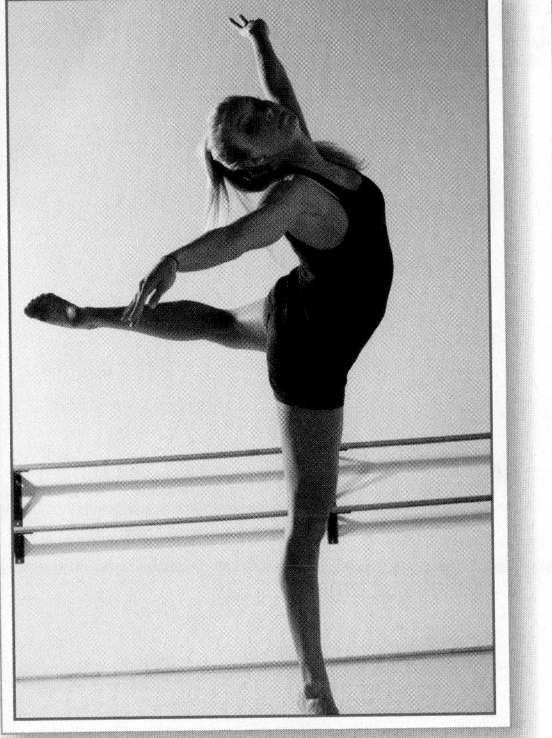

6 Questions personnelles PARLER/ÉCRIRE

1. En général, qu'est-ce que tu fais pendant les vacances de Noël?
2. Est-ce que tu vas voyager pendant les grandes vacances? Où vas-tu aller? Combien de temps *(How long)* est-ce que tu vas rester là-bas?
3. Qu'est-ce que tu aimes faire quand tu es à la plage?
4. Est-ce que tu voyages souvent? Comment voyages-tu?

COMMUNAUTÉS

During summer vacation, some American teenagers spend a month in a French-speaking region doing community service. At the same time they have the opportunity to meet other young people and to use their French skills.

You can go on the Internet to research some of the non-profit organizations that sponsor such exchanges. It is not too early to begin planning ahead.

À votre tour!

Digital performance space

OBJECTIFS

Now you can . . .
- discuss your weekend and vacation plans
- talk about individual sports

1 Écoutez bien!

ÉCOUTER On weekends, you can stay in and take care of things at home, or you can go out and have fun. Listen carefully to what the people are saying. If they refer to an indoor activity, mark A. If they refer to an outdoor activity, mark B.

	1	2	3	4	5	6
A: À l'intérieur						
B: À l'extérieur						

A. À l'intérieur

B. À l'extérieur

2 Composition: Le week-end prochain

ÉCRIRE Make plans for next weekend. Prepare a list of activities describing . . .

- four things that you are going to do at home
- four things that you are going to do outside

▶ **Samedi, je vais ranger ma chambre. Après, je . . .**

3 Composition: Mes sports préférés

ÉCRIRE Describe two sports that you engage in during each of the following times of year.

- Pendant les vacances d'été
- En hiver
- En toute *(any)* saison

4 Créa-dialogue 

PARLER Des amis parlent de leurs projets. Avec un(e) camarade de classe, choisissez une scène et composez le dialogue correspondant.

▶ —Où vas-tu vendredi?
—Je vais en ville.
—Qu'est-ce que tu vas faire là-bas?
—Je vais faire des achats.

▶		
vendredi	en ville	

1. samedi matin			2. samedi après-midi			3. à Noël	à Aspen	
4. pendant les vacances de printemps	en Floride		5. en juillet			6. en août		
7. demain matin	?		8. dimanche après-midi	?	?	9. cet été	?	?

5 Conversation dirigée  

PARLER Avec un(e) camarade, composez un dialogue basé sur les instructions suivantes. Thomas demande à Hélène si elle a des projets de vacances.

Thomas		Hélène
asks Hélène where she is going this summer	→ ←	says that she is going to the ocean with friends
asks her if they are going to travel by car	→ ←	answers that they are going to travel by train because they do not have a car
asks her if she is going to go sailing	→ ←	answers yes and says that she is also going to windsurf
says good-bye to Hélène and wishes her a good vacation **(Bonnes vacances!)**	→	answers good-bye

LESSON REVIEW
my.hrw.com

Vive le week-end!

AUDIO

Le week-end, nous avons nos occupations préférées. Certaines personnes aiment aller en ville et rencontrer leurs amis.

D'autres préfèrent rester à la maison et bricoler. Qu'est-ce que les personnes suivantes ont fait le week-end dernier?

Others / do things around the house
did … do
last

Le week-end

Le week-end dernier

J'aime acheter des vêtements.

J'ai acheté des vêtements.

bought

Tu aimes réparer ton vélo.

Tu as réparé ton vélo. *fixed*

M. Lambert aime travailler dans le jardin.

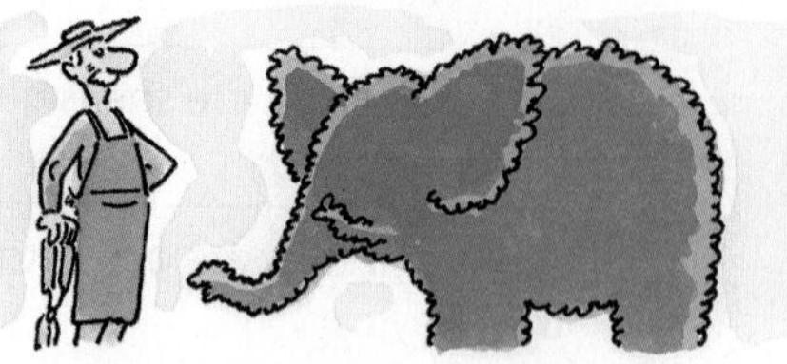

Il a travaillé dans le jardin. *worked*

Nous aimons organiser des boums.

Nous avons organisé une boum. *organized*

Le week-end

Vous aimez jouer au foot.

Pluton et Philibert aiment rencontrer leurs amis.

Le week-end dernier

Vous avez joué au foot. *played*

Ils ont rencontré leurs amis. *met*

Et toi?

Indique si oui ou non tu as fait les choses suivantes le week-end dernier. Pour cela complète les phrases suivantes.

1. (J'ai/Je n'ai pas) … acheté des vêtements.
2. (J'ai/Je n'ai pas) … réparé mon vélo.
3. (J'ai/Je n'ai pas) … travaillé dans le jardin.
4. (J'ai/Je n'ai pas) … organisé une boum.
5. (J'ai/Je n'ai pas) … joué au foot.
6. (J'ai/Je n'ai pas) … rencontré mes amis.

NOTE Culturelle

Le week-end

Le week-end ne commence pas° le vendredi soir pour tout le monde.° Dans beaucoup d'écoles françaises, les élèves ont classe le samedi matin. Pour eux, le week-end commence seulement° le samedi à midi.

Que font les jeunes Français le samedi? Ça dépend. Beaucoup° vont en ville. Ils vont dans des magasins pour regarder, essayer° et parfois° acheter des vêtements. Ils vont au café ou au cinéma avec leurs copains. Certains° préfèrent louer un film et rester chez eux ou aller chez des copains. Parfois ils vont à une soirée. Là on écoute de la musique, on mange des sandwichs et on danse …

En général, le dimanche est réservé aux activités familiales.° Un week-end, on invite des cousins. Un autre° week-end, on rend visite aux grands-parents … Le dimanche, on déjeune° et on dîne en famille.° Le soir, on regarde la télé et souvent on fait ses devoirs pour les classes du lundi matin.

ne commence pas *does not begin* **tout le monde** *everyone* **seulement** *only* **Beaucoup** *Many* **essayer** *try on* **parfois** *sometimes* **Certains** *Some of them* **activités familiales** *family activities* **Un autre** *Another* **déjeune** *has lunch* **en famille** *at home (with the family)*

A Les expressions avec *avoir*

Note the use of **avoir** in the following sentences:

J'ai faim.	***I am hungry.***
Brigitte **a soif.**	*Brigitte* ***is thirsty.***

French speakers use **avoir** in many expressions where English speakers use the verb *to be.*

VOCABULAIRE Expressions avec *avoir*

avoir chaud	*to be (feel) warm*	Quand **j'ai chaud** en été, je vais à la plage.
avoir froid	*to be (feel) cold*	Est-ce que tu **as froid?** Voici ton pull.
avoir faim	*to be hungry*	Tu **as faim?** Est-ce que tu veux une pizza?
avoir soif	*to be thirsty*	J'**ai soif.** Je voudrais une limonade.
avoir raison	*to be right*	Est-ce que les profs **ont** toujours **raison?**
avoir tort	*to be wrong*	Marc ne fait pas ses devoirs. Il **a tort!**
avoir de la chance	*to be lucky*	J'**ai de la chance.** J'ai des amis sympathiques.

1 Tort ou raison?

PARLER/ÉCRIRE Informez-vous sur les personnes suivantes et dites si, à votre avis, elles ont tort ou raison.

▶ Les élèves ne font pas leurs devoirs.
Ils ont tort!

▶ Tu écoutes le prof.
Tu as raison!

1. Catherine est généreuse avec ses copines.
2. Nous aidons nos parents.
3. Tu fais tes devoirs.
4. Vous êtes très impatients avec vos amis.
5. Mes copains étudient le français.
6. Jean-François dépense son argent inutilement *(uselessly)*.
7. M. Legros mange trop *(too much)*.
8. Alain et Nicolas sont impolis *(impolite)*.
9. Vous rangez votre chambre.
10. Léa est polie *(polite)* avec les voisins.

2 De bonnes questions

PARLER/ÉCRIRE Étudiez ce que font les personnes suivantes. Ensuite, posez une question logique sur chaque personne. Pour cela, utilisez l'une des expressions suivantes:

avoir faim — avoir soif — avoir chaud — avoir froid — avoir de la chance

▶ Philippe va au restaurant.
Est-ce que Philippe a faim?

1. Tu veux un soda.
2. Jean-Pierre mange une pizza.
3. Cécile porte un manteau.
4. Vous gagnez à la loterie.
5. Vous faites des sandwichs.
6. Tu mets ton blouson.
7. Mes copains vont aller à la piscine.
8. Ces élèves n'étudient pas beaucoup, mais ils réussissent toujours à leurs examens.
9. Tu as des grands-parents très généreux.

@HOMETUTOR
my.hrw.com

B Le passé composé des verbes en *-er*

The sentences below describe past events. In the French sentences, the verbs are in the PASSÉ COMPOSÉ. Note the forms of the passé composé and its English equivalents.

Hier j'**ai réparé** mon vélo.	*Yesterday I **fixed** my bicycle.*
Le week-end dernier, Marc **a organisé** une boum.	*Last weekend, Marc **organized** a party.*
Pendant les vacances, nous **avons visité** Paris.	*During vacation, we **visited** Paris.*

FORMS

The PASSÉ COMPOSÉ is composed of two words. For most verbs, it is formed as follows:

PRESENT of **avoir** + PAST PARTICIPLE

Note the forms of the passé composé for **visiter.**

PASSÉ COMPOSÉ		PRESENT OF AVOIR + PAST PARTICIPLE	
J'**ai visité**	Québec.	j' **ai**	**visité**
Tu **as visité**	Paris.	tu **as**	
Il/Elle/On **a visité**	Montréal.	il/elle/on **a**	
Nous **avons visité**	Genève.	nous **avons**	
Vous **avez visité**	Strasbourg.	vous **avez**	
Ils/Elles **ont visité**	Fort-de-France.	ils/elles **ont**	

→ For all **-er** verbs, the past participle is formed by replacing the **-er** of the infinitive by **-é**.

jouer	→	**joué**	Nous **avons joué** au tennis.
parler	→	**parlé**	Éric **a parlé** à Nathalie.
téléphoner	→	**téléphoné**	Vous **avez téléphoné** à Cécile.

LEARNING ABOUT LANGUAGE

The PASSÉ COMPOSÉ, as its name indicates, is a "past" tense "composed" of two parts. It is formed like the present perfect tense in English

AUXILIARY VERB +	PAST PARTICIPLE of the main verb
Nous **avons**	**travaillé.**
We have	*worked.*

USES

The passé composé is used to describe past actions and events. It has several English equivalents.

J'ai visité Montréal. { *I **visited** Montreal.* / *I **have visited** Montreal.* / *I **did visit** Montreal.* }

3 Achats

PARLER/ÉCRIRE Samedi dernier *(Last Saturday)*, les personnes suivantes ont fait des achats. Dites ce que chaque personne a acheté.

▶ Philippe (des CD)
Philippe a acheté des CD.

▶ Philippe
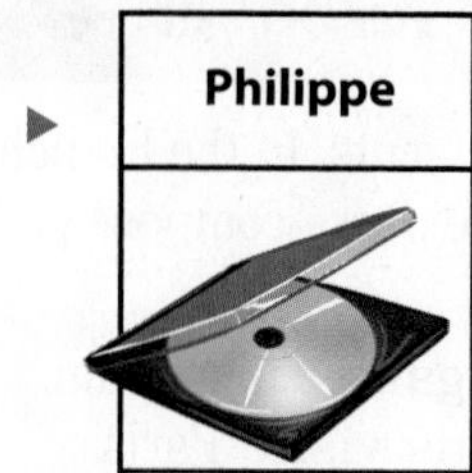

1. Pauline	2. moi
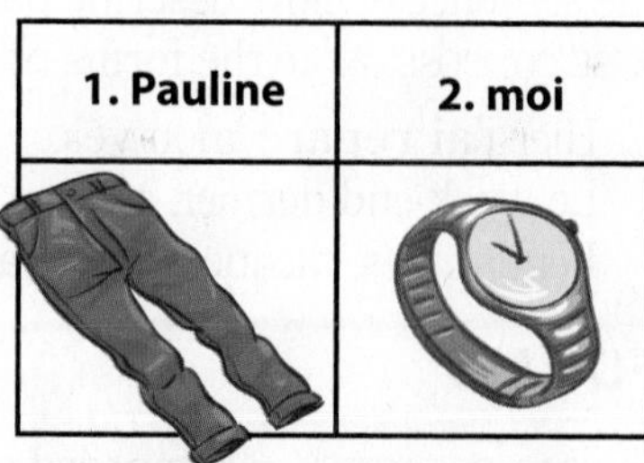	

3. toi	4. vous	5. nous	6. Stéphanie et Isabelle	7. Patrick et Jean-Paul	8. M. et Mme Dupont

4 Vive la différence! 

PARLER Caroline et Jean-Pierre sont des copains, mais ils aiment faire des choses différentes. Ils parlent de ce qu'ils ont fait ce week-end.

▶ jouer au volley (au tennis)

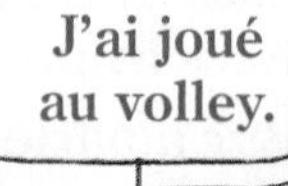

1. dîner au restaurant (chez moi)
2. inviter mon cousin (un ami)
3. téléphoner à ma tante (à mon grand-père)
4. aider ma mère (mon père)
5. nettoyer la cuisine (le garage)
6. réparer ma mobylette (mon vélo)
7. assister à un match de foot (à un concert)
8. laver mes tee-shirts (mes jeans)
9. regarder un film (une comédie)
10. ranger ma chambre (le salon)

5 La boum 

PARLER Anne et Éric organisent une boum ce week-end. Anne demande à Éric s'il a fait les choses suivantes. Il répond oui.

▶ acheter des sodas? **—Tu as acheté des sodas?**
—Mais oui, j'ai acheté des sodas.

1. préparer les sandwichs?
2. ranger le salon?
3. réparer la télé?
4. apporter un DVD?
5. inviter nos copains?
6. téléphoner aux voisins?

6 Un jeu

PARLER/ÉCRIRE Décrivez ce que certaines personnes ont fait samedi dernier. Pour cela, faites des phrases logiques en utilisant les éléments des Colonnes A, B et C.

▶ **Vous avez assisté à un concert de jazz.**

A	B	C
nous	acheter	une boum
vous	assister	un musée
Marc	dîner	des vêtements
Hélène et Juliette	jouer	un film
Éric et Stéphanie	organiser	aux jeux vidéo
mes copains	louer	dans le jardin
les voisins	travailler	dans un restaurant vietnamien
	visiter	à un concert de jazz

VOCABULAIRE Expressions pour la conversation

▶ ***How to indicate the order in which actions take place:***

d'abord	*first*	**D'abord**, nous avons invité nos copains à la boum.
après	*after, afterwards*	**Après**, tu as préparé des sandwichs.
ensuite	*then, after that*	**Ensuite**, Jacques a acheté des jus de fruit.
enfin	*at last*	**Enfin**, vous avez décoré le salon.
finalement	*finally*	**Finalement**, j'ai apporté ma radio.

7 Dans quel ordre?

PARLER/ÉCRIRE Décrivez ce que les personnes suivantes ont fait dans l'ordre logique.

▶ nous (manger / préparer la salade / acheter des pizzas)
D'abord, nous avons acheté des pizzas.
Après, nous avons préparé la salade.
Ensuite, nous avons mangé.

1. Alice (travailler / trouver un job / acheter une moto)
2. les touristes canadiens (voyager en avion / visiter Paris / réserver les billets [*tickets*])
3. tu (assister au concert / acheter un billet / acheter le programme)
4. vous (danser / apporter des CD / inviter des copains)
5. nous (payer l'addition [*check*] /dîner / trouver un restaurant)

C Le passé composé: forme négative

Compare the affirmative and negative forms of the passé composé in the sentences below.

AFFIRMATIVE	NEGATIVE	
Alice **a travaillé.**	Éric **n'a pas travaillé.**	*Éric **has not worked.*** *Éric **did not work.***
Nous **avons visité** Paris.	Nous **n'avons pas visité** Lyon.	*We **have not visited** Lyon.* *We **did not visit** Lyon.*

In the negative, the passé composé follows the pattern:

negative form of **avoir** + PAST PARTICIPLE

Note the negative forms of the passé composé of **travailler.**

PASSÉ COMPOSÉ (NEGATIVE)		PRESENT of avoir (NEGATIVE) + PAST PARTICIPLE		
Je **n'ai**	**pas travaillé.**	je **n'ai**	**pas**	
Tu **n'as**	**pas travaillé.**	tu **n'as**	**pas**	
Il/Elle/On **n'a**	**pas travaillé.**	il/elle/on **n'a**	**pas**	
				travaillé
Nous **n'avons**	**pas travaillé.**	nous **n'avons**	**pas**	
Vous **n'avez**	**pas travaillé.**	vous **n'avez**	**pas**	
Ils/Elles **n'ont**	**pas travaillé.**	ils/elles **n'ont**	**pas**	

8 Oublis *(Things forgotten)*

PARLER Nicole demande à Jean-Marc s'il a fait *(did)* les choses suivantes. Jean-Marc a oublié *(forgot)*.

▸ acheter *Paris-Match*?

1. apporter tes livres?
2. étudier?
3. téléphoner à ta tante?
4. inviter tes copains?
5. ranger ta chambre?
6. laver tes chemises?
7. louer un film?
8. aider ta mère?
9. nettoyer le garage?
10. chercher le programme de télé?
11. trouver ton livre?

@HOMETUTOR
my.hrw.com

9 Quel mauvais temps!

PARLER/ÉCRIRE Ce week-end, il a fait mauvais et les personnes suivantes sont restées *(stayed)* chez elles. Dites qu'elles n'ont pas fait les choses suivantes.

▶ nous/nager
Nous n'avons pas nagé.

1. vous/jouer au tennis
2. Philippe/rencontrer ses copains à la plage
3. Nathalie/dîner en ville
4. les voisins/travailler dans le jardin
5. Mlle Lacaze/laver sa voiture
6. mes copains/organiser un pique-nique
7. nous/assister au match de foot
8. toi/visiter le musée

10 Une question d'argent

PARLER/ÉCRIRE Les personnes suivantes n'ont pas beaucoup d'argent. Décrivez leur choix. Pour cela, dites ce qu'elles ont fait et ce qu'elles n'ont pas fait.

▶ nous/dîner au restaurant ou chez nous?
Nous avons dîné chez nous.
Nous n'avons pas dîné au restaurant.

1. Philippe/acheter un tee-shirt ou une chemise?
2. vous/manger un steak ou un sandwich?
3. nous/assister au concert ou au match de foot?
4. les touristes/voyager en car ou en avion?
5. mes voisins/louer une petite maison ou un grand appartement?
6. Marc/passer dix jours ou trois semaines à Paris?

11 Impossibilités

PARLER/ÉCRIRE Sans *(Without)* certaines choses il n'est pas possible de faire certaines activités. Expliquez cela logiquement en choisissant une personne de la Colonne A, un objet de la Colonne B et une activité de la Colonne C.

▶ **Je n'ai pas d'aspirateur. Je n'ai pas nettoyé le salon.**

A	B	C
je	une raquette	surfer sur l'Internet
vous	un billet *(ticket)*	voyager en Europe
nous	un passeport	nettoyer le salon
Frédéric	un ordinateur	regarder la comédie
Éric et Olivier	une télé	assister au concert
Claire et Caroline	un aspirateur *(vacuum cleaner)*	jouer au tennis

D Les questions au passé composé

Compare the statements and questions in the passé composé.

STATEMENT	QUESTION	
Tu as travaillé.	Tu as travaillé?	*Did you work?*
	Est-ce que tu as travaillé?	
Philippe a voyagé cet été.	**Quand est-ce que** Philippe a voyagé?	*When did Philippe travel?*
	Où est-ce qu'il a voyagé?	*Where did he travel?*

For most verbs, questions in the passé composé are formed as follows:

interrogative form of **avoir** + PAST PARTICIPLE

	YES/NO QUESTIONS	INFORMATION QUESTIONS
WITH INTONATION	Tu as voyagé?	—
	Paul a téléphoné?	—
WITH est-ce que	**Est-ce que** tu as voyagé?	**Avec qui est-ce que** tu as voyagé?
	Est-ce qu´Alice a téléphoné?	**À qui est-ce qu´**Alice a téléphoné?

→ When the subject is a pronoun, questions in the passé composé can also be formed by inversion.

As-tu assisté au match de foot? — *Did you go to the soccer game?*
Avec qui **avez-vous joué** au foot? — *With whom did you play soccer?* *Who(m) did you play soccer with?*

12 Expériences personnelles 

PARLER Demandez à vos camarades s'ils ont déjà *(already)* fait les choses suivantes.

▶ visiter Paris?

Est-ce que tu as visité Paris?
Oui, j'ai visité Paris.
(Non, je n'ai pas visité Paris.)

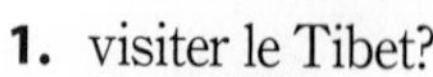

1. visiter le Tibet?
2. voyager en Alaska?
3. piloter un avion?
4. dîner dans un restaurant vietnamien?
5. manger des escargots *(snails)*?
6. gagner à la loterie?
7. assister à un match de catch *(wrestling)*?
8. rencontrer un fantôme *(ghost)*?

13 Curiosité 

PARLER Lisez ce que les personnes suivantes ont fait et posez des questions sur leurs activités.

▶ Paul a joué au tennis. (avec qui?)
Avec qui est-ce qu'il a joué au tennis?

1. Thomas a visité Québec. (quand?)
2. Corinne a téléphoné. (à quelle heure?)
3. Nathalie a voyagé en Italie. (comment?)
4. Marthe a acheté une robe. (où?)
5. Léa a rencontré sa copine. (où?)
6. Michèle a visité Genève. (avec qui?)
7. Philippe a trouvé un job. (où?)
8. Éric et Véronique ont dîné en ville. (dans quel restaurant?)
9. Les voisins ont téléphoné. (quand?)

14 Jérôme et Valérie 

PARLER Jérôme est très curieux. Il veut toujours savoir ce que Valérie a fait. Valérie répond à ses questions.

▶ où/dîner? (dans un restaurant italien)
JÉRÔME: **Où est-ce que tu as dîné?**
VALÉRIE: **J'ai dîné dans un restaurant italien.**

1. avec qui / jouer au tennis? (avec Marc)
2. quand / assister au concert? (samedi après-midi)
3. qui / inviter au café? (ma copine Nathalie)
4. où / rencontrer Pierre? (dans la rue)
5. où / acheter ta veste? (au Bon Marché)
6. combien / payer ce jeu vidéo? (10 euros)
7. à qui / téléphoner? (à ma grand-mère)
8. chez qui / passer le week-end? (chez une amie)

15 Conversation 

PARLER Demandez à vos camarades ce qu'ils ont fait hier.

▶ à quelle heure / dîner?

1. avec qui / dîner?
2. à qui / téléphoner?
3. quel programme / regarder à la télé?
4. quel programme / écouter à la radio?
5. qui / rencontrer après les classes?
6. quand / étudier?

Dis, Hélène, à quelle heure est-ce que tu as dîné?
J'ai dîné à six heures.

Prononciation 

ain = /ɛ̃/ aine = /ɛn/ in = /ɛ̃/ ine = /in/

Les lettres «ain» et «in»

sa main

semaine

magasin

magazine

When the letters "**ain**," "**aim**," "**in**," "**im**" are at the end of a word or are followed by a *consonant*, they represent the nasal vowel /ɛ̃/.

REMEMBER: Do not pronounce an /n/ after the nasal vowel /ɛ̃/.

Répétez: /ɛ̃/ **demain faim train main voisin cousin jardin magasin maintenant intelligent intéressant important**

When the letters "**ain**," "**aim**," "**in(n)**," "**im**" are followed by a *vowel*, they do NOT represent a nasal sound.

Répétez: /ɛn/ **semaine américaine**
/ɛm/ **j'aime**
/in/ **voisine cousine cuisine magazine cinéma Corinne finir**
/im/ **timide dimanche Mimi centime**
Alain Minime a un rendez-vous important demain matin, avenue du Maine.

À votre tour!

OBJECTIFS

Now you can . . .
- talk with friends about what you did and did not do last weekend
- talk about past events in general

1 Allô!

PARLER Reconstituez la conversation entre Alain et Christine. Pour cela, faites correspondre les réponses de Christine avec les questions d'Alain.

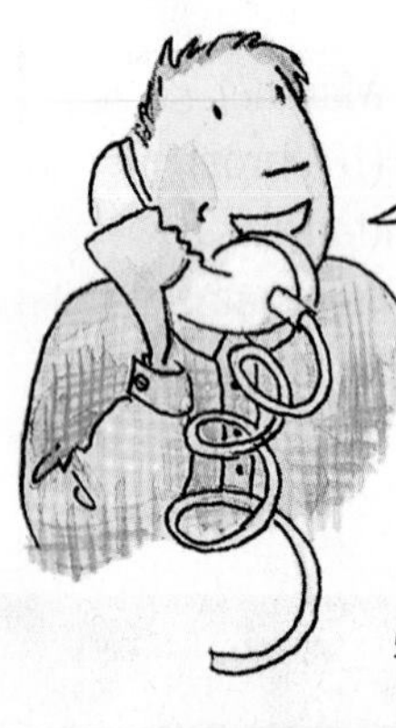

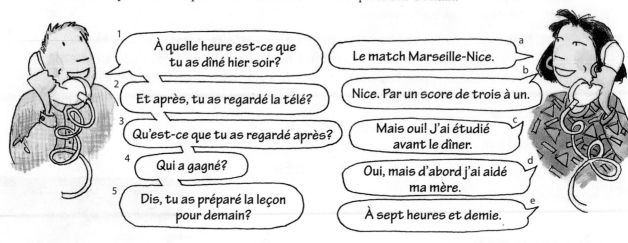

1. À quelle heure est-ce que tu as dîné hier soir?
2. Et après, tu as regardé la télé?
3. Qu'est-ce que tu as regardé après?
4. Qui a gagné?
5. Dis, tu as préparé la leçon pour demain?

a. Le match Marseille-Nice.
b. Nice. Par un score de trois à un.
c. Mais oui! J'ai étudié avant le dîner.
d. Oui, mais d'abord j'ai aidé ma mère.
e. À sept heures et demie.

2 Dis-moi . . .

PARLER *I will tell you a few things that I did yesterday after school and a few things that I did not do, then you will tell me what you did and did not do.*

- J'ai étudié.
- J'ai dîné avec mes parents.
- J'ai téléphoné à une copine.
- Je n'ai pas rangé ma chambre.
- Je n'ai pas rencontré mes copains.
- Je n'ai pas regardé la télé.

Et maintenant, dis-moi . . .

3 Créa-dialogue

PARLER Demandez à vos camarades s'ils ont fait les choses suivantes le week-end dernier. En cas de réponse affirmative, continuez la conversation.

▶ —Est-ce que tu as dîné au restaurant?
—Oui, j'ai dîné au restaurant.
—Avec qui?
—Avec mes cousins.
—Où est-ce que vous avez dîné?
—Nous avons dîné Chez Tante Lucie (à l'Hippopotamus, etc.).

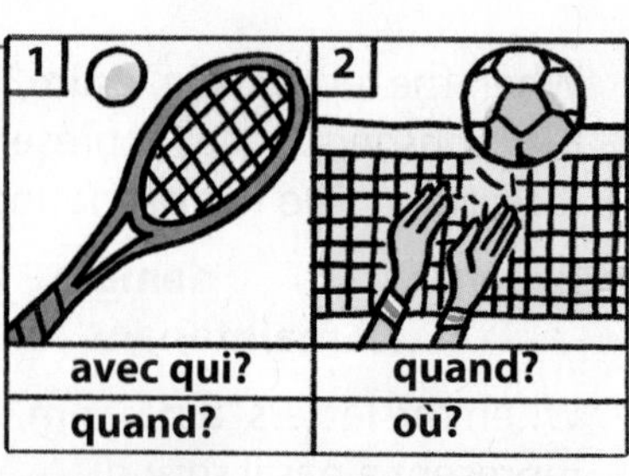

4 Composition: Hier soir *(Last night)* 

ÉCRIRE In one or two paragraphs describe what you did yesterday evening. You may wish to use the following suggestions:

- étudier (quoi?)
- dîner (à quelle heure?)
- manger (quoi?)
- téléphoner (à qui?)
- parler (de quoi?)
- écouter (quel type de musique?)
- regarder (quel programme à la télé?)
- aider (qui? comment?)
- ranger (quoi?)

STRATEGY Writing

Narrating the past When you write about past events, it is helpful to indicate the order in which these events occurred. In your composition, you can indicate the sequence in which you did certain things last night by using expressions such as **d'abord, après, ensuite, enfin,** and **finalement**.

Comment dit-on ...?

How to wish somebody a nice time:

Bon week-end! *(Have a nice weekend!)*

Bonnes vacances! *(Have a good vacation!)*

Bonne journée! *(Have a nice day!)*

Bon voyage! *(Have a good trip!)*

LESSON REVIEW
my.hrw.com

Leçon 23

Conversation et Culture

L'alibi

AUDIO

l'inspecteur Leflic

Êtes-vous bon (bonne) détective? Pouvez-vous trouver la solution du mystère suivant?

Samedi dernier à deux heures de l'après-midi, il y a eu une panne d'électricité dans la petite ville de Marcillac-le-Château. La panne a duré une heure. Pendant la panne, un cambrioleur a pénétré dans la Banque Populaire de Marcillac-le-Château. Bien sûr, l'alarme n'a pas fonctionné et c'est seulement lundi matin que le directeur de la banque a remarqué le cambriolage: un million d'euros.

Lundi après-midi, l'inspecteur Leflic a interrogé quatre suspects, mais chacun a un alibi.

Can / following / there was / power failure / lasted / burglar / entered / only / noticed / burglary / police detective / each one

Sophie Filou

Euh, … excusez-moi, Monsieur l'Inspecteur.
Ma mémoire n'est pas très bonne.
Voyons, qu'est-ce que j'ai fait samedi après-midi?
Ah oui, j'ai fini un livre.
Le titre du livre? *Le crime ne paie pas!*

Let's see / did I do / finished / title

Marc Laroulette

Qu'est-ce que j'ai fait samedi?
J'ai rendu visite à mes copains.
Nous avons joué aux cartes.
C'est moi qui ai gagné!

visited

Patrick Lescrot

Voyons, samedi dernier …
Ah oui … cet après-midi-là, j'ai invité des amis chez moi.
Nous avons regardé la télé.
Nous avons vu le match de foot France-Allemagne.
Quel match! Malheureusement, c'est la France qui a perdu!
Dommage!

saw / Germany / Unfortunately / lost

Pauline Malin

Ce n'est pas moi, Monsieur l'Inspecteur!
Samedi j'ai fait un pique-nique à la campagne avec une copine.
Nous avons choisi un coin près d'une rivière.
Ensuite, nous avons fait une promenade à vélo.
Nous avons eu de la chance!
Il a fait un temps extraordinaire!

chose / spot / were lucky / The weather was great!

Lisez attentivement les quatre déclarations. À votre avis, qui est le cambrioleur ou la cambrioleuse? Pourquoi? (Vous pouvez comparer votre réponse avec la réponse de l'inspecteur à la page 337.)

carefully

Compréhension

Certains événements ont eu lieu *(took place)* samedi dernier. Indiquez si oui ou non les événements suivants ont eu lieu.

1. Le directeur de la banque a vu *(saw)* le cambrioleur.
2. Un cambriolage a eu lieu *(took place)* à Marcillac-le-Château.
3. L'inspecteur Leflic a arrêté *(arrested)* quatre personnes.
4. Sophie Filou a vu le film *Le crime ne paie pas* à la télé.
5. Marc Laroulette a perdu un million d'euros.
6. L'Allemagne a gagné un match de foot.
7. Pauline Malin a fait une promenade à vélo à la campagne.
8. Il a fait beau.

Et toi?

Dis si oui ou non tu as fait les choses suivantes le week-end dernier.

1. (J'ai/Je n'ai pas) … rendu visite à mes copains.
2. (J'ai/Je n'ai pas) … vu un match de foot à la télé.
3. (J'ai/Je n'ai pas) … fini un livre.
4. (J'ai/Je n'ai pas) … fait une promenade à vélo.
5. (J'ai/Je n'ai pas) … fait un pique-nique.

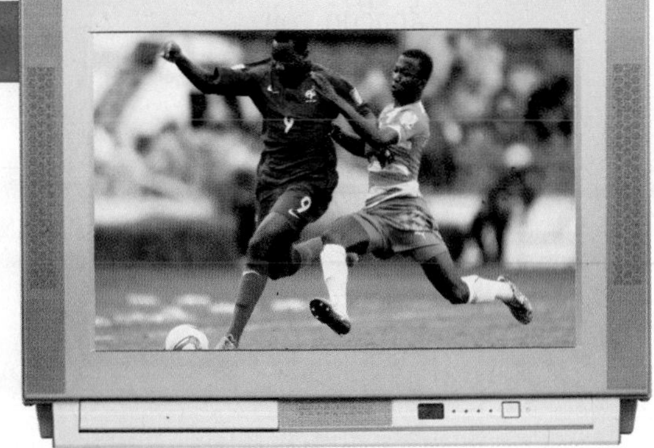

NOTE Culturelle

Les jeunes Français et la télé

Combien d'heures par° jour est-ce que tu regardes la télé? Une heure? deux heures? trois heures? plus? moins? En général, les jeunes Français regardent la télé moins souvent et moins longtemps° que les jeunes Américains: en moyenne° 1 heure 15 les jours d'école et 2 heures 15 les autres° jours (mercredi, samedi et dimanche). Dans beaucoup de familles, les parents contrôlent l'usage° de la télé. Souvent ils exigent° que leurs enfants finissent leurs devoirs avant de regarder la télé. Ainsi,° beaucoup de jeunes regardent la télé seulement° après le dîner.

Quels sont leurs programmes favoris? Les jeunes Français aiment surtout° les films, les programmes de sport, les variétés et les jeux télévisés,° comme «Qui veut gagner° des millions?». Les séries américaines sont aussi très populaires.

par *per* **moins longtemps** *for a shorter time* **en moyenne** *on an average of* **autres** *other* **usage** *use* **exigent** *insist* **Ainsi** *Thus* **seulement** *only* **surtout** *especially* **jeux télévisés** *game shows* **gagner** *to win*

A Le verbe *voir*

The verb **voir** *(to see)* is irregular. Note the forms of **voir** in the present tense.

INFINITIVE	voir	
PRESENT	Je **vois** Marc. Tu **vois** ton copain. Il/Elle/On **voit** un accident.	Nous **voyons** un film. Vous **voyez** un match de baseball. Ils/Elles **voient** le professeur.

1 Week-end à Paris

PARLER/ÉCRIRE Les personnes suivantes passent le week-end à Paris. Décrivez ce que chacun voit.

▶ Olivier **Olivier voit Notre-Dame.**

▶ Notre-Dame

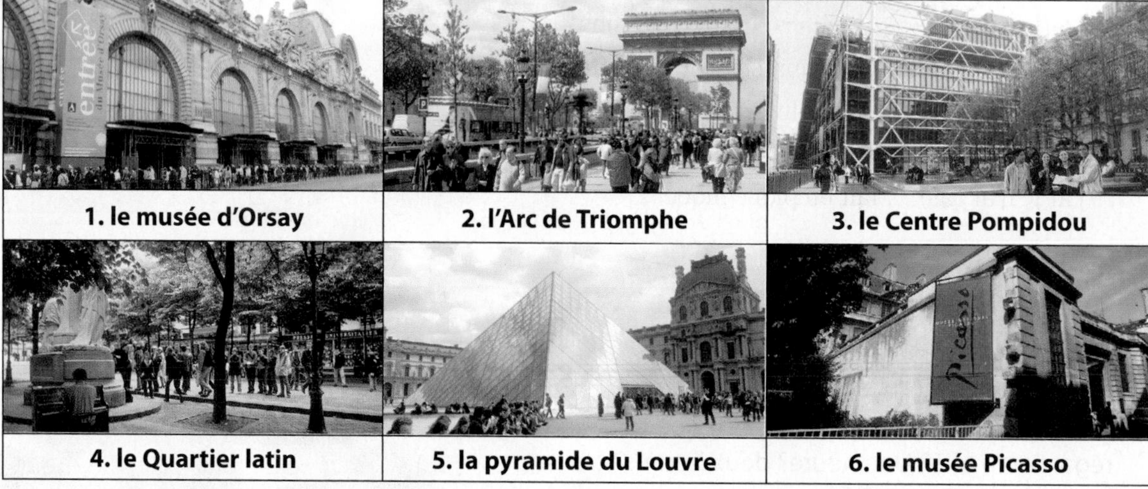

1. le musée d'Orsay
2. l'Arc de Triomphe
3. le Centre Pompidou
4. le Quartier latin
5. la pyramide du Louvre
6. le musée Picasso

1. nous
2. toi
3. moi
4. Sophie
5. vous
6. les touristes japonais

2 Questions personnelles PARLER/ÉCRIRE

1. Est-ce que tu vois bien? Est-ce que tu portes des lunettes?
2. Est-ce que tu vois tes amis pendant les vacances? Est-ce que tu vois tes professeurs?
3. Est-ce que tu vois souvent tes cousins? Est-ce que tu vois tes cousins pendant les vacances? à Noël?
4. Qu'est-ce que tu préfères voir à la télé? un match de football ou un match de baseball?
5. Quand tu vas au cinéma, quels films aimes-tu voir? les comédies? les films d'aventures? les films policiers *(detective movies)*?

@HOMETUTOR
my.hrw.com

B Le passé composé des verbes réguliers en *-ir* et *-re*

Note the passé composé of the verbs below, paying special attention to the ending of the past participle.

choisir	J'ai **choisi** cette casquette.	Je **n'ai pas choisi** cette chemise.
finir	Nous **avons fini** le magazine.	Nous **n'avons pas fini** le livre.
vendre	Tu **as vendu** ton vélo.	Tu **n'as pas vendu** ta moto.
attendre	Jacques **a attendu** Paul.	Il **n'a pas attendu** François.
répondre	J'**ai répondu** au professeur.	Tu **n'as pas répondu** à la question.

The past participle of regular **-ir** and **-re** verbs is formed as follows:

-ir → -i	-re → -u
chois**ir** → chois**i**	vend**re** → vend**u**
fin**ir** → fin**i**	attend**re** → attend**u**

3 Besoins d'argent *(Money needs)*

PARLER/ÉCRIRE Parce qu'elles ont besoin d'argent, les personnes suivantes ont vendu certains objets. Dites ce que chaque personne a vendu.

▶ Philippe/sa guitare — **Philippe a vendu sa guitare.**

1. M. Roche/sa voiture
2. mes copains/leur tablette
3. moi/mon appareil-photo
4. toi/ton skate
5. les voisins/leur piano
6. nous/nos livres
7. vous/votre ordinateur
8. François et Vincent/ leurs CD

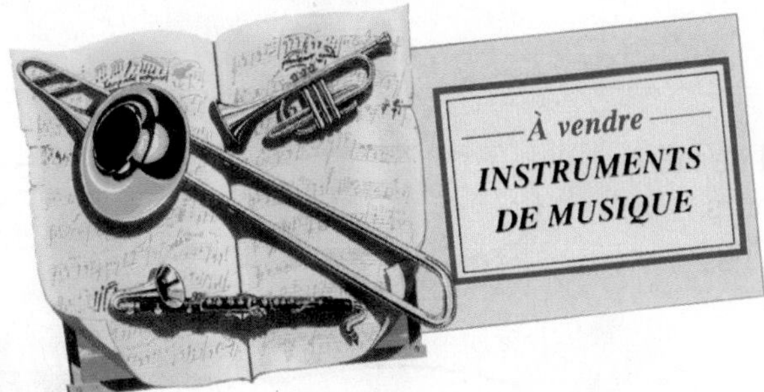

4 Bravo!

PARLER/ÉCRIRE Les personnes suivantes méritent *(deserve)* des félicitations *(congratulations)*. Expliquez pourquoi.

▶ les élèves/réussir à l'examen — **Les élèves ont réussi à l'examen.**

1. M. Bedon/maigrir
2. Mlle Legros/perdre dix kilos
3. Florence/gagner le match de tennis
4. les élèves/finir la leçon
5. moi/ranger ma chambre
6. nous/choisir une classe difficile
7. toi/finir les exercices
8. Marc/rendre visite à un copain à l'hôpital
9. vous/attendre vos copains
10. les élèves/répondre en français

5 Non!

PARLER Jean-Louis répond négativement aux questions de Béatrice. Jouez les deux rôles.

▶ gagner le match/perdre

1. étudier ce week-end/rendre visite à un copain
2. acheter un DVD/choisir un CD
3. finir ce livre/regarder la télé
4. vendre ta guitare/vendre mon appareil-photo
5. téléphoner à Marc/rendre visite à son cousin
6. maigrir/grossir
7. répondre à la lettre/téléphoner

6 Aujourd'hui et hier

PARLER/ÉCRIRE Dites ce que les personnes suivantes font aujourd'hui et ce qu'elles ont fait hier.

▶ Paul/acheter un blouson/un pantalon
Aujourd'hui, Paul achète un blouson.
Hier, il a acheté un pantalon.

1. moi/téléphoner à mon cousin/à mes copains
2. toi/finir ce livre/ce magazine
3. nous/manger des sandwichs/une pizza
4. Mélanie/choisir une jupe/un chemisier
5. les élèves/réussir à l'examen de français/ à l'examen d'anglais
6. Philippe/vendre sa radio/ses vieux CD
7. Philippe et Jean-Pierre/rendre visite à leurs cousins/à leur grand-mère
8. les touristes/attendre le train/le car

7 Excuses

PARLER Quand Michel ne fait pas une chose, il a toujours une excuse. Jouez le dialogue entre Michel et sa soeur Laure.

▶ étudier/perdre mon livre

1. travailler/jouer au foot
2. répondre/entendre la question
3. jouer au tennis/perdre ma raquette
4. acheter une veste/choisir un blouson
5. finir le livre/regarder la télé
6. rendre visite à Marc/étudier
7. réussir à l'examen/perdre mes notes
8. écouter de la musique/perdre mon MP3

@HOMETUTOR
my.hrw.com

C Le passé composé des verbes *être, avoir, faire, mettre* et *voir*

The verbs **être, avoir, faire, mettre,** and **voir** have irregular past participles.

être	→	**été**	Nous **avons été** à Paris.
avoir	→	**eu**	M. Lambert **a eu** un accident.
faire	→	**fait**	Qu'est-ce que tu **as fait** hier?
mettre	→	**mis**	Nous **avons mis** des jeans.
voir	→	**vu**	J'**ai vu** un bon film.

→ In the passé composé, the verb **être** has two different meanings:

Mme Lebrun **a été** malade. — *Mme Lebrun **has been** sick.*
Elle **a été** à l'hôpital. — *She **was** in the hospital.*

8 Dialogue 

PARLER Demandez à vos camarades s'ils ont fait les choses suivantes récemment *(recently)*.

▶ faire une promenade?
—Est-ce que tu as fait une promenade récemment?
—Oui, j'ai fait une promenade. (Non, je n'ai pas fait de promenade.)

1. faire un pique-nique?
2. faire une promenade en voiture?
3. être malade *(sick)*?
4. avoir la grippe *(flu)*?
5. avoir une dispute *(fight)* avec ton copain?
6. avoir une bonne surprise?
7. avoir un «A» en français?
8. voir un film?
9. voir tes cousins?
10. mettre des affiches dans ta chambre?

9 Pourquoi? 

PARLER Avec vos camarades de classe, parlez des personnes suivantes.

▶ Fabrice est content.
(avoir un «A» à l'examen)

Fabrice est content.
Ah bon? Pourquoi?
Il a eu un «A» à l'examen.

1. Mes copains sont furieux. (avoir un «F» à l'examen)
2. Pauline est très contente. (voir son copain)
3. Mon père n'est pas content. (avoir une dispute avec son chef [*boss*])
4. Philippe est pâle. (voir un accident)
5. Juliette est fatiguée *(tired)*. (faire du jogging)
6. Alice et Laure sont bronzées *(tanned)*. (être à la mer)
7. Mon frère est fatigué. (faire de la gymnastique [*to work out*])
8. Patrick et Marc sont contents. (voir un bon film)
9. Isabelle est très élégante. (mettre une jolie robe)

10 Vive les vacances!

PARLER/ÉCRIRE Dites où les personnes suivantes ont été pendant les vacances. Dites aussi si oui ou non elles ont fait les choses entre parenthèses. Soyez logique *(Be logical)*.

VIVE LES VACANCES
viva
RÉSEAU DE VILLAGES
VACANCES ANIMÉS

▶ Christophe: à la piscine (étudier/nager)
Christophe a été à la piscine. Il n'a pas étudié. Il a nagé.

1. Élodie: à la montagne (nager/faire du VTT)
2. nous: à la campagne (visiter des monuments/faire du camping)
3. vous: à Paris (parler italien/voir la tour Eiffel)
4. moi: à la mer (faire de la planche à voile/travailler)
5. mes parents: en Égypte (voir les pyramides/visiter Paris)
6. vous: dans un club de sport (faire de la gymnastique/grossir)
7. Christine: à la plage (mettre des lunettes de soleil/jouer au tennis)

VOCABULAIRE *Quand?*

	maintenant	avant	après
le jour	**aujourd'hui**	**hier**	**demain**
le matin	**ce matin**	**hier matin**	**demain matin**
l'après-midi	**cet après-midi**	**hier après-midi**	**demain après-midi**
le soir	**ce soir**	**hier soir**	**demain soir**
le jour	**samedi**	**samedi dernier** *(last)*	**samedi prochain** *(next)*
le week-end	**ce week-end**	**le week-end dernier**	**le week-end prochain**
la semaine	**cette semaine**	**la semaine dernière**	**la semaine prochaine**
le mois	**ce mois-ci**	**le mois dernier**	**le mois prochain**

11 Quand? 

PARLER Demandez à vos camarades quand ils ont fait les choses suivantes. Ils vont répondre en utilisant une expression du **Vocabulaire**.

Quand est-ce que tu as fait tes devoirs?
J'ai fait mes devoirs hier après-midi.
(vendredi soir, le week-end dernier, ...)

▶ faire tes devoirs?

1. faire des achats?
2. ranger ta chambre?
3. rencontrer tes voisins?
4. voir ton copain?
5. voir un film?
6. avoir un examen?
7. faire une promenade à pied?
8. être en ville?
9. mettre *(set)* la table?

@HOMETUTOR
my.hrw.com

12 Le passé et le futur

PARLER/ÉCRIRE Décrivez ce que vous avez fait (phrases 1 à 5) et ce que vous allez faire (phrases 6 à 10). Dites la vérité … ou utilisez votre imagination!

1. Ce matin, j'ai … _____
2. Hier matin, j'ai … _____
3. Samedi après-midi, j'ai … _____
4. La semaine dernière, j'ai … _____
5. Le mois dernier, j'ai … _____
6. Ce soir, je vais … _____
7. Demain soir, je vais … _____
8. Vendredi soir, je vais … _____
9. Le week-end prochain, je vais … _____
10. La semaine prochaine, je vais … _____

13 Questions personnelles PARLER/ÉCRIRE

1. En général, est-ce que tu étudies avant ou après le dîner?
2. En général, est-ce que tu regardes la télé avant ou après le dîner?
3. À quelle heure est-ce que tu as dîné hier soir?
4. Quel programme de télé est-ce que tu as regardé hier après-midi?
5. Qu'est-ce que tu vas faire le week-end prochain?
6. Où vas-tu aller le week-end prochain?

Prononciation  gn = /ɲ/

Les lettres «gn»

The letters **"gn"** represent a sound similar to the **"ny"** in *canyon*. First, practice with words you know.

Répétez: **espagnol gagner mignon**
la montagne la campagne

espagnol

Now try saying some new words. Make them sound French!

Répétez: **Champagne Espagne** *(Spain)* **un signe**
la vigne *(vineyard)* **la ligne** *(line)* **un signal**
la dignité ignorer magnétique magnifique Agnès

Agnès Mignard a gagné son match. C'est magnifique!

(L'alibi, p. 330)

La Réponse de L'Inspecteur:

C'est Patrick Lescrot le cambrioleur. Samedi après-midi, il y a eu une panne d'électricité. Patrick Lescrot n'a pas pu *(was not able to)* regarder la télé. Son alibi n'est pas valable *(valid)*.

À votre tour!

OBJECTIFS

Now you can . . .
- talk about what you did last week
- find out what others did recently

1 Allô!

PARLER Reconstituez la conversation entre Robert et Julien. Pour cela, faites correspondre les réponses de Julien avec les questions de Robert.

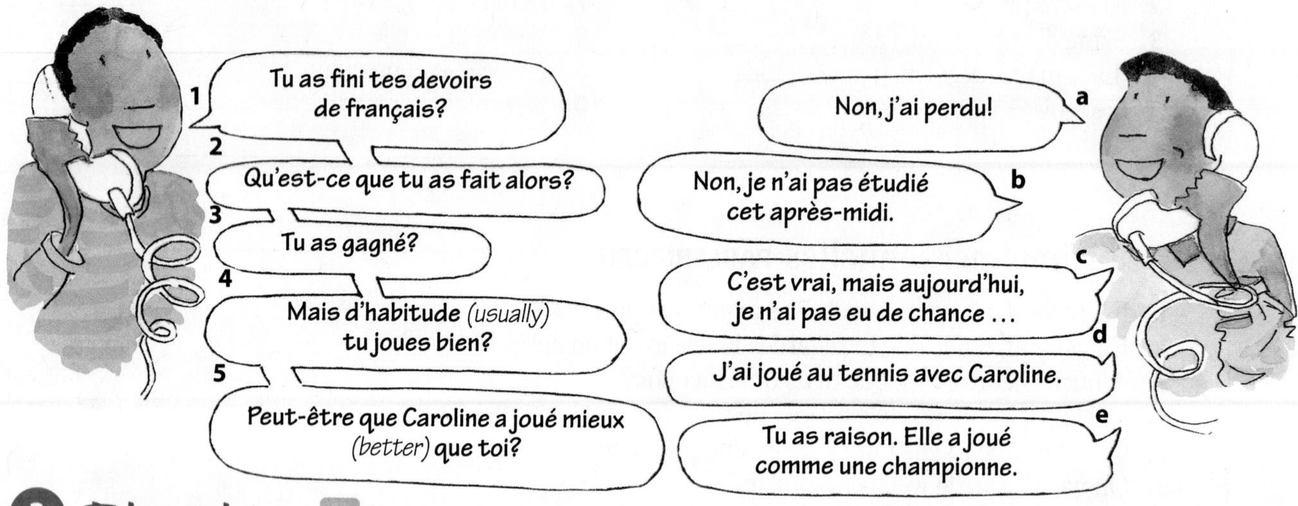

1 Tu as fini tes devoirs de français?
2 Qu'est-ce que tu as fait alors?
3 Tu as gagné?
4 Mais d'habitude (usually) tu joues bien?
5 Peut-être que Caroline a joué mieux (better) que toi?
a Non, j'ai perdu!
b Non, je n'ai pas étudié cet après-midi.
c C'est vrai, mais aujourd'hui, je n'ai pas eu de chance . . .
d J'ai joué au tennis avec Caroline.
e Tu as raison. Elle a joué comme une championne.

2 Dis-moi . . .

PARLER *I will tell you about some nice things that happened to me recently; then you will tell me about three nice things that happened to you.*

- J'ai réussi à mon examen d'anglais. (J'ai eu un «A».)
- J'ai eu un rendez-vous avec une personne très intéressante.
- J'ai vu un très bon film.

Et maintenant, dis-moi . . .

3 Créa-dialogue

PARLER Avec vos camarades, discutez de ce que vous avez fait récemment *(recently)*. Vous pouvez utiliser les expressions et les activités suggérées. Continuez la conversation avec des questions supplémentaires.

Quand?

dimanche après-midi	lundi dernier
hier soir	la semaine dernière
samedi soir	le mois dernier
le week-end dernier	

Quoi?

jouer aux jeux vidéo	dîner au restaurant
faire des achats	voir un film
faire du skate	avoir un rendez-vous
voir mes cousins	rendre visite à un copain
	faire du roller

▶ —Qu'est-ce que tu as fait dimanche après-midi?
—J'ai joué au tennis avec ma soeur.
—Est-ce que tu as gagné?
—Non, j'ai perdu.
—Dommage!

4 Le week-end dernier 

ÉCRIRE Write a short composition in which you describe what you did last weekend. You may adopt some of the following suggestions. Do not use **aller.**

- voir (qui? où? quand?)
- voir (quel film? où?)
- faire (de quel sport? de quelle activité? avec qui?)
- jouer (à quel jeu? à quel sport?)
- jouer (de quel instrument? où?)
- avoir un rendez-vous (avec qui?)
- faire une promenade (où? avec qui?)
- dîner (où? avec qui?)
- être (à quel endroit? avec qui? quand?)
- faire des achats (où? quand?)
- acheter (quoi? pourquoi?)
- regarder (quel programme de télé? quel DVD?)
- assister (à quel match? à quel concert?)

▶ **Vendredi soir, j'ai vu le film *Casablanca* au Palace avec mon copain . . .**

Comment dit-on ...?

How to wish someone good luck or give encouragement:

Bonne chance!

Bon courage!

Leçon 24

Conversation et Culture

Qui a de la chance?

AUDIO

VENDREDI APRÈS-MIDI

Anne et Valérie parlent de leurs projets pour le week-end.

Anne: Qu'est-ce que tu vas faire samedi soir?

Valérie: Je vais aller au cinéma avec Jean-Pierre.

Anne: Tu as de la chance! Moi, je dois rester à la maison.

Valérie: Mais pourquoi?

Anne: Les amis de mes parents viennent chez nous ce week-end. Mon père insiste pour que je reste pour le dîner. Quelle barbe! *that / What a pain!*

Valérie: C'est vrai! Tu n'as pas de chance!

LUNDI MATIN

Anne et Valérie parlent de leur week-end.

Anne: Alors, tu as passé un bon week-end?

Valérie: Euh non, pas très bon.

Anne: Mais tu es sortie avec Jean-Pierre! *went out*

Valérie: C'est vrai. Je suis allée au cinéma avec lui ... *went*
Nous avons vu un très, très mauvais film!
Après le film, j'ai eu une dispute avec *quarrel*
Jean-Pierre. Et, en plus, j'ai perdu *in addition*
mon porte-monnaie ... et je suis rentrée *wallet / went back*
chez moi à pied! Et toi, tu es restée chez toi? *stayed*

Anne: Non.

Valérie: Comment? Les amis de tes parents ne sont pas venus? *didn't come*

Anne: Si, si, ils sont venus ... avec leur fils!

Valérie: Et alors?

Anne: Eh bien, c'est un garçon très sympa et très amusant ... *sympa = sympathique*
Après le dîner, nous sommes allés au *went*
Zénith.* Nous avons assisté à un concert de rock absolument extraordinaire. Après, nous sommes allés dans un café et nous avons fait des projets pour le week-end prochain.

Valérie: Qu'est-ce que vous allez faire?

Anne: Nous allons faire une promenade à la campagne dans la nouvelle voiture de sport de Thomas. (C'est le nom de mon nouveau copain!)

Valérie: Toi, vraiment, tu as de la chance!

*Une salle (*hall*) de concert à Paris, parc de la Villette.

Compréhension

1. Qu'est-ce que Valérie va faire samedi soir?
2. Pourquoi est-ce qu'Anne doit (*must*) rester à la maison?
3. Est-ce que Valérie a aimé le film?
4. Qu'est-ce qu'elle a perdu?
5. Comment est-ce qu'elle est rentrée chez elle?
6. Où et avec qui est-ce qu'Anne a dîné?
7. Où est-ce qu'elle est allée après le dîner?
8. Qu'est-ce qu'elle va faire le week-end prochain?
9. Comment s'appelle son nouveau copain?

Et toi?

Dis si oui ou non tu as fait les choses suivantes samedi dernier.

1. (Je suis/Je ne suis pas) … allé(e) en ville.
2. (Je suis/Je ne suis pas) … allé(e) au cinéma.
3. (Je suis/Je ne suis pas) … allé(e) à un concert.
4. (Je suis/Je ne suis pas) … rentré(e) chez moi pour le dîner.
5. (Je suis/Je ne suis pas) … resté(e) chez moi le soir.

NOTE Culturelle

Les jeunes Français et la musique

«Pour moi, la musique c'est tout!»° déclare Anne, une jeune Française de quinze ans. Sa copine Hélène est d'accord: «Aujourd'hui, on ne peut pas° vivre° sans° musique.»

Comme les jeunes Américains, les jeunes Français sont des «fanas»° de la musique. Ils aiment particulièrement le rock, le rap français ou américain, la techno, le pop, le reggae et le ska, mais certains préfèrent la musique classique. Le week-end, ils vont au concert écouter les stars de la chanson° française, anglaise ou américaine.

Le 21 juin de chaque année, les jeunes célèbrent la «Fête de la Musique» avec tous° les Français. C'est une grande fête nationale avec des concerts publics gratuits° dans toutes les villes et tous les villages de France. Ce jour-là, 800 000 musiciens jouent pour 60 millions de spectateurs. Pour la «Fête de la Musique» tout le monde° fait de la musique.

tout *everything* **ne peut pas** *cannot* **vivre** *live* **sans** *without* **fanas = fanatiques** **chanson** *song* **tous** *all* **gratuits** *free* **tout le monde** *everyone*

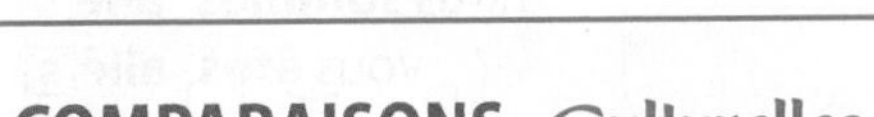

COMPARAISONS Culturelles

- Do you think American teenagers would agree with Anne: **"On ne peut pas vivre sans musique?"** Explain.
- Do French and American teenagers listen to the same types of music?
- Do you think that the United States should declare a national music day like the French **"Fête de la Musique"**? Why or why not?

A Le passé composé avec *être*

Note the forms of the passé composé of **aller** in the sentences below, paying attention to the endings of the past participle **(allé).**

Jean-Paul **est allé** au cinéma.	*Jean-Paul **went** to the movies.*
Mélanie **est allée** à la plage.	*Mélanie **went** to the beach.*
Éric et Patrick **sont allés** en ville.	*Éric and Patrick **went** downtown.*
Mes copines **sont allées** à la campagne.	*My friends **went** to the country.*

The passé composé of **aller** and certain verbs of motion is formed with **être** according to the pattern:

PRESENT of **être** + PAST PARTICIPLE

→ When the passé composé of a verb is conjugated with **être** (and not with **avoir**), the PAST PARTICIPLE *agrees* with the SUBJECT in gender and number.

INFINITIVE	aller	
PASSÉ COMPOSÉ	je **suis** **allé** tu **es** **allé** il **est** **allé**	je **suis** **allée** tu **es** **allée** elle **est** **allée**
	nous **sommes** **allés** vous **êtes** **allés** ils **sont** **allés**	nous **sommes** **allées** vous **êtes** **allées** elles **sont** **allées**
NEGATIVE	je **ne suis pas** **allé**	je **ne suis pas** **allée**
INTERROGATIVE	est-ce que tu **es** **allé?** tu **es** **allé?** (**es**-tu **allé?**)	est-ce que tu **es** **allée?** tu **es** **allée?** (**es**-tu **allée?**)

→ When **vous** refers to a single person, the past participle is in the singular:

Mme Mercier, est-ce que vous êtes **allée** au concert hier soir?

@HOMETUTOR
my.hrw.com

1 À Paris

PARLER/ÉCRIRE Des amis sont allés à Paris samedi dernier. Chacun est allé à un endroit différent. Dites qui est allé aux endroits suivants. Complétez chaque phrase avec le sujet approprié et la forme correspondante du verbe **être.**

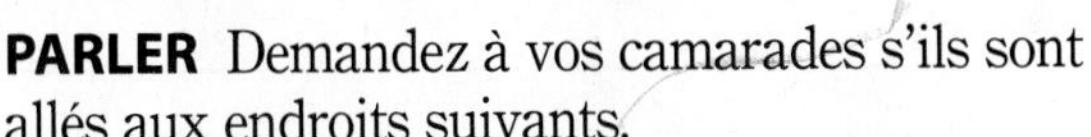

▸ **Anne et Monique sont allées au Louvre.**

1. … allée à la tour Eiffel.
2. … allé au Centre Pompidou.
3. … allés au Stade de France.
4. … allées aux Galeries Lafayette.
5. … allé à la Villette.
6. … allés au Zénith.
7. … allé au musée d'Orsay.
8. … allées au Quartier latin.

2 Conversation

PARLER Demandez à vos camarades s'ils sont allés aux endroits suivants.

▸ ce matin/à la bibliothèque?

1. hier matin/à l'école?
2. hier soir/au cinéma?
3. dimanche dernier/au restaurant?
4. samedi dernier/dans les magasins?
5. l'été dernier/chez tes cousins?
6. le week-end dernier/à la campagne?
7. le mois dernier/à un concert?
8. la semaine dernière/chez le coiffeur *(barber, hairdresser)*?
9. les vacances dernières/à la mer?

Ce matin, est-ce que tu es allé à la bibliothèque?
Oui, je suis allé à la bibliothèque.
(Non, je ne suis pas allé à la bibliothèque.)

3 Le week-end dernier

PARLER/ÉCRIRE Dites ce que les personnes de la Colonne A ont fait en choisissant une activité de la Colonne B. Puis dites où ces personnes sont allées en choisissant un endroit de la Colonne C. Soyez logiques!

A	B	C
je	voir des clowns	à la campagne
tu	nager	au zoo
nous	dîner en ville	dans un magasin de chaussures
Catherine	regarder les éléphants	à la bibliothèque
vous	choisir des livres	à la plage
mon petit frère	faire un pique-nique	au restaurant
André et Thomas	acheter des sandales	au cirque *(circus)*
les filles	faire du roller	dans la rue

▸ **J'ai nagé. Je suis allé(e) à la plage.**

4 Week-end 

PARLER Des amis parlent de leur week-end. Jouez ces dialogues.

▶ en ville / acheter des vêtements

Où est-ce que tu es allée?
Je suis allée en ville.
Ah bon! Qu'est-ce que tu as fait?
J'ai acheté des vêtements.

1. au stade / regarder un match de foot
2. à la plage / jouer au volley
3. à une boum / danser
4. à la campagne / faire une promenade à pied
5. au Bon Marché / acheter un blouson
6. dans un restaurant italien / manger des spaghetti

VOCABULAIRE Quelques verbes conjugués avec *être* au passé composé

INFINITIVE	PAST PARTICIPLE		
aller	**allé**	*to go*	Nous **sommes allés** en ville.
arriver	**arrivé**	*to arrive*	Vous **êtes arrivés** à midi.
rentrer	**rentré**	*to return, go back, come back*	Nous **sommes rentrés** à la maison à onze heures.
rester	**resté**	*to stay*	Les touristes **sont restés** à l'hôtel Ibis.
venir	**venu**	*to come*	Qui **est venu** hier?

5 Qui est resté à la maison?

PARLER/ÉCRIRE Samedi après-midi, les personnes suivantes ont fait certaines choses. Dites si oui ou non elles sont restées à la maison.

▶ Paul a regardé la télé. **Il est resté à la maison.**
▶ Mélanie a fait des achats. **Elle n'est pas restée à la maison.**

1. Mlle Joly a lavé sa voiture.
2. Nous avons fait une promenade à vélo.
3. Tu as nettoyé le garage.
4. Éric et Olivier ont joué aux jeux vidéo.
5. Christine et Isabelle ont travaillé dans le jardin.
6. Vous avez fait du roller.
7. Mes cousins ont fait de la voile.
8. J'ai fait du jogging.

@HOMETUTOR
my.hrw.com

6 La journée de Sandrine

PARLER/ÉCRIRE Pendant les vacances, Sandrine travaille dans une agence de tourisme. Le soir, elle raconte (*tells about*) sa journée à son père.

▶ aller au bureau *(office)*

1. arriver à neuf heures
2. téléphoner à un client anglais
3. parler avec des touristes japonais
4. aller au restaurant à midi et demi
5. rentrer au bureau à deux heures
6. copier des documents
7. préparer des billets *(tickets)* d'avion
8. rester jusqu'à *(until)* six heures
9. dîner en ville
10. rentrer à la maison à neuf heures

7 Une question de circonstances *(A matter of circumstances)*

PARLER/ÉCRIRE Nos activités dépendent souvent des circonstances. Dites si oui ou non les personnes suivantes ont fait les choses indiquées.

▶ On est mardi aujourd'hui.
- les élèves/rester à la maison?

Les élèves ne sont pas restés à la maison.

1. On est dimanche.
   - M. Boulot/travailler?
   - nous/aller à l'école?
   - vous/dîner à la cantine *(school cafeteria)*?
2. Il fait très beau aujourd'hui.
   - moi/aller à la campagne?
   - mes copines/regarder la télé?
   - toi/venir à la piscine avec nous?
3. Il fait très mauvais!
   - Marc/faire un pique-nique?
   - Hélène et Juliette/rester à la maison?
   - ma mère/rentrer à la maison à pied?
4. Mes copains et moi, nous n'avons pas beaucoup d'argent.
   - toi/aller dans un restaurant cher?
   - mes copains/venir chez moi en taxi?
   - moi/acheter des vêtements?

B La construction négative *ne ... jamais*

Compare the following negative constructions.

Éric **ne** parle **pas** à Paul.	*Éric does* **not** *speak to Paul.*
Éric **ne** parle **jamais** à Paul.	*Éric* **never** *speaks to Paul.*
Nous **n'**étudions **pas** le dimanche.	*We do* **not** *study on Sundays.*
Nous **n'**étudions **jamais** le dimanche.	*We* **never** *study on Sundays.*

To say that one NEVER does something, French speakers use the construction **ne ... jamais,** as follows:

SUBJECT	+	**ne**	+	VERB	+	**jamais ...**
NOUS		**ne**		regardons		**jamais** la télé.

→ **Ne** becomes **n'** before a vowel sound.

Nous **n'**allons **jamais** à l'opéra.

→ Note the use of **ne ... jamais** in the passé composé:

Nous **n'**avons **jamais** visité Québec.	*We* ***never*** *visited Quebec.*
Je **ne** suis **jamais** allé à Genève.	*I* ***never*** *went to Geneva.*

8 Jamais le dimanche

PARLER/ÉCRIRE Le dimanche les personnes suivantes ne font jamais ce qu'elles font pendant la semaine. Exprimez cette situation.

▶ François va à l'école.
Le dimanche, il ne va jamais à l'école.

1. Anne étudie.
2. Marc travaille.
3. Nous parlons français.
4. Vous allez à la bibliothèque.
5. M. Bernard va en ville.
6. Les élèves mangent à la cantine.
7. Tu rends visite à tes copains.
8. Vous dînez chez vous.
9. Je range ma chambre.
10. Je lave la voiture.

9 Et toi?

PARLER/ÉCRIRE Dites si vous avez jamais *(ever)* fait les choses suivantes.

▶ aller en France
Oui, je suis allé(e) en France.
Non, je ne suis jamais allé(e) en France.

1. aller en Chine?
2. visiter Paris?
3. voyager en limousine?
4. voir un opéra?
5. voir un fantôme *(ghost)*?
6. téléphoner au Président?
7. surfer sur l'Internet en français?
8. dîner dans un restaurant vietnamien?
9. jouer aux échecs?
10. faire une promenade en scooter?

@HOMETUTOR
my.hrw.com

C Les expressions *quelqu'un, quelque chose* et leurs contraires

Compare the affirmative and negative constructions in heavy print.

—Tu attends **quelqu'un?** — *Are you waiting for* ***someone (anyone)?***
—Non, je **n'**attends **personne.** — *No, I'm* ***not*** *waiting for* ***anyone.***

—Vous faites **quelque chose** ce soir? — *Are you doing* ***something (anything)*** *tonight?*
—Non, nous **ne** faisons **rien.** — *No, we're* ***not*** *doing* ***anything.***
No, we're doing ***nothing.***

To refer to unspecified people or things, French speakers use the following expressions:

quelqu'un	someone, anyone somebody, anybody	**ne ... personne**	no one, not anyone nobody, not anybody
quelque chose	something, anything	**ne ... rien**	nothing, not anything

→ Like all negative expressions, **personne** and **rien** require **ne** before the verb.
→ In short answers, **personne** and **rien** may be used alone.

Qui est là? **Personne.**
Qu'est-ce que tu fais? **Rien.**

10 Florence est malade

PARLER Florence est malade *(sick)* aujourd'hui. Elle répond négativement aux questions de Paul.

▶ dîner avec quelqu'un?

Tu dînes avec quelqu'un?
Non, je ne dîne avec personne.

1. inviter quelqu'un?
2. faire quelque chose ce soir?
3. manger quelque chose à midi?
4. regarder quelque chose à la télé?
5. attendre quelqu'un ce matin?
6. voir quelqu'un cet après-midi?
7. préparer quelque chose pour le dîner?
8. rencontrer quelqu'un après le dîner?

Prononciation

qu = /k/

Les lettres «qu»

The letters "**qu**" represent the sound /k/.

Répétez: **qui quand quelque chose quelqu'un quatre**
quatorze Québec Monique Véronique sympathique
un pique-nique le ski nautique
Véronique pense que Monique aime la musique classique.

un bouquet

OBJECTIFS

Now you can ...
- say where you went and when you came back
- talk about things you have never done

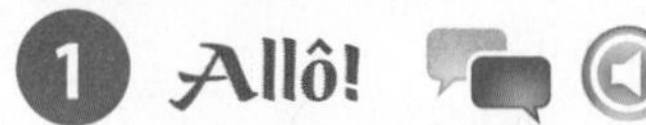

PARLER Reconstituez la conversation entre Sophie et Charlotte. Pour cela, faites correspondre les réponses de Charlotte avec les questions de Sophie.

5 À quelle heure es-tu rentrée chez toi?
a Oui, des sandwichs.
b À onze heures et demie.
c Un vieux western avec Gary Cooper.
d Nous sommes allées dans un café sur le boulevard Saint Michel.

PARLER *I will tell you about some places I have never visited. Then you will tell me about a few places where you have been.*

- Je ne suis jamais allée à la Martinique.
- Je n'ai jamais vu la Statue de la Liberté.
- Je n'ai jamais été à New York.
- Je n'ai jamais visité San Francisco.

Et maintenant, dis-moi ...

3 Créa-dialogue

PARLER Avec vos copains, discutez de ce que vous avez fait récemment *(recently)*. Utilisez les suggestions suivantes.

▸ —Tu es resté(e) chez toi hier matin?
—Oui, je suis resté(e) chez moi.
—Qu'est-ce que tu as fait?
—J'ai rangé ma chambre.

▸ —Tu es resté(e) chez toi hier matin?
—Non, je ne suis pas resté(e) chez moi.
—Qu'est-ce que tu as fait?
—Je suis allé(e) à l'école.

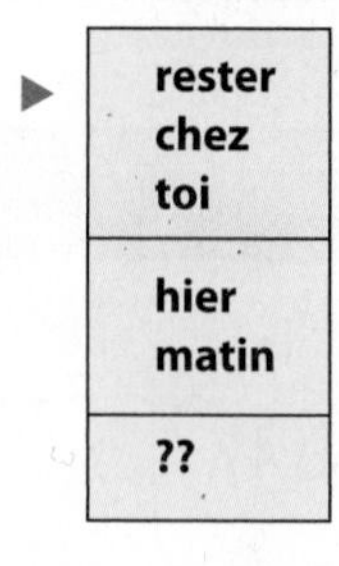

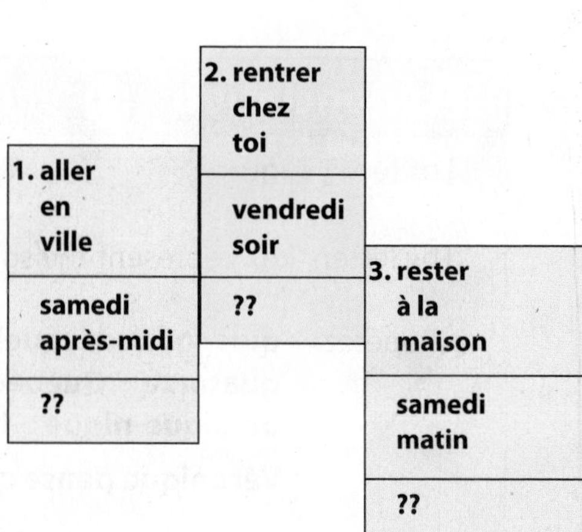

1. aller en ville
samedi après-midi
??
2. rentrer chez toi
vendredi soir
??
3. rester à la maison
samedi matin
??

4 Composition: Samedi dernier 

ÉCRIRE Read what Céline did last Saturday. Then write a short composition in the **passé composé** telling how a friend of yours (real or imaginary) spent the day. Use only familiar vocabulary.

Le matin, Céline est restée à la maison. Elle a rangé sa chambre et après elle a fini ses devoirs.

L'après-midi, elle est allée au cinéma avec son copain Trinh. Ils ont vu une comédie. Ensuite ils sont allés dans un magasin de vêtements. Céline a acheté un tee-shirt et Trinh a acheté une nouvelle casquette. Finalement, Céline est rentrée chez elle.

Le soir, elle a dîné avec ses parents. Après, elle est restée dans sa chambre. Elle a surfé sur l'Internet et elle a téléchargé de la musique reggae. Elle adore la musique reggae!

▶ Samedi dernier
Le matin, mon ami Kevin n'est pas resté à la maison. Il a fait du jogging et après . . .

STRATEGY Writing

Narration in the *passé composé* Read the description of Céline's activities again. Note that the author wrote **Céline est restée, elle est allée,** and **Céline est rentrée,** adding a final "e" to the past participles because the subject, **Céline/elle** is feminine. In referring to Céline and Trinh, the author wrote **ils sont allés** and added a final "s" to **allé** because the subject, **ils,** is plural.

When you are writing in the passé composé, it is important to go back over your composition and check all the verb forms. If you have used the verbs **aller, venir, arriver, rester,** or **rentrer,** look to be sure that you formed the passé composé with **être,** rather than **avoir,** and that in each case the past participle agrees with the subject.

Comment dit-on ...?

How to celebrate a happy occasion:

Bon anniversaire!

Bonne année!

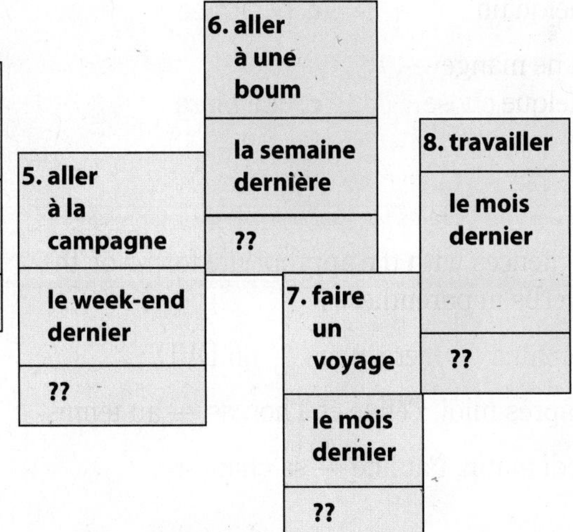

4. aller à la plage
dimanche dernier
??
5. aller à la campagne
le week-end dernier
??
6. aller à une boum
la semaine dernière
??
7. faire un voyage
le mois dernier
??
8. travailler
le mois dernier
??

Tests de contrôle

By taking the following tests, you can check your progress in French and also prepare for the unit test. Write your answers on a separate sheet of paper.

Review...
new words and expressions
- verbs: p. 310
- sports: pp. 312, 313
- expressions with **avoir:** p. 320
- expressions of time: p. 336
- **quelqu'un** and **quelque chose:** p. 34

1 The right choice

Choose the expressions (a), (b), or (c) which best complete the following sentences.

1. Céline va au cinéma. Elle va — une comédie.
a. aider **b.** rencontrer **c.** voir

2. Thomas va au stade. Il va — un match de foot.
a. assister à **b.** attendre **c.** nettoyer

3. Mathieu va rester à la maison. Il va — la voiture de sa mère.
a. aider **b.** laver **c.** rencontrer

4. Charlotte va au café. Elle va — ses copines.
a. rencontrer **b.** assister à **c.** louer

5. Julien est à la mer. Il fait —.
a. du ski **b.** du roller **c.** de la planche à voile

6. Léa est à la montagne. Elle fait —.
a. de la voile **b.** de l'escalade **c.** ses devoirs

7. Clément met un pull parce qu'il a —.
a. faim **b.** chaud **c.** froid

8. Mélanie commande *(orders)* un soda parce qu'elle a —.
a. soif **b.** tort **c.** de la chance

9. Je suis allé au cinéma—.
a. demain **b.** hier soir **c.** samedi prochain

10. Je vais aller à une boum —.
a. hier matin **b.** demain après-midi **c.** la semaine dernière

11. Catherine est au café. Elle attend —.
a. un **b.** quelqu'un **c.** personne

12. Pierre n'a pas faim. Il ne mange —.
a. rien **b.** quelque chose **c.** une pizza

Review...
the passé composé
- **-er** verbs: p. 321
- **-ir** and **-re** verbs: p. 333
- irregular verbs: p. 335

2 The right verb

Complete the following sentences with the appropriate forms of the **passé composé** of the verbs in parentheses.

1. (louer) La semaine dernière, nous — un DVD.

2. (jouer) Hier après-midi, Céline et Thomas — au tennis.

3. (ranger) Samedi matin, Pauline — sa chambre.

4. (finir)	Est-ce que vous — les exercices?
5. (vendre)	À qui est-ce que tu — ton vélo?
6. (avoir)	Monsieur Lescure — un accident avec sa nouvelle voiture.
7. (faire)	Pendant les vacances, les élèves — un voyage au Canada.
8. (être)	Moi, j'— à Paris l'année dernière.
9. (voir)	Quel film est-ce que tu — mardi soir?
10. (mettre)	Mathieu — un CD de rock.

3 Être or avoir?

Review...
- **passé composé** with **être:** pp. 342 and 344

Complete the following sentences with the **passé composé** forms of the verbs in parentheses. Be sure to use the appropriate forms of **être** or **avoir.**

1. (acheter)	Nous — un livre sur Paris.	**5. (arriver)**	Pierre — à l'aéroport.
2. (aller)	Marie — à la tour Eiffel.	**6. (rentrer)**	Nous — le 15 août.
3. (rester)	Mes copains — à l'hôtel.	**7. (visiter)**	Tu — le musée d'Orsay.
4. (téléphoner)	Ils — à des amis.	**8. (venir)**	Mes amis — avec nous.

4 Non!

Review...
- the negative **passé composé:** p. 324

Transform the statements below into **negative** sentences. Replace the underlined words with the expressions in parentheses.

1. Léa a voyagé <u>en bus</u>. **(en train)**
2. J'ai joué <u>au foot</u> hier. **(au basket)**
3. Tu es resté <u>à l'hôtel</u>. **(chez tes cousins)**
4. Éric a invité <u>sa cousine</u>. **(son copain)**

5 Composition: Thanksgiving

Digital performance space

Write a short paragraph of five or six sentences about what you and your family did last Thanksgiving. Did you travel somewhere or did people come to your house? What did you do together? Use the **passé composé,** limiting yourself to words and expressions that you know in French.

STRATEGY Writing

a Make a list of the verbs you will use to describe your activities. Review which ones use **avoir** in the **passé composé** and which use **être**.

	avoir	être
<u>diner</u> chez mes cousins	X	

b Organize your ideas and write your paragraph.

c Check the **passé composé** forms of all the verbs in your composition.

Vocabulaire

POUR COMMUNIQUER

Talking about past activities

Qu'est-ce que tu as fait hier?	*What did you do yesterday?*
J'ai vu un film.	*I saw a film.*
Je suis allé au cinéma.	*I went to the movies.*
Je n'ai pas travaillé.	*I didn't work.*
Je ne suis pas allé à l'école.	*I didn't go to school.*

Explaining why

Pourquoi est-ce que tu es allé en ville?	*Why did you go downtown?*
Je suis allé en ville pour louer un DVD.	*I went downtown to rent a DVD.*

Talking about one's activities

Est-ce que tu fais	**du roller?**	*Do you do*	*in-line skating?*
	de la voile?		*sailing?*
	de l'escalade?		*rock climbing?*
Marc ne fait pas de sport.		*Marc doesn't do sports.*	

MOTS ET EXPRESSIONS

Activités sportives

le jogging	*jogging*	**l'escalade**	*rock climbing*
le roller	*in-line skating*	**la natation**	*swimming*
le skate	*skateboarding*	**la planche à voile**	*windsurfing*
le ski	*skiing*	**la voile**	*sailing*
le ski nautique	*water-skiing*		
le snowboard	*snowboarding*		
le sport	*sport(s)*		
le VTT	*mountain biking*		

Équipement sportif

des rollers	*in-line skates*
un skate	*skateboard*
un snowboard	*snowboard*
un VTT	*mountain bike*

Vacation travel

un autocar, un car	*touring bus*
un avion	*plane*
un bateau	*boat, ship*
un train	*train*

Vacation destinations

la campagne	*countryside*
la mer	*ocean, shore*
la montagne	*mountains*

Les contraires

souvent	*often*	**ne ... jamais**	*never*
quelque chose	*something, anything*	**ne ... rien**	*nothing, not anything*
quelqu'un	*someone, anyone, somebody*	**ne ... personne**	*no one, not anyone, nobody*

Interactive Flashcards @HOMETUTOR my.hrw.com

Verbes en *-er*

aider	*to help*
assister à	*to go to, to attend*
laver	*to wash*
louer	*to rent*
nettoyer	*to clean*
passer	*to spend*
préparer	*to prepare*
ranger	*to clean, to pick up*
rencontrer	*to meet*
réparer	*to fix*

Verbes irréguliers

avoir chaud/froid	*to be (feel) hot/cold*
avoir faim/soif	*to be hungry/thirsty*
avoir raison/tort	*to be right/wrong*
avoir de la chance	*to be lucky*
faire des achats	*to go shopping*
faire les devoirs	*to do homework*
faire un pique-nique	*to have a picnic*
voir	*to see*

Le passé composé avec *avoir*

parler	**j'ai parlé**	*I spoke*
finir	**j'ai fini**	*I finished*
vendre	**j'ai vendu**	*I sold*
avoir	**j'ai eu**	*I had*
être	**j'ai été**	*I was, I have been*
faire	**j'ai fait**	*I did*
mettre	**j'ai mis**	*I put*
voir	**j'ai vu**	*I saw*

Le passé composé avec *être*

aller	**je suis allé(e)**	*I went*
arriver	**je suis arrivé(e)**	*I arrived*
rentrer	**je suis rentré(e)**	*I came back*
rester	**je suis resté(e)**	*I stayed*
venir	**je suis venu(e)**	*I came*

Le calendrier

Noël	*Christmas*
un jour	*day*
un mois	*month*
l'après-midi	*afternoon*
le matin	*morning*
le soir	*evening*
le week-end	*weekend*
Pâques	*Easter*
une semaine	*week*
les vacances	*vacation*
les grandes vacances	*summer vacation*

Expressions pour indiquer quand

aujourd'hui	*today*
hier	*yesterday*
demain	*tomorrow*
prochain(e)	*next*
dernier (dernière)	*last*
d'abord	*first*
avant	*before*
pendant	*during*
après	*after, afterwards*
ensuite	*then, after that*
enfin	*at last*
finalement	*finally*

Expressions utiles

pour	*in order to*
seul(e)	*alone*

Le roller: un sport qui roule!°

Beaucoup de jeunes Français participent aux sports d'équipe° comme° le foot, le basket et le volley, mais certains préfèrent les sports individuels comme le jogging ou la natation. Aujourd'hui, beaucoup de jeunes pratiquent aussi les «sports de glisse»° comme le roller, le skate, la planche à voile (en été) et le ski et le snowboard (en hiver).

Le roller est particulièrement populaire parce qu'il peut être pratiqué en toute° saison et par les gens de tout âge. Deux millions de Français font régulièrement du roller, principalement dans les grandes villes et surtout° dans la région parisienne. «Pour moi,» dit Clément, 15 ans, «le roller est l'occasion° de me faire des nouveaux copains.» Mélanie, 17 ans, dit qu'elle fait du roller «parce que j'ai l'impression de vitesse,° d'indépendance et de liberté. Je suis libre° comme un oiseau.» Pour Charlotte, 21 ans, «le roller est un excellent moyen° de faire de l'exercice et de rester en bonne forme° physique.»

Pour certaines personnes qui habitent dans les grandes villes, le roller est un nouveau moyen de transport urbain. Philippe Tardieu, un jeune avocat° de la région parisienne, va à son bureau° en roller. «Le roller est plus économique, moins polluant° et souvent plus rapide que l'auto. Le roller, ça roule...!»

Le roller a beaucoup d'avantages, mais c'est aussi un sport qui peut être dangereux si on ne fait pas attention. Pour faire du roller, on doit être en bonne forme physique et avoir l'équipement nécessaire. On doit toujours porter un casque pour se protéger° la tête. On doit aussi porter des genouillières pour se protéger les genoux° et des protège-poignets pour se protéger les poignets.°

On peut faire du roller dans la rue ou sur toute surface plane, mais il est préférable de pratiquer ce sport dans les endroits réservés pour cette activité. Dans les grandes villes, il y a des «rollerparks» où les jeunes peuvent aussi faire du roller acrobatique et jouer au hockey sur roller.

À Paris, une association sportive nommée Pari-Roller organise tous les vendredis soirs° une grande randonnée° en roller dans les rues de la ville. Cette randonnée commence à dix heures du soir et finit à une heure du matin. Il y a souvent 12 000 (douze mille) participants de tout âge accompagnés de policiers en roller. Pendant cet événement, les rues du circuit sont interdites° aux voitures. Pour beaucoup de Parisiens, cet événement est l'occasion de redécouvrir° leur ville dans une ambiance° d'amitié, de bonne humeur et de fête populaire.

roule *rolls* **équipe** *team* **comme** *like* **glisse** *gliding* **toute** *any* **surtout** *above all* **occasion** *opportunity* **vitesse** *speed* **libre** *free* **moyen** *means* **forme** *shape* **avocat** *lawyer* **bureau** *office* **polluant** *polluting* **protéger** *to protect* **genoux** *knees* **poignets** *wrists* **tous les vendredis soirs** *every Friday evening* **randonnée** *long ride* **interdites** *closed* **redécouvrir** *to rediscover* **ambiance** *atmosphere*

Additional readings @ **my.hrw.com**
FRENCH InterActive Reader

L'équipement du roller

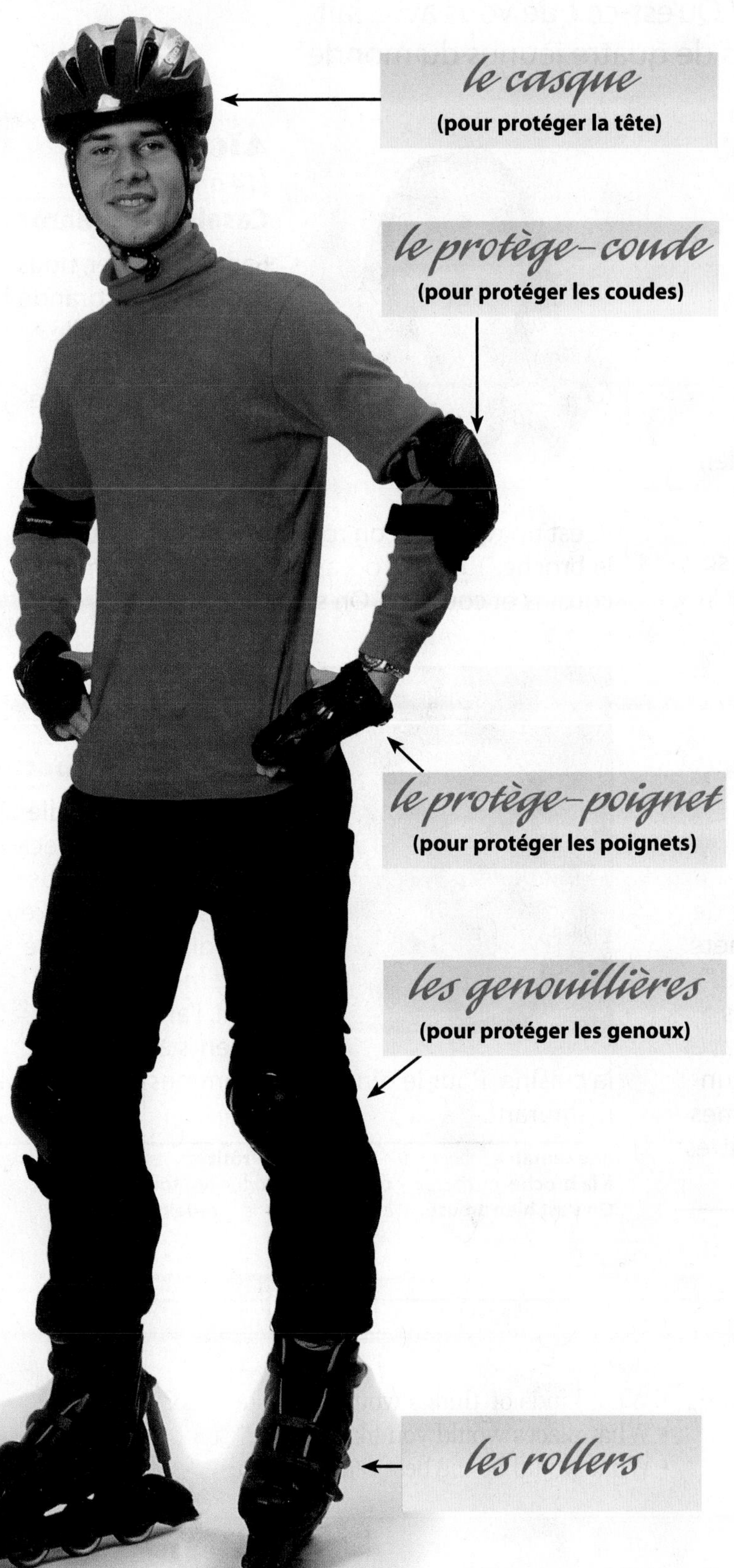

Compréhension

Faites correspondre *(Match)* les personnes et leurs opinions.

a. Clément
b. Mélanie
c. Charlotte
d. Philippe

1. «Le roller, ça roule!»
2. «Le roller est moins polluant que l'auto.»
3. «Quand je fais du roller, je suis libre comme un oiseau.»
4. «Le roller est l'occasion de me faire des nouveaux copains.»
5. «Le roller est un excellent moyen de faire de l'exercice.»
6. «Quand je fais du roller, j'ai l'impression de vitesse.»
7. «En ville, le roller est un bon moyen de transport.»

Et vous?

Classez *(Rank)* les avantages du roller par ordre d'importance personnelle — de 6 (plus important) à 1 (moins important). Comparez votre classement avec vos camarades.

Le roller, c'est ...

- un moyen de faire de l'exercice
- un moyen de rester en forme
- un moyen de rencontrer des copains
- un moyen de transport urbain
- l'impression d'indépendance
- l'impression de vitesse

Les activités du week-end

Qu'est-ce que vous faites le week-end? Qu'est-ce que vous avez fait le week-end dernier? Voici les réponses de quatre jeunes du monde° francophone.

Pierre
(16 ans)
Basse Terre, Guadeloupe

Le samedi, je joue généralement au foot. Je fais partie° de l'équipe° junior de mon village. Le week-end dernier, nous avons fait un match. Nous avons bien joué, mais nous avons perdu! Après le match, je suis allé à la plage. Le soir, je suis allé chez des copains. Nous avons mis de la musique et nous avons dansé.

Élisabeth
(15 ans)
Bruxelles, Belgique

Samedi matin, j'ai fait des achats. J'ai choisi un cadeau pour l'anniversaire de mon père. (J'ai acheté une cravate en soie.°) L'après-midi, je suis allée au ciné-club avec un copain. Nous avons vu *Les Temps modernes*, un vieux film de Charlie Chaplin. Après, nous sommes allés dans un café et nous avons rencontré d'autres° copains. J'ai passé la soirée° en famille.

monde *world* **fais partie** *am a member* **équipe** *team*
soie *silk* **d'autres** *other* **soirée** *evening*

Aïcha
(14 ans)
Casablanca, Maroc

Samedi dernier, nous avons eu une grande réunion de famille chez mon oncle Karim. Une centaine° de personnes sont venues. Nous avons fait un «méchoui». (C'est un repas° où on rôtit° un mouton° entier à la broche.°) J'ai eu l'occasion° de voir tous° mes cousins et cousines. On s'est bien amusé.°

Yvan
(14 ans)
Montréal, Québec

Le matin, je suis allé à un rollerpark avec des copains et nous avons joué au hockey. À midi, je suis rentré chez moi. L'après-midi, j'ai aidé mes parents à repeindre° la cuisine. Pour le dîner, nous sommes allés au restaurant.

une centaine *about 100* **repas** *meal* **rôtit** *roasts* **mouton** *sheep*
à la broche *on the spit* **occasion** *opportunity* **tous** *all*
On s'est bien amusé. *We had a good time.* **repeindre** *repaint*

CONNEXIONS

Pick one of the above French-speaking cities, and find out more about it on the Internet. Imagine that you will be spending a week in that city.

- What kinds of things would you like to do?
- What places would you like to visit?
- What would be the best season to go?

Additional readings @ **my.hrw.com**
FRENCH InterActive Reader

STRATEGY Reading

More cognate patterns
Here are two important cognate patterns that will help you read French more easily.

- French verbs in **-er** sometimes correspond to English verbs in *-ate*.

FRENCH	ENGLISH	FRENCH	ENGLISH
situer	*situate*	**situé**	*situated*
indiquer	*indicate*	**indiqué**	*indicated*

- The ending **-ment** usually corresponds to the English ending *-ly*.

généralement *generally*

Activité écrite: Une carte postale

Imaginez que vous avez passé le week-end avec l'une des quatre personnes: Pierre, Yvan, Élisabeth ou Aïcha. Dans une carte postale, décrivez ce week-end de votre point de vue personnel.

Chers amis,

J'ai passé le week-end avec Yvan. Nous avons ....

Writing Hint Be sure to use the **passé composé.**

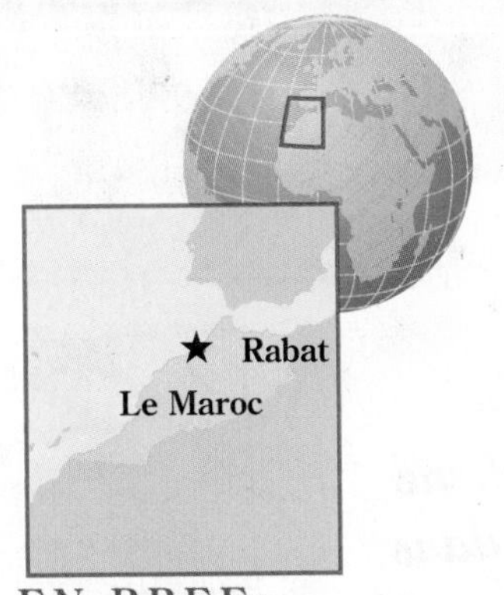

EN BREF: LE MAROC

Population: 30 millions
Capitale: Rabat
Langues: arabe, français, espagnol

Le Maroc est un pays° d'Afrique du Nord° situé entre la Méditerranée au nord, l'Atlantique à l'est° et le Sahara au sud.° Autrefois° administré par la France, ce pays est maintenant gouverné par un roi,° le roi Mohammed VI. Le sud du pays est habité par les Touareg, un peuple nomade qui traverse le Sahara en caravanes de chameaux.°

De culture islamique, le Maroc est un pays moderne avec une longue tradition intellectuelle et artistique. Les artisans marocains créent° des produits d'excellente qualité: textiles, céramiques et objets de cuir° et de cuivre.°

Il y a aujourd'hui un million de Marocains qui habitent en France où ils ont introduit le couscous, le thé à la menthe° et d'autres° spécialités de leur pays.

pays *country* **nord** *north* **est** *east* **sud** *south* **Autrefois** *In the past* **roi** *king* **chameaux** *camels* **créent** *create* **cuir** *leather* **cuivre** *copper* **menthe** *mint* **d'autres** *other*

Les quatre erreurs de Sophie

Pendant les vacances, Sophie Lambert, une jeune Française, a fait un grand voyage dans les pays° francophones. Dans chaque° pays où elle est allée, elle a écrit° des cartes postales à ses copains. Dans chaque carte postale, Sophie a fait une erreur.° Quelle est cette erreur? (Les erreurs de Sophie concernent la géographie ou les gens.) Lisez attentivement chaque carte et cherchez l'erreur que Sophie a faite.

pays *countries* **chaque** *each* **a écrit** *wrote* **erreur** *error, mistake*

Marrakech, le 10 juillet
Ma chère Pauline,
Je suis au Maroc. C'est un pays d'Afrique du Sud° où on parle arabe et où beaucoup de gens parlent aussi français. Samedi, je suis allée à la «médina» qui est le vieux quartier° de Marrakech. Là, j'ai acheté un beau sac de cuir° à un artisan local.
Amitiés,
Sophie

Sud *south* **quartier** *district* **cuir** *leather*

Québec, le 25 juillet
Mon cher Guillaume,
Je passe une semaine à Québec, la capitale du Canada. Hier j'ai téléphoné à une copine et nous sommes allées dans la vieille ville. Ensuite, nous sommes allées à la Citadelle et nous avons vu le changement de la garde.° Ici, les gens parlent un français un peu ancien.° Par exemple, pour dire «au revoir», on dit° «bonjour». C'est amusant, non?
Amicalement,
Sophie

changement de la garde *changing of the guard* **ancien** *old* **dit** *says*

Additional readings @ **my.hrw.com**
FRENCH InterActive Reader

Fort-de-France, le 3 août

Ma chère Élodie,

Un grand bonjour de la Martinique qui est une petite île° de l'Océan Pacifique. Je suis arrivée ici la semaine dernière. Ici, il fait toujours chaud et les gens vont à la plage toute l'année!° Hier j'ai acheté un maillot de bain et des lunettes de soleil dans une boutique de l'hôtel. Ensuite, j'ai nagé et j'ai fait de la planche à voile et de la plongée sous-marine.° J'ai vu des poissons de toutes les couleurs!

Affectueusement,

Sophie

île *island* **toute l'année** *all year long*
plongée sous-marine *scuba diving*

Port-au-Prince, le 14 août

Mon cher Mathieu,

Je suis arrivée à Haïti dimanche dernier. J'ai trouvé une chambre dans une pension° à Port-au-Prince, la capitale du pays. Les gens d'ici parlent créole et espagnol. Hier soir, je suis allée écouter un orchestre de musique «compas». Génial! J'aime aussi la cuisine créole. C'est épicé,° mais c'est très bon!

Amitiés,

Sophie

pension *boarding house* **épicé** *spicy, hot*

Les 4 erreurs:

1. *Le Maroc est en Afrique du Nord (et non pas en Afrique du Sud).*
2. *La capitale du Canada est Ottawa (et non pas Québec).*
3. *La Martinique est dans l'Océan Atlantique (et non pas dans l'Océan Pacifique).*
4. *À Haïti, on parle créole et français (et non pas espagnol).*

Unité 8

Les repas

LEÇON 25 **LE FRANÇAIS PRATIQUE** Les repas et la nourriture

LEÇON 26 À la cantine

LEÇON 27 Un client difficile

LEÇON 28 Pique-nique

THÈME ET OBJECTIFS

Food and meals

Eating well is not only essential for our health, it should be an enjoyable experience as well.

In this unit, you will learn ...

- to talk about your favorite foods
- to describe the different meals of the day
- to prepare a shopping list and do the grocery shopping
- to order a meal in a restaurant
- to set the table

You will also be able ...

- to ask people to do things for you

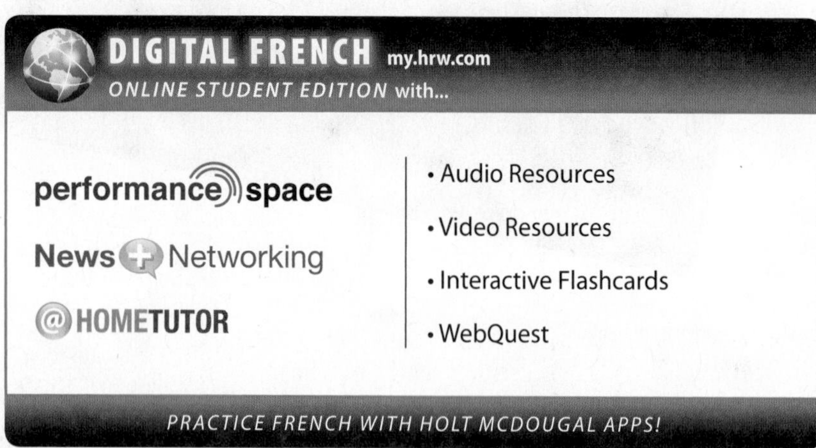

Des trésors sont cachés dedans ...
MUSÉE DU VIEIL AIX
ようこそ
EST OUVERT
OUS LES JOURS SANS
INTERRUPTION

Leçon 25

Vocabulaire et Culture

Les repas et la nourriture

LE FRANÇAIS PRATIQUE

DVD AUDIO

Accent sur ... Les repas français

For the French, a meal is more than just food served on a plate. It is a happy social occasion where people gather around a table to enjoy one another's company. Dinner is the most important family time of the day. Parents and children sit down together and talk about the day's events and topics of common interest. Special events are celebrated by more elaborate meals.

In traditional homes, children do not go to the refrigerator to fix their own sandwiches nor do they help themselves to snacks. They are expected to sit down at the table with everyone else at mealtime, eat what is served, join in the conversation, and not ask to be excused until the adults are finished.

Le petit déjeuner (breakfast)

Le petit déjeuner français traditionnel est un repas simple: tartines° de pain avec du beurre° et de la confiture° et un grand bol de café au lait ou de chocolat chaud. Dans les familles modernes, les enfants mangent «à l'américaine»: ils prennent° des céréales et du jus d'orange.

tartines *slices* **beurre** *butter* **confiture** *jam* **prennent** *have*

Le déjeuner (lunch)

Le déjeuner est généralement servi entre° midi et demi et une heure et demie. Il se compose de hors-d'oeuvre divers (saucisson,° radis,° salade de concombres, etc.), d'un plat principal (viande° ou poisson° avec des légumes°), d'une salade verte, d'un fromage° et d'un dessert (gâteau,° fruits ou glace). Le café est toujours servi à la fin du repas.

entre *between* **saucisson** *salami* **radis** *radishes* **viande** *meat* **poisson** *fish* **légumes** *vegetables* **fromage** *cheese* **gâteau** *cake*

@HOMETUTOR
my.hrw.com

Le goûter *(afternoon snack)*

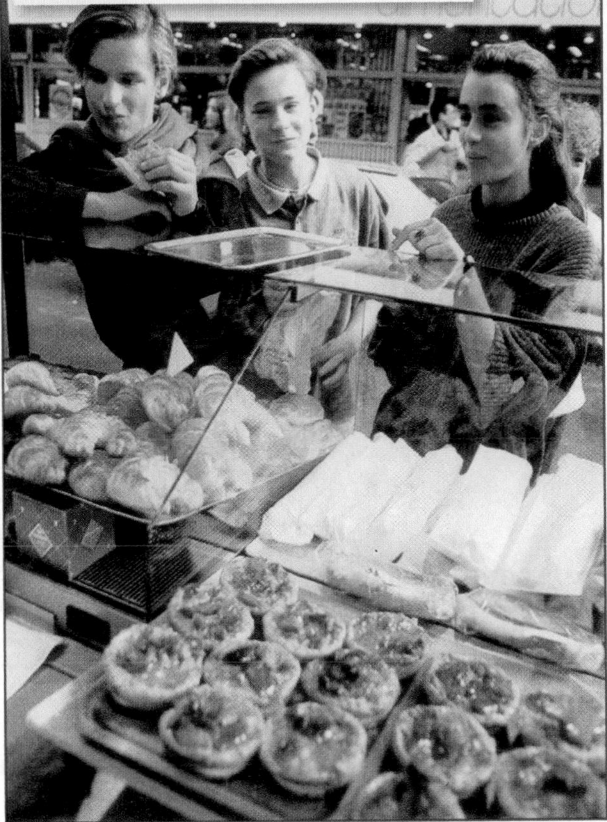

Après les cours, beaucoup de jeunes vont à la pâtisserie. Là, ils achètent un pain au chocolat,° un croissant ou un éclair.

pain au chocolat *chocolate croissant*

Le dîner *(dinner)*

Le dîner est le repas familial principal. Il est servi entre huit heures et neuf heures avec tout le monde° présent. C'est un repas simple qui se compose d'une soupe, d'un plat principal (viande ou poisson, omelette ou pâtes°), d'une salade et d'un dessert léger° (yaourt ou fruit).

tout le monde *everybody*
pâtes *pasta* **léger** *light*

A VOCABULAIRE Les repas et la table

▶ How to talk about meals:

—En général, à quelle heure est-ce que tu **prends le petit déjeuner** *(have breakfast)*?
—Je prends le petit déjeuner à sept heures et demie.
—Où est-ce que tu vas **déjeuner** *(to have lunch)* aujourd'hui?
—Je vais déjeuner à **la cantine de l'école** *(school cafeteria)*.

Les repas et la nourriture

NOMS		VERBES	
un repas	*meal*		
le petit déjeuner	*breakfast*	**prendre le petit déjeuner**	*to have breakfast*
le déjeuner	*lunch*	**déjeuner**	*to have lunch*
le dîner	*dinner*	**dîner**	*to have dinner*
la nourriture	*food*		
la cuisine	*cooking, cuisine*		

—Tu peux **mettre** *(set)* la table?
—D'accord. Je vais mettre la table.

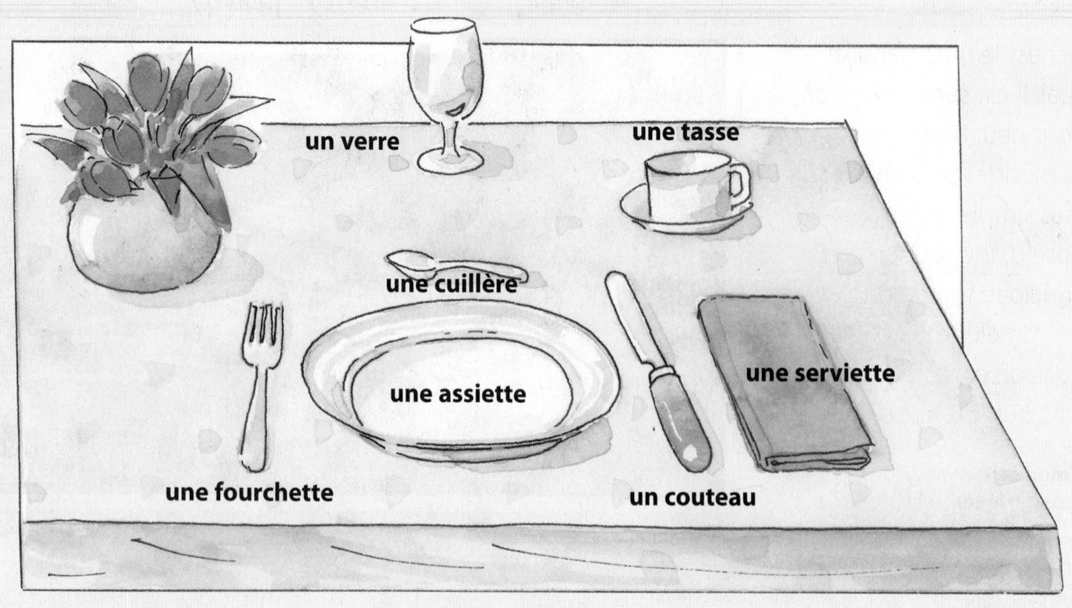

@HOMETUTOR
my.hrw.com

1 Et toi?

PARLER/ÉCRIRE Exprime tes préférences. Pour cela complète les phrases suivantes.

1. Mon repas préféré est …	• le petit déjeuner • le déjeuner • le dîner
2. Je préfère déjeuner …	• chez moi • dans un fast-food • à la cantine de l'école • …?
3. En général, la nourriture de la cantine de l'école est …	• excellente • mauvaise • bonne • …?
4. Je préfère dîner …	• chez moi • au restaurant • chez mes copains • …?
5. Je préfère la nourriture …	• mexicaine • chinoise • italienne • …?
6. Quand je dois aider pour le dîner, je préfère …	• préparer la salade • laver les assiettes • mettre la table • …?

2 Questions personnelles PARLER/ÉCRIRE

1. À quelle heure est-ce que tu prends ton petit déjeuner le lundi? Et le dimanche?
2. En général, à quelle heure est-ce que tu dînes?
3. Où est-ce que tu déjeunes pendant la semaine? le samedi? le dimanche?
4. Où est-ce que tu as déjeuné hier? Avec qui?
5. Où est-ce que tu vas dîner ce soir? Avec qui?
6. Est-ce que tu vas souvent au restaurant? Quand? Avec qui? Quel est ton restaurant préféré?
7. Est-ce que tu as jamais *(ever)* déjeuné dans un restaurant français? (dans un restaurant mexicain? dans un restaurant italien? dans un restaurant chinois? dans un restaurant vietnamien?) Quand et avec qui?
8. Est-ce que tu mets la table chez toi? Qui a mis la table pour le petit déjeuner? Et pour le dîner?

3 Au restaurant 

PARLER Vous êtes dans un restaurant français. Vous avez commandé *(ordered)* les choses suivantes. Le serveur a oublié *(forgot)* d'apporter le nécessaire (les ustensiles, etc.).

Monsieur, je voudrais un verre pour le jus d'orange.
Pardon. Voici un verre.

▶ pour le jus d'orange

1. pour l'eau minérale *(mineral water)*
2. pour le thé
3. pour la soupe
4. pour les frites
5. pour le steak
6. pour le gâteau *(cake)*

B VOCABULAIRE La nourriture et les boissons

How to express food preferences:

—Est-ce que tu aimes **le poisson** *(fish)*?
—Oui, j'aime le poisson mais je préfère **la viande** *(meat)*.
—Quelle viande est-ce que tu aimes?
—J'aime **le rosbif** *(roast beef)* et **le poulet** *(chicken)*.

Les Plats

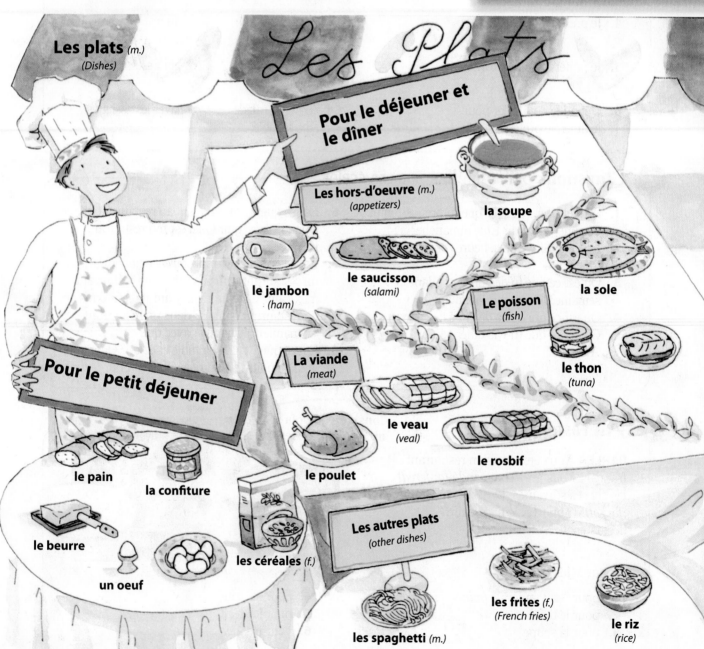

Les plats *(m.)* *(Dishes)*

Pour le déjeuner et le dîner

Les hors-d'oeuvre *(m.)* *(appetizers)*
- **la soupe**
- **le jambon** *(ham)*
- **le saucisson** *(salami)*

Le poisson *(fish)*
- **la sole**
- **le thon** *(tuna)*

La viande *(meat)*
- **le veau** *(veal)*
- **le poulet**
- **le rosbif**

Les autres plats *(other dishes)*
- **les spaghetti** *(m.)*
- **les frites** *(f.)* *(French fries)*
- **le riz** *(rice)*

Pour le petit déjeuner

- **le pain**
- **la confiture**
- **le beurre**
- **un oeuf**
- **les céréales** *(f.)*

Quelle viande est-ce que tu aimes?
J'aime le rosbif et le poulet.

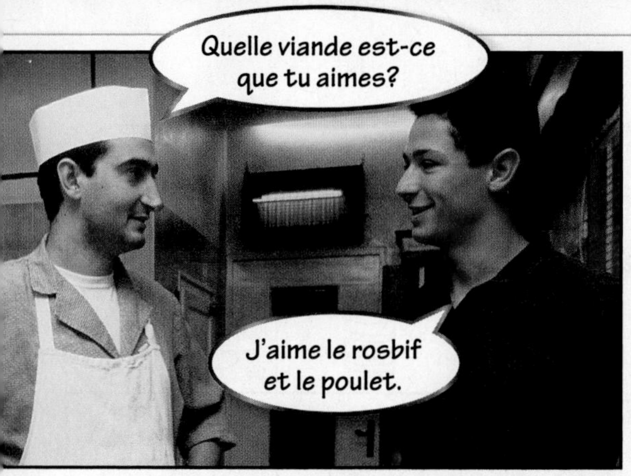

@HOMETUTOR
my.hrw.com

aimer	*to like*	Alice **aime** le poulet.
préférer	*to prefer*	Philippe **préfère** le rosbif.
détester	*to hate*	Paul **déteste** le poisson.

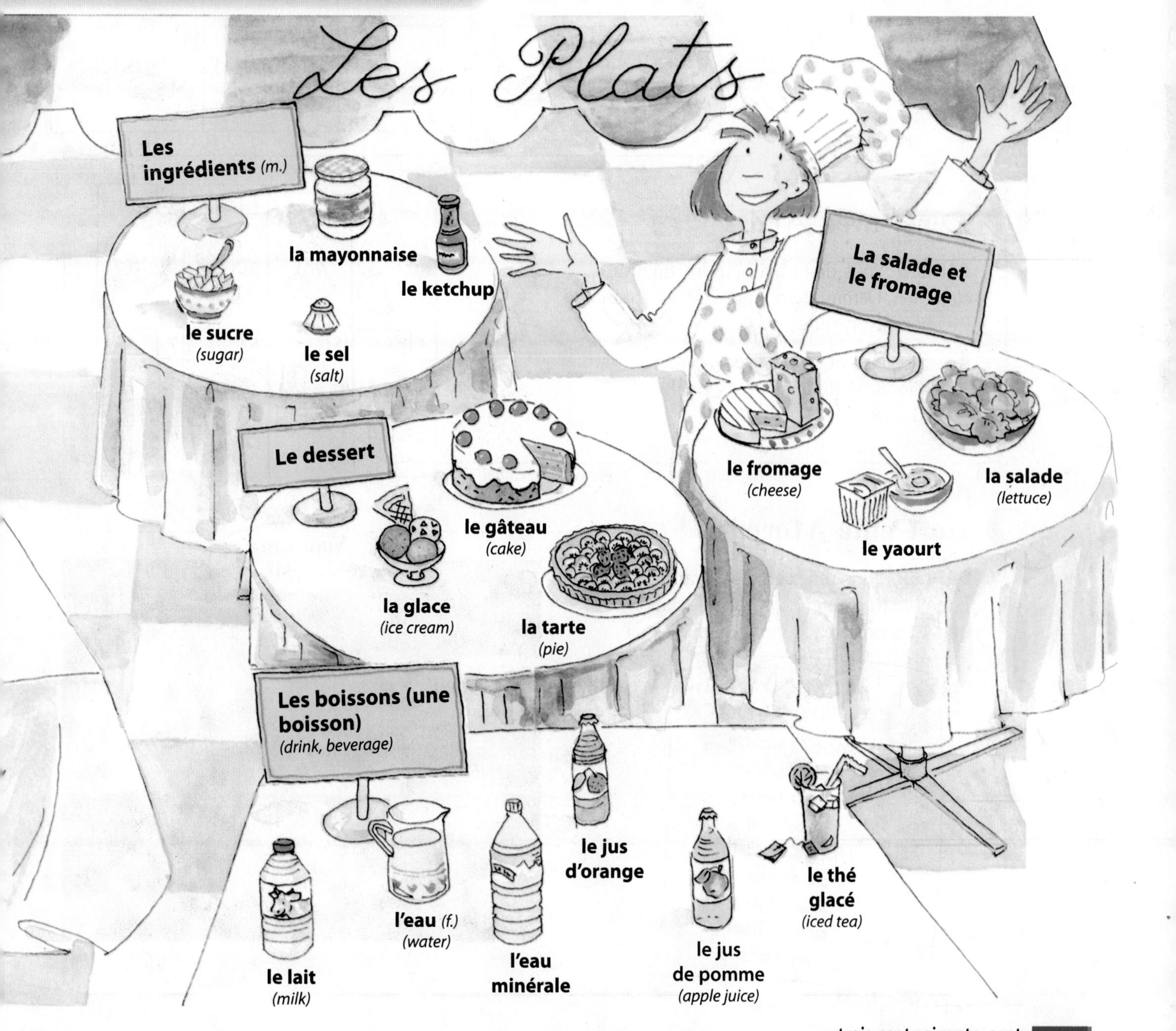

Les Plats
Les ingrédients (m.)
la mayonnaise
le ketchup
le sucre (sugar)
le sel (salt)
Le dessert
le gâteau (cake)
la glace (ice cream)
la tarte (pie)
La salade et le fromage
le fromage (cheese)
la salade (lettuce)
le yaourt
Les boissons (une boisson) (drink, beverage)
le lait (milk)
l'eau (f.) (water)
l'eau minérale
le jus d'orange
le jus de pomme (apple juice)
le thé glacé (iced tea)

4 Vous aimez ça?

PARLER/ÉCRIRE Dites si oui ou non vous aimez les choses suivantes.

- J'aime …
- J'aime beaucoup …
- Je n'aime pas …
- Je déteste …

▶ **J'aime le fromage. (Je n'aime pas le fromage.)**

5 Dîner avec André 

PARLER Vous dînez avec André, un ami canadien. Demandez à André de vous passer les choses suivantes.

▶ **—S'il te plaît, André, passe-moi le pain.**
—Tiens. Voilà le pain.
—Merci.

6 La Petite Marmite 

PARLER Vous dînez au restaurant français La Petite Marmite. Le garçon demande ce que vous préférez. Répondez-lui.

La Petite Marmite
menu

▶
- soupe / saucisson
- viande / poisson
- poulet / veau
- sole / thon
- frites / spaghetti
- fromage / salade
- yaourt / glace
- tarte / gâteau
- thé / café

Vous avez choisi?
Oui, j'ai choisi la soupe.

@HOMETUTOR
my.hrw.com

7 Dans le réfrigérateur ou sur la table?

PARLER Choisissez un produit et demandez à vos camarades où est le produit. Ils vont dire si le produit est dans le réfrigérateur ou sur la table.

▶ Où est la confiture?
Elle est sur la table.
RIZ

8 Les préférences

PARLER/ÉCRIRE Indiquez les préférences culinaires des personnes suivantes en complétant les phrases.

1. J'aime …
2. Je déteste …
3. Ma mère aime …
4. Mon petit frère (ma petite soeur) déteste …
5. Mon copain aime …
6. Ma copine déteste …
7. Les enfants aiment …
8. En général, les Italiens aiment …
9. En général, les Japonais aiment …

9 Les courses *(Food shopping)*

ÉCRIRE Vous passez les vacances en France avec votre famille. Faites la liste des courses pour les repas suivants.

▶ un repas végétarien

1. un pique-nique à la campagne
2. un bon petit déjeuner
3. un repas d'anniversaire
4. le dîner de ce soir
5. le déjeuner de demain
6. un repas de régime *(diet)*

LISTE

▶ *Un repas végétarien:*
- *oeufs*
- *salade*
- *fromage*
- *pain*
- *yaourt*
- *eau minérale*

C VOCABULAIRE Les fruits et les légumes *(Fruits and vegetables)*

▶ ***How to shop for food:***

À la maison

—Où vas-tu?
—Je vais au **marché**.
Je vais **faire les courses** *(to do the food shopping)*.
—Qu'est-ce que tu vas acheter?
—Je vais acheter des **tomates** et des **oranges**.

Où vas-tu?
Je vais au marché.

Au marché

—Pardon, madame. Combien coûtent les **pommes?**
—Elles coûtent un euro cinquante le kilo.
—Donnez-moi deux **kilos de** pommes, s'il vous plaît.
—Voilà. Ça fait trois euros.

Pardon, madame. Combien coûtent les pommes?
Elles coûtent un euro 50 le kilo.

10 *Qu'est-ce que vous préférez?*

PARLER/ÉCRIRE Indiquez vos préférences.

▶ pour le petit déjeuner: (un oeuf ou des céréales?) **Je préfère des céréales.**

1. pour le petit déjeuner:	(un pamplemousse ou une banane?)
2. après le déjeuner:	(une pomme ou une poire?)
3. avec le poulet:	(des haricots verts ou des petits pois?)
4. avec le steak:	(des pommes de terre ou des carottes?)
5. comme *(as)* salade:	(une salade de tomates ou une salade de concombres *(cucumbers)*?)
6. pour le dessert:	(une tarte aux cerises ou une tarte aux poires?)
7. comme glace:	(une glace à la vanille ou une glace à la fraise?)

11 *Les achats*

PARLER Vos copains reviennent du marché. Demandez ce qu'ils ont acheté.

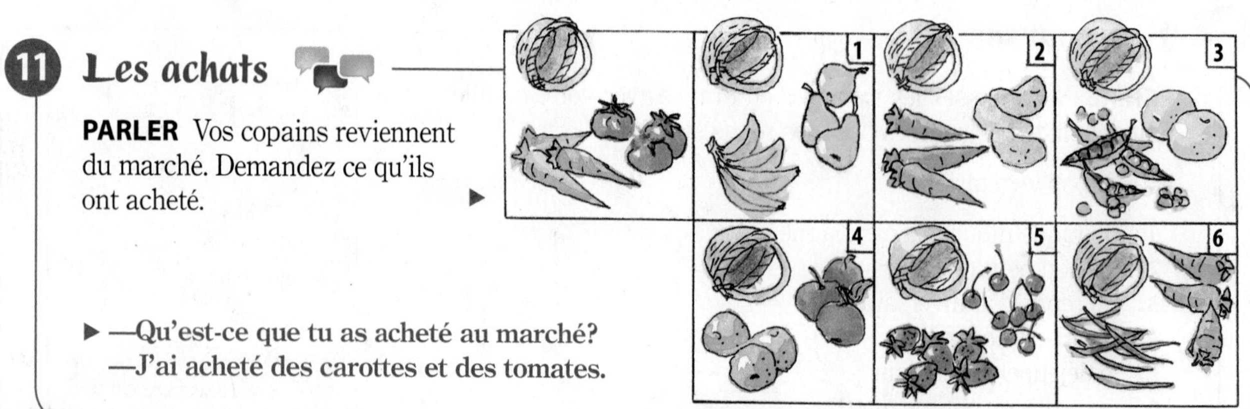

▶ **—Qu'est-ce que tu as acheté au marché?**
—J'ai acheté des carottes et des tomates.

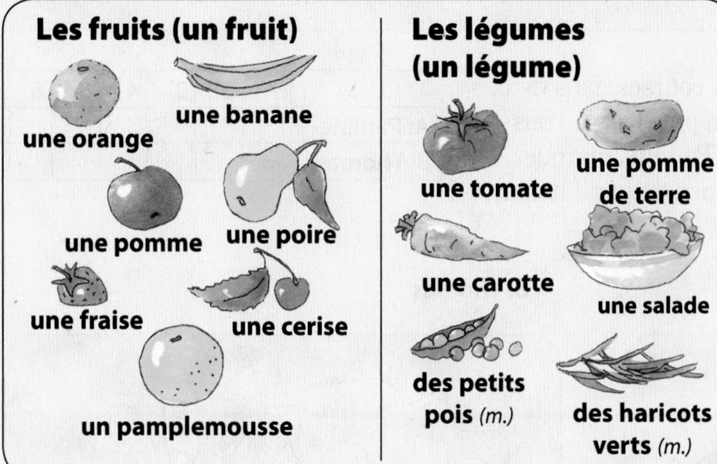

NOTE Culturelle

Le marché

In France, as in the United States, most people do their food shopping at the supermarket **(le supermarché).** However, to have fresher fruits and vegetables, many people still go to the local open-air market **(le marché)** where farmers come to sell their produce.

LES QUANTITÉS

une livre (de)	*pound*	
un kilo (de)	*kilo (2.2 pounds)*	
une douzaine (de)	*dozen*	

Donnez-moi | **une livre** de tomates.
un kilo de pommes.
une douzaine d'oeufs.

12 Au marché

PARLER Vous êtes au marché. Demandez au vendeur combien coûtent certaines choses. Dites aussi quelle quantité vous voulez acheter.

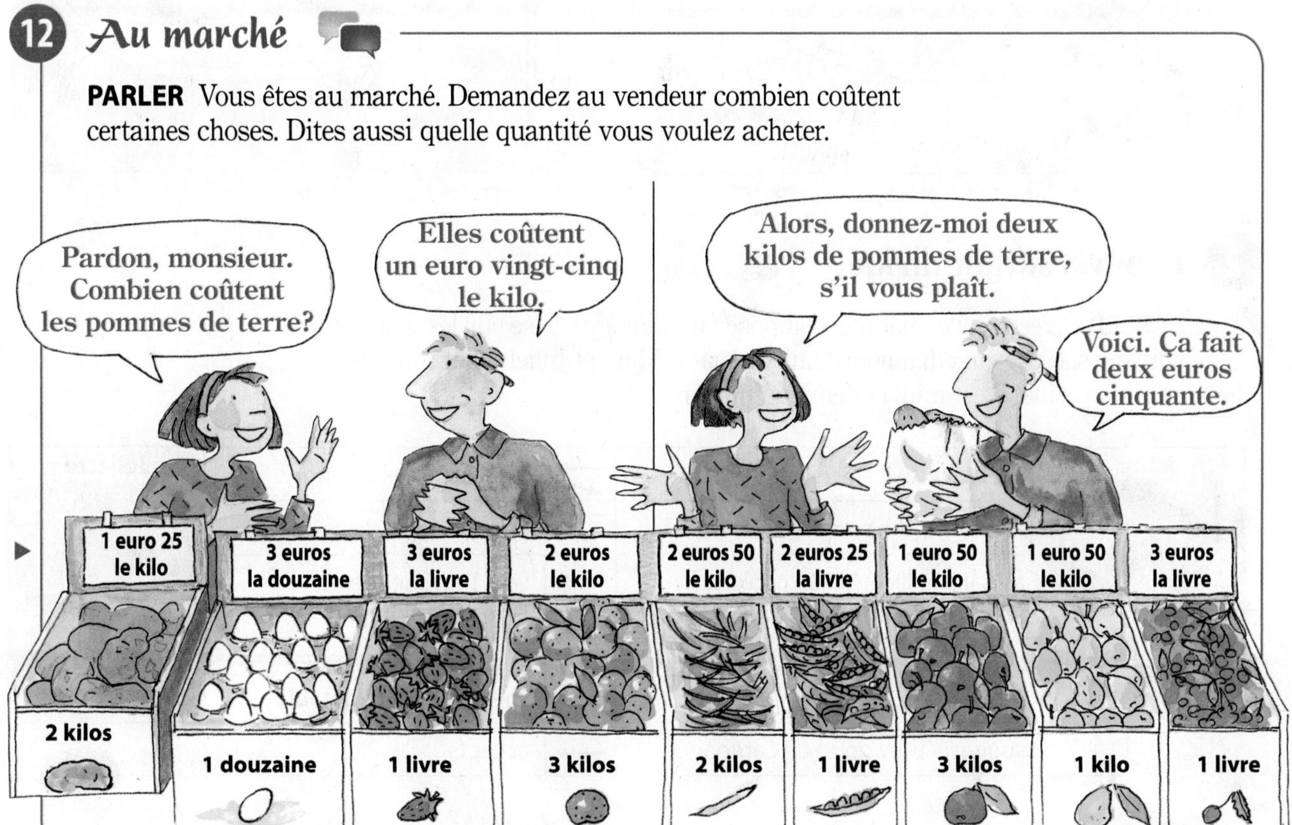

À votre tour!

OBJECTIFS

Now you can ...
- talk about what you like to eat and drink
- prepare a shopping list

1 Écoutez bien!

ÉCOUTER Pauline et Thomas ont fait les courses dans deux supermarchés différents. Écoutez bien les phrases. Si vous entendez le nom d'un produit acheté par Pauline, marquez A. Si vous entendez le nom d'un produit acheté par Thomas, marquez B.

	1	2	3	4	5	6
A: Pauline						
B: Thomas						

A. Pauline

B. Thomas

2 Conversation dirigée

PARLER Avec un(e) camarade, composez un dialogue basé sur les instructions suivantes. C'est samedi aujourd'hui. Ce matin Marc et Juliette ont fait des achats en ville. Il est midi et demi maintenant.

Marc			Juliette
asks Juliette if she is hungry	→ ←	says she is very hungry	
asks her if she wants to have lunch	→ ←	answers yes	
asks if she likes Italian cooking **(la cuisine italienne)**	→ ←	says that she prefers French cooking	
asks her if she likes meat	→ ←	says she does, but that she also likes vegetables	
suggests they go to La Campagne	→	accepts	

3 Créa-dialogue  

PARLER Vous voyagez en France avec un(e) ami(e). Essayez de découvrir *(try to discover)* ce que votre ami(e) aime manger. Proposez à votre ami(e) de déjeuner dans le restaurant correspondant à ses préférences.

▶ **—Tu aimes la viande?**
—Non, je n'aime pas la viande.
—Tu aimes les légumes?
—Non, je n'aime pas les légumes.
—Tu aimes le poisson?
—Oui, j'aime beaucoup le poisson.
—On déjeune à La Marine?
—D'accord.

▶ 

1 

2 

3 

4 

5 

6 

7 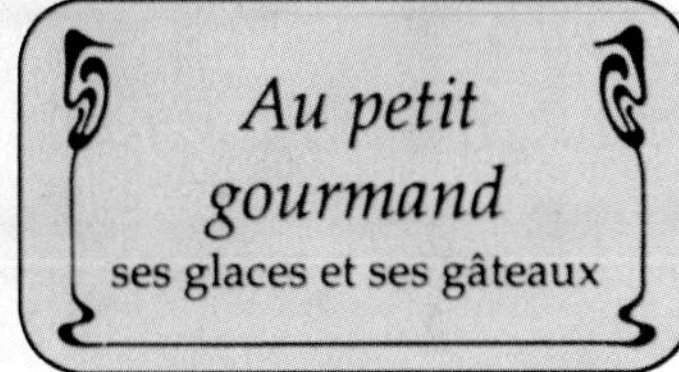

4 Comparaisons 

ÉCRIRE Avec un(e) camarade de classe, préparez le menu de trois repas américains et trois repas français typiques. Comparez ces menus.

Repas américains	Repas français
• petit déjeuner ______	• petit déjeuner ______
• déjeuner ______	• déjeuner ______
• dîner ______	• dîner ______

CONNEXIONS

La France exporte beaucoup de produits alimentaires *(food products)*, en particulier des fromages et des eaux minérales.

Allez dans votre supermarché local et visitez le rayon *(department)* de ces produits.

- Est-ce qu'il y a des fromages français? Quelles sortes de fromage?
- Est-ce qu'il y a des eaux minérales françaises? Quelles marques *(brands)*?

Leçon 26

À la cantine

AUDIO

Il est midi et demi. Suzanne va à la cantine. Elle rencontre Jean-Marc.

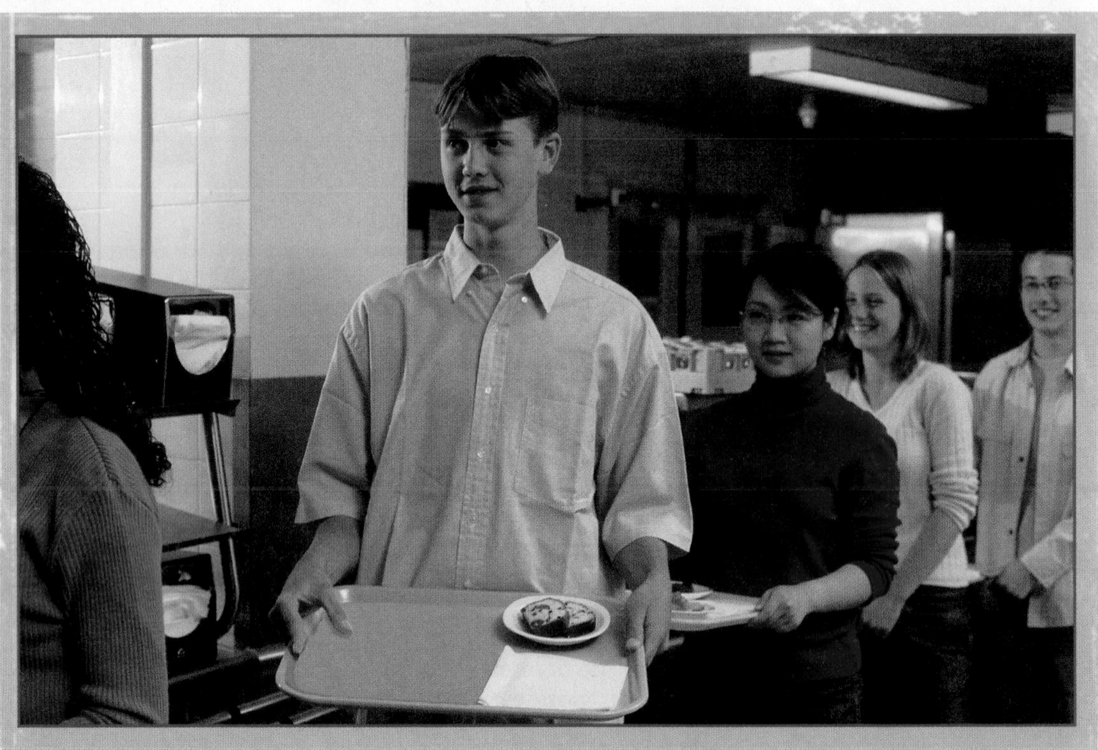

Suzanne: Est-ce que tu veux déjeuner avec moi?
Jean-Marc: Ça dépend. Qu'est-ce qu'il y a aujourd'hui?
Suzanne: Il y a du poisson!
Jean-Marc: Du poisson?
Suzanne: Oui, du poisson.
Jean-Marc: Quelle horreur! Bon, aujourd'hui, je ne veux pas déjeuner. — *How disgusting!*
Suzanne: Il y a aussi du gâteau.
Jean-Marc: Du gâteau! Hm …
Suzanne: Et de la glace!
Jean-Marc: Une minute … je vais prendre un plateau. — *to take / tray*

Compréhension

1. À quelle heure est-ce que Suzanne va déjeuner?
2. Qui est-ce qu'elle rencontre?
3. Est-ce que Jean-Marc aime le poisson?
4. Qu'est-ce qu'il aime?
5. Est-ce qu'il va déjeuner avec Suzanne? Pourquoi?

@HOMETUTOR
my.hrw.com

Et toi?

1. En général, où est-ce que tu déjeunes?
2. À quelle heure est-ce que tu déjeunes?
3. En général, est-ce que tu aimes la nourriture de la cantine?
4. Qu'est-ce que tu fais quand tu n'aimes pas la nourriture de la cantine?

NOTE Culturelle

À la cantine

Où est-ce que tu déjeunes pendant la semaine? Quand on habite près de l'école, on peut° rentrer à la maison. Quand on habite loin, on déjeune à la cantine. À midi, beaucoup de jeunes Français déjeunent à la cantine de leur école.

À la cantine, chacun° prend° un plateau et va chercher° sa nourriture. Cette nourriture est généralement bonne, abondante° et variée. Le menu change chaque° jour de la semaine. Un repas typique inclut° les plats suivants:

- **un hors-d'oeuvre**
  salade de concombres, salade de pommes de terre, carottes râpées,° jambon …
- **un plat principal° chaud**
  poulet, steak, côtelette de porc°
- **une garniture°**
  spaghetti, frites, petits pois, purée de pommes de terre°
- **une salade verte**
- **du fromage**
- **un dessert**
  glace ou fruit
- **une boisson**
  eau minérale, limonade, jus de fruit

Où est-ce que tu préférerais° déjeuner? À ton école ou dans une école française?

peut *can* **chacun** *each one* **prend** *takes* **chercher** *to get*
abondante *plentiful* **chaque** *each* **inclut** *includes*
râpées *grated* **principal** *main* **côtelette de porc** *pork chop*
garniture *side dish* **purée de pommes de terre** *mashed potatoes*
est-ce que tu préférerais *would you prefer*

A Le verbe *vouloir*

Note the forms of the irregular verb **vouloir** *(to want).*

vouloir				
PRESENT	Je **veux**	aller au café.	Nous **voulons** une glace.
	Tu **veux**	déjeuner.	Vous **voulez** des spaghetti.
	Il/Elle/On **veut**	dîner.	Ils/Elles **veulent** des frites.
PASSÉ COMPOSÉ	J'**ai voulu**	dîner chez Maxim's.	

→ When making a request, French speakers often use **je voudrais** *(I would like),* which is more polite than **je veux** *(I want).*

Je voudrais un café. — ***I would like** a cup of coffee.*
Je voudrais dîner. — ***I would like** to have dinner.*

→ When accepting an offer, French speakers often use the expression **je veux bien.**

— Est-ce que tu veux déjeuner avec moi? — *Do you want to have lunch with me?*
— Oui, **je veux bien.** — *Yes, **I do.** (Yes, **I want to.**)*

1 Vive la différence!

PARLER/ÉCRIRE Nous sommes samedi. Des amis vont en ville. Pour le déjeuner, chacun veut faire des choses différentes.

▶ Cécile/aller dans un café
Cécile veut aller dans un café.

1. nous/manger des frites
2. toi/manger une pizza
3. vous/aller dans un restaurant italien
4. moi/aller dans un restaurant chinois
5. Patrick et Alain/déjeuner à midi
6. Isabelle/déjeuner à une heure

2 Oui ou non?

PARLER/ÉCRIRE Dites si oui ou non les personnes entre parenthèses veulent faire les choses indiquées.

▶ Il est midi. (nous/déjeuner?)
Oui, nous voulons déjeuner.

▶ C'est samedi. (les élèves/étudier?)
Non, les élèves ne veulent pas étudier.

1. Il fait froid. (Éric/jouer au foot?)
2. Il fait beau. (mes copains/aller à la plage?)
3. La nourriture est mauvaise. (vous/déjeuner à la cantine?)
4. Il y a des spaghetti. (moi/dîner?)
5. Il y a une excellente comédie. (toi/regarder la télé?)
6. C'est dimanche. (nous/travailler)

3 Expression personnelle

PARLER/ÉCRIRE Complétez les phrases suivantes avec une expression personnelle.

1. Ce week-end, je voudrais …
   Je ne veux pas …
2. Cet été, je voudrais …
   Je ne veux pas …
3. Après l'école, je voudrais …
   Je ne veux pas …
4. Dans la vie *(life),* je voudrais …
   Je ne veux pas …

@HOMETUTOR
my.hrw.com

B Le verbe *prendre*

Note the forms of the irregular verb **prendre** *(to take)*.

	prendre	
PRESENT	Je **prends** une pizza.	Nous **prenons** le train.
	Tu **prends** un sandwich.	Vous **prenez** l'avion.
	Il/Elle/On **prend** une salade.	Ils/Elles **prennent** des photos.
PASSÉ COMPOSÉ	J'**ai pris** un steak.	

→ The singular forms follow the pattern of regular **-re** verbs. The plural forms are irregular.

VOCABULAIRE Verbes comme *prendre*

prendre	*to take*	Nous **prenons** le métro.
	to have (food)	Est-ce que tu **prends** un café?
apprendre	*to learn*	Nous **apprenons** le français.
apprendre à + *infinitive*	*to learn how to*	Sophie **apprend à** jouer de la guitare.
comprendre	*to understand*	Est-ce que vous **comprenez** l'espagnol?

4 Qu'est-ce qu'ils prennent?

PARLER/ÉCRIRE Dites ce que les personnes suivantes prennent. Pour cela, choisissez une expression logique de la liste.

un bateau	une salade
un taxi	une limonade
le bus	un steak-frites
des photos	

▶ Philippe a faim. **Il prend un steak-frites.**

1. J'ai très soif.
2. Vous n'avez pas très faim.
3. Hélène a un nouvel appareil-photo.
4. Tu vas à l'aéroport.
5. Nous allons à l'école.
6. Les touristes vont à la Statue de la Liberté.

5 Questions personnelles PARLER/ÉCRIRE

1. À quelle heure est-ce que tu prends le petit déjeuner le lundi? Et le dimanche?
2. Est-ce que tu prends le bus pour aller à l'école? Et tes copains?
3. Est-ce que tu prends des photos? Avec quel appareil?
4. Quand tu fais un grand voyage, est-ce que tu prends l'autocar? le train? l'avion?
5. Est-ce que tu apprends le français? l'italien? l'espagnol? Et ton copain?
6. Est-ce que tu apprends à jouer du piano? à jouer de la guitare? à faire du snowboard? à faire de la planche à voile?
7. Où as-tu appris à nager? À quel âge?
8. Est-ce que tu comprends quand le prof parle français? Et les autres *(other)* élèves?
9. À ton avis, est-ce que les adultes comprennent les jeunes? Est-ce que les jeunes comprennent les adultes?

C L'article partitif: *du, de la*

LEARNING ABOUT LANGUAGE

The pictures on the left represent <u>*whole*</u> items: a whole chicken, a whole cake, a whole head of lettuce, a whole fish. The nouns are introduced by INDEFINITE ARTICLES: **un, une.**

The pictures on the right represent a <u>*part*</u> or <u>*some quantity*</u> of these items: a serving of chicken, a slice of cake, some leaves of lettuce, a piece of fish. The nouns are introduced by PARTITIVE ARTICLES: **du, de la.**

Voici ...

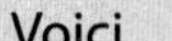

Voilà ...

un poulet

du poulet

un gâteau

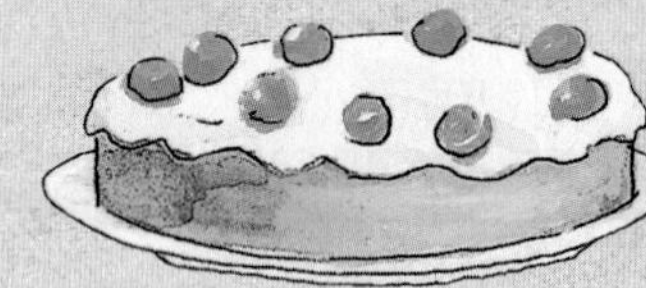

du gâteau

une salade

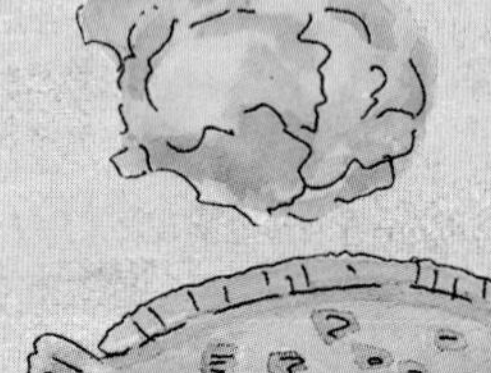

de la salade

une sole

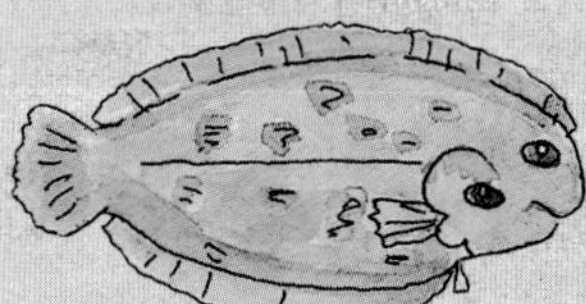

de la sole

FORMS

The PARTITIVE ARTICLE is used to refer to A CERTAIN QUANTITY or A CERTAIN AMOUNT OF SOMETHING and corresponds to the English *some* or *any*. It has the following forms:

MASCULINE	**du**	*some*	**du** fromage, **du** pain
FEMININE	**de la**	*some*	**de la** salade, **de la** limonade

→ Note that **du** and **de la** become **de l'** before a vowel sound.

de l'eau minérale

USES

Note how the partitive article is used in the sentences below.

Philippe mange **du** fromage.	*Philippe is eating (some) cheese.*
Nous prenons **de la** salade.	*We are having (some) salad.*
—Est-ce que tu veux **du** lait?	*Do you want (any, some) milk?*
—Non, mais je voudrais **de l'**eau.	*No, but I would like some water.*

→ While the words *some* or *any* are often omitted in English, the articles **du** and **de la** must be used in French.

→ Partitive articles may also be used with nouns designating things other than foods and beverages. For example:

Tu as **de l'argent?**	*Do you have (any) money?*

Partitive articles are often, but not always, used after the following expressions and verbs.

voici	**Voici du** pain.	*Here is (some) bread.*
voilà	**Voilà de la** mayonnaise.	*Here is (some) mayonnaise.*
il y a	Est-ce qu'**il y a de la** salade?	*Is there (any) salad?*
acheter	Nous **achetons du** fromage.	*We are buying (some) cheese.*
avoir	Est-ce que tu **as de la** limonade?	*Do you have (any) lemon soda?*
manger	Marc **mange du** rosbif.	*Marc is eating (some) roast beef.*
prendre	Est-ce que vous **prenez du** café?	*Are you having (any) coffee?*
vouloir	Est-ce que tu **veux de la** glace?	*Do you want (any) ice cream?*

Voici un gâteau.

Voici du gâteau.

6 Le menu

PARLER/ÉCRIRE Vous avez préparé un dîner pour le Club Français. Dites à un(e) camarade ce qu'il y a au menu.

▶ la viande **Il y a de la viande.**

1. le rosbif
2. le poulet
3. la salade
4. le fromage
5. la glace
6. la tarte
7. l'eau minérale
8. le jus d'orange

7 Au choix 

PARLER Vous déjeunez avec votre famille. Offrez aux membres de votre famille le choix entre les choses suivantes. Ils vont indiquer leurs préférences.

▶ le jus ou l'eau minérale?

Tu veux du jus ou de l'eau minérale?
Je voudrais de l'eau minérale.

1. la soupe ou la salade?
2. le poisson ou la viande?
3. le rosbif ou le poulet?
4. le ketchup ou la mayonnaise?
5. le fromage ou le yaourt?
6. le beurre ou la margarine?
7. le gâteau ou la tarte?
8. le jus d'orange ou le jus de pomme?

8 Qu'est-ce qu'on met?

PARLER/ÉCRIRE Dites quels produits de la liste on met dans ou sur les choses suivantes.

▶ **On met <u>du beurre</u> (<u>de la confiture</u>) sur le pain.**

1. On met … dans le café.
2. On met … dans le thé.
3. On met … dans la soupe.
4. On met … dans un sandwich.
5. On met … sur un hamburger.
6. On met … sur un hot dog.
7. On met … dans les céréales.
8. On met … sur un toast.

le fromage
le jambon
le beurre
la confiture
le ketchup
la mayonnaise
le sel
la crème
le sucre
la moutarde (mustard)
le lait

9 Les courses

PARLER/ÉCRIRE M. Simon a fait les courses. Dites ce qu'il a acheté.

▶ **Il a acheté de la viande.**

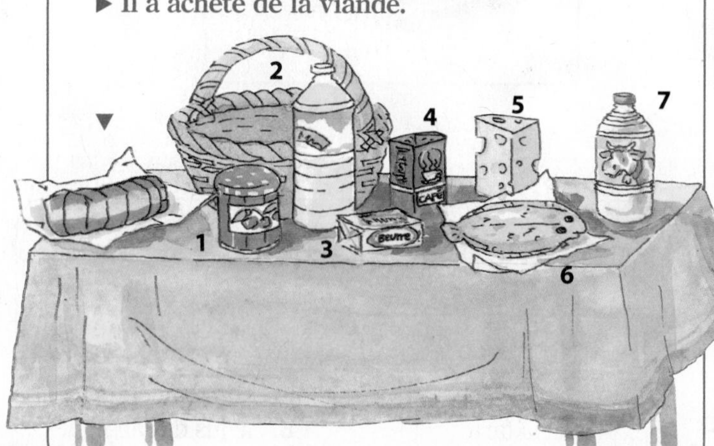

10 Le Cochon d'Or

LIRE/PARLER Émilie est allée au restaurant. Voici l'addition. Dites ce qu'elle a pris.

▶ **Émilie a pris de la salade de tomates.**

RESTAURANT
Le Cochon d'Or

salade de tomates	3€
poulet	4€
salade	3€
fromage	3€
glace	3€50
eau minérale	2€50
	19 €

11 Au café

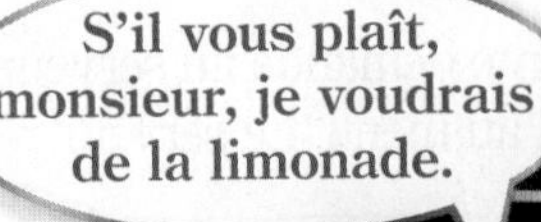

S'il vous plaît, monsieur, je voudrais de la limonade.

Voici de la limonade, mademoiselle.

PARLER Au café, une cliente commande *(orders)* les choses suivantes. Le serveur apporte ces choses.

▼

12 Menus

PARLER/ÉCRIRE Préparez des menus pour les personnes suivantes. Dites ce que vous allez acheter pour chaque personne.

▶ une personne qui aime manger
Je vais acheter du rosbif, du fromage, de la glace ...

1. une personne malade *(sick)*
2. un(e) athlète
3. un petit enfant
4. un végétarien (une végétarienne)
5. une personne qui veut maigrir
6. un invité *(guest)* japonais
7. une invitée française
8. un invité américain

D L'article partitif dans les phrases négatives

Note the forms of the partitive articles in the negative sentences below.

AFFIRMATIVE	NEGATIVE	
Tu manges **du jambon?**	Non, je **ne** mange **pas de jambon.**	*No, I don't eat ham.*
Tu veux **de la salade?**	Non, merci, je **ne** veux **pas de salade.**	*Thanks, I don't want any salad.*
Il y a **de l'eau minérale?**	Non, il **n'**y a **pas d'eau minérale.**	*No, there is no mineral water.*

In negative sentences, the PARTITIVE ARTICLE follows the pattern:

du, de la (de l') →	**ne ... pas de (d')**
Marc prend **du** café.	Éric **ne** prend **pas de** café.
Sophie prend **de la** limonade.	Alain **ne** prend **pas de** limonade.
Anne prend **de l**'eau.	Nicole **ne** prend **pas d**'eau.

13 Un mauvais restaurant

PARLER Une cliente demande au serveur s'il y a certaines choses au menu. Le serveur répond négativement.

▶ le rosbif

Est-ce que vous avez du rosbif?
Je regrette mademoiselle, mais nous n'avons pas de rosbif.

1. le jambon
2. le melon
3. le thon
4. la sole
5. le veau
6. le yaourt
7. le jus de pamplemousse
8. l'eau minérale
9. la tarte aux pommes
10. le gâteau au chocolat

14 Au régime *(On a diet)*

PARLER Les personnes suivantes sont au régime parce qu'elles veulent maigrir. Répondez négativement aux questions suivantes.

▶ —Est-ce qu'Anne mange du pain?
—**Non, elle ne mange pas de pain.**

1. Est-ce que Marc prend de la mayonnaise?
2. Est-ce que Pauline veut du gâteau?
3. Est-ce que Jean-Pierre mange de la glace?
4. Est-ce qu'Alice prend du beurre?
5. Est-ce que Monsieur Ledodu veut de la tarte?
6. Est-ce que Mademoiselle Poix met de la crème dans son café?

15 Conversation

PARLER Demandez à vos camarades s'ils mangent souvent les choses suivantes.

▶ du poisson

Est-ce que vous mangez souvent du poisson?
Oui, je mange souvent du poisson.
Non, je ne mange pas souvent de poisson.

1. de la confiture
2. du veau
3. du pain français
4. du fromage français
5. de la tarte aux fraises
6. de la soupe
7. du rosbif
8. du poulet
9. du thon
10. de la glace

16 Dans le réfrigérateur

PARLER Vous préparez le dîner. Demandez à un(e) camarade s'il y a les choses suivantes dans le réfrigérateur.

▶ le lait —**Est-ce qu'il y a du lait?**
—**Non, il n'y a pas de lait.**

1. le jus d'orange?
2. le pain?
3. la glace?
4. le beurre?
5. le jambon?
6. l'eau minérale?
7. le jus de pomme?
8. le fromage?
9. la mayonnaise?
10. le ketchup?

E Le verbe *boire*

Note the forms of the irregular verb **boire** *(to drink)*.

INFINITIVE	boire	
PRESENT	Je **bois** du lait. Tu **bois** de l'eau. Il/Elle/On **boit** du soda.	Nous **buvons** du café. Vous **buvez** du thé glacé. Ils/Elles **boivent** du jus d'orange.
PASSÉ COMPOSÉ	J'ai **bu** du jus de tomate.	

17 Les boissons

PARLER Philippe et ses amis ont soif. Chacun *(Each person)* boit quelque chose de différent. ▶ **Philippe boit de l'eau.**

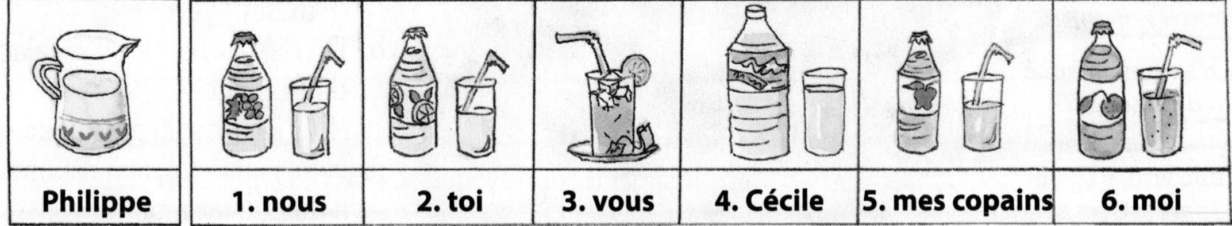

▶ Philippe | 1. nous | 2. toi | 3. vous | 4. Cécile | 5. mes copains | 6. moi

18 Expression personnelle

PARLER/ÉCRIRE Complétez les phrases suivantes avec la forme appropriée du verbe **boire** et une expression de votre choix. Attention: utilisez le passé composé dans les phrases 6 à 8.

1. Au petit déjeuner, je …
2. Au petit déjeuner, mes parents …
3. À la cantine de l'école, nous …
4. Quand il fait chaud, on …
5. Quand il fait froid, on …
6. Hier soir au dîner, j' …
7. Hier matin, au petit déjeuner, ma mère …
8. À la dernière boum, nous …

Prononciation  ou = /u/ u = /y/

Les lettres «ou» **et** «u»

The letters "**ou**" always represent the sound /u/.

Répétez: /u/ **vous nous poulet soupe fourchette couteau douzaine**

la poule

le pull

The letter "**u**" always represents the sound /y/.

Répétez: /y/ **tu du une légume jus sucre bien sûr avenue musée**

Now distinguish between the two vowel sounds:

Répétez: /u/ – /y/ **poule** *(hen)* – **pull** **roue** *(wheel)* – **rue** **vous** – **vue** *(view)* **je joue** – **le jus**

Vous buvez du jus de pamplemousse. Je voudrais de la soupe, du poulet et du jus de raisin.

À votre tour!

OBJECTIFS

Now you can . . .
- describe what you eat and drink at meals
- talk about food shopping

1 Allô!  

PARLER Reconstituez la conversation entre Frédéric et Sandrine. Pour cela, faites correspondre les réponses de Sandrine avec les questions de Frédéric.

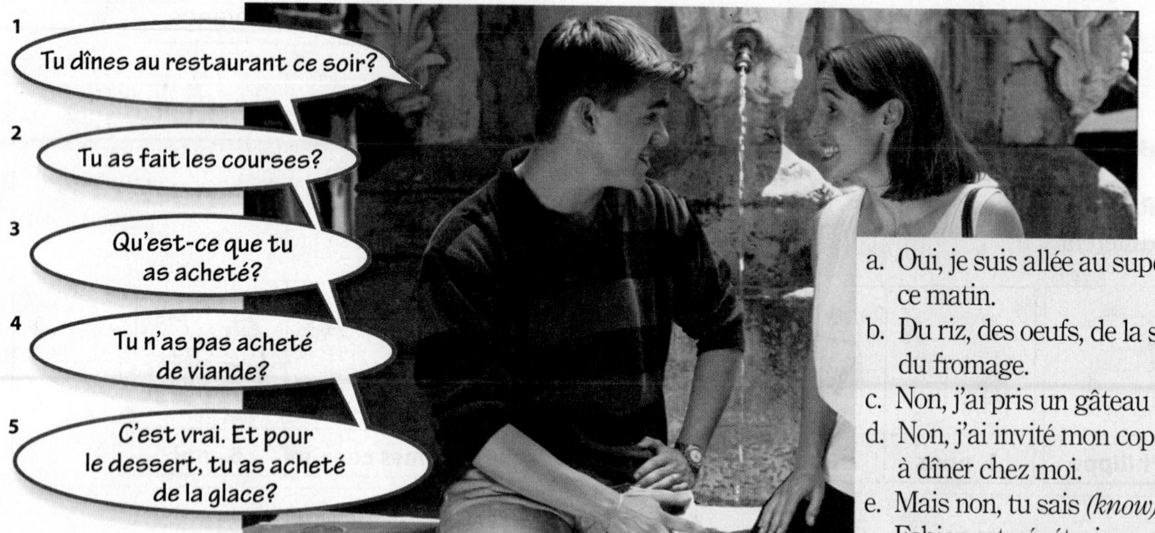

1 Tu dînes au restaurant ce soir?
2 Tu as fait les courses?
3 Qu'est-ce que tu as acheté?
4 Tu n'as pas acheté de viande?
5 C'est vrai. Et pour le dessert, tu as acheté de la glace?

a. Oui, je suis allée au supermarché ce matin.
b. Du riz, des oeufs, de la salade et du fromage.
c. Non, j'ai pris un gâteau au chocolat.
d. Non, j'ai invité mon copain Fabien à dîner chez moi.
e. Mais non, tu sais *(know)* bien que Fabien est végétarien.

2 Dis-moi . . . 

I will tell you about my breakfast this morning

- J'ai pris le petit déjeuner à sept heures.
- J'ai mangé du pain avec du beurre et de la confiture.
- J'ai bu du jus d'orange.

PARLER *Now choose one of the meals you had yesterday and tell me . . .*
- *at what time you had that meal*
- *what you ate*
- *what you drank*

3 Créa-dialogue  

PARLER Avec vos camarades, décrivez où vous êtes allé(e)s et ce que vous avez fait aux endroits suivants.

▶ **au supermarché acheter**

4 Composition: Un bon repas 

Imaginez que vous êtes allé(e) *(went)* dans un bon restaurant pour une occasion spéciale. Décrivez le repas. Voici quelques suggestions:

- Dans quel restaurant êtes-vous allé(e)?
- Avec qui et pour quelle occasion?
- Qu'est-ce que vous avez mangé comme *(as)* hors d'oeuvre?
- Comme plat principal?
- Comme dessert?
- Qu'est-ce que vous avez bu?
- Qu'est-ce que les autres (*other*) personnes ont mangé et bu?
- Est-ce que tout le monde *(everyone)* a aimé le repas?

STRATEGY Writing

Writing about food When you are writing in French about what you ate and drank at a recent meal, you have to decide whether you had a whole item (for example, **une pizza**) or whether you had a portion of that item (for example, **de la pizza**).

Before you begin your composition, make a list of the foods and beverages that you and your friends had. Then, next to each item, write the appropriate article (**un/une** or **du/de la/de l'**). Use this list as you write your composition.

un steak
du poulet

Comment dit-on ...?

How to show your appreciation for good food:

Hm ... C'est délicieux!

C'est exquis!

C'est fameux!

1. à la cantine manger	2. au restaurant manger	3. au marché acheter	4. à la boum boire

5. à la cuisine prendre	6. au café boire	7. dans un restaurant chinois ??
	? ?	? ?

Leçon 27 — Conversation et Culture

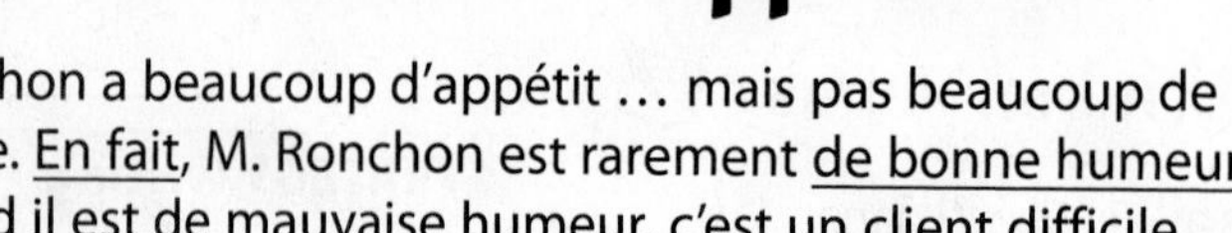

Un client difficile

DVD  AUDIO 

M. Ronchon a beaucoup d'appétit … mais pas beaucoup de patience. En fait, M. Ronchon est rarement de bonne humeur. Et quand il est de mauvaise humeur, c'est un client difficile. Aujourd'hui, par exemple, au restaurant …

En fait: As a matter of fact / de bonne humeur: in a good mood / par exemple: for instance

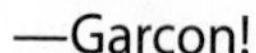

—Garçon! *(Waiter!)*

—J'arrive! *(I'm coming!)*

—Qu'est-ce que vous avez comme hors-d'oeuvre? *(comme: as, for)*

—Nous avons du jambon et du saucisson.

—Apportez-moi tout ça … avec du pain et du beurre! *(tout ça: all of that)*

—Bien, monsieur.

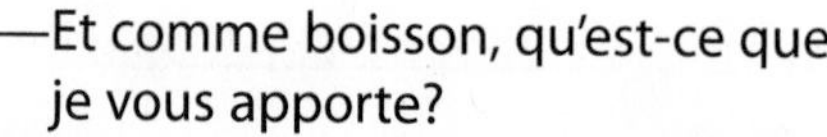

—Et comme boisson, qu'est-ce que je vous apporte?

—Donnez-moi de l'eau minérale … Dépêchez-vous! J'ai soif! *(Dépêchez-vous: Hurry up!)*

—Apportez-moi du poulet et des frites … Vite! J'ai très faim! *(Vite: Fast)*

—Je vous apporte ça tout de suite. *(tout de suite: right away)*

—Et apportez-moi aussi du fromage, de la glace, de la tarte aux pommes et de la tarte aux abricots … Mais, qu'est-ce que vous attendez? *(abricots: apricots)*

—Tout de suite, monsieur, tout de suite.

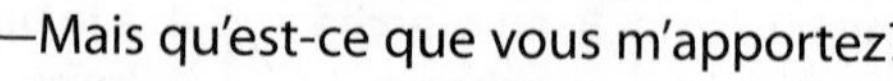

—Mais qu'est-ce que vous m'apportez?

—Je vous apporte l'addition! *(addition: check)*

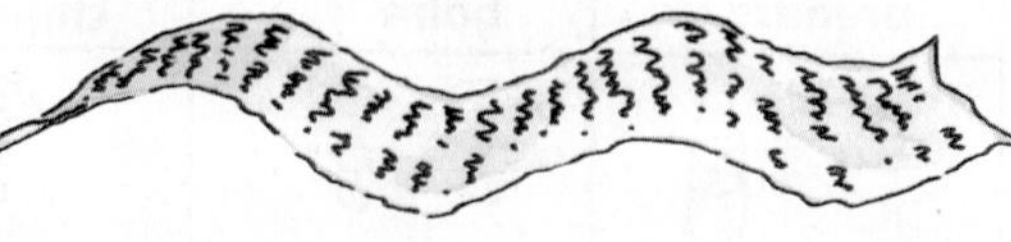

@HOMETUTOR
my.hrw.com

Compréhension

1. En général, est-ce que M. Ronchon est de bonne humeur ou de mauvaise humeur?
2. Qu'est-ce qu'il va prendre comme hors-d'oeuvre?
3. Qu'est-ce qu'il va prendre comme plat principal *(main course)*?
4. Qu'est-ce qu'il va boire?
5. Qu'est-ce qu'il va manger comme dessert?
6. Qu'est-ce que le garçon apporte après le dessert?
7. Quelle est la réaction de M. Ronchon? Est-ce qu'il est de bonne humeur ou de mauvaise humeur?

Et toi?

1. En général, est-ce que tu es de bonne humeur?
2. Et aujourd'hui, est-ce que tu es de bonne ou de mauvaise humeur?
3. En général, est-ce que tu as beaucoup d'appétit?
4. Est-ce que tu es une personne patiente?
5. Quand tu vas au restaurant avec un copain (une copine), qui paie l'addition?

NOTE Culturelle

Les restaurants français et la cuisine française

Les Français aiment manger chez eux, mais ils aiment aussi aller au restaurant. Pour les gens pressés,° il y a la restauration rapide° et les pizzerias.

Pour les gens qui veulent faire un bon repas, il y a toutes° sortes de restaurants spécialisés: auberges,° restaurants régionaux, restaurants de poisson, … Il y a aussi les «grands restaurants» où la cuisine est extraordinaire … et très chère!

La cuisine française a une réputation internationale. Pour beaucoup de personnes, c'est la meilleure° cuisine du monde.°

Les Américains ont emprunté° un grand nombre de mots° au vocabulaire de la cuisine française. Est-ce que tu connais les mots suivants: **soupe, sauce, mayonnaise, omelette, filet mignon, tarte, purée, soufflé?** Est-ce que tu aimes **les croissants? les crêpes? la mousse au chocolat?**

pressés *in a hurry* **restauration rapide** *fast food* **toutes** *all*
auberges *country inns* **meilleure** *best* **du monde** *in the world*
ont emprunté *have borrowed* **mots** *words*

INTERNET ACTIVITY

Go to the sites of restaurants in France and read their menus. Which menu/restaurant do you find tempting?

A Les pronoms compléments *me, te, nous, vous*

In the sentences below, the pronouns in heavy print are called OBJECT PRONOUNS. Note the form and the position of these pronouns in the sentences below.

Anne **me** parle.	Elle **m'**invite.	*Anne talks **to me**.*	*She invites **me**.*
Mes amis **te** parlent.	Ils **t'**invitent.	*My friends talk **to you**.*	*They invite **you**.*
Tu **nous** parles.	Tu **nous** invites.	*You talk **to us**.*	*You invite **us**.*
Je **vous** parle.	Je **vous** invite.	*I am talking **to you**.*	*I invite **you**.*

FORMS

The OBJECT PRONOUNS that correspond to the subject pronouns **je, tu, nous, vous** are:

me ↓ **m'** (+ VOWEL SOUND)	*me, to me*	**nous**	*us, to us*
te ↓ **t'** (+ VOWEL SOUND)	*you, to you*	**vous**	*you, to you*

POSITION

In French, object pronouns usually come before the verb, according to the following patterns:

AFFIRMATIVE			NEGATIVE			
SUBJECT + OBJECT PRONOUN + VERB ...			SUBJECT + **ne** + OBJECT PRONOUN + VERB + **pas** ...			
Paul	**nous**	invite.	Éric	ne	**nous**	invite **pas.**

1 D'accord! 

PARLER Demandez à vos camarades de faire les choses suivantes pour vous. Ils sont d'accord pour faire ces choses.

▸ **téléphoner ce soir?**

Tu me téléphones ce soir?
D'accord, je te téléphone ce soir.

1. téléphoner demain?
2. attendre après la classe?
3. inviter à ta fête/soirée?
4. inviter à dîner?
5. rendre visite ce week-end?
6. rendre visite cet été?
7. acheter une glace?
8. apporter un sandwich?
9. vendre ton lecteur MP3?
10. écouter?

2 Pauvre Chloé! 

PARLER Charlotte a de la chance. Sa copine Chloé n'a pas de chance. Jouez les deux rôles.

▶ **mon copain/inviter**

Mon copain m'invite.
Tu as de la chance. Mon copain ne m'invite pas.

1. ma tante/inviter au restaurant
2. mes cousins/téléphoner souvent
3. mon frère/écouter
4. mes parents/comprendre
5. mes voisins/inviter à dîner
6. ma copine/aider avec mes devoirs
7. mon grand-père/acheter des cadeaux *(gifts)*
8. mes amis/attendre après la classe

VOCABULAIRE Les services personnels 

aider quelqu'un	*to help*	J'**aide** mes copains avec les devoirs.
amener quelqu'un	*to bring*	Le taxi **amène** les touristes à la gare *(train station).*
apporter quelque chose **à** quelqu'un	*to bring*	Le serveur **apporte** le menu **aux** clients.
donner quelque chose **à** quelqu'un	*to give*	Mme Marin **donne** 10 euros **à** sa fille.
montrer quelque chose **à** quelqu'un?	*to show*	Est-ce que tu **montres** tes photos **à** ton copain?
prêter quelque chose **à** quelqu'un	*to lend, loan*	Est-ce que tu **prêtes** tes CD **à** tes amis?

3 Questions personnelles

PARLER/ÉCRIRE Réponds affirmativement ou négativement aux questions suivantes.

1. Est-ce que tes copains t'aident avec tes devoirs?
2. Est-ce que ta mère ou ton père t'aide avec les devoirs de français?
3. Est-ce que ton père ou ta mère te prête sa voiture?
4. Est-ce que ton frère ou ta soeur te prête ses CD?
5. Est-ce que tes profs te donnent des conseils *(advice)*?
6. Est-ce que ton copain te montre ses photos?
7. Est-ce que tes cousins t'apportent des cadeaux *(gifts)* quand ils viennent chez toi?
8. Est-ce que tes parents t'amènent au restaurant pour ton anniversaire?

SAMEDI devoirs

MATIÈRES	pour le	TEXTES
histoire	*lundi*	*questions 1-15 page 475*
français	*mardi*	*examen chapitre 8*

4 Bons services

PARLER/ÉCRIRE Informez-vous sur les personnes suivantes. Dites ce que leurs amis ou leurs parents font pour eux. Pour cela, complétez les phrases avec les pronoms **me (m'), te (t'), nous** ou **vous**.

▶ J'organise une boum. **Ma soeur me prête ses CD.**
▶ Nous avons faim. **Cécile nous apporte des sandwichs.**

1. Nous organisons un pique-nique. Nos copains ... aident.
2. Tu as soif. Je ... apporte un soda.
3. Vous préparez l'examen. Le prof ... donne des conseils *(advice)*.
4. J'ai besoin d'argent. Mon cousin ... prête vingt euros.
5. Tu es chez les voisins. Ils ... montrent leur appartement.
6. Nous sommes à l'hôpital. Nos amis ... rendent visite.
7. Vous êtes sympathiques. Je ... invite chez moi.
8. Nous allons prendre l'avion. Le taxi ... amène à l'aéroport.

B Les pronoms compléments à l'impératif

Compare the position and the form of the object pronouns when the verb is in the imperative.

AFFIRMATIVE	NEGATIVE
Téléphone-**moi** ce soir!	Ne **me** téléphone pas demain!
Invite-**moi** samedi!	Ne **m'**invite pas dimanche!
Apporte-**nous** du thé!	Ne **nous** apporte pas de café!

When the IMPERATIVE verb is AFFIRMATIVE, the object pronouns come *after* the verb.
→ **me** becomes **moi**
When the imperative verb is negative, the object pronouns come *before* the verb.

5 Prêts *(Loans)*

PARLER Demandez à vos copains de vous prêter les choses suivantes. Ils vont accepter.

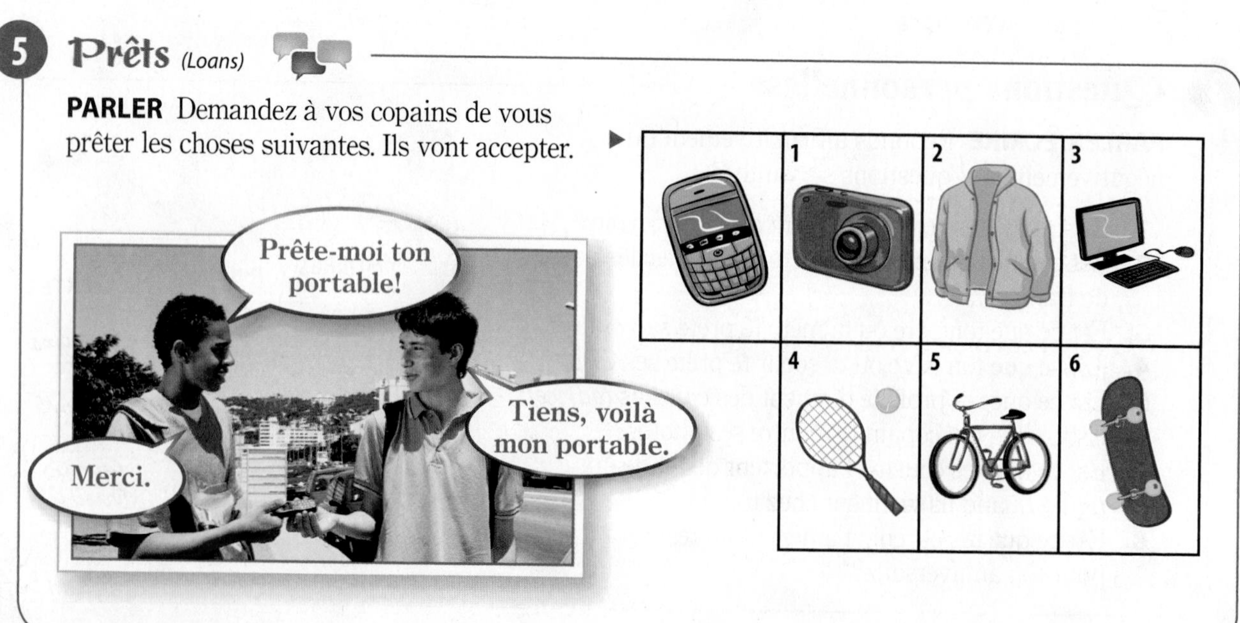
Prête-moi ton portable!
Tiens, voilà mon portable.
Merci.
▶
1
2
3
4
5
6

@HOMETUTOR my.hrw.com

6 À Paris

PARLER/ÉCRIRE Vous visitez Paris. Demandez certains services aux personnes suivantes.

▶ au garçon de café *(waiter)*
• apporter un sandwich
S'il vous plaît, apportez-moi un sandwich.

1. au garçon de café
   • apporter de l'eau
   • apporter une limonade
   • donner un croissant
2. à la serveuse *(waitress)* du restaurant
   • montrer le menu
   • donner du pain
   • apporter l'addition *(check)*
3. au chauffeur de taxi *(cab driver)*
   • amener au musée d'Orsay
   • montrer Notre-Dame
   • aider avec les bagages
4. à un copain parisien
   • téléphoner ce soir
   • donner ton adresse
   • prêter ton plan *(map)* de Paris

7 Quel service? 

PARLER Demandez à vos camarades certains services. Pour cela complétez les phrases en utilisant ces verbes.

aider	amener	apporter
donner	montrer	prêter

▶ J'ai soif. … de la limonade.
S'il te plaît, apporte-moi (donne-moi) de la limonade.

▶ J'ai faim. … un sandwich
S'il te plaît, apporte-moi (donne-moi) un sandwich.

1. Je ne comprends pas les devoirs de maths. … avec le problème.
2. Je voudrais téléphoner à ta cousine. … son numéro de téléphone.
3. Je n'ai pas d'argent pour aller au cinéma. … dix dollars.
4. Je voudrais voir tes photos. … tes photos.
5. J'ai soif. … de l'eau minérale.
6. J'organise une boum. … tes CD.
7. Je vais peindre *(to paint)* ma chambre. … avec ce projet.
8. Je vais à l'aéroport. … là-bas avec ta voiture.
9. Je ne sais pas où tu habites. … ton adresse.

8 Non! 

PARLER Proposez à vos camarades de faire les choses suivantes pour eux. Ils vont refuser et donner une explication.

▶ téléphoner ce soir (Je ne suis pas chez moi.)

1. téléphoner demain soir (Je dois faire mes devoirs.)
2. inviter ce week-end (Je vais à la campagne.)
3. inviter dimanche (Je dîne chez mes cousins.)
4. attendre après la classe (Je dois rentrer chez moi.)
5. acheter un sandwich (Je n'ai pas faim.)
6. rendre visite ce soir (Je vais au cinéma.)

Je te téléphone ce soir?
Sony
Non, ne me téléphone pas. Je ne suis pas chez moi.

C Les verbes *pouvoir* et *devoir*

FORMS

Note the forms of the irregular verbs **pouvoir** *(can, may, be able)* and **devoir** *(must, have to)*.

INFINITIVE	pouvoir		devoir	
PRESENT	Je **peux**	venir.	Je **dois**	rentrer avant midi.
	Tu **peux**	travailler.	Tu **dois**	gagner de l'argent.
	Il/Elle/On **peut**	voyager.	Il/Elle/On **doit**	visiter Paris.
	Nous **pouvons**	dîner ici.	Nous **devons**	regarder le menu.
	Vous **pouvez**	rester.	Vous **devez**	finir vos devoirs.
	Ils/Elles **peuvent**	aider.	Ils/Elles **doivent**	mettre la table.
PASSÉ COMPOSÉ	J'**ai pu**	étudier.	J'**ai dû**	faire mes devoirs.

USES

- **Pouvoir** has several English equivalents.

can	Est-ce que tu **peux** venir au pique-nique?	***Can*** *you come to the picnic?*
may	Est-ce que je **peux** prendre la voiture?	***May*** *I take the car?*
to be able	Jacques ne **peut** pas réparer sa mobylette.	*Jacques* ***is*** *not* ***able*** *to fix his moped.*

- **Devoir** is used to express an OBLIGATION.

must	Vous **devez** faire vos devoirs.	*You* ***must*** *do your homework.*
to have to	Est-ce que je **dois** ranger ma chambre?	***Do*** *I* ***have to*** *pick up my room?*

→ **Devoir** is usually followed by an infinitive. It cannot stand alone.

Est-ce que tu **dois étudier** ce soir?	*Do you* ***have to study*** *tonight?*
Oui, je **dois étudier**.	*Yes, I* ***have to (study).***
Non, je **ne dois pas étudier**.	*No, I* ***don't have to (study).***

9 Le coût de la vie *(The cost of living)*

PARLER/ÉCRIRE Décrivez ce que les personnes suivantes peuvent acheter avec leur argent.

▶ Philippe a quinze euros.
Il peut acheter des lunettes de soleil.

1. Alice et Françoise ont vingt euros.
2. J'ai cent euros.
3. Tu as soixante euros.
4. Vous avez quatre-vingts euros.
5. Ma copine a soixante-cinq euros.
6. Nous avons cinquante euros.
7. Mon frère a vingt-cinq euros.

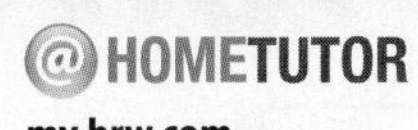
@HOMETUTOR
my.hrw.com

10 Obligations?

PARLER Demandez à vos camarades s'ils doivent faire les choses suivantes.

▶ étudier?

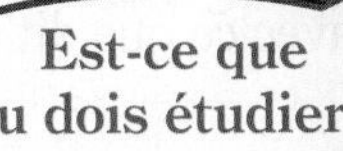
Est-ce que
tu dois étudier?

Oui, je dois
étudier.
(Non, je ne dois pas
étudier.)

1. étudier ce soir?
2. ranger ta chambre?
3. mettre la table?
4. réussir à l'examen?
5. aller chez le dentiste cette semaine?
6. parler au professeur après la classe?
7. être poli(e) *(polite)* avec tes voisins?
8. rentrer chez toi après la classe?

11 Excuses

PARLER/ÉCRIRE Thomas demande à ses amis de repeindre *(to repaint)* sa chambre avec lui, mais chacun a une excuse. Dites que les personnes suivantes ne peuvent pas aider Thomas. Dites aussi ce qu'elles doivent faire.

▶ Hélène (étudier)
Hélène ne peut pas aider Thomas.
Elle doit étudier.

1. nous (faire les courses)
2. Lise et Rose (acheter des vêtements)
3. moi (aider ma mère)
4. toi (nettoyer le garage)
5. Alice (rendre visite à sa grand-mère)
6. vous (déjeuner avec vos cousins)
7. mon frère et moi (laver la voiture)
8. Nathalie et toi (préparer l'examen)

12 Expression personnelle

PARLER/ÉCRIRE Complétez les phrases suivantes avec vos idées personnelles.

1. Chez moi, je peux …
   Je ne peux pas …
2. À l'école, nous devons …
   Nous ne devons pas …
3. À la maison, je dois …
   Mes frères (Mes soeurs) doivent …
4. Quand on est riche, on peut …
   On doit …
5. Quand on est malade *(sick)*, on doit …
   On ne doit pas …
6. Quand on veut maigrir, on doit …
   On ne peut pas …

Prononciation

s = /z/ ss = /s/

Les lettres «s» et «ss»

Be sure to distinguish between "**s**" and "**ss**" in the middle of a word.

poison **poisson**

Répétez: /z/ **mauvaise cuisine fraise mayonnaise quelque chose magasin**

/s/ **poisson saucisson dessert boisson assiette pamplemousse**

/z/–/s/ **poison – poisson désert** *(desert)* **– dessert**
Comme dessert nous choisissons une tarte aux fraises.

À votre tour!

OBJECTIFS

Now you can . . .
- ask people for favors
- say what your friends do for you

 Allô!  

PARLER Reconstituez la conversation entre Corinne et Philippe. Pour cela, faites correspondre les réponses de Philippe avec ce que dit Corinne.

Corinne
1 Dis, Philippe, j'ai besoin d'un petit service.
2 Prête-moi ta mobylette, s'il te plaît.
3 Dans ce cas, apporte-moi Paris-Match.
4 Alors, achète-moi aussi le nouvel album d'Astérix.
5 Je t'ai prêté vingt euros hier!
Philippe
a C'est vrai ... Bon, je t'achète tout ça (all that).
b D'accord! Je vais aller à la librairie (bookstore) Duchemin.
c Écoute, je n'ai pas assez d'argent.
d Ah, je ne peux pas. Je dois aller en ville cet après-midi.
e Qu'est-ce que je peux faire pour toi?

2 Créa-dialogue 

PARLER Demandez certains services à vos camarades. Ils vont vous demander pourquoi. Répondez à leurs questions. Ils vont accepter le service.

▶ —S'il te plaît, prête-moi ton vélo!
—Pourquoi?
—Parce que je voudrais faire une promenade à la campagne.
—D'accord, je te prête mon vélo.

	▶ prêter	1. prêter	2. prêter	3. apporter	4. prêter	5. donner	6. donner
QUEL SERVICE?					$5.00	$20.00	??
POURQUOI?	faire une promenade à la campagne	jouer au tennis	téléphoner à Pauline	prendre des photos	acheter une glace	??	??

3 Au restaurant 

PARLER Avec un(e) camarade, préparez un dialogue original correspondant à la situation suivante.

You are having dinner at a French restaurant called Sans-Souci. You have a friendly but inexperienced waiter/ waitress (played by your classmate) who forgets to bring you what you need. However, whenever you mention something, he/she agrees to bring it right away **(tout de suite)**.

Tell your waiter/waitress …

- to please show you the menu **(le menu)**
- to please give you some water
- to bring you a napkin
- to give you a beverage (of your choice)
- to bring you a dessert (of your choice)
- to bring you the silverware that you need for eating the dessert

Comment dit-on …?

How to show your reaction to bad food:

Pouah! … C'est infect! … C'est dégoûtant! C'est infâme!

4 Composition: Bonnes relations 

ÉCRIRE Select a person you like (a friend, a neighbor, a relative, a teacher) and write a short paragraph mentioning at least four things this person does for you. You may want to use some of the following verbs:

acheter	amener	aider
donner	inviter	montrer
prêter	rendre visite	téléphoner

J'ai une bonne copine.
Elle s'appelle Stéphanie.
Elle est très sympathique. Elle
me téléphone souvent
et le week-end, elle m'invite
chez elle. Elle est très
intelligente et quand je ne
comprends pas, elle m'aide
avec mes devoirs de français.
Elle me donne toujours
des conseils (advice) excellents.

Now tell me about a friend of yours and let me know some of the things this friend does for you.

Pique-nique

AUDIO

Mélanie et Jean-Marc organisent un pique-nique ce week-end. Ils préparent la liste des invités. Qui vont-ils inviter? — *guests*

Pique-nique:
Stéphanie
Frédéric
Fatima
Olivier
Ousmane
Sophie

Mélanie: Tu connais Stéphanie?

Jean-Marc: Oui, je la connais. C'est une copine.

Mélanie: Je l'invite au pique-nique?

Jean-Marc: Bien sûr. Invite-la.

Mélanie: Et son cousin Frédéric, tu le connais?

Jean-Marc: Oui, je le connais un peu.

Mélanie: Je l'invite aussi?

Jean-Marc: Non, ne l'invite pas. Il est trop snob.

Mélanie: Comment? Tu le trouves snob? Moi, je le trouve intelligent et sympathique. Et puis, il a une voiture et nous avons besoin d'une voiture pour transporter tout le monde …

Jean-Marc: Mélanie, tu es géniale … C'est vrai, Frédéric n'est pas aussi snob que ça … Téléphonons-lui tout de suite et invitons-le au pique-nique!

Comment? = *What?*; *puis* = *also*; *tout le monde* = *everyone*; *géniale* = *brilliant*; *aussi snob que ça* = *that snobbish*; *tout de suite* = *right away*

NOTE Culturelle

Un pique-nique français

Quand ils vont à la campagne, les Français adorent faire des pique-niques. Un pique-nique est un repas froid assez simple. Il y a généralement du poulet froid et des oeufs durs° et aussi du jambon, du saucisson ou du pâté* pour les sandwichs. Quand on a l'équipement nécessaire, on peut aussi faire des grillades° sur un barbecue. Comme dessert, il y a des fruits (bananes, oranges, pommes, poires, raisin°). Comme boisson, il y a de l'eau minérale, des sodas et des jus de fruit.

*The French have created dozens of varieties of **pâté**, ranging from the expensive and refined **foie gras** (made from the livers of fattened geese) to the everyday **pâté de campagne** (a type of cold meat loaf served in thin slices with bread).

durs *hard-boiled* **grillades** *grilled meat* **raisin** *grapes* *(Note that* **raisin** *is always in the singular.)*

Compréhension

1. Qui est Stéphanie?
2. Qui est Frédéric?
3. Est-ce que Jean-Marc a une bonne ou une mauvaise opinion de Frédéric? Pourquoi?
4. Et Mélanie, comment est-ce qu'elle trouve Frédéric?
5. Finalement, est-ce que Jean-Marc va inviter Frédéric au pique-nique? Pourquoi?

Et toi?

1. Est-ce que tu aimes faire des pique-niques?
2. Quand tu fais un pique-nique avec des copains, où allez-vous?
3. Qui invites-tu?
4. En général, qu'est-ce qu'on mange à un pique-nique américain?
5. Qu'est-ce qu'on boit?
6. Dans ta famille, est-ce qu'on fait des barbecues? Où? Qui est le «chef»? Qu'est-ce qu'on mange et qu'est-ce qu'on boit?

A Le verbe *connaître*

Note the forms of the irregular verb **connaître** *(to know)*.

INFINITIVE	connaître	
PRESENT	Je **connais** Stéphanie. Tu **connais** son cousin? Il/Elle/On **connaît** ces garçons.	Nous **connaissons** Paris. Vous **connaissez** Montréal? Ils/Elles **connaissent** ce café.
PASSÉ COMPOSÉ	**J'ai connu** ton frère pendant les vacances.	

→ In the passé composé, **connaître** means to *meet for the first time.*

→ The French use **connaître** to say that they *know* or *are acquainted with people or places.* To say that they *know information,* they use **je sais, tu sais.** Compare:

PEOPLE/PLACES	INFORMATION
Je **connais** Éric.	Je **sais** où il habite.
Tu **connais** Frédéric.	Tu **sais** à quelle heure il vient?
Je **connais** un bon restaurant.	Je **sais** qu'il est près du théâtre.

Je connais Éric.

Je sais où il habite.

1 On ne peut pas tout connaître

PARLER/ÉCRIRE Les personnes suivantes connaissent la première personne ou la première chose entre parenthèses. Elles ne connaissent pas la deuxième.

▶ Philippe (Isabelle/sa soeur)
Philippe connaît Isabelle.
Il ne connaît pas sa soeur.

1. nous (Paul/ses copains)
2. vous (le prof d'anglais/le prof de maths)
3. moi (les voisins/leurs amis)
4. toi (Paris/Bordeaux)
5. les touristes (le Louvre/le musée d'Orsay)
6. mon copain (ce café/ce restaurant)

2 Questions personnelles PARLER/ÉCRIRE

1. Est-ce que tu connais New York? Chicago? San Francisco? Montréal? Quelles villes est-ce que tu connais bien?
2. Dans ta ville est-ce que tu connais un bon restaurant? Comment est-ce qu'il s'appelle? Est-ce que tu connais un supermarché? un centre commercial? Comment est-ce qu'ils s'appellent?
3. Est-ce que tu connais des monuments à Paris? Quels monuments?
4. Est-ce que tu connais bien tes voisins? Est-ce qu'ils sont sympathiques? Est-ce que tu connais personnellement le directeur (la directrice) de ton école? Est-ce qu'il (elle) est strict(e)?
5. Quels acteurs de cinéma est-ce que tu connais? Quelles actrices? Quels musiciens? Quels athlètes professionnels?

@HOMETUTOR
my.hrw.com

B Les pronoms compléments: *le, la, les*

In the questions below, the nouns in heavy type follow the verb directly. They are the DIRECT OBJECTS of the verb. Note the forms and position of the DIRECT OBJECT PRONOUNS which are used to replace those nouns in the answers.

Tu connais **Éric?**	Oui, je **le** connais. Je **l'**invite souvent.	*Yes, I know* ***him****.* *I invite* ***him*** *often.*
Tu connais **Stéphanie?**	Oui, je **la** connais. Je **l'**invite aussi.	*Yes, I know* ***her****.* *I invite* ***her*** *also.*
Tu connais **mes copains?**	Je **les** connais bien. Je **les** invite.	*I know* ***them*** *well.* *I invite* ***them****.*
Tu connais **mes amies?**	Je **les** connais aussi. Je **les** invite souvent.	*I know* ***them*** *too.* *I invite* ***them*** *often.*

FORMS AND USES

Direct object pronouns have the following forms:

	SINGULAR		PLURAL
MASCULINE	**le** ↓ **l'** (+ VOWEL SOUND)	*him, it*	**les** *them*
FEMININE	**la** ↓ **l'** (+ VOWEL SOUND)	*her, it*	

→ The direct object pronouns **le, la, l', les** can refer to either people or things.

Tu vois **Nicole?**	Oui, je **la** vois.	*Yes, I see* ***her.***
Tu vois **ma voiture?**	Oui, je **la** vois.	*Yes, I see* ***it.***
Tu comprends **le professeur?**	Oui, je **le** comprends.	*Yes, I understand* ***him.***
Tu comprends **ce mot** *(word)*?	Oui, je **le** comprends.	*Yes, I understand* ***it.***

POSITION

Direct object pronouns generally come *before* the verb according to the following patterns:

	AFFIRMATIVE			NEGATIVE				
	SUBJECT + **le/la/les** + VERB …			SUBJECT + **ne** + **le/la/les** + VERB + **pas** …				
Éric?	Je	**le**	connais bien.	Tu	**ne**	**le**	connais	**pas.**
Ces filles?	Nous	**les**	invitons.	Vous	**ne**	**les**	invitez	**pas.**

3 À la boum de Delphine

PARLER Pierre connaît tous les invités *(all the guests)* à la boum de Delphine, mais Lise ne les connaît pas. Jouez les trois rôles.

▶ ces garçons?

Tu connais ces garçons?
Oui, je les connais.
Et toi, Lise?
Non, je ne les connais pas.

1. Christophe?
2. Jacqueline?
3. Anne et Valérie?
4. Jérôme et Jean-François?
5. la fille là-bas?
6. cette étudiante?
7. ma cousine?
8. les cousins de Véronique?
9. la copine de Jacques?
10. ses frères?

4 Un choix difficile

PARLER Vous allez passer le mois de juillet en France. Vous êtes limité(e) à 20 kilos de bagages. Un(e) camarade demande si vous allez prendre les choses suivantes. Répondez affirmativement ou négativement.

▶ ta raquette?
—Tu prends ta raquette?
—Oui, je la prends.
(Non, je ne la prends pas.)

1. ta tablette?
2. ton livre de français?
3. ta guitare?
4. ton MP3?
5. tes magazines?
6. ton maillot de bain?
7. ton skate?
8. tes tee-shirts?
9. tes sandales?

5 Questions et réponses

PARLER Julien pose des questions à Luc en utilisant les éléments des colonnes A et B. Jérôme répond logiquement en utilisant les éléments des colonnes B et C et un pronom complément. Avec un(e) camarade, jouez les deux rôles.

A	B	C
où	rencontrer tes copains	le samedi matin
quand	voir ta cousine	à 8 heures du matin
à quelle heure	regarder la télé	à 9 heures du soir
	ranger ta chambre	à Mod' Shop
	faire les courses	au café Le Pont Neuf
	acheter tes vêtements	dans un supermarché
	prendre le petit déjeuner	le week-end
		pendant les vacances
		dans la cuisine
		dans le salon

@HOMETUTOR
my.hrw.com

C La place des pronoms à l'impératif

Note the position of the object pronoun when the verb is in the imperative.

	AFFIRMATIVE COMMAND	NEGATIVE COMMAND
J'invite **Frédéric?**	Oui, invite-**le!**	Non, ne **l'**invite pas!
Je prends **la guitare?**	Oui, prends-**la!**	Non, ne **la** prends pas!
J'achète **les sandales?**	Oui, achète-**les!**	Non, ne **les** achète pas!

In AFFIRMATIVE COMMANDS, the object pronoun comes *after* the verb and is joined to it by a hyphen.
In NEGATIVE COMMANDS, the object pronoun comes *before* the verb.

6 Invitations

PARLER/ÉCRIRE Vous préparez une liste de personnes à inviter à une boum. Vous êtes limité(e)s à quatre *(4)* des personnes suivantes. Faites vos suggestions d'après les modèles.

▶ Caroline est sympathique.
Invitons-la!
▶ Jean-Louis est pénible.
Ne l'invitons pas!

1. Sylvie est très sympathique.
2. Cécile et Anne aiment danser.
3. Jacques est stupide.
4. Robert joue bien de la guitare.
5. Ces filles sont intelligentes.
6. Martin et Thomas sont snobs.
7. Nicolas n'est pas mon ami.
8. Ces garçons sont pénibles.
9. Cette fille est gentille.
10. Tes copains sont méchants.

7 Le pique-nique

PARLER Élodie demande à Mathieu si elle doit prendre certaines choses pour le pique-nique.

▶ ma guitare (oui)

Est-ce que je prends ma guitare?
Oui, prends-la!

1. la limonade (oui)
2. les sandwichs (non)
3. la salade (oui)
4. le lait (non)
5. le gâteau (non)
6. mon appareil-photo (oui)
7. mes lunettes de soleil (oui)
8. les impers (non)

8 Oui ou non?

PARLER Votre petit cousin de Québec passe deux semaines chez vous. Il vous demande s'il doit ou peut faire les choses suivantes. Répondez affirmativement ou négativement.

1. Je fais les courses?
2. Je regarde tes photos?
3. Je range ma chambre?
4. J'achète le journal *(newspaper)*?
5. J'invite les voisins à déjeuner?
6. Je prépare le dîner?
7. Je prends ton vélo?
8. Je loue les DVD?
9. J'aide ta mère?
10. Je mets la télé?

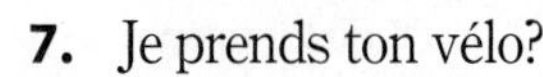

Je fais les devoirs?
Oui, fais-les.
(Non, ne les fais pas.)
QUÉBEC

D Les pronoms compléments *lui, leur*

In the questions below, the nouns in heavy type are INDIRECT OBJECTS. These nouns represent PEOPLE and are introduced by **à.**

Note the forms and position of the corresponding INDIRECT OBJECT PRONOUNS in the answers on the right.

Tu téléphones **à Philippe?**	Oui, je **lui** téléphone.
Tu parles **à Juliette?**	Non, je ne **lui** parle pas.
Tu téléphones **à tes amis?**	Oui, je **leur** téléphone.
Tu prêtes ton vélo **à tes cousines?**	Non, je ne **leur** prête pas mon vélo.

FORMS

INDIRECT OBJECT pronouns replace **à** + noun representing people. They have the following forms:

	SINGULAR	PLURAL
MASCULINE/FEMININE	**lui** *to him, to her*	**leur** *to them*

POSITION

Like other object pronouns, **lui** and **leur** come before the verb, except in affirmative commands.

Voici Henri. Parle-**lui!** Prête-**lui** ton vélo!

→ In negative sentences, **lui** and **leur,** like other object pronouns, come between **ne** and the verb.

Voici Éric.	Je ne **lui** téléphone pas.
Voici mes voisins.	Je ne **leur** parle pas.

9 Au téléphone 

PARLER Demandez à vos camarades s'ils téléphonent aux personnes suivantes.

▶ ta copine

pharmacie
Tu téléphones à ta copine?
cosmetologie
homéopathie
Oui, je lui téléphone.
(Non, je ne lui téléphone pas.)

1. ton copain
2. tes cousins
3. ta grand-mère
4. ton prof de français
5. tes voisins
6. ta tante favorite

@HOMETUTOR
my.hrw.com

VOCABULAIRE Verbes suivis *(followed)* d'un complément indirect

parler à	*to speak, talk (to)*	Je **parle à** mon copain.
rendre visite à	*to visit*	Nous **rendons visite à** nos voisins.
répondre à	*to answer*	Tu **réponds au** professeur.
téléphoner à	*to phone, call*	Jérôme **téléphone à** Juliette.
demander à	*to ask*	Je ne **demande** pas d'argent **à** mes frères.
donner à	*to give (to)*	Tu **donnes** ton adresse **à** ta copine.
montrer à	*to show (to)*	Nous **montrons** nos photos **à** nos amis.
prêter à	*to lend, loan (to)*	Je ne **prête** pas mon baladeur **à** ma soeur.

➔ **Répondre** is a regular **-re** verb.
Je réponds à François. **J'ai répondu** à Catherine.

➔ The verbs **téléphoner, répondre,** and **demander** take indirect objects in French, but not in English. Compare:

téléphoner	Nous **téléphonons**	**à**	Paul.	Nous **lui téléphonons.**
	*We **are calling***	…	*Paul.*	*We **are calling him.***

répondre	Tu **réponds**	**à**	tes parents.	Tu **leur réponds.**
	*You **answer***	…	*your parents.*	*You **answer them.***

demander	Je **demande**	**à**	Sylvie	…	son stylo.	Je **lui demande** son stylo.
	*I **am asking***	…	*Sylvie*	*for*	*her pen.*	*I **am asking her** for her pen.*

10 Les copains de Léa

PARLER/ÉCRIRE Léa a beaucoup de copains. Décrivez ce que chacun fait pour elle. Complétez les phrases avec **Léa** ou **à Léa.**

▸ Françoise invite Léa.
Patrick rend visite à Léa.

1. Marc téléphone …
2. Jean-Paul voit … samedi prochain.
3. Sophie prête son vélo …
4. Mélanie écoute …
5. François donne son adresse …
6. Philippe regarde … pendant la classe.
7. Antoine attend … après la classe.
8. Nathalie parle …
9. Pauline invite … au concert.
10. Pierre répond …
11. Céline montre ses photos …
12. Thomas demande … son numéro de téléphone.
13. Éric rend visite …

11 Joyeux anniversaire!

PARLER Choisissez un cadeau d'anniversaire pour les personnes suivantes. Un(e) camarade va vous demander ce que vous donnez à chaque personne.

▶ à ton copain

Qu'est-ce que tu donnes à ton copain?
Je lui donne un livre.

1. à ton petit frère
2. à ta mère
3. à ta grand-mère
4. à ta copine
5. à tes cousins
6. à ton (ta) prof
7. à tes copains

Cadeaux
- un pull
- un jeu vidéo
- une cravate
- un livre
- des billets *(tickets)* de théâtre
- un magazine
- ma photo
- une boîte *(box)* de chocolats
- un gâteau
- ??

12 Questions personnelles

PARLER/ÉCRIRE Réponds aux questions suivantes. Utilise **lui** ou **leur** dans tes réponses.

1. Le week-end, est-ce que tu rends visite à tes copains? à ton oncle?
2. Est-ce que tu prêtes tes livres à ta soeur? à ton frère? à tes copains?
3. Est-ce que tu demandes de l'argent à ton père? à ta mère?
4. Est-ce que tu demandes des conseils *(advice)* à tes parents? à tes professeurs?
5. Est-ce que tu donnes de bons conseils à tes copains?
6. Est-ce que tu montres tes photos à ton frère? à ta soeur? à ta copine? à ton copain? à tes cousins?
7. En classe, est-ce que tu réponds en français à ton professeur?
8. Quand tu as un problème, est-ce que tu parles à tes copains? à ton professeur? à tes grands-parents? à tes parents?

E Les verbes *dire et écrire*

Note the forms of the irregular verbs **dire** *(to say, tell)* and **écrire** *(to write)*.

INFINITIVE	dire	écrire
PRESENT	je **dis**	j' **écris**
	tu **dis**	tu **écris**
	il/elle/on **dit**	il/elle/on **écrit**
	nous **disons**	nous **écrivons**
	vous **dites**	vous **écrivez**
	ils/elles **disent**	ils/elles **écrivent**
PASSÉ COMPOSÉ	**j'ai dit**	**j'ai écrit**

→ Note the use of **que/qu'** *(that)* after **dire** and **écrire.**

Florence **dit que** Frédéric est sympathique. — *Florence **says (that)** Frédéric is nice.*
Alain **écrit qu'**il est allé à un pique-nique. — *Alain **writes (that)** he went on a picnic.*

→ **Décrire** *(to describe)* follows the same pattern as **écrire.**

@HOMETUTOR
my.hrw.com

13 Correspondance

PARLER/ÉCRIRE Pendant les vacances, on écrit beaucoup de lettres. Dites à qui les personnes suivantes écrivent.

▶ Juliette/à Marc
Juliette écrit à Marc.

1. nous/à nos copains
2. toi/à ta cousine
3. moi/à ma grand-mère
4. Nicolas/à ses voisins
5. vous/à vos parents
6. les élèves/au professeur

14 La boum

PARLER/ÉCRIRE Des amis sont à une boum. Décrivez ce que chacun dit.

▶ toi/la musique est super
Tu dis que la musique est super.

1. Nicole/les sandwichs sont délicieux
2. nous/les invités *(guests)* sont sympathiques
3. Pauline/Jérôme danse bien
4. moi/ces garçons dansent mal
5. vous/vous n'aimez pas ce CD
6. mes copains/ils vont organiser une soirée le week-end prochain

15 Questions personnelles PARLER/ÉCRIRE

1. Est-ce que tu aimes écrire?
2. Pendant les vacances, est-ce que tu écris à tes copains? à tes voisins? à ton(ta) meilleur(e) *(best)* ami(e)?
3. À Noël, est-ce que tu écris des cartes *(cards)*? À qui?
4. À qui as-tu écrit un mail récemment *(recently)*?
5. Est-ce que tu dis toujours la vérité *(truth)*?
6. À ton avis, est-ce que les journalistes disent toujours la vérité? Et les politiciens?

Prononciation 

on = /ɔ̃/ on(n)e = /ɔn/

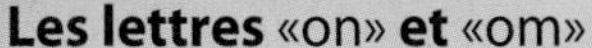

Les lettres «on» et «om»

Be sure to distinguish between the nasal and non-nasal vowel sounds.

REMEMBER: Do not pronounce an /n/ or /m/ after the nasal vowel /ɔ̃/.

lion

lionne

Répétez: /ɔ̃/ **mon ton son bon avion montrer répondre invitons blouson**

/ɔn/ **téléphone Simone donner connais mayonnaise personne bonne**

/ɔm/ **fromage promenade tomate pomme dommage comment**

/ɔ̃/–/ɔn/ **lion–lionne bon–bonne Simon–Simone Yvon–Yvonne**

Monique donne une pomme à Raymond.
Simone connaît mon oncle Léon.

À votre tour!

OBJECTIFS

Now you can . . .
- talk about people you know and don't know
- use pronouns to refer to people and things

1 Allô!

PARLER Reconstituez la conversation entre Olivier et Sophie. Pour cela, faites correspondre les réponses de Sophie avec les questions d'Olivier.

1 Qu'est-ce que tu fais ce week-end?
2 Tu m'invites?
3 Et Catherine? Tu l'invites aussi?
4 C'est ma nouvelle copine.
5 Tu veux son numéro de téléphone?
6 C'est le 01.44.32.28.50.

a. Je lui téléphone tout de suite *(right away)*.
b. Oui, je ne l'ai pas.
c. Bien sûr, je t'invite.
d. J'organise une fête.
e. Catherine? Je ne la connais pas. Qui est-ce?
f. Ah oui, je vois qui c'est maintenant. Eh bien, d'accord! Je l'invite.

2 Créa-dialogue

PARLER Avec vos camarades, discutez de certaines choses que vous faites. Posez plusieurs questions sur chaque activité.

▶ regarder la télé?	1. inviter tes amis?	2. voir tes cousins?
à quelle heure?	quand? à quelle occasion?	quand? où?

3. faire les courses?	4. aider ta mère?	5. faire tes devoirs?	6. téléphoner à tes copains?	7. rendre visite à ta grand-mère?	8. écrire à ton cousin?
quand? où?	quand? comment?	quand? où?	quand? pourquoi?	quand? pourquoi?	pourquoi?

3 Composition: Les personnes dans ma vie *(life)*

Select three people from the list and write a short paragraph about each one. Give their names, say when you see them, and describe several things you do for them as well as one thing that you can't do. In your descriptions use the suggested verbs … and your imagination!

- un cousin/une cousine
- un frère/une soeur
- un copain/une copine
- un voisin/une voisine
- mon meilleur *(best)* ami
- ma meilleure amie
- un professeur de français (d'anglais, de maths, d'histoire)

téléphoner	voir	prêter	inviter
écrire	connaître	donner	rendre visite
répondre	parler	aider	

Ma cousine s'appelle Denise. Je lui écris des mails et elle me répond toujours. Je la vois...

Comment dit-on ...?

How to tell someone to leave you alone:

Laisse-moi tranquille!

Fiche-moi la paix!

Tests de contrôle

By taking the following tests, you can check your progress in French and also prepare for the unit test. Write your answers on a separate sheet of paper.

Review...
- foods and beverages: pp. 366-367
- partitive article: pp. 378-379

1 Foods and beverages

Give the names of the foods and beverages you see on the table. With each one, be sure to use the appropriate partitive article: **du, de la,** or **de l'.**

Sur la table, il y a ...

1. __	**3.** __	**5.** __	**7.** __	**9.** __
2. __	**4.** __	**6.** __	**8.** __	**10.** __

Review...
- new verbs: pp. 364, 370, 377, 383, 389, and 404

2 The right choice

Complete each of the following sentences with the appropriate forms of the verbs in the box. Be logical in your choice of verbs and do not use the same word more than once.

apprendre
boire
comprendre
déjeuner
donner
écrire
faire
montrer
prendre
prêter

1. Caroline — ses photos de vacances à sa copine.
2. Madame Durand — au restaurant La Marmite.
3. Monsieur Lemaire — les courses au supermarché Prisunic.
4. À la piscine, mon petit frère — à nager.
5. Les gens généreux — de l'argent aux pauvres *(poor people)*.
6. Nicolas — un mail à sa cousine.
7. Est-ce que tu — bien quand le professeur parle français?
8. Au petit déjeuner, je — du jus d'orange.
9. Pauline — des photos avec son nouvel appareil-photo.
10. Catherine — souvent son vélo à sa soeur.

3 The right verb

Complete the following sentences with the appropriate forms of the present tense of the verb in parentheses.

(vouloir) **1.** Cécile — voyager. Ses copines — visiter Paris.

(prendre) **2.** Les touristes — le train. Nous — le bus.

(apprendre) **3.** Élodie — l'anglais. Ses copains — l'espagnol.

(boire) **4.** Nous — du thé. Les enfants — du lait.

(pouvoir) **5.** Mes amis — venir à la boum. Est-ce que vous — rester?

(devoir) **6.** Éric — étudier. Nous — aider nos parents.

(connaître) **7.** Isabelle — Céline. Nous — ses copains.

(écrire) **8.** Tu — une lettre. Mes cousins — un mail.

(dire) **9.** Je — «oui». Mais vous, vous — «non».

Review...
- irregular verbs: pp. 376, 377, 383, 392, 398, and 404

4 The right pronoun

Complete the following sentences with the appropriate pronoun in parentheses that replaces the underlined words.

▶ Je connais <u>Céline</u>. Je **la** connais. **(le, la)**

1. Nous invitons <u>Pierre</u>. Nous — invitons à la boum. **(l', le)**
2. Tu écris <u>à Charlotte</u>. Tu — écris. **(la, lui)**
3. J'aide <u>mes parents</u>. Je — aide. **(l', les)**
4. Vous téléphonez <u>à Mathieu</u>. Vous — téléphonez souvent. **(le, lui)**
5. J'écoute <u>mes CD</u>. Je — écoute. **(les, leur)**
6. Nous parlons <u>à nos amis</u>. Nous — parlons. **(les, leur)**
7. Tu regardes <u>ces photos</u>. Tu — regardes avec Léa. **(les, leur)**
8. Vous lavez <u>la voiture</u>. Vous — lavez. **(la, lui)**

Review...
- object pronouns: pp. 399 and 402

5 Composition: Mon repas d'anniversaire

Digital performance space

Write a short paragraph of five or six sentences describing what you would like for a special birthday dinner. Use only vocabulary and expressions that you know in French.

STRATEGY Writing

a First write out your menu.

b Then plan your paragraph, perhaps explaining why you are choosing certain items.

c Read over your composition to check that you are using the correct article with each food item.

hors d'oeuvre: ______________
viande ou poisson: ______________
autres plats: ______________
____
dessert: ______________
boissons: ______________

Vocabulaire

POUR COMMUNIQUER

Saying where you will eat

Je vais déjeuner	**à la maison.**	*I will have lunch*	*at home.*
	à la cantine (de l'école)		*at the (school) cafeteria*
	au restaurant		*at the restaurant*

Planning a meal

Il faut ...

aller au marché	*go to the market*
faire les courses	*do the food shopping*
acheter la nourriture	*buy the food*
choisir les boissons	*choose the beverages*
préparer le repas	*fix the meal*
faire la cuisine	*do the cooking*
mettre le couvert	*set the table*

Saying what foods you like and dislike

J'aime [le rosbif].	*I like roast beef.*
Je préfère [la glace].	*I prefer ice cream.*
Je déteste [les frites].	*I detest French fries.*

Shopping for food, asking for certain quantities

Je voudrais ...

du beurre	*(some) butter*	**une livre de beurre**	*a pound of butter.*
de la sole	*(some) sole*	**un kilo de sole**	*a kilo (2.2 pounds) of sole*
des oeufs	*(some) eggs*	**une douzaine d'oeufs**	*a dozen eggs*

MOTS ET EXPRESSIONS

Les repas *(Meals)*

le petit déjeuner	*breakfast*	**prendre le petit déjeuner**	*to have breakfast*
le déjeuner	*lunch*	**déjeuner**	*to have lunch*
le dîner	*dinner*	**dîner**	*to have dinner*

Le couvert *(Place settings)*

un couteau	*knife*	**une assiette**	*plate*
un verre	*glass*	**une cuillère**	*spoon*
		une fourchette	*fork*
		une serviette	*napkin*
		une tasse	*cup*

La nourriture et les plats

un dessert	*dessert*	**le poulet**	*chicken*	**les céréales**	*cereal*
le fromage	*cheese*	**le riz**	*rice*	**les frites**	*French fries*
le gâteau	*cake*	**le rosbif**	*roast beef*	**la glace**	*ice cream*
un hors-d'oeuvre	*appetizer*	**le saucisson**	*salami*	**la nourriture**	*food*
le jambon	*ham*	**les spaghetti**	*spaghetti*	**la salade**	*salad*
le pain	*bread*	**le thon**	*tuna*	**la sole**	*sole*
un plat	*dish*	**le veau**	*veal*	**la soupe**	*soup*
le poisson	*fish*	**le yaourt**	*yogurt*	**la tarte**	*pie*
				la viande	*meat*

Interactive Flashcards
@HOMETUTOR
my.hrw.com

Les fruits et les légumes

un fruit	*fruit*	**une banane**	*banana*	**une poire**	*pear*
des haricots verts	*green beans*	**une carotte**	*carrot*	**une pomme**	*apple*
un légume	*vegetable*	**une cerise**	*cherry*	**une pomme de terre**	*potato*
un pamplemousse	*grapefruit*	**une fraise**	*strawberry*	**une salade**	*(head of) lettuce*
des petits pois	*peas*	**une orange**	*orange*	**une tomate**	*tomato*

Les ingrédients

le beurre	*butter*	**la confiture**	*jam*
le ketchup	*ketchup*	**la mayonnaise**	*mayonnaise*
un oeuf	*egg*		
le sel	*salt*		
le sucre	*sugar*		

Les boissons

le jus d'orange	*orange juice*	**une boisson**	*beverage*
le jus de pomme	*apple juice*	**l'eau**	*water*
le lait	*milk*	**l'eau minérale**	*mineral water*
le thé glacé	*iced tea*		

Interacting with others

Est-ce que Paul	**me**	**connaît?**	*Does Paul know*	*me ?*
	te			*you?*
	nous			*us?*
	vous			*you?*
	le			*him?*
	la			*her?*
	les			*them?*
Est-ce que Sophie	**me**	**parle?**	*Is Sophie talking*	*to me?*
	te			*to you?*
	nous			*to us?*
	vous			*to you?*
	lui			*to him/her?*
	leur			*to them?*

Verbes réguliers

aider	*to help*
amener	*to bring (people)*
apporter	*to bring (things)*
demander (à)	*to ask*
donner (à)	*to give (to)*
montrer (à)	*to show (to)*
prêter (à)	*to lend, to loan (to)*
répondre (à)	*to answer*

Verbes irréguliers

apprendre	*to learn*
apprendre à + *infinitive*	*to learn how to*
boire	*to drink*
comprendre	*to understand*
connaître	*to know*
décrire	*to describe*
devoir	*must, to have to*
dire	*to say, to tell*
écrire (à)	*to write (to)*
pouvoir	*can, may, to be able*
prendre	*to take, to have (a meal)*
vouloir	*to want*

Bon appétit, Aurélie!

Nous avons demandé à Aurélie de décrire ses repas. Voici sa réponse.

À midi, je mange à la cantine de l'école et le soir à la maison. C'est ma mère qui fait les courses et c'est mon père qui prépare le dîner. Il adore ça! Il fait une cuisine assez traditionnelle, mais bien équilibrée.° En général, on commence par une salade de concombres ou de tomates. Ensuite, il y a de la viande, par exemple, un bifteck ou du poulet, avec des haricots verts ou des pommes de terre. Parfois, on mange du cassoulet° en boîte.° Après, il y a une salade verte et des fromages divers. Comme dessert, il y a du yaourt ou un fruit. Avec le repas, on boit de l'eau minérale.

Quand mon père n'a pas envie de faire la cuisine, on va au restaurant. Dans notre quartier, il y a un restaurant vietnamien que nous aimons bien. Mon plat préféré, c'est le riz avec des crevettes° et des petits pois.

Quand je sors avec mes copains, on va dans les fast-food. J'aime bien aller dans les pizzerias parce qu'on peut choisir ses ingrédients. En général, je prends une pizza avec du fromage, des olives et des anchois. Avec la pizza, je bois souvent un soda.

PIZZA PIZZA PIZZA PIZZA PIZZA

équilibrée *balanced*
cassoulet *bean stew with pork or duck*
en boîte *canned* **crevettes** *shrimp*

COMPARAISONS *Culturelles*

Comparez les repas d'Aurélie avec vos repas. Qu'est-ce que vous mangez pour le dîner? Faites une liste des similarités et des différences.

	AURÉLIE	LES SIMILARITÉS AVEC MOI	LES DIFFÉRENCES AVEC MOI
À la maison	________	________	________
Au restaurant avec la famille	________	________	________
Au restaurant avec les copains	________	________	________

Additional readings @ my.hrw.com
FRENCH InterActive Reader

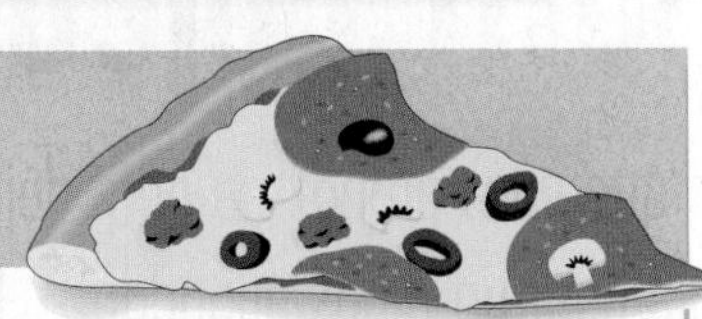

ALLOpizza

MENU

		26 cm. 1 pers.	31 cm. 2/3 pers.	40 cm. 3/4 pers.
ITALIENNE	sauce tomate, origan, mozzarella, anchois, olives	7,50 €	12 €	15 €
4 SAISONS	sauce tomate, mozzarella, crème, olives, tomates fraîches, champignons	7,50 €	12 €	15 €
3 FROMAGES	sauce tomate, mozzarella, origan, chèvre, Roquefort	8 €	13 €	17 €
PESCATORE	sauce tomate, mozzarella, origan, oignons, saumon, champignons	8 €	13 €	17 €
ANGLAISE	sauce tomate, mozzarella, origan, bacon, oeuf, pommes de terre	9 €	14 €	20 €
TEXANE	sauce tomate, mozzarella, origan, boeuf épicé, pepperoni, oignons	9 €	14 €	20 €

02-47-66-89-89

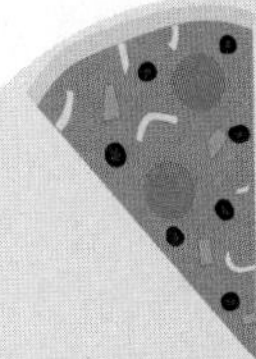

Petit dictionnaire

anchois *anchovies*
frais/fraîche *fresh*
boeuf épicé *spicy beef*
oignon *onion*
champignon *mushroom*
origan *oregano*
chèvre *goat cheese*
saumon *salmon*

Et vous?

Formez un groupe de 4 à 5 personnes. Imaginez que vous êtes en France. Vous voulez dîner et vous avez décidé de commander des pizzas. Faites une liste de ce que chacun veut commander.

NOM	TYPE DE PIZZA	DIMENSION	PRIX
John	Texane	31 cm.	14 €
•			
•			
•			
•			
•			

Le petit déjeuner *en France*

«Qu'est-ce que vous prenez au petit déjeuner?» Aux États-Unis, le petit déjeuner est généralement un repas abondant.° En France, c'est un repas simple.

Fabrice (13 ans)

Chez nous, nous sommes très traditionnels. Je mange du pain avec du beurre et de la confiture. Je bois un grand bol° de café au lait.

Mathieu (16 ans)

Chez nous, on prend le petit déjeuner «à l'américaine». Je mange des céréales et je bois du jus d'orange.

Sandrine (16 ans)

Je mange des tartines de pain° grillé° et je bois du lait chaud ou du chocolat avec beaucoup de sucre. Le dimanche, il y a parfois° des croissants. (Ça dépend si quelqu'un veut faire les courses!)

Sylvie (15 ans)

Le matin, je n'ai pas très faim. En général, je mange une tartine, c'est tout.° Je prends avec moi une barre de céréales ou une barre chocolatée que je mange avant° la première classe.

abondant *abundant, copious* **bol** *deep bowl* **tartines de pain** *slices of bread* **grillé** *toasted* **parfois** *sometimes* **tout** *all* **avant** *before*

COMPARAISONS *Culturelles*

Comparez le petit déjeuner des cinq jeunes Français avec votre petit déjeuner.

- Qui a le petit déjeuner le plus semblable *(most similar)*? Expliquez.
- Qui a le petit déjeuner le plus différent? Expliquez.

Activité écrite

Décrivez le petit déjeuner chez vous:

- pendant la semaine
- le dimanche matin

Additional readings @ **my.hrw.com**
FRENCH InterActive Reader

Stéphanie (13 ans)

Je suis martiniquaise. En général, je mange du pain et de la confiture comme° tout le monde.° Parfois ma mère prépare un petit déjeuner martiniquais typique. On mange du blaff de poisson° et des bananes vertes cuites.° On mange aussi des ananas,° des papayes et de la gelée de goyave.° C'est délicieux!

comme *like* **tout le monde** *everyone* **blaff de poisson** *fish stew* **cuites** *cooked* **ananas** *pineapple* **gelée de goyave** *guava jelly*

NOTE Culturelle

La cuisine créole

La cuisine créole est une cuisine régionale typique de la Martinique et de la Guadeloupe. C'est une cuisine assez épicée° qui utilise les produits locaux,° principalement les produits de la mer° et les fruits exotiques.

Voici certaines spécialités:

boudin créole	*spicy sausage*
colombo	*rice with spicy meat sauce*
blaff de poisson	*fish stew*
matoutou crabes	*stewed crabs served with rice*
crabes farcis	*stuffed crabs*
langoustes grillées	*(small) lobsters, broiled*

épicée *hot (spicy)* **locaux** *local* **mer** *sea*

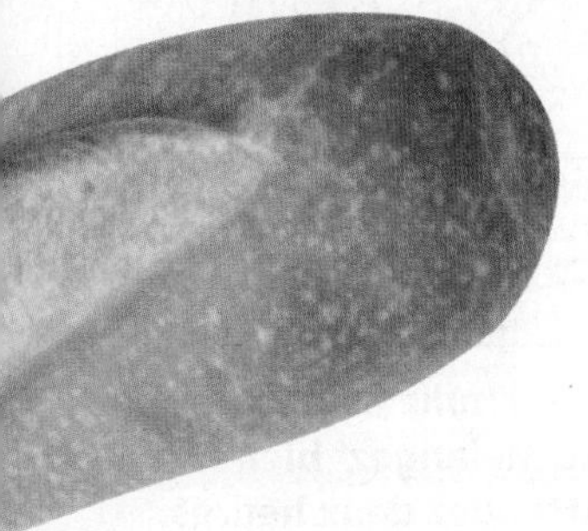

CONNEXIONS

Haitian people have their own creole cuisine which is somewhat different from that of Martinique. Find out about Haitian cuisine by visiting a local Haitian restaurant or by surfing the Internet.

- What products do Haitians use in their cooking?
- What are some typical dishes?

Les crêpes

Les crêpes sont d'origine bretonne.° Aujourd'hui, on vend les crêpes dans les «crêperies». On peut aussi faire des crêpes à la maison. Voici une recette° très simple.

les ingrédients

3 oeufs
3 cuillères à soupe de sucre
une pincée° de sel
2 tasses de lait
1 tasse de farine°
1 cuillère à soupe d'huile°
du beurre

les ustensiles

un petit bol **un grand bol**

un fouet **une poêle**

D'abord: Pour faire la pâte°

Mettez les oeufs dans le petit bol. Battez-les° bien avec le fouet.

Ajoutez° le sucre, le sel et un peu de lait.

Mettez la farine dans le grand bol. Versez° le contenu° du petit bol dans le grand bol.

Ajoutez l'huile et le reste du lait. Mélangez° bien la pâte. Attendez deux heures.

bretonne *from Brittany* **recette** *recipe* **pincée** *pinch* **farine** *flour* **huile** *oil* **pâte** *batter* **Battez-les** *Beat them* **Ajoutez** *Add* **Versez** *Pour* **contenu** *contents* **Mélangez** *Mix, Stir*

STRATEGY Reading

Using illustrations When you are reading, the context is not only the printed word. Sometimes the illustrations can help you understand the text. As you read the recipe, try guessing the meanings of the new words by studying the pictures.

Additional readings @ my.hrw.com
FRENCH
InterActive Reader

Ensuite: Pour faire les crêpes

Chauffez° la poêle. Mettez du beurre dans la poêle.

Mettez une cuillère de pâte dans la poêle.

Agitez° la poêle pour étendre° la pâte.

Retournez° la crêpe quand elle est dorée.°

Si vous êtes adroit(e), faites sauter° la crêpe en l'air. Si vous n'êtes pas adroit(e), abstenez-vous!°

Enfin: Pour servir les crêpes

Mettez la crêpe sur une assiette chaude. Faites les autres° crêpes.

Mettez du sucre ou de la confiture sur chaque° crêpe.

Au choix, roulez-la° ou pliez-la° en quatre.

Chauffez *Heat* **Agitez** *Shake* **étendre** *spread* **Retournez** *Turn over* **dorée** *golden brown* **faites sauter** *flip* **abstenez-vous** *don't try* **autres** *other* **chaque** *each* **roulez-la** *roll it* **pliez-la** *fold it*

Tête à tête Pair Activities

CONTENTS

Sports, jeux et musique — Élève B

Jean-Paul and Stéphanie are very active.

- Look at the illustrations on the right to find out about Stéphanie's pastimes. (Your partner has similar illustrations showing Jean-Paul's pastimes.)

▶ Take turns asking each other questions to discover which games and instruments Jean-Paul and Stéphanie play.

Élève A: **Jean-Paul joue de la flûte. Et Stéphanie?**

Élève B: **Stéphanie ne joue pas de la flûte, mais elle joue de la clarinette. Est-ce que Jean-Paul joue aux échecs? ...**

Stéphanie

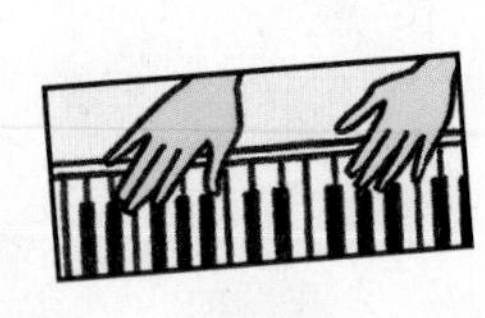

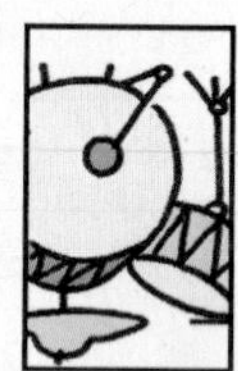

Which pastimes do Jean-Paul and Stéphanie have in common?

Sports, jeux et musique — Élève A

Jean-Paul and Stéphanie are very active.

- Look at the illustrations on the right to find out about Jean-Paul's pastimes. (Your partner has similar illustrations showing Stéphanie's pastimes.)

▶ Take turns asking each other questions to discover which games and instruments Jean-Paul and Stéphanie play.

Élève A: **Jean-Paul joue de la flûte. Et Stéphanie?**

Élève B: **Stéphanie ne joue pas de la flûte, mais elle joue de la clarinette. Est-ce que Jean-Paul joue aux échecs? ...**

Jean-Paul

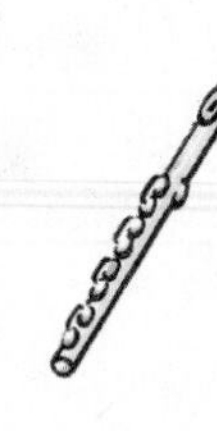

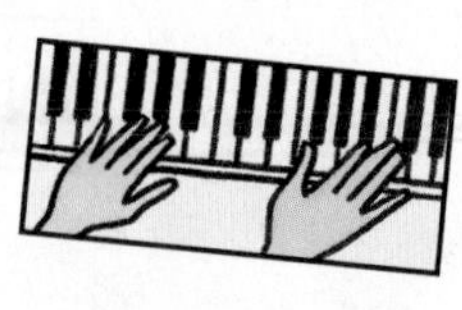

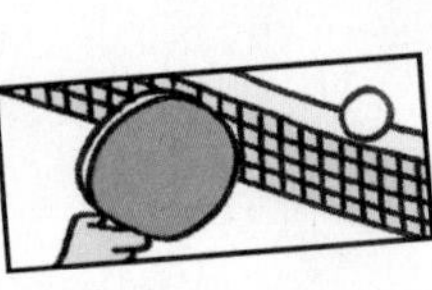

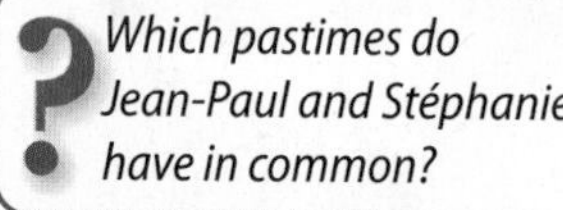

Which pastimes do Jean-Paul and Stéphanie have in common?

Vêtements — Élève B

You and your partner are shopping for clothes.

- You each have a maximum of 250 euros to spend.
- Choose five (5) different items from the picture on the right.

▶ Ask each other questions to find out what each of you is planning to buy.
Also find out the color and price of the five items your partner is buying.

Élève A: Est-ce que tu vas acheter une chemise?

Élève B: Oui, je vais acheter une chemise. [Non, je ne vais pas acheter de chemise.]

Élève A: De quelle couleur?

Élève B: Je vais acheter une chemise bleue.

Élève A: Combien est-ce qu'elle coûte?

Élève B: Elle coûte 35 euros.

How many similar items are the two of you going to buy?

Vêtements — Élève A

You and your partner are shopping for clothes.

- You each have a maximum of 250 euros to spend.
- Choose five (5) different items from the picture on the right.

▶ Ask each other questions to find out what each of you is planning to buy.
Also find out the color and price of the five items your partner is buying.

Élève A: Est-ce que tu vas acheter une chemise?

Élève B: Oui, je vais acheter une chemise. [Non, je ne vais pas acheter de chemise.]

Élève A: De quelle couleur?

Élève B: Je vais acheter une chemise bleue.

Élève A: Combien est-ce qu'elle coûte?

Élève B: Elle coûte 35 euros.

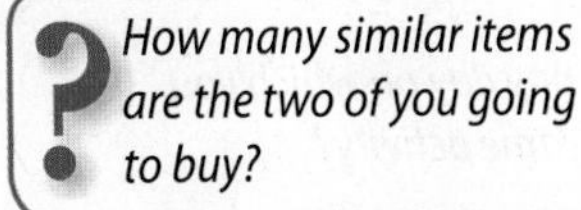

How many similar items are the two of you going to buy?

Vacances en France — Élève B

Last July, you and your partner spent a week in France, but you were each in different cities. You went to Nice on the French Riviera.

- The calendar on the right shows where you went each day.
- On a separate piece of paper, complete the calendar with an activity that corresponds logically to each place.

▶ Then find out where your partner went each day and what he/she did there. Your partner will ask you similar questions.

Élève A: Où es-tu allé(e) lundi?
Élève B: Lundi je suis allé(e) au stade.
Élève A: Et qu'est-ce que tu as fait là-bas?
Élève B: J'ai ... [joué au foot/fait du jogging/assisté à un match de foot ...]

	Où?	Activité
lundi	le stade	?
mardi	la piscine	?
mercredi	le club de sport	?
jeudi	la mer	?
vendredi	les magasins	?
samedi	la campagne	?
dimanche	la plage	?

? *Is there any day on which you did the same activity?*

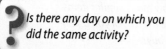

Vacances en France — Élève A

Last July, you and your partner spent a week in France, but you were each in different cities. You went to Annecy which is on a lake in the Alps.

- The calendar on the right shows where you went each day.
- On a separate piece of paper, complete the calendar with an activity that corresponds logically to each place.

▶ Then find out where your partner went each day and what he/she did there. Your partner will ask you similar questions.

Élève A: Où es-tu allé(e) lundi?
Élève B: Lundi je suis allé(e) au stade.
Élève A: Et qu'est-ce que tu as fait là-bas?
Élève B: J'ai ... [joué au foot/fait du jogging /assisté à un match de foot ...]

	Où?	Activité
lundi	le club de sport	?
mardi	la plage	?
mercredi	la montagne	?
jeudi	le cinéma	?
vendredi	le centre commercial	?
samedi	la campagne	?
dimanche	la piscine	?

? *Is there any day on which you did the same activity?*

Au supermarché — Élève B

You and your partner have been food shopping in two different supermarkets. On the right are the items you brought home.

▶ Find out about your partner's purchases by asking what he/she bought in the following categories:

- viande?
- poisson?
- dessert?
- fruits?
- légumes?
- boissons?

Your partner will ask you similar questions.

Élève A: Est-ce que tu as acheté de la viande?
Élève B: Oui, j'ai acheté du jambon. Et toi, est-ce que tu as acheté de la viande aussi?
Élève A: Moi, j'ai acheté ...

Which items did you buy that were the same?

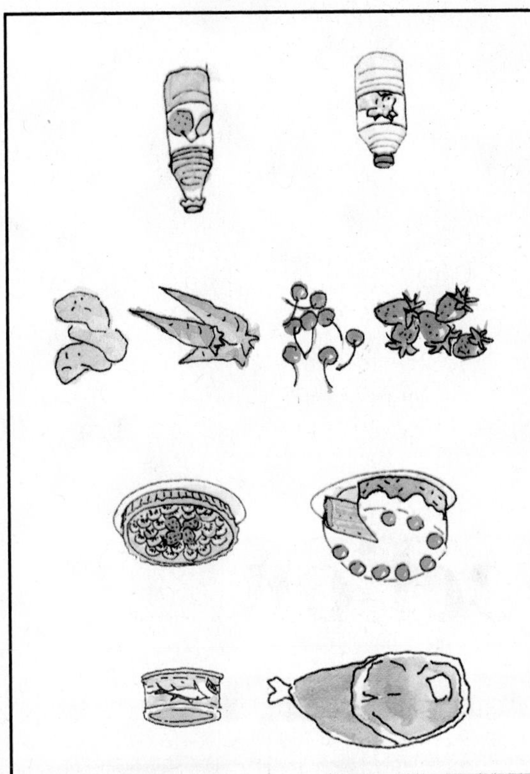

Au supermarché — Élève A

You and your partner have been food shopping in two different supermarkets. On the right are the items you brought home.

▶ Find out about your partner's purchases by asking what he/she bought in the following categories:

- viande?
- poisson?
- dessert?
- fruits?
- légumes?
- boissons?

Your partner will ask you similar questions.

Élève A: Est-ce que tu as acheté de la viande?
Élève B: Oui, j'ai acheté du jambon. Et toi, est-ce que tu as acheté de la viande aussi?
Élève A: Moi, j'ai acheté ...

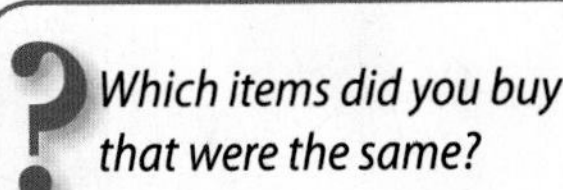

Which items did you buy that were the same?

Reference Section

CONTENTS

APPENDIX A RAPPEL 1 *Les noms, les articles et les adjectifs*

Les noms et les articles

In French, all nouns are MASCULINE or FEMININE, SINGULAR or PLURAL.
Nouns are often introduced by ARTICLES.

Definite Article *(the)*

	SINGULAR	PLURAL		
MASCULINE	**le (l')**	**les**	**le** garçon, **l'**ami	**les** garçons, **les** amis
FEMININE	**la (l')**	**les**	**la** fille, **l'**amie	**les** filles, **les** amies

Indefinite Article *(a, an; some)*

	SINGULAR	PLURAL		
MASCULINE	**un**	**des**	**un** copain	**des** copains
FEMININE	**une**	**des**	**une** copine	**des** copines

→ **Des** often corresponds to the English *some*. Although the word *some* is often omitted in English, the article **des** must be used in French.
J'ai **des** cousins à Paris.
*I have **(some)** cousins in Paris.*

→ After a NEGATIVE verb, **un, une,** and **des** become **de (d').**
J'ai **une** soeur. Je n'ai pas **de** frères.

Note also:

	MASCULINE	FEMININE
my	**mon**	**ma (mon)**
	mon frère **mon** ami	**ma** soeur **mon** amie
your	**ton**	**ta (ton)**
	ton frère **ton** ami	**ta** soeur **ton** amie

Les adjectifs de description

FORMS

In French, descriptive adjectives AGREE with the nouns they modify.
REGULAR adjectives have the following endings:

	SINGULAR	PLURAL		
MASCULINE	—	-s	**intelligent**	**intelligents**
FEMININE	-e	-es	**intelligente**	**intelligentes**

→ Adjectives that end in **-e** in the masculine remain the same in the feminine.
un garçon **timide** une fille **timide**

→ Adjectives that end in **-s** in the masculine singular remain the same in the masculine plural.
un ami **français** des amis **français**

POSITION

Most adjectives come AFTER the noun they modify.
une fille **intelligente** *an intelligent girl*

A few adjectives come before the noun.
une **petite** voiture *a small car*

Les personnes

VOCABULAIRE La famille

un frère	*brother*	**une soeur**	*sister*
un père	*father*	**une mère**	*mother*
un grand-père	*grandfather*	**une grand-mère**	*grandmother*
un cousin		**une cousine**	
un oncle	*uncle*	**une tante**	*aunt*

Les animaux domestiques *(Pets)*

un chien **un chat**

VOCABULAIRE D'autres personnes *(Other people)*

un garçon	*boy*	**une fille**	*girl*
un ami	*friend*	**une amie**	
un copain	*friend*	**une copine**	
un camarade	*classmate*	**une camarade**	
un élève	*high school student*	**une élève**	
un étudiant	*college student*	**une étudiante**	
un prof	*professor, teacher*	**une prof**	
un homme	*man*	**une femme**	*woman*
un monsieur	*man, gentleman*	**une dame**	*lady*
un voisin	*neighbor*	**une voisine**	
des gens	*people*	**une personne**	

Adjectifs de description

VOCABULAIRE La nationalité

américain
anglais
canadien (canadienne)
chinois
espagnol
français
italien (italienne)
japonais
mexicain
suisse

VOCABULAIRE La description physique

blond	**brun**	**jeune***	*young*
grand*	**petit**	**beau (belle)***	*good-looking, beautiful, handsome*
		joli	*pretty*

VOCABULAIRE La personnalité

amusant	**bon (bonne)***	*good*	**mauvais***	*bad*
intéressant	**gentil (gentille)**	*nice, kind*	**bête**	*not smart, stupid*
intelligent	**mignon (mignonne)**	*cute*	**méchant**	*nasty*
timide	**sportif (sportive)**	*athletic*		
	sympathique	*nice, pleasant*		

→ Adjectives marked with an asterisk **[*]** usually come before the noun.
Cécile est une **jolie** fille.

Quelques objets (A few objects)

VOCABULAIRE Dans le garage

un vélo	*bike*	**une auto**	
un scooter	*motorscooter*	**une bicyclette**	
		une mobylette	*moped*
		une moto	*motorcycle*
		une voiture	*car*

VOCABULAIRE À la maison

un objet		**une chose**	*thing*
un crayon	*pencil*	**une affiche**	*poster*
un stylo	*pen*		
un livre	*book*		
un ordinateur	*computer*	**une calculatrice**	*pocket calculator*
un sac		**une raquette**	
un appareil-photo	*camera*	**une montre**	*watch*
un téléphone		**une guitare**	
un portable	*cell phone*		
un (lecteur) MP3	*MP3 player*	**une radio**	
un CD		**une télé**	*TV*

VOCABULAIRE Une chambre (*bedroom*)

APPENDIX A

VOCABULAIRE Au café

Les plats *(dishes)*

un croissant
une crêpe
un hamburger
une glace *(ice cream)*
un hot-dog
une omelette
un sandwich
une pizza
un steak
une salade
un steak-frites

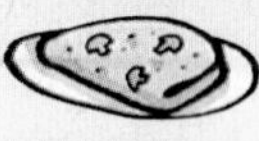

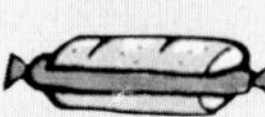

Les boissons *(drinks, beverages)*

un café
une limonade
un chocolat *(cocoa)*
un thé *(tea)*
un jus de pomme *(apple juice)*
un jus d'orange
un jus de raisin *(grape juice)*
un jus de tomate
un soda *(soft drink)*

VOCABULAIRE Les couleurs

De quelle couleur...? *What color...?*

— **De quelle couleur** est la moto?
— Elle est rouge.

blanc (blanche)	noir (noire)	bleu (bleue)	rouge (rouge)	jaune (jaune)	vert (verte)	marron (marron)	orange (orange)

➔ Colors are adjectives and take adjective endings.
un vélo **vert** une voiture **verte**

NOTE: The colors **marron** and **orange** are INVARIABLE: they have the same form in the masculine and feminine.

APPENDIX A RAPPEL 2 *Les verbes*

Les verbes réguliers en -er: formes affirmatives et négatives

	AFFIRMATIVE	NEGATIVE	ENDINGS
INFINITIVE	**parler**		
STEM	**parl-**		
PRESENT	je parl**e**	je **ne** parl**e** **pas**	**-e**
	tu parl**es**	tu **ne** parl**es** **pas**	**-es**
	il/elle parl**e**	il/elle **ne** parl**e** **pas**	**-e**
	nous parl**ons**	nous **ne** parl**ons** **pas**	**-ons**
	vous parl**ez**	vous **ne** parl**ez** **pas**	**-ez**
	ils/elles parl**ent**	ils/elles **ne** parl**ent** **pas**	**-ent**

→ For verbs ending in **-ger,** the **nous-** form is written with **-geons:** nous man**geons,** nous na**geons**

Les verbes irréguliers: *être, avoir, faire*

être *(to be)*	**avoir** *(to have)*	**faire** *(to do, make)*
je **suis**	j' **ai**	je **fais**
tu **es**	tu **as**	tu **fais**
il/elle **est**	il/elle **a**	il/elle **fait**
nous **sommes**	nous **avons**	nous **faisons**
vous **êtes**	vous **avez**	vous **faites**
ils/elles **sont**	ils/elles **ont**	ils/elles **font**

APPENDIX A

VOCABULAIRE Quelques activités

aimer	*to like, love*
chanter	*to sing*
danser	*to dance*
dîner	*to have supper, dinner*
écouter le professeur	*to listen to the teacher*
écouter la radio	*to listen to the radio*
étudier	*to study*
habiter à	*to live in*
jouer au basket	*to play basketball*
jouer au foot	*to play soccer*
jouer au tennis	
jouer aux jeux vidéo	*to play video games*
manger	*to eat*
marcher	*to walk*
nager	*to swim*
organiser une boum	*to organize a party*
parler	*to speak*
regarder un magazine	*to look at a magazine*
regarder la télé	*to watch TV*
téléphoner	*to phone, call*
travailler	*to work*
visiter	*to visit (a place)*
voyager	*to travel*

→ When referring to things, **marcher** means *to work, to function.*

Je **marche** parce que ma voiture ne **marche** pas.

VOCABULAIRE Expressions avec *être, avoir* et *faire*

être		
être d'accord	*to agree*	Pourquoi est-ce que tu n'**es** pas **d'accord** avec moi?
avoir		
avoir … ans	*to be … [years old]*	Ma cousine **a quinze ans.**
avoir faim	*to be/feel hungry*	Je mange un sandwich parce que j'**ai faim.**
avoir soif	*to be/feel thirsty*	Tu **as soif**? Voici une limonade.
faire:		
faire attention	*to pay attention*	Les élèves **font attention** en classe.
faire un match	*to play a game*	Mes cousins **font un match** de tennis.
faire une promenade	*to go for a walk*	Nous **faisons une promenade** en ville.
faire un voyage	*to take a trip*	Cécile **fait un voyage** à Québec.

RAPPEL 3 *Les nombres, la date, l'heure et le temps*

A VOCABULAIRE Les nombres

▶ How to count:

0 to 19			
0	**zéro**	10	**dix**
1	**un**	11	**onze**
2	**deux**	12	**douze**
3	**trois**	13	**treize**
4	**quatre**	14	**quatorze**
5	**cinq**	15	**quinze**
6	**six**	16	**seize**
7	**sept**	17	**dix-sept**
8	**huit**	18	**dix-huit**
9	**neuf**	19	**dix-neuf**

20 to 59			
20	**vingt**	30	**trente**
21	**vingt et un**	31	**trente et un**
22	**vingt-deux**	32	**trente-deux**
23	**vingt-trois**		**...**
24	**vingt-quatre**	40	**quarante**
25	**vingt-cinq**	41	**quarante et un**
26	**vingt-six**	46	**quarante-six**
27	**vingt-sept**		**...**
28	**vingt-huit**	50	**cinquante**
29	**vingt-neuf**	51	**cinquante et un**
		59	**cinquante-neuf**

60 to 100			
60	**soixante**	80	**quatre-vingts**
61	**soixante et un**	81	**quatre-vingt-un**
62	**soixante-deux**	82	**quatre-vingt-deux**
63	**soixante-trois**	88	**quatre-vingt-huit**
	...		**...**
70	**soixante-dix**	90	**quatre-vingt-dix**
71	**soixante et onze**	91	**quatre-vingt-onze**
72	**soixante-douze**	99	**quatre-vingt-dix-neuf**
76	**soixante-seize**	100	**cent**

→ Note the use of **et** in the numbers 21, 31, 41, 51, 61, 71.

B VOCABULAIRE La date

▶ *How to give the date:*

Quel jour est-ce aujourd'hui?
C'est jeudi.

Quelle est la date?
C'est le trois janvier.
C'est le dix-sept mai.

Quand est-ce, ton anniversaire?
C'est le vingt-deux novembre.

Les jours de la semaine:

lundi	**mercredi**	**vendredi**	**dimanche**
mardi	**jeudi**	**samedi**	

Les mois de l'année:

janvier	**avril**	**juillet**	**octobre**
février	**mai**	**août**	**novembre**
mars	**juin**	**septembre**	**décembre**

→ The first of the month is **le premier.** Demain, c'est **le premier** juillet.

C VOCABULAIRE L'heure

▶ ***How to tell time:***

Quelle heure est-il?
Il est ...

une heure

dix heures

midi

minuit

une heure et quart

neuf heures et demie

cinq heures moins le quart

une heure dix

dix heures vingt

deux heures moins vingt

six heures moins cinq

—À quelle heure est le film?
—Il est à huit heures et demie.

→ In French, official time is given on a 24-hour clock. Compare:

	CONVERSATIONAL TIME	OFFICIAL TIME
10 A.M.	Il est **dix heures du matin.**	Il est **dix heures.**
1 P.M.	Il est **une heure de l'après-midi.**	Il est **treize heures.**
9 P.M.	Il est **neuf heures du soir.**	Il est **vingt et une heures.**

D VOCABULAIRE Le temps

▶ ***How to talk about the weather:***

Quel temps fait-il?

Il fait	**beau.**	*It's nice.*
	bon.	*It's fine, pleasant.*
	chaud.	*It's hot.*
	froid.	*It's cold.*
	mauvais.	*It's bad.*

Il pleut. *It's raining.*
Il neige. *It's snowing.*

Les saisons:

le printemps	*spring*
l'été	*summer*
l'automne	*fall*
l'hiver	*winter*

APPENDIX 1 MAP *France*

[1]Also known as Île-de-France
[2]Also known as Nord-Pas-de-Calais
[3]Also known as Provence-Alpes-Côte d'Azur *(Bottin 1989)*

APPENDIX 1

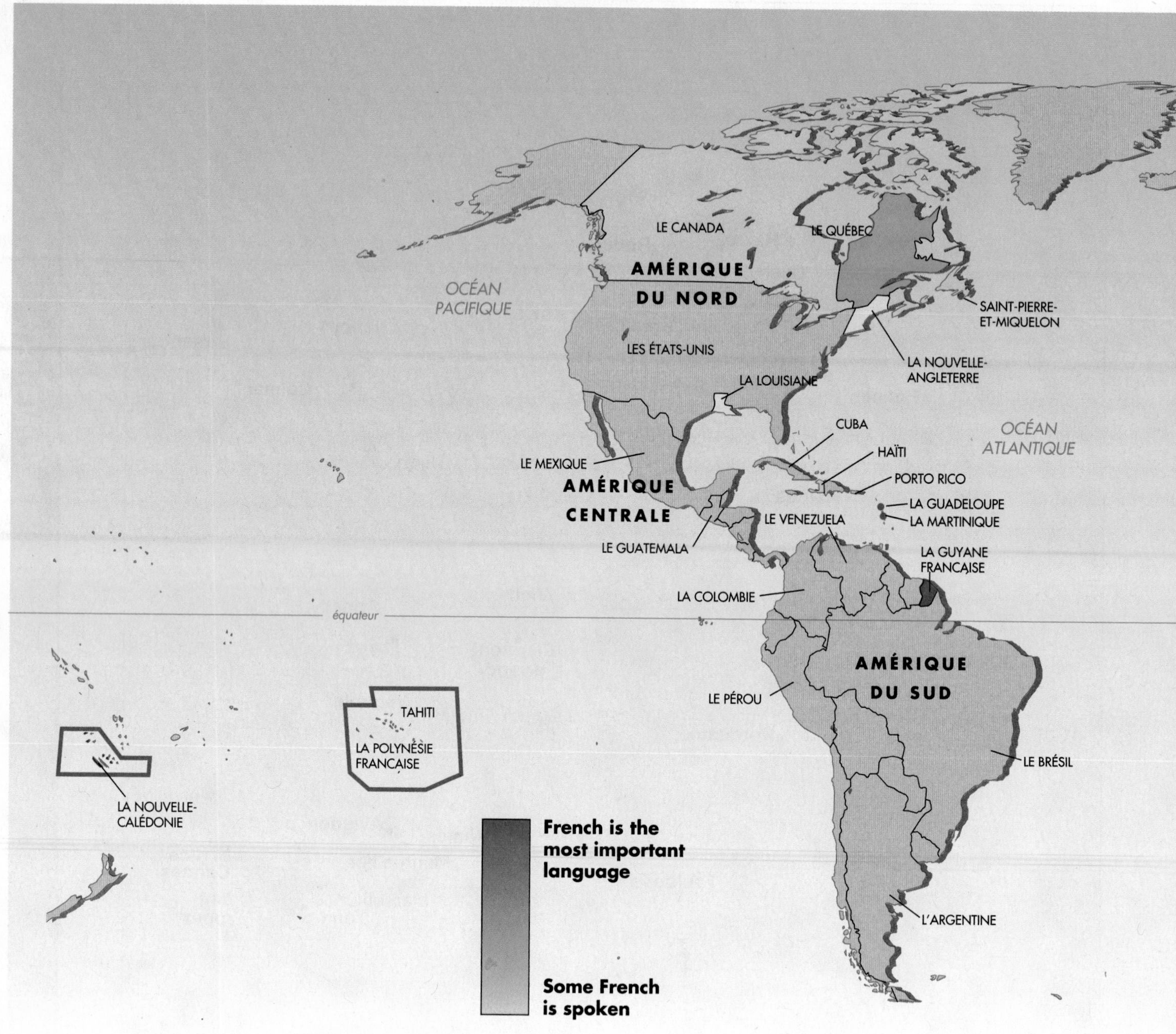

LE CANADA
LE QUÉBEC
AMÉRIQUE DU NORD
OCÉAN PACIFIQUE
SAINT-PIERRE-ET-MIQUELON
LES ÉTATS-UNIS
LA NOUVELLE-ANGLETERRE
LA LOUISIANE
CUBA
OCÉAN ATLANTIQUE
HAÏTI
LE MEXIQUE
PORTO RICO
AMÉRIQUE CENTRALE
LA GUADELOUPE
LA MARTINIQUE
LE VENEZUELA
LE GUATEMALA
LA GUYANE FRANÇAISE
LA COLOMBIE
équateur
AMÉRIQUE DU SUD
LE PÉROU
TAHITI
LA POLYNÉSIE FRANÇAISE
LE BRÉSIL
LA NOUVELLE-CALÉDONIE
French is the most important language
Some French is spoken
L'ARGENTINE

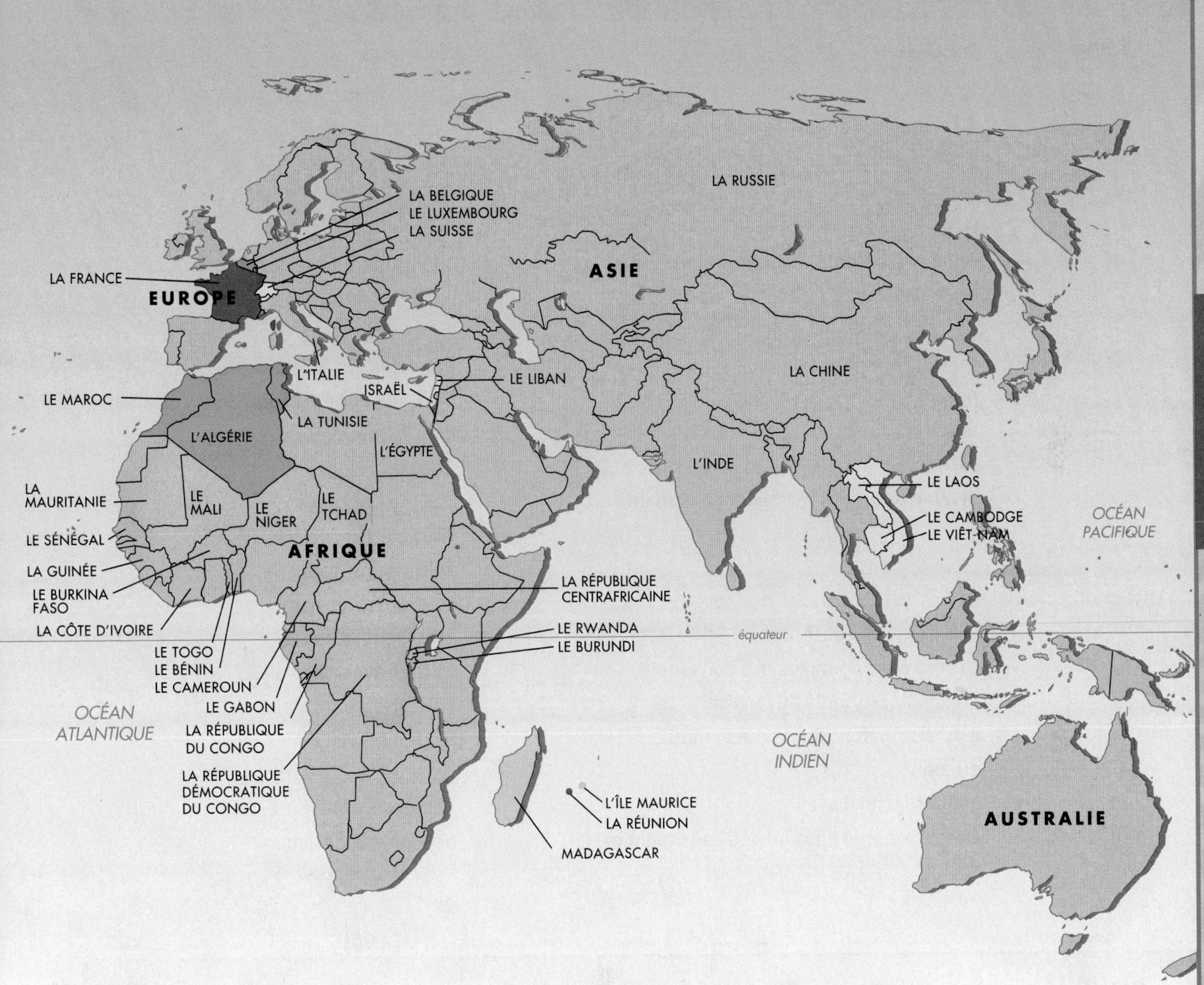
LA BELGIQUE
LE LUXEMBOURG
LA SUISSE
LA FRANCE
EUROPE
LA RUSSIE
ASIE
LA CHINE
L'ITALIE
ISRAËL
LE LIBAN
LE MAROC
LA TUNISIE
L'ALGÉRIE
L'ÉGYPTE
L'INDE
LE LAOS
LA MAURITANIE
LE MALI
LE NIGER
LE TCHAD
LE CAMBODGE
LE VIÊT-NAM
OCÉAN PACIFIQUE
LE SÉNÉGAL
AFRIQUE
LA GUINÉE
LE BURKINA FASO
LA RÉPUBLIQUE CENTRAFRICAINE
LA CÔTE D'IVOIRE
LE RWANDA
LE BURUNDI
équateur
LE TOGO
LE BÉNIN
LE CAMEROUN
LE GABON
OCÉAN ATLANTIQUE
LA RÉPUBLIQUE DU CONGO
OCÉAN INDIEN
LA RÉPUBLIQUE DÉMOCRATIQUE DU CONGO
L'ÎLE MAURICE
LA RÉUNION
AUSTRALIE
MADAGASCAR

APPENDIX 2 SOUND-SPELLING CORRESPONDENCES

VOWELS

SOUND	SPELLING	EXAMPLES
/a/	**a, à, â**	Madame, là-bas, théâtre
/i/	**i, î**	visite, Nice, dîne
	y (initial, final, or between consonants)	Yves, Guy, style
/u/	**ou, où, oû**	Toulouse, où, août
/y/	**u, û**	tu, Luc, sûr
/o/	**o** (final or before silent consonant)	piano, idiot, Margot
	au, eau	jaune, Claude, beau
	ô	hôtel, drôle, Côte d'Ivoire
/ɔ/	**o**	Monique, Noël, jolie
	au	Paul, restaurant, Laure
/e/	**é**	Dédé, Québec, télé
	e (before silent final **z, t, r**)	chez, et, Roger
	ai (final or before final silent consonant)	j'ai, mai, japonais
/ɛ/	**è**	Michèle, Ève, père
	ei	seize, neige, tour Eiffel
	ê	tête, être, Viêt-nam
	e (before two consonants)	elle, Pierre, Annette
	e (before pronounced final consonant)	Michel, avec, cher
	ai (before pronounced final consonant)	française, aime, Maine
/ə/	**e** (final or before single consonant)	je, Denise, venir
/ɸ/	**eu, oeu**	deux, Mathieu, euro, oeufs
	eu (before final **se**)	nerveuse, généreuse, sérieuse
/œ/	**eu** (before final pronounced consonant except /z/)	heure, neuf, Lesieur,
	oeu	soeur, coeur, oeuf
	oe	oeil

NASAL VOWELS

SOUND	SPELLING	EXAMPLES
/ɑ̃/	**an, am**	France, quand, lampe
	en, em	Henri, pendant, décembre
/ɔ̃/	**on, om**	non, Simon, bombe
/ɛ̃/	**in, im**	Martin, invite, impossible
	yn, ym	syndicat, sympathique, Olympique
	ain, aim	Alain, américain, faim
	(o) + in	loin, moins, point
	(i) + en	bien, Julien, viens
	un, um	un, Lebrun, parfum
/œ̃/	**un, um**	un, Lebrun, parfum

SEMI - VOWELS

SOUND	SPELLING	EXAMPLES
/j/	**i, y** (before vowel sound)	bien, piano, Lyon
	-il, -ill (after vowel sound)	oeil, travaille, Marseille, fille
/ɥ/	**u** (before vowel sound)	lui, Suisse, juillet
/w/	**ou** (before vowel sound)	oui, Louis, jouer
/wa/	**oi, oî**	voici, Benoît
	oy (before vowel)	voyage

CONSONANTS

SOUND	SPELLING	EXAMPLES
/b/	**b**	Barbara, banane, Belgique
/k/	**c** (before **a, o, u,** or consonant)	casque, cuisine, classe
	ch(r)	Christine, Christian, Christophe
	qu, q (final)	Québec, qu'est-ce que, cinq
	k	kilo, Kiki, ketchup
/ʃ/	**ch**	Charles, blanche, chez
/d/	**d**	Didier, dans, médecin
/f/	**f**	Félix, franc, neuf
	ph	Philippe, téléphone, photo
/g/	**g** (before **a, o, u,** or consonant)	Gabriel, gorge, légumes, gris
	gu (before **e, i, y**)	vague, Guillaume, Guy
/ɲ/	**gn**	mignon, champagne, Allemagne
/ʒ/	**j**	je, Jérôme, jaune
	g (before **e, i, y**)	rouge, Gigi, gymnastique
	ge (before **a, o, u**)	orangeade, Georges, nageur
/l/	**l, ll**	Lise, elle, cheval
/m/	**m**	Maman, moi, tomate
/n/	**n**	banane, Nancy, nous
/p/	**p**	peu, Papa, Pierre
/r/	**r, rr**	arrive, rentre, Paris
/s/	**c** (before **e, i, y**)	ce, Cécile, Nancy
	ç (before **a, o, u**)	ça, garçon, déçu
	s (initial or before consonant)	sac, Sophie, reste
	ss (between vowels)	boisson, dessert, Suisse
	t (before **i** + vowel)	attention, Nations Unies, natation
	x	dix, six, soixante
/t/	**t**	trop, télé, Tours
	th	Thérèse, thé, Marthe
/v/	**v**	Viviane, vous, nouveau
/gz/	**x**	examen, exemple, exact
/ks/	**x**	Max, Mexique, excellent
/z/	**s** (between vowels)	désert, Louise, télévision
	z	Suzanne, zut, zéro

APPENDIX 3 Numbers

A VOCABULAIRE CARDINAL NUMBERS

0 to 19

0	**zéro**	10	**dix**
1	**un (une)**	11	**onze**
2	**deux**	12	**douze**
3	**trois**	13	**treize**
4	**quatre**	14	**quatorze**
5	**cinq**	15	**quinze**
6	**six**	16	**seize**
7	**sept**	17	**dix-sept**
8	**huit**	18	**dix-huit**
9	**neuf**	19	**dix-neuf**

20 to 59

20	**vingt**	31	**trente et un (une)**
21	**vingt et un (une)**	32	**trente-deux**
22	**vingt-deux**	40	**quarante**
23	**vingt-trois**	41	**quarante et un (une)**
30	**trente**	50	**cinquante**

60 to 99

60	**soixante**	81	**quatre-vingt-un (une)**
70	**soixante-dix**	82	**quatre-vingt-deux**
71	**soixante et onze**	90	**quatre-vingt-dix**
72	**soixante-douze**	91	**quatre-vingt-onze**
80	**quatre-vingts**		

100 to 1 000 000

100	**cent**	600	**six cents**
101	**cent un (une)**	700	**sept cents**
102	**cent deux**	800	**huit cents**
200	**deux cents**	900	**neuf cents**
201	**deux cent un**	1 000	**mille**
300	**trois cents**	2 000	**deux mille**
400	**quatre cents**	1 000 000	**un million**
500	**cinq cents**		

Notes

1. The word **et** occurs only in the numbers 21, 31, 41, 51, 61, and 71: **vingt et un**, **soixante et onze**
2. **Un** becomes **une** before a feminine noun: **trente et une filles**
3. **Quatre-vingts** becomes **quatre-vingt** before another number: **quatre-vingt-cinq**
4. **Cents** becomes **cent** before another number: **trois cent vingt**
5. **Mille** never adds an **-s:** **quatre mille**

B VOCABULAIRE ORDINAL NUMBERS

1er (ère)	**premier (première)**	5e	**cinquième**	9e	**neuvième**
2e	**deuxième**	6e	**sixième**	10e	**dixième**
3e	**troisième**	7e	**septième**	11e	**onzième**
4e	**quatrième**	8e	**huitième**	12e	**douzième**

Note: **Premier** becomes **première** before a feminine noun: **la première histoire**

C VOCABULAIRE METRIC EQUIVALENTS

1 gramme	= 0.035 ounces	**1 ounce**	= 28,349 grammes
1 kilogramme	= 2.205 pounds	**1 pound**	= 0,453 kilogrammes
1 litre	= 1.057 quarts	**1 quart**	= 0,946 litres
1 mètre	= 39.37 inches	**1 foot**	= 30,480 centimètres
1 kilomètre	= 0.62 miles	**1 mile**	= 1,609 kilomètres

APPENDIX 4 VERBS

A. REGULAR VERBS

Infinitive	*Present*		*Passé Composé*	
parler *(to talk, speak)*	je **parle** tu **parles** il **parle**	nous **parlons** vous **parlez** ils **parlent**	j'**ai parlé** tu **as parlé** il **a parlé**	nous **avons parlé** vous **avez parlé** ils **ont parlé**
	IMPERATIVE: **parle, parlons, parlez**			
finir *(to finish)*	je **finis** tu **finis** il **finit**	nous **finissons** vous **finissez** ils **finissent**	j'**ai fini** tu **as fini** il **a fini**	nous **avons fini** vous **avez fini** ils **ont fini**
	IMPERATIVE: **finis, finissons, finissez**			
vendre *(to sell)*	je **vends** tu **vends** il **vend**	nous **vendons** vous **vendez** ils **vendent**	j'**ai vendu** tu **as vendu** il **a vendu**	nous **avons vendu** vous **avez vendu** ils **ont vendu**
	IMPERATIVE: **vends, vendons, vendez**			

B. *-er* VERBS WITH SPELLING CHANGES

Infinitive	*Present*		*Passé Composé*
acheter *(to buy)*	j' **achète** tu **achètes** il **achète**	nous **achetons** vous **achetez** ils **achètent**	j'**ai acheté**
	Verb like **acheter:** amener *(to bring, take along)*		
espérer *(to hope)*	j'**espère** tu **espères** il **espère**	nous **espérons** vous **espérez** ils **espèrent**	j'**ai espéré**
	Verb like **espérer:** célébrer *(to celebrate)*, préférer *(to prefer)*		
commencer *(to begin, start)*	je **commence** tu **commences** il **commence**	nous **commençons** vous **commencez** ils **commencent**	j'**ai commencé**
manger *(to eat)*	je **mange** tu **manges** il **mange**	nous **mangeons** vous **mangez** ils **mangent**	j'**ai mangé**
	Verbs like **manger:** nager *(to swim)*, voyager *(to travel)*		
payer *(to pay, pay for)*	je **paie** tu **paies** il **paie**	nous **payons** vous **payez** ils **paient**	j'**ai payé**
	Verbs like **payer:** nettoyer *(to clean)*		

APPENDIX 4 VERBS *continued*

C. IRREGULAR VERBS

Infinitive	*Present*		*Passé Composé*
avoir *(to have, own)*	j'**ai** tu **as** il **a**	nous **avons** vous **avez** ils **ont**	**j'ai eu**
	IMPERATIVE: **aie, ayons, ayez**		
être *(to be)*	je **suis** tu **es** il **est**	nous **sommes** vous **êtes** ils **sont**	**j'ai été**
	IMPERATIVE: **sois, soyons, soyez**		
aller *(to go)*	je **vais** tu **vas** il **va**	nous **allons** vous **allez** ils **vont**	je **suis allé(e)**
	IMPERATIVE: **va, allons, allez**		
boire *(to drink)*	je **bois** tu **bois** il **boit**	nous **buvons** vous **buvez** ils **boivent**	**j'ai bu**
connaître *(to know)*	je **connais** tu **connais** il **connaît**	nous **connaissons** vous **connaissez** ils **connaissent**	j'ai **connu**
devoir *(to have to, should, must)*	je **dois** tu **dois** il **doit**	nous **devons** vous **devez** ils **doivent**	**j'ai dû**
dire *(to say, tell)*	je **dis** tu **dis** il **dit**	nous **disons** vous **dites** ils **disent**	**j'ai dit**
dormir *(to sleep)*	je **dors** tu **dors** il **dort**	nous **dormons** vous **dormez** ils **dorment**	**j'ai dormi**
écrire *(to write)*	j'**écris** tu **écris** il **écrit**	nous **écrivons** vous **écrivez** ils **écrivent**	**j'ai écrit**
	Verbs like **écrire:** décrire *(to describe)*		
faire *(to make do)*	je **fais** tu **fais** il **fait**	nous **faisons** vous **faites** ils **font**	j'ai **fait**

Infinitive	*Present*		*Passé Composé*
lire *(to read)*	je **lis** tu **lis** il **lit**	nous **lisons** vous **lisez** ils **lisent**	j'**ai lu**
mettre *(to put, place)*	je **mets** tu **mets** il **met**	nous **mettons** vous **mettez** ils **mettent**	j'**ai mis**
Verb like **mettre:** promettre *(to promise)*			
ouvrir *(to open)*	j'**ouvre** tu **ouvres** il **ouvre**	nous **ouvrons** vous **ouvrez** ils **ouvrent**	j'**ai ouvert**
Verbs like **ouvrir:** découvrir *(to discover)*, offrir *(to offer)*			
partir *(to leave)*	je **pars** tu **pars** il **part**	nous **partons** vous **partez** ils **partent**	je **suis parti(e)**
pouvoir *(to be able, can)*	je **peux** tu **peux** il **peut**	nous **pouvons** vous **pouvez** ils **peuvent**	j'**ai pu**
prendre *(to take)*	je **prends** tu **prends** il **prend**	nous **prenons** vous **prenez** ils **prennent**	j'**ai pris**
Verbs like **prendre:** apprendre *(to learn)*, comprendre *(to understand)*			
savoir *(to know)*	je **sais** tu **sais** il **sait**	nous **savons** vous **savez** ils **savent**	j'**ai su**
sortir *(to go out, get out)*	je **sors** tu **sors** il **sort**	nous **sortons** vous **sortez** ils **sortent**	je **suis sorti(e)**
venir *(to come)*	je **viens** tu **viens** il **vient**	nous **venons** vous **venez** ils **viennent**	je **suis venu(e)**
Verb like **venir:** revenir *(to come back)*			
voir *(to see)*	je **vois** tu **vois** il **voit**	nous **voyons** vous **voyez** ils **voient**	j'**ai vu**

C. IRREGULAR VERBS continued

INFINITIVE	PRESENT		PASSÉ COMPOSÉ
vouloir *(to want)*	je **veux** tu **veux** il **veut**	nous **voulons** vous **voulez** ils **veulent**	j'**ai voulu**

D. VERBS WITH *ÊTRE* IN THE *PASSÉ COMPOSÉ*

aller *(to go)*	je **suis allé(e)**	**passer** *(to go by, through)*	je **suis passé(e)**
arriver *(to arrive, come)*	je **suis arrivé(e)**	**rentrer** *(to go home)*	je **suis rentré(e)**
descendre *(to go down)*	je **suis descendu(e)**	**rester** *(to stay)*	je **suis resté(e)**
entrer *(to enter, go in)*	je **suis entré(e)**	**revenir** *(to come back)*	je **suis revenu(e)**
monter *(to go up)*	je **suis monté(e)**	**sortir** *(to go out, get out)*	je **suis sorti(e)**
mourir *(to die)*	il/elle **est mort(e)**	**tomber** *(to fall)*	je **suis tombé(e)**
naître *(to be born)*	je **suis né(e)**	**venir** *(to come)*	je **suis venu(e)**
partir *(to leave)*	je **suis parti(e)**		

FRENCH-ENGLISH VOCABULARY

The French-English vocabulary contains active and passive words from the text, as well as the important words of the illustrations used with in the units. Obvious passive cognates have not been listed.

The numbers following an entry indicate the lesson in which the word or phrase is activated. R1, 2, or 3 indicates vocabulary from one of the **Rappel** sections in the Reprise Unit; (**I** stands for the list of classroom expressions at the end of the first **Images** section in Book 1A; **E** stands for **Entracte**, and **AX** stands for **Appendix**.)

Nouns: If the article of a noun does not indicate gender, the noun is followed by *m. (masculine)* or *f. (feminine)*. If the plural *(pl.)* is irregular, it is given in parentheses.

Adjectives: Adjectives are listed in the masculine form. If the feminine form is irregular, it is given in parentheses. Irregular plural forms *(pl.)* are also given in parentheses.

Verbs: Verbs are listed in the infinitive form. An asterisk (*) in front of an active verb means that it is irregular. (For forms, see the verb charts in Appendix 4C.) Irregular present tense forms are listed when they are used before the verb has been activated. Irregular past participle *(p.p.)* forms are listed separately.

Words beginning with an **h** are preceded by a bullet (•) if the **h** is aspirate; that is, if the word is treated as if it begins with a consonant sound.

A

a: il y a there is, there are [9]
à at, in, to [6], **14**
  à côté next door; next to
  à demain see you tomorrow [4B]
  à droite on (to) the right [13]
  à gauche on (to) the left [13]
  à la mode popular; in fashion; fashionable **17**
  à mon avis in my opinion **19**
  à partir de as of, beginning
  à pied on foot **14**
  à quelle heure? at what time? **R3**
  à qui? to whom? **R3**
  à samedi! see you Saturday! [4B]
  à vélo by bicycle **14**
abolir to abolish
abondant plentiful, copious, large
abord: d'abord (at) first **22**
un **abricot** apricot
absolument absolutely
un **accent** accent mark, stress
accepter to accept
des **accessoires** *m.* accessories **17**
un **accord** agreement
  d'accord okay, all right [5]
  être d'accord to agree [6], **AX**
un **achat** purchase
  faire des achats to go shopping **21**
acheter to buy **17, 18**
  acheter + du, de la *(partitive)* to buy (some) **26**
un **acteur, une actrice** actor, actress
une **activité** activity
l' **addition** *f.* check
adorer to love
une **adresse** address [13]
  quelle est ton adresse? what's your address? [13]
adroit skilled, skillful
un(e) **adulte** adult
aéronautique aeronautic, aeronautical
un **aéroport** airport
affectueusement affectionately *(at the end of a letter)*
une **affiche** poster [9]
affirmativement affirmatively
l' **Afrique** *f.* Africa
l' **âge** *m.* age
  quel âge a-t-il/elle? how old is he/she? [9], **R1**
  quel âge as-tu? how old are you? [2C], **R1**
  quel âge a ton père/ta mère? how old is your father/your mother? [2C]
âgé old
une **agence** agency
une **agence de tourisme** tourist office
une **agence de voyages** travel agency
agiter to shake
agité agitated
ah! ah!, oh!
ah bon? oh? really? [8]
ah non! ah, no!
ai *(see* **avoir**): **j'ai** I have [9]
  j'ai... ans I'm ... (years old) [2C]
aider to help **21, 27**
une **aile** wing
aimer to like [7], **25**
  est-ce que tu aimes...? do you like ...? [5], **R3**
  j'aime... I like ... [5], **R3**
  j'aimerais I would like
  je n'aime pas... I don't like ... [5], **R3**
ainsi thus
aîné older
  un frère aîné older brother
  une soeur aînée older sister
ajouter to add
l' **Algérie** *f.* Algeria *(country in North Africa)*
  algérien (algérienne) Algerian
l' **Allemagne** *f.* Germany
  allemand German
* **aller** to go **14**
  aller + *inf.* to be going to + *inf.* **14**
  allez *(see* **aller**): **allez-vousen** go away!
  allez-y come on!, go ahead!, do it!
  comment allez-vous? how are you? [1C]
allô! hello! *(on the telephone)*
allons *(see* **aller**): **allons-y** let's go! **14**
alors so, then [11]
une **alouette** lark
les **Alpes** *f.* (the) Alps
l' **alphabet** *m.* alphabet

FRENCH-ENGLISH VOCABULARY *continued*

l' **Alsace** *f.* Alsace *(province in eastern France)*
amener to bring *(a person)* **18, 27**
américain American [1B, 11]
à l'américaine American-style
un **Américain, une Américaine** American person
l' **Amérique** *f.* America
un **ami, une amie** (close) friend [2A], **AX**
amicalement love *(at the end of a letter)*
l' **amitié** *f.* friendship
amitiés best regards *(at the end of a letter)*
amusant funny, amusing [11]
amuser to amuse
s'amuser to have fun
on s'est bien amusé! we had a good time!
un **an** year
avoir... ans to be ... (years old) [10]
il/elle a... ans he/she is ... (years old) [2C], **R1**
j'ai... ans I'm ... (years old) [2C], **R1**
l'an dernier last year
par an per year
un **ananas** pineapple
ancien (ancienne) former, old, ancient
un **âne** donkey
un **ange** angel
anglais English [1B, 11]
un **Anglais, une Anglaise** English person
un **animal** (*pl.* **animaux**) animal
les **animaux domestiques** pets **AX**
une **animation** live entertainment
animé animated, lively
une **année** year [4B]
bonne année! Happy New Year! **24**
toute l'année all year long
un **anniversaire** birthday [4B]
bon anniversaire! happy birthday! **24**
c'est quand, ton anniversaire? when is your birthday? [4B], **AX**
mon anniversaire est le (2 mars) my birthday is (March 2nd) [4B], **AX**
un **annuaire** telephone directory
un **anorak** ski jacket
les **antiquités** *f.* antiquities, antiques
août *m.* August [4B], **AX**
un **appareil-photo** (*pl.* **appareils-photo**) (still) camera [9]
un **appartement** apartment [13]
s' **appeller** to be named, called
comment s'appelle...? what's ...'s name? [2B]
comment s'appelle-t-il/elle? what's his/her name? [9]
comment t'appelles-tu? what's your name? [1A], **R1**
il/elle s'appelle... his/her name is ... [2B]
je m'appelle... my name is ... [1A], **R1**
apporter to bring *(things)* **18**
apporter quelque chose à quelqu'un to bring something to someone **27**
apporte-moi (apportez-moi) bring me [I]
* **apprendre (à)** + *inf.* to learn (to) **26**
apprécier to appreciate
approprié appropriate
après after **21**; after, afterwards **22, 23**
d'après according to
l'après-midi *m.* afternoon **21**
cet après-midi this afternoon **23**
de l'après-midi in the afternoon, P.M. [4A]
demain après-midi tomorrow afternoon **23**
hier après-midi yesterday afternoon **23**
l' **arabe** *m.* Arabic *(language)*
un **arbre** tree
un arbre généalogique family tree
l' **arche** *f.* **de Noé** Noah's Ark
l' **argent** *m.* money **20**
l'argent de poche allowance, pocket money
arrêter to arrest; to stop
arriver to arrive, come **14**
j' arrive! I'm coming!
une arrivée arrival
un **arrondissement** district
un **artifice: le feu d'artifice** fireworks
un **artiste, une artiste** artist
as (*see* **avoir**): **est-ce que tu as...?** do you have ...? [9]
un **ascenseur** elevator
un **aspirateur** vacuum cleaner
asseyez-vous! sit down! [I]
assez rather [11]; enough
assieds-toi! sit down! [I]
une **assiette** plate **25**
assister à to go to, attend **21**
associer to associate
athlétique athletic **AX**
l' **Atlantique** *m.* Atlantic Ocean
attendre to wait, wait for **20**
attention *f.*: **faire attention** to be careful, pay attention [8]
attentivement carefully
au (à + le) to (the), at (the), in (the) [6], **14**
au revoir! good-bye! [1C]
une **auberge** inn
une auberge de campagne country inn **27**
aucun: ne... aucun none, not any
aujourd'hui today [4B], **23**
aujourd'hui, c'est... today is ... [4B]
aussi also, too [1B, 7]
aussi... que as ... as **19**
une **auto (automobile)** car, automobile [9]
une auto-école driving school
un autobus bus
un autocar touring bus **21**
l' **automne** *m.* autumn, fall **AX**
en automne in (the) autumn, fall [4C]
autre other **25**
d'autres others
un(e) autre another
aux (à + les) to (the), at (the), in (the) **14**
avant before **21**
avant hier the day before yesterday
en avant let's begin
avantageux (avantageuse) reasonable, advantageous
avec with [6]
avec moi, avec toi with me, with you [5]
avec qui? with who(m)? [8], **R3**
une **avenue** avenue [13]
un **avion** airplane, plane **21**
en avion by airplane **21**
un **avis** opinion
avis de recherche missing person's bulletin
à mon avis in my opinion **19**

à votre avis in your opinion
* **avoir** to have [10]
avoir... ans to be ... (years old) [10], **AX**
avoir besoin de to need **20**
avoir chaud to be warm, hot **22**
avoir de la chance to be lucky **22**
avoir envie de to feel like, want **20**
avoir faim to be hungry [10], **AX**
avoir froid to be cold **22**
avoir lieu to take place
avoir raison to be right **22**
avoir soif to be thirsty [10], **22, AX**
avoir tort to be wrong **22**
avril *m.* April [4B] , **AX**

B

le **baby-foot** tabletop soccer game
le **babysitting: faire du babysitting** to baby-sit
les **bagages** *m.* bags, baggage
bain: un maillot de bain bathing suit **17**
une **banane** banana **25**
une **bande dessinée** comic strip
des bandes dessinées comics
la **Bannière étoilée** Star-Spangled Banner
une **banque** bank
une **barbe: quelle barbe!** what a pain! *(colloq.)*
bas: en bas downstairs [13]
au bas at the bottom
le **baseball** baseball **15**
basé based
le **basket (basketball)** basketball **15**
jouer au basket to play basketball [5]
des **baskets** *m.* hightops (sneakers) **17**
un **bateau** boat, ship **21**
un bateau-mouche sightseeing boat
la **batterie** drums **15**
battre to beat
bavard talkative
beau (bel, belle; *m.pl.* **beaux)** handsome, good-looking, beautiful [9, 12], **19**
il est beau he is good-looking, handsome [9]
il fait beau it's beautiful (nice) out [4C]
un beau-frère stepbrother, brother-in-law
un beau-père stepfather, father-in-law
beaucoup (de) much, very much, many, a lot [7]
la **beauté** beauty
un **bec** beak
bel (*see* **beau**) beautiful, handsome **19**
la **Belgique** Belgium
belle (*see* **beau**) beautiful [9, 12], **19**
elle est belle she is beautiful [9]
une belle-mère stepmother, mother-in-law
une belle-soeur stepsister, sister-in-law
les **Bermudes** *f.* Bermuda
le **besoin** need
avoir besoin de to need, to have to **20**
des besoins d'argent money needs
bête dumb, silly [11], **AX**
le **beurre** butter **25**
une **bibliothèque** library [13]
une **bicyclette** bicycle [9], **AX**
bien well, very well, carefully [7]
bien sûr of course [5]
ça va bien everything's fine (going well) [1C]
ça va très bien I'm (everything's) very well [1C]
c'est bien that's good (fine) [12]
eh bien! well! **18**
je veux bien (...) I'd love to (...), I do, I want to [5], **26**
oui, bien sûr... yes, of course ... [5]
très bien very well [7]
bientôt: à bientôt! see you soon!
bienvenue welcome
le **bifteck** steak
un bifteck de tortue turtle steak
bilingue bilingual
un **billet** bill, paper money **20;** ticket
la **biologie** biology
une **biscotte** dry toast
blaff de poisson *m.* fish stew
blanc (blanche) white [E1, 12], **AX**
Blanche-Neige Snow White
blanchir to blanch, turn white
bleu blue [E1, 12], **AX**
blond blonde [9], **AX**
il/elle est blond(e) he/she is blond [9]
un **blouson** jacket **17**
* **boire** to drink **26**
une **boisson** drink, beverage [3B], **25**
une **boîte** box
un **bol** deep bowl
bon (bonne) good [12]
bon marché *(inv.)* inexpensive **17**
ah **bon?** oh, really? [8]
de bonne humeur in a good mood
il fait bon the weather's good (pleasant) [4C]
le **bonheur** happiness
bonjour hello [1A, 1C]
une **botte** boot **17**
une **bouche** mouth [E2]
une **boucherie** butcher shop
le **boudin** sausage
une **boulangerie** bakery
un **boulevard** boulevard [13]
une **boum** party *(colloq.)* **14**
une **boutique** boutique, shop **17**
boxe: un match de boxe boxing match
un **bras** arm [E2]
brésilien (brésilienne) Brazilian
la **Bretagne** Brittany *(province in northwestern France)*
bricoler to do things around the house
broche: à la broche on the spit
bronzé tan
un **bruit** noise
brun brown, dark-haired [9], **AX**
il/elle est brun(e) he/she has dark hair [9]
brunir to turn brown
Bruxelles Brussels
le **bulletin de notes** report card
un **bureau** desk [I, 9]; office
un **bus** bus
en bus by bus **14**
un **but** goal; end

C

ça that, it
ça fait combien? ça fait... how much is that (it)? that (it) is ... [3C]
ça, là-bas that (one), over there [9]

ça va? how's everything? how are you? [1C]
ça va everything's fine, I'm OK [1C]
ça va (très) bien, ça va bien everything's going very well, everything's fine (going well) [1C]
ça va comme ci, comme ça everything's (going) so-so [1C]
ça va (très) mal things are going (very) badly [1C]
regarde ça look at that [9]
une **cabine d'essayage** fitting room
les **cabinets** *m.* toilet
un **cadeau** (*pl.* **cadeaux**) gift, present
cadet (cadette) younger
un frère cadet (a) younger brother
une soeur cadette (a) younger sister
le **café** coffee [3B]
un café au lait coffee with hot milk
un café café *(French coffee shop)* [6]
au café to (at) the café [6]
un **cahier** notebook [I, 9]
une **calculatrice** calculator [9]
un **calendrier** calendar
un **camarade, une camarade** classmate [9], **AX**
le **Cambodge** Cambodia *(country in Asia)*
un **cambriolage** burglary
un **cambrioleur** burglar
une **caméra** movie camera
la **campagne** countryside **21**
à la campagne to (in) the countryside **21**
une auberge de campagne country inn
le **Canada** Canada
canadien (canadienne) Canadian [1B, 11], **AX**
un **Canadien, une Canadienne** Canadian person
un **canard** duck
la **cantine de l'école** school cafeteria **25**
un **car** touring bus **21**
un car scolaire school bus
une **carotte** carrot **25**
des carottes râpées grated carrots
un **carré** square
le Vieux Carré *the French Quarter in New Orleans*
une **carte** map [I]; card
une **carte postale** postcard
les **cartes** *f.* (playing) cards **15**
jouer aux cartes to play cards **15**
un **cas** case
en cas de in case of
une **casquette** (baseball) cap **17**
le **catch** wrestling
une **cathédrale** cathedral
une **cave** cellar
un **CD** CD, compact disc [9], **AX**
ce (c') this, that, it
ce n'est pas that's/it's not [12]
ce que what
ce sont these are, those are, they are [12]
c'est it's, that's [2A, 9, 12]
c'est + *day of the week* it's ... [4B], **AX**
c'est + *name or noun* it's ... [2A]
c'est bien/mal that's good/bad [12]
c'est combien? how much is that/it? [3C]
c'est le ([12] octobre) it's (October [12]) [4B], **AX**
qu'est-ce que c'est? what is it? what's that? [9]
qui est-ce? who's that/this? [9]
ce (cet, cette; ces) this, that, these, those **18**
ce... -ci this... (over here) **18**
ce mois-ci this month **23**
ce n'est pas it's (that's) not [12]
ce soir this evening, tonight **23**
une **cédille** cedilla
une **ceinture** belt **17**
cela that
célèbre famous
cent one hundred [2B], **17, AX**
cent un, cent deux 101, 102, **17, AX**
deux cents, trois cents, ... neuf cents 200, 300, ... 900 **17**
une **centaine** about a hundred
un **centime** centime *(1/100 of a euro)*
un **centre** center
un **centre commercial** shopping center [13]
les **céréales** *f.* cereal **25**
une **cerise** cherry **25**
certain certain
certains some of them
ces (*see* **ce**) these, those **18**
c'est (*see* **ce**)
cet (*see* **ce**) this, that **18**
cette (*see* **ce**) this, that **18**
chacun each one, each person
une **chaise** chair [I, 9]
une **chaîne** (TV) channel
une **chaîne hi-fi** stereo set [9], **AX**
une mini-chaîne compact stereo
la **chaleur** heat, warmth
une **chambre** bedroom [9, 13]
un **champion, une championne** champion
la **chance** luck
avoir de la chance to be lucky **22**
bonne chance! good luck! **23**
une **chanson** song
chanter to sing [5, 7], **AX**
un **chanteur, une chanteuse** singer
un **chapeau** (*pl.* **chapeaux**) hat **17**
chaque each, every
charmant charming
un **chat** cat [2C, **E4**]
un **château** (*pl.* **châteaux**) castle
chatter to chat (online)
chaud warm, hot
avoir chaud to be warm (hot) *(people)* **22**
il fait chaud it's warm (hot) *(weather)* [4C]
chauffer to warm, heat up
un **chauffeur** driver
une **chaussette** sock **17**
une **chaussure** shoe **17**
un **chef** boss; chef
une **chemise** shirt **17**
un **chemisier** blouse **17**
cher (chère) expensive; dear **17**
chercher to look for, to get, to find **17**
je cherche... I'm looking for...**17**
un **cheval** (*pl.* **chevaux**) horse [E4]
les **cheveux** *m.* hair [E2]
chez + *person* at (to) someone's house **14;** at (to) the office of
chez moi (toi, lui...) (at) home **15**
chic *(inv.)* nice; elegant, in style
une chic fille a great girl
un **chien** dog [2C], **AX**
la **chimie** chemistry
chinois Chinese [11], **AX**
le **chinois** Chinese *(language)*

le **chocolat** hot chocolate, cocoa [3B]
une glace au chocolat chocolate ice cream
choisir to choose **19**
un **choix** choice
au choix choose one, your choice
une **chorale** choir
une **chose** thing [9], **AX**
quelque chose something **24**
chouette great, terrific [12], **17**
le **cidre** cider
un **cinéaste, une cinéaste** film maker
un **cinéma** movie theater [13]
au cinéma to (at) the movies, movie theater [6]
cinq five [1A]
cinquante fifty [1C]
cinquième fifth **16**
une **circonstance** circumstance
cité: la Cité Interdite Forbidden City
une **clarinette** clarinet **15**
une **classe** class
en classe in class [6]
classique classical
un **clavier** keyboard **15**
un **client, une cliente** customer
un **clip** music video
un **cochon** pig
un **coiffeur, une coiffeuse** hairdresser
un **coin** spot
une **coïncidence** coincidence
le **Colisée** the Coliseum *(a large stadium built by the Romans)*
des **collants** *m.* (pair of) tights, pantyhose **17**
un **collège** junior high school
une **colonie** colony
une **colonne** column
combien how much **20**
combien coûte...? how much does...cost? [3C], **17**
combien de how much, how many **20**
combien de temps? how long?
combien d'heures? how many hours?
ça fait combien? how much is this (it)? [3C]
c'est combien? how much is this (it)? [3C]
commander to order
comme like, as, for
comme ci, comme ça so-so
ça va comme ci, comme ça everything's so-so [1C]
commencer to begin, start
comment? how? [8], **R3;** what?
comment allez-vous? how are you? [1C]
comment est-il/elle? what's he/she like? what does he/she look like? [9]
comment dit-on... en français? how do you say ... in French? [I]
comment lire reading hints
comment s'appelle...? what's... 's name? [2B], **R1**
comment s'appelle-t-il/elle? what's his/her name? [9]
comment t'appelles-tu? what's your name? [1A]
comment trouves-tu...? what do you think of...? **17**
comment vas-tu? how are you? [1C]
un **commentaire** comment, commentary
commercial: un centre commercial shopping center [13]
le **commérage** gossip
communiquer to communicate
un **compact (disc), un CD** compact disc, CD [9]
complément object
compléter to complete
* **comprendre** to understand **26**
je (ne) comprends (pas) I (don't) understand [I]
compter to count (on); to expect, intend
concerne: en ce qui concerne as for
un **concert** concert **14**
un **concombre** cucumber
la **confiture** jam **25**
confortable comfortable [13]
une **connaissance** acquaintance
faire connaissance (avec) to become acquainted (with)
* **connaître** to know, be acquainted with; *(in passé composé)* to meet for the first time **28**
tu connais...? do you know...? are you acquainted with...? [2B]
connu (*p.p. of* **connaître**) knew, met **28**
un **conseil** piece of advice, counsel
des **conseils** *m.* advice
un **conservatoire** conservatory
une **consonne** consonant
se **contenter** to limit oneself
le **contenu** contents
continuer to continue [13]
une **contradiction** disagreement
une **contravention** (traffic) ticket
cool cool, neat
un **copain, une copine** friend, pal [2A]
un petit copain, une petite copine boyfriend, girlfriend
copier to copy
une **copine** friend [2A]
coréen (coréenne) Korean
un **corps** body
correspondant corresponding
correspondre to correspond, agree
la **Corse** Corsica *(French island off the Italian coast)*
un **costume** man's suit
la **Côte d'Azur** Riviera *(southern coast of France on the Mediterranean)*
la **Côte d'Ivoire** Ivory Coast *(French-speaking country in West Africa)*
côté: à côté (de) next door; next to
une **côtelette de porc** pork chop
le **cou** neck [E2]
une **couleur** color [12]
de quelle couleur ...? what color ...? [12]
un **couloir** hall, corridor
coup: dans le coup with it
courage: bon courage! good luck! **23**
courageux (courageuse) courageous
le **courrier électronique** e-mail, electronic mail
une **course** race
faire les courses to go shopping *(for food)* **25**
court short **17**
un **cousin, une cousine** cousin [2C], **16**
le **coût: le coût de la vie** cost of living
un **couteau** (*pl.* **couteaux**) knife **25**
coûter to cost
combien coûte...? how much does...cost? [3C], **17**
il (elle) coûte... it costs... [3C]

un **couturier, une couturière** fashion designer
un **couvert** place setting **25**
un **crabe** crab
des matoutou crabes stewed crabs with rice
la **craie** chalk
un morceau de craie piece of chalk [I]
une **cravate** tie **17**
un **crayon** pencil [I, 9]
créer to create
un **crétin** idiot
une **crêpe** crepe (pancake) [3A]
une **crêperie** crepe restaurant
une **crevaison** flat tire
une **croisade** crusade
un **croissant** crescent (roll) [3A]
une **cuillère** spoon **25**
une cuillère à soupe soup spoon
la **cuisine** cooking **25**
une **cuisine** kitchen [13]
cuit cooked
culturel (culturelle) cultural
curieux (curieuse) curious, strange
la **curiosité** curiosity
le **cybercafé** internet café
un **cyclomoteur** moped

D

d'abord (at) first **22**
d'accord okay, all right
être d'accord to agree [6]
oui, d'accord yes, okay [5]
une **dame** lady, woman *(polite term)* [2A], **AX**
les **dames** *f.* checkers *(game)* **15**
dangereux (dangereuse) dangerous
dans in [9]
danser to dance [5, 7], **AX**
la **date** date [4B], **AX**
quelle est la date? what's the date? [4B]
de (d') of, from, about [6], **15**
de l'après-midi in the afternoon [4A]
de quelle couleur...? what color ...? [12], **AX**
de qui? of whom? [8]
de quoi? about what?
de temps en temps from time to time
pas de not any, no [10]
débarquer to land
décembre *m.* December [4B], **AX**
décider (de) to decide (to)
une **déclaration** statement
décoré decorated
* **découvrir** to discover
* **décrire** to describe
décrivez... describe...
un **défaut** shortcoming
un **défilé** parade
dégoûtant: c'est dégoûtant! it's (that's) disgusting **27**
dehors outside
en dehors de outside of
déjà already; ever
déjeuner to eat (have) lunch **25**
le **déjeuner** lunch **25**
le **petit déjeuner** breakfast **25**
délicieux (délicieuse) delicious **26**
demain tomorrow [4B], **AX**
à demain! see you tomorrow! [4B]
demain, c'est... (jeudi) tomorrow is ... (Thursday) [4B]
demander (à) to ask **28**
demandez ... ask ...
demi half
un demi-frère half-brother
une demi-soeur half-sister
demi: ... heures et demie half past ... [4A], **AX**
midi et demi half past noon [4A], **AX**
minuit et demi half past midnight [4A]
démodé out of style, unfashionable **17**
un **démon** devil
une **dent** tooth
un **départ** departure
se **dépêcher: dépêchez-vous!** hurry up!
dépend: ça dépend that depends
une **dépense** expense
dépenser to spend (money) **20**
dernier (dernière) last **23**
derrière behind, in back of [9], **R2**
des some, any [10]; of (the), from (the), about (the) **15**
la **description physique** physical description **AX**
le **désert** desert
désirer to wish, want
vous désirez? what would you like? may I help you? [3B], **17**
désolé sorry
le **dessert** dessert **25**
le **dessin** art, drawing
un **dessin animé** cartoon
détester to hate, detest [1C]
deux two [1A], **AX**
deuxième second **16**
le deuxième étage third floor
devant in front of [9], **R2**
développer to develop
deviner to guess
* **devoir** to have to, should, must **27**
un **devoir** homework assignment [I]
les **devoirs** *m.* homework
faire mes devoirs to do my homework **21**
d'habitude usually
différemment differently
différent different
difficile hard, difficult [12]
la **dignité** dignity
dimanche *m.* Sunday [4B], **AX**
le **dîner** dinner, supper **25**
dîner to have dinner [7], **25**
dîner au restaurant to have dinner at a restaurant [5]
* **dire** to say, tell **28**
que veut dire...? what does... mean? [I]
directement straight
un **directeur, une directrice** director, principal
dirigé directed, guided
dis! (*see* **dire**) say!, hey! [12]
dis donc! say there!, hey there! [12]
discuter to discuss
une **dispute** quarrel, dispute
dit (*p.p. of* **dire**) said
dit (*see* **dire**): **comment dit-on... en français?** how do you say...in French? [I]
dites... (*see* **dire**) say..., tell...
dix ten [1A, 1B], **AX**
dix-huit eighteen [1B], **AX**
dixième tenth **16**
dix-neuf nineteen [1B], **AX**
dix-sept seventeen [1B], **AX**
un **dock** docking station [9]
un **docteur** doctor
dois (*see* **devoir**): **je dois** I have to (must) [5], **R3**

domestique domestic
les animaux *m.* **domestiques** pets [2C]
dommage! too bad! [7]
donner (à) to give (to) **27, 28**
donne-moi… give me… [3A], [I]
donnez-moi… give me [3B], [I]
s'il te plaît, donne-moi… please, give me… [3B]
doré golden brown
* **dormir** to sleep
le **dos** back [E2]
une **douzaine** dozen **25**
douze twelve [1B]
douzième twelfth **16**
droit: tout droit straight [13]
droite right à droite to (on) the right [13]
drôle funny [12]
du (de + le) of (the), from (the) **15; some, any 26**
du matin in the morning, A.M. [4A]
du soir in the evening, P.M. [4A]
dû (*p.p. of* **devoir**) had to **27**
dur hard
des oeufs *(m.)* **durs** hard-boiled eggs
durer to last
un **DVD** DVD [9]
dynamique dynamic

E

l' **eau** *f.* (*pl.* **eaux**) water **25**
l' **eau minérale** mineral water **25**
un **échange** exchange
les **échecs** *m.* chess **15**
une **éclosion** hatching
une **école** school [13]
économiser to save money
écouter to listen to [I], [7]
écouter la radio to listen to the radio [5]
écouter des CD to listen to CDs **21**
l' **écran** *m.* screen (computer)
* **écrire** to write **28**
l' **éducation** *f.* education
l'éducation civique civics
l'éducation physique physical education
une **église** church [13]
égyptien (égyptienne) Egyptian
eh bien! well! **18**
électronique: une guitare électrique electric guitar
élégant elegant **17**
un **éléphant** elephant [E4]
un **élève, une élève** pupil, student [9], **AX**
élevé high
elle she, it [3C, 6, 10]; her **15**
elle coûte… it costs … [3C]
elle est (canadienne) she's (Canadian) [2B]
elle s'appelle… her name is … [2B]
embrasser: je t'embrasse love and kisses *(at the end of a letter)*
un **emploi du temps** time-table *(of work)*
emprunter à to borrow from
en in, on, to, by
en avion by airplane, plane **21**
en bas (haut) downstairs (upstairs) [13]
en bus (métro, taxi, train, voiture) by bus (subway, taxi, train, car) **14**
en ce qui concerne as for
en face opposite, across (the street)
en fait in fact
en famille at home
en plus in addition
en scène on stage
en solde on sale
va-t'en! go away! **14**
un **endroit** place **14**
un **enfant, une enfant** child **16**
enfin at last **22**
ensuite then, after that **22**
entendre to hear **20**
entier (entière) entire
l' **entracte** *m.* interlude
entre between
une **entrée** entry *(of a house)*
un **entretien** discussion
envers toward
l' **envie** *f.* envy; feeling
avoir envie de to want; to feel like, want to **20**
envoyer to send
envoyer un mail to send an e-mail
épicé hot (spicy)
une **épicerie** grocery store
les **épinards** *m.* spinach
une **équipe** team
une **erreur** error, mistake
es (*see* **être**)
tu es + *nationality* you are … [1B]
tu es + *nationality?* are you …? [1B]
tu es de…? are you from …? [1B]
l' **escalade** *f.* rock climbing **21**
faire de l'escalade to go rock climbing **21**
un **escalier** staircase
un **escargot** snail
l' **Espagne** *f.* Spain
espagnol Spanish [11], **AX**
parler espagnol to speak Spanish [5]
espérer to hope **18**
un **esprit** spirit
essayer to try on, to try
l' **essentiel** *m.* the important thing
est (*see* **être**)
est-ce que (qu')…? *phrase used to introduce a question* [6]
c'est… it's …, that's … [2A, 2C, 12]
c'est le + *date* it's … [4B]
il/elle est + *nationality* he/she is … [2B]
n'est-ce pas…? isn't it? [6]
où est…? where is …? [6]
quel jour est-ce? what day is it? [4B]
qui est-ce? who's that (this)? [2A, 9]
l' **est** *m.* east
et and [1B, 6]
et demi(e), et quart half past, quarter past [4A]
et toi? and you? [1A]
établir to establish
un **étage** floor of a building, story
les **États-Unis** *m.* United States
été (*p.p. of* **être**) been, was **23**
l' **été** *m.* summer, **AX**
en été in (the) summer [4C]
l'heure d'été daylight savings time
étendre to spread
une **étoile** star
étrange strange
étranger (étrangère) foreign
* **être** to be [6]
être à to belong to
être d'accord to agree [6], **AX**

une étude study
un étudiant, une étudiant(e) (college) student [9], **AX**
étudier to study [5, 7]
eu (*p.p. of* **avoir**) had **23**
il y a eu there was
euh… er …, uh …
euh non… well, no
un euro euro; monetary unit of Europe
européen (européenne) European
eux they, them **15**
eux-mêmes themselves
un événement event **14**
un examen exam, test
réussir à un examen to pass an exam, a test
excusez-moi excuse me [13]
un exemple example
par exemple for instance
un exercice exercise
faire des exercices to exercise
exiger to insist
expliquer to explain
expliquez… explain …
exprimer to express
exquis: c'est exquis! it's exquisite! **26**
extérieur: à l'extérieur outside
extraordinaire extraordinary
il a fait un temps extraordinaire! the weather was great!

F

face: en face (de) opposite, across (the street) from
facile easy [12]
faible weak
la faim hunger
avoir faim to be hungry **22**
j'ai faim I'm hungry [3A]
tu as faim? are you hungry? [3A]
* **faire** to do, make [8]
faire attention to pay attention, be careful [8], **AX**
faire de + *activity* to do, play, study, participate in **21**
faire des achats to go shopping **21**
faire beau *(weather)* to be nice out **AX**
faire les courses to go shopping **25**
faire mauvais *(weather)* to be bad out **AX**
faire mes devoirs to do my homework **21**
faire les magasins to go shopping (browsing from store to store)
faire partie de to be a member of
faire sauter to flip
faire un match to play a game *(match)* [8], **AX**
faire un pique-nique to have a picnic **21**
faire un voyage to take a trip [8], **AX**
faire une promenade to take a walk [8]
faire une promenade à pied (à vélo, en voiture) to take a walk (a bicycle ride, a drive) **14**
fait (*p.p. of* **faire**) did, done, made **23**
fait: en fait in fact
fait (*see* **faire**): **ça fait combien?** how much is that (it)? [3C]
ça fait… euros that's (it's) … euros [3C]
il fait (beau, etc.) it's (beautiful, etc.) *(weather)* [4C]
quel temps fait-il? what (how) is the weather? [4C]
fameux: c'est fameux! it's superb! **26**
familial with the family
une famille family [2C], **16**
en famille at home
un fana, une fana fan *(person)*
un fantôme ghost
la farine flour
fatigué tired
faux (fausse) false [12]
favori (favorite) favorite
les félicitations *f.* congratulations
une femme woman [9], **AX; wife 16**
une fenêtre window [I, 9]
fermer to close [I]
une fête party, holiday
le feu d'artifice fireworks
une feuille sheet, leaf [I]
une feuille de papier sheet of paper [I]
un feuilleton series, serial story *(in newspaper)*
février *m.* February [4B], **AX**
fiche-moi la paix! leave me alone! *(colloq.)* **28**
la fièvre fever
une fille girl [2A], **AX; daughter 16**
un film movie **14, 21**
un film policier detective movie
un fils son **16**
la fin end
finalement finally **22**
fini (*p.p. of* **finir**) over, finished **23**
finir to finish **19**
flamand Flemish
un flamant flamingo
une fleur flower
un fleuve river
un flic cop *(colloq.)*
une flûte flute **15**
une fois time
à la fois at the same time
la folie: à la folie madly
folklorique: une chanson folklorique folksong
fonctionner to work, function
fondé founded
le foot (football) soccer **15**
le football américain football
jouer au foot to play soccer [5]
une forêt forest
formidable great!
fort strong
plus fort louder [I]
un fouet whisk
une fourchette fork **25**
la fourrure fur
un manteau de fourrure fur coat
frais: il fait frais it's cool *(weather)* [4C], **AX**
une fraise strawberry **25**
un franc franc *(former monetary unit of France)* [3C]
ça fait… francs that's (it's) … francs [3C]
français French [1B, 11]
comment dit-on… en français? how do you say… in French? [I]
parler français to speak French [5]
le français French *(language)*
un Français, une Française French person
la France France [6]
en France in France [6]
francophone French-speaking

un **frère** brother [2C], **16**
des **frites** *f.* French fries **25**
un steak-frites steak and French fries [3A]
froid cold
avoir froid to be (feel) cold *(people)* **22**
il fait froid it's cold out *(weather)* [4C]
le **fromage** cheese **25**
un sandwich au fromage cheese sandwich
un **fruit** fruit **25**
furieux (furieuse) furious
une **fusée** rocket

G

gagner to earn, to win **20**
un **garage** garage [13]
un **garçon** boy [2A], **AX; waiter**
une **gare** train station
une **garniture** side dish
un **gâteau** (*pl.* **gâteaux**) cake **25**
gauche left
à gauche to (on) the left [13]
une **gelée** jelly
généralement generally
généreux (généreuse) generous
la **générosité** generosity
génial brilliant: terrific [12]
des **gens** *m.* people [10], **AX**
gentil (gentille) nice, kind [11]; sweet
la **géographie** geography
une **girafe** giraffe [E4]
une **glace** ice cream [3A], **25;** mirror, ice
glacé iced
un thé glacé iced tea **25**
un **goûter** afternoon snack
une **goyave** guava
grand tall [9]; big, large [12]; big *(size of clothing)* **17**
un grand magasin department store **17**
une grande surface big store, self-service store
grandir to get tall; to grow up
une **grand-mère** grandmother [2C], **16**
un **grand-père** grandfather [2C], **16**
les **grands-parents** *m.* grandparents **16**
grec (grecque) Greek
un **grenier** attic
une **grillade** grilled meat
une **grille** grid
grillé: le pain grillé toast
une tartine de pain grillé buttered toast
la **grippe** flu
gris gray [12], **AX**
gros (grosse) fat, big
grossir to gain weight, get fat **19**
la **Guadeloupe** Guadeloupe *(French island in the West Indies)*
une **guerre** war
une **guitare** guitar [9], **15**
un **gymnase** gym

H

habillé dressed
habiter (à) to live (in + *city*) [7]
Haïti Haiti *(French- and Creole-speaking country in the West Indies)*
un • **hamburger** hamburger [3A]
les • **haricots** *m.* **verts** green beans **25**
la • **hâte** haste
en hâte quickly
• **haut** high
en haut upstairs [13]
plus haut above
• **hélas!** too bad!
hésiter to hesitate
l' **heure** *f.* time, hour; o'clock [4A]
... heure(s) (dix) (ten) past ... [4A], **AX**
... heure(s) et demie half past ... [4A], **AX**
... heure(s) et quart quarter past ... [4A], **AX**
... heure(s) moins (dix) (ten) of ... [4A], **AX**
... heure(s) moins le quart quarter to ... [4A], **AX**
à... heures at ... o'clock [6], **AX**
à quelle heure...? at what time ...? [8], **AX**
à quelle heure est...? at what time is ...? [4A], **AX**
il est... heure(s) it's ... o'clock [4A], **AX**
par heure per hour, an hour
quelle heure est-il? what time is it? [4A]
heureux (heureuse) happy
hier yesterday **23**
avant-hier the day before yesterday
un **hippopotame** hippopotamus [E4]
une **histoire** story, history
l' **hiver** *m.* winter [4C], **AX**
en hiver in (the) winter [4C]
• **hollandais** Dutch
un **homme** man [9]
honnête honest
un **hôpital** (*pl.* **hôpitaux**) hospital [13]
une **horreur** horror
quelle horreur! what a scandal! how awful!
un • **hors-d'oeuvre** appetizer **25**
un • **hot dog** hot dog [3A]
un **hôte, une hôtesse** host, hostess
un **hôtel** hotel [13]
un **hôtel de police** police department
l' **huile** *f.* oil
• **huit** eight [1A], **AX**
huitième eighth **16**
l' **humeur** *f.* mood
de bonne humeur in a good mood
un **hypermarché** shopping center

ici here [6]
une **idée** idea
c'est une bonne idée! it's (that's) a good idea! **20**
ignorer to be unaware of
il he, it [3C, 6, 10]
il est it is [12]
il/elle est + *nationality* he/she is ... [2B]
il y a there is, there are [9], **R2**
il y a + du, de la *(partitive)* there is (some) **26**
il y a eu there was
il n'y a pas de... there is/are no ... [10], **R2**
est-ce qu'il y a...? is there, are there ...? [9]
qu'est-ce qu'il y a...? what is there ...? [9]
une **île** island
illustré illustrated
un **immeuble** apartment building [13]
un **imper (imperméable)** raincoat **17**
l' **impératif** *m.* imperative (command) mood

impoli impolite
l' **importance** *f.* importance
ça n'a pas d'importance it doesn't matter
importé imported
impressionnant impressive
l' **imprimante** *f.* printer
inactif (inactive) inactive
inclure to include
l' **indicatif** *m.* area code
indiquer to indicate, show
indiquez… indicate …
infâme: c'est infâme! that's (it's) awful! **27**
infect: c'est infect! that's revolting! *(colloq.)* **27**
les **informations** *f.* news
l' **informatique** *f.* computer science
s' **informer (de)** to find out about
un **ingénieur** engineer
un **ingrédient** ingredient **25**
un **inspecteur, une inspectrice** police detective
un **instrument** instrument **15**
intelligent intelligent [11], **AX**
intéressant interesting [11], **AX**
l' **intérieur** *m.* interior, inside
l' **Internet** *m.* the Internet
surfer sur l'Internet (sur le Net) to surf the Internet
interroger to question
interviewer to interview
inutilement uselessly
un **inventaire** inventory
un **invité, une invitée** guest
inviter to invite [7]
israélien (israélienne) Israeli
italien (italienne) Italian [11], **AX**
un **Italien, une Italienne** Italian person

J

j' (*see* **je**)
jamais ever; never
jamais le dimanche! never on Sunday!
ne… jamais never **24**
la **Jamaïque** Jamaica
une **jambe** leg [E2]
un **jambon** ham **25**
janvier *m.* January [4B], **AX**
japonais Japanese [11], **AX**
un **jardin** garden [13]
jaune yellow [E1, 12], **AX**
jaunir to turn yellow
je I [6]
un **jean** pair of jeans **15**
un **jeu** (*pl.* **jeux**) game **17**
les jeux d'ordinateur computer games
les jeux télévisés TV game shows
les jeux vidéo video games
jeudi *m.* Thursday [4B], **AX**
jeune young [9], **AX**
les **jeunes** *m.* young people
un **job** (part-time) job
le **jogging** jogging **21**
faire du jogging to jog **21**
un **jogging** jogging suit **25**
joli pretty *(for girls, women)* **17**; *(for clothing)* **17**
plus joli(e) que prettier than
jouer to play [7]
jouer à + *game, sport* to play a game, sport **15**
jouer aux jeux vidéo to play video games [5]
jouer au tennis (volley, basket, foot) to play tennis (volleyball, basketball, soccer) [5]
jouer de + *instrument* to play a musical instrument **15**
un **jour** day [4B], **21**
le Jour de l'An New Year's Day
par jour per week, a week
quel jour est-ce? what day is it? [8], **AX**
un **journal** (*pl.* **journaux**) newspaper
une **journée** day, whole day
bonne journée! have a nice day!
joyeux (joyeuse) happy
juillet *m.* July [8], **AX**
le quatorze juillet Bastille Day *(French national holiday)*
juin *m.* June [4B], **AX**
un **jumeau** (*pl.* **jumeaux**), une **jumelle** twin
une **jupe** skirt **17**
le **jus** juice
le jus d'orange orange juice [3B], **25**
le jus de pomme apple juice [3B], **25**
le jus de raisin grape juice [3B], **AX**
le jus de tomate tomato juice [3B], **AX**
jusqu'à until
juste right, fair
le mot juste the right word

K

un **kangourou** kangaroo [E4]
le **ketchup** ketchup **25**
un **kilo** kilogram
un kilo (de) a kilogram (of) **25**

L

l' (*see* **le, la**)
la the [2B], [10]; her, it **28**
là here, there [6]
là-bas over there [6]
ça, là-bas that (one), over there [9]
ce… -là that … (over there) **18**
oh là là! uh, oh!; oh, dear!; wow!; oh, yes!
laid ugly
laisser (un message) to leave (a message)
laisser: laisse-moi tranquille! leave me alone! **28**
le **lait** milk **25**
une **lampe** lamp [9]
une **langue** language
large wide
laver to wash **21**
se **laver** to wash (oneself), wash up
le the [2B], [10]; him, it **28**
le + *number* + *month* the … [4B]
le (lundi) on (Mondays) [10]
une **leçon** lesson
un **lecteur MP3** MP3 player [9]
un **légume** vegetable **25**
lent slow
les the [10]; them **28**
une **lettre** letter
leur(s) their **16**
leur (to) them **28**
se **lever: lève-toi!** stand up! [I]
levez-vous! stand up! [I]
un **lézard** lizard [E4]
le **Liban** Lebanon *(country in the Middle East)*
libanais Lebanese
libéré liberated

une **librairie** bookstore
libre free
un **lieu** place, area
avoir lieu to take place
une **ligne** line
limité limited
la **limonade** lemon soda [3B]
un **lion** lion [E4]
* **lire** to read
comment lire reading hints
lisez… (*see* **lire**) read … [I]
une **liste** list
une liste des courses shopping list
un **lit** bed [9], **AX**
un **living** living room *(informal)*
un **livre** book [I, 9]
une **livre** metric pound **25**
local (*m.pl.* **locaux**) local
une **location** rental
logique logical
logiquement logically
loin far [13]
loin d'ici far (from here)
le **loisir** leisure, free time
un **loisir** leisure-time activity
Londres London
long (longue) long **17**
longtemps (for) a long time
moins longtemps que for a shorter time
le **loto** lotto, lottery, bingo
louer to rent **21**
un **loup** wolf [E4]
lui him **15;** (to) him/her **28**
lui-même: en lui-même to himself
lundi *m.* Monday [4B], **AX**
des **lunettes** *f.* glasses **17**
des lunettes de soleil sunglasses **17**
le **Luxembourg** Luxembourg
un **lycée** high school

m' (*see* **me**)
M. (monsieur) Mr. (Mister) [1C]
ma my [2C], **16**
et voici ma mère and this is my mother [2C]
ma chambre my bedroom [9]
une **machine** machine
une machine à coudre sewing machine
Madagascar Madagascar *(French-speaking island off of East Africa)*
Madame (Mme) Mrs., ma'am [1C]
Mademoiselle (Mlle) Miss [1C]
un **magasin** store, shop [13], **17**
faire les magasins to go shopping (browsing from store to store)
un grand magasin department store **17**
magnétique magnetic
un **magnétophone** tape recorder
un **magnétoscope** VCR (videocassette recorder)
magnifique magnificent
mai *m.* May [4B], **AX**
maigre thin, skinny
maigrir to lose weight, get thin **19**
un **mail** e-mail
un **maillot de bain** bathing suit **17**
une **main** hand [E2]
maintenant now [7], **23**
mais but [6]
j'aime…, mais je préfère… I like …, but I prefer … [5]
je regrette, mais je ne peux pas… I'm sorry, but I can't … [5]
mais oui! sure! [6]
mais non! of course not! [6]
une **maison** house [13]
à la maison at home [6]
mal badly, poorly [1C], [7]
ça va mal things are going badly [1C]
ça va très mal things are going very badly [1C]
c'est mal that's bad [12]
malade sick
malheureusement unfortunately
malin clever
manger to eat [7], **AX**
j'aime manger I like to eat [5]
manger + du, de la *(partitive)* to eat (some) **26**
une salle à manger dining room [13]
un **manteau** (*pl.* **manteaux**) overcoat **17**
un manteau de fourrure fur coat
un **marchand, une marchande** merchant, shopkeeper, dealer
un **marché** open-air market **25**
un marché aux puces flea market
bon marché *(inv.)* inexpensive **17**
marcher to work, to run *(for objects)* [9], **AX;** to walk *(for people)* [9], **AX**
il/elle (ne) marche (pas) bien it (doesn't) work(s) well [9]
est-ce que la radio marche? does the radio work? [9]
mardi *m.* **Tuesday** [4B], **AX**
le Mardi gras Shrove Tuesday
un **mari** husband **16**
le **mariage** wedding, marriage
marié married
une **marmite** covered stew pot
le **Maroc** Morocco *(country in North Africa)*
une **marque** brand (name)
une **marraine** godmother
marrant fun
marron *(inv.)* brown [12]
mars *m.* March [4B], **AX**
martiniquais from Martinique
la **Martinique** Martinique *(French island in the West Indies)*
un **match** game, (sports) match **14**
faire un match to play a game, (sports) match [8]
les **maths** *f.* math
le **matin** morning **21;** in the morning AX
ce matin this morning **23**
demain matin tomorrow morning **23**
du matin in the morning, A.M. [4A]
hier matin yesterday morning **23, AX**
des **matoutou crabes** *m.* stewed crabs with rice
mauvais bad [12]
c'est une mauvaise idée that's a bad idea
il fait mauvais it's bad *(weather)* [4C]
la **mayonnaise** mayonnaise **25**
me (to) me **27**
méchant mean, nasty [11]

un **médecin** doctor
  un médecin de nuit doctor on night duty
la **Méditerranée** Mediterranean Sea
meilleur(e) better, best **19**
mélanger to mix, stir
même same; even
  eux-mêmes themselves
  les mêmes choses the same things
une **mémoire** memory
mentionner to mention
la **mer** ocean, shore **21**
  à la mer to (at) the sea **21**
merci thank you [1C]
  oui, merci yes, thank you [5]
mercredi *m.* Wednesday [4B], **AX**
une **mère** mother [2C], **16**
mériter to deserve
mes my **16**
la **messagerie vocale** voice mail
le **métro** subway
en **métro** by subway **14**
* **mettre** to put on, to wear **17; to put, to place, to turn on 18**
  mettre la table to set the table **25**
mexicain Mexican [11], **AX**
midi *m.* noon [4A]
  il est midi it is noontime **AX**
mieux better
mignon (mignonne) cute [11], **AX**
militaire military
mille one thousand [2B], **17**
minérale: l'eau *f.* minérale mineral water **25**
une **mini-chaîne** compact stereo [9]
minuit *m.* midnight [4A]
  il est minuit it is midnight **AX**
mis (*p.p. of* **mettre**) put, placed **23**
mixte mixed
Mlle Miss [1C]
Mme Mrs. [1C]
une **mob (mobylette)** motorbike, moped [9], **AX**
moche plain, ugly **17**
la **mode** fashion
  à la mode popular; in fashion; fashionable **17**
moderne modern [13]
moi me [1A], **15; (to) me 27**
  moi, je m'appelle (Marc) me, my name is (Marc) [1A]
  avec moi with me [5]
  donne-moi give me [3A]
  donnez-moi give me [3B]
  excusez-moi... excuse me ... [13]
  prête-moi... lend me ... [3C]
  s'il te plaît, donne-moi... please give me ... [3B]
un **moine** monk
moins less
  moins de less than
  moins... que less ... than **19**
  ... heure(s) moins (dix) (ten) of ... [4A]
  ... heure(s) moins le quart quarter of ... [4A]
un **mois** month [4B], **21**
  ce mois-ci this month **23**
  le mois dernier last month **23**
  le mois prochain next month **23**
  par mois per month, a month
mon (ma; mes) my [2C], **16**
  mon anniversaire est le... my birthday is the ... [4B]
  voici mon père this is my father [2C]
le **monde** world
  du monde in the world
  tout le monde everyone
la **monnaie** money; change
Monsieur (M.) Mr., sir [1C]
  un monsieur (*pl.* **messieurs**) gentleman, man *(polite term)* [2A]
une **montagne** mountain **21**
  à la montagne to (at) the mountains **21**
une **montre** watch [9], **AX**
montrer à to show ... to **27, 28**
  montre-moi (montrez-moi) show me [I]
un **morceau** piece
  un morceau de craie piece of chalk [I]
un **mot** word
une **moto** motorcycle [9]
la **moutarde** mustard
un **mouton** sheep
moyen (moyenne) average, medium
en **moyenne** on the average
un **moyen** means
un **MP3** MP3 player [9]
muet (muette) silent
le **multimédia** multimedia
un **musée** museum [13]
la **musique** music **15**

N

n' (*see* **ne**)
nager to swim [7], **AX**
  j'aime nager I like to swim [5]
une **nationalité** nationality [1B], **AX**
nautique: le ski nautique water-skiing **21**
ne (n')
  ne... aucun none, not any
  ne... jamais never **24**
  ne... pas not [6]
  ne... personne nobody **24**
  ne... plus no longer
  ne... rien nothing **24**
  n'est-ce pas? right?, no?, isn't it (so)?, don't you?, aren't you? [6]
né born
nécessaire necessary
négatif (négative) negative
négativement negatively
la **neige** snow
  neiger to snow
  il neige it's snowing [4C], **AX**
le **Net** the Internet
nettoyer to clean **21**
neuf nine [1A]
neuvième ninth **16**
un **neveu** (*pl.* **neveux**) nephew
un **nez** nose [E2]
une **nièce** niece
un **niveau** (*pl.* **niveaux**) level
Noël m. Christmas
  à Noël at Christmas **21**
noir black [E1, 12]
un **nom** name; noun
un **nombre** number
nombreux (nombreuses) numerous
nommé named
non no [1B, 6]
  non plus neither
  mais non! of course not! **[6]**
le **nord** north
le **nord-est** northeast
normalement normally
nos our **16**
une **note** grade
notre (*pl.* **nos**) our **16**

la **nourriture** food **25**
nous we [6]; us **15;** (to) us **27**
nouveau (nouvel, nouvelle; *m.pl.* **nouveaux)** new **19**
la **Nouvelle-Angleterre** New England
la **Nouvelle-Calédonie** New Caledonia *(French island in the South Pacific)*
novembre *m.* November [4B], **AX**
le onze novembre Armistice Day
la **nuit** night
un **numéro** number

O

objectif (objective) objective
un **objet** object [9], **AX**
une **occasion** occasion; opportunity
occupé occupied
un **océan** ocean
octobre *m.* October [4B], **AX**
une **odeur** odor
un **oeil** (*pl.* **yeux**) eye [E2]
un **oeuf** egg **25**
officiel (officielle) official
offert (*p.p. of* **offrir**) offered
* **offrir** to offer, to give
oh là là! uh,oh!, oh, dear!, wow!, oh, yes!
un **oiseau** (*pl.* **oiseaux**) bird
une **omelette** omelet [3A]
on one, they, you, people **20**
on est... today is ...
on va dans un café? shall we go to a café?
on y va let's go
comment dit-on... en français? how do you say ... in French? [I]
un **oncle** uncle [2C], **16**
onze eleven [1B], **AX**
opérer to operate
l' **or** *m.* gold
orange *(inv.)* orange *(color)* [E1, 12]
une orange orange *(fruit)*
le jus d'orange orange juice [3B], **25**
un **ordinateur** computer [9]
un **ordinateur portable** laptop computer
une **oreille** ear [E2]
organiser to organize [7]
organiser une boum to organize a party **AX**
originairement originally
l' **origine** *f.* origin, beginning
d'origine bretonne from Brittany
orthographiques: les signes *m.* **orthographiques** spelling marks
ou or [1B, 6]
où where [6, 8], **R3**
où est...? where is ...? [6]
où est-ce? where is it? [13]
d'où? from where? **15**
oublier to forget
l' **ouest** *m.* west
oui yes [1B, 6]
oui, bien sûr... yes, of course ... [5]
oui, d'accord... yes, okay ... [5]
oui, j'ai... yes, I have ... [9]
oui, merci... yes, thank you ... [5]
mais oui! sure! [6]
un **ouragan** hurricane
un **ours** bear [E4]
ouvert open
* **ouvrir** to open
ouvre... (ouvrez...) open ... [I]

P

le **pain** bread **25**
pâle pale
un **pamplemousse** grapefruit **25**
une **panne** breakdown
une panne d'électricité power failure
un **pantalon** pants, trousers **17**
une **panthère** panther
une **papaye** papaya
le **papier** paper
une feuille de papier a sheet (piece) of paper [I]
Pâques *m.* Easter **21**
à Pâques at Easter **21**
par per
par exemple for example
par jour per day
un **parc** park [13]
un parc public city park
parce que (parce qu') because [8]
pardon excuse me [13], **17**
les **parents** *m.* parents, relatives **16**
paresseux (paresseuse) lazy
parfait perfect
rien n'est parfait nothing is perfect
parfois sometimes
parisien (parisienne) Parisian
parler to speak, talk [I, 7]
parler à to speak (talk) to **28**
parler (français, anglais, espagnol) to speak (French, English, Spanish) [5]
un **parrain** godfather
une **partie** part
* **partir** to leave
à partir de as of, beginning
partitif (partitive) partitive
pas not
ne... pas not [6]
pas de not a, no, not any [10], **26**
pas du tout not at all, definitely not **15**
pas possible not possible
pas toujours not always [5]
pas très bien not very well
le **passé composé** compound past tense
passer to spend (time) **21;** to pass by
passionnément passionately
une **pâte** dough
patient patient
le **patinage** ice skating, roller skating
une **patinoire** skating rink
une **pâtisserie** pastry, pastry shop
une **patte** foot, paw *(of bird or animal)*
pauvre poor **20**
payer to pay, pay for **20**
un **pays** country
un **PC portable** laptop computer
la **peau** skin, hide
* **peindre** to paint
peint painted
une **pellicule** film (camera)
pendant during **21**
pénétrer to enter
pénible bothersome, a pain [12]
penser to think **17**
penser de to think of **17**
penser que to think that **17**
qu'est-ce que tu penses de...? what do you think of ...? **17**
une **pension** inn, boarding house
Pentecôte *f.* Pentecost
perdre to lose, to waste **20**
perdu (*p.p. of* **perdre**) lost

FRENCH-ENGLISH VOCABULARY *continued*

un **père** father [2C], **16**
* **permettre** to permit
un **perroquet** parrot
la **personnalité** personality **AX**
personne (de) nobody **24**
ne... personne nobody, not anybody, not anyone **24**
une personne person [2A]
personnel (personnelle) personal
personnellement personally
péruvien (péruvienne) Peruvian
petit small, short [9, 12], **17**
il/elle est petit(e) he/she is short [9]
un petit copain, une petite copine boyfriend, girlfriend
plus petit(e) smaller
le petit déjeuner breakfast **25**
prendre le petit déjeuner to have breakfast **25**
le petit-fils, la petite-fille grandson, granddaughter
les petits pois *m.* peas **25**
peu little, not much
un peu a little, a little bit [7]
un peu de a few
peut (*see* **pouvoir**)
peut-être perhaps, maybe [6]
peux (*see* **pouvoir**)
je peux I can **R3**
je ne peux pas I cannot **R3**
est-ce que tu peux...? can you ...? [5], **R3**
je regrette, mais je ne peux pas... I'm sorry, but I can't ... [5]
la **photo** photography
une **phrase** sentence [I]
la **physique** physics
un **piano** piano **15**
une **pie** magpie [E4]
une **pièce** coin **20;** room
un **pied** foot [E2]
à pied on foot **14**
faire une promenade à pied to take a walk **14**
piloter to pilot (a plane)
une **pincée** pinch
le **ping-pong** Ping-Pong **15**
un **pique-nique** picnic **14**
faire un pique-nique to have a picnic **21**
une **piscine** swimming pool [13]
une **pizza** pizza [3A]
un **placard** closet

une **plage** beach [13]
plaît: s'il te plaît please *(informal)* [3A]; excuse me (please)
s'il te plaît, donne-moi... please, give me ... [3B]
s'il vous plaît please *(formal)* [3B]; excuse me (please)
un **plan** map
la **planche à voile** windsurfing **21**
faire de la planche à voile to windsurf **21**
une **plante** plant
un **plat** dish, course *(of a meal)* **25**
le **plat principal** main course
un **plateau** tray
pleut: il pleut it's raining [4C], **AX**
plier to fold
plumer to pluck
plus more
plus de more than
plus joli que prettier than
plus... que more ... than, ... -er than **19**
en plus in addition
le plus the most
ne... plus no longer, no more
non plus neither
plusieurs several
une **poche** pocket
l'argent *m.* **de poche** allowance, pocket money
une **poêle** frying pan
un **point de vue** point of view
une **poire** pear **25**
pois: les petits pois *m.* peas **25**
un **poisson** fish [E4], **25**
un poisson rouge goldfish
blaff de poisson fish stew
poli polite
un **politicien, une politicienne** politician
un **polo** polo shirt **17**
une **pomme** apple
le jus de pomme apple juice [3B], **25**
une **pomme de terre** potato **25**
une purée de pommes de terre mashed potatoes
le **porc: une côtelette de porc** pork chop
un **portable** cell phone [9]
une **porte** door [I, 9]
un **porte-monnaie** change purse, wallet
porter to wear **17**

portugais Portuguese
poser: poser une question to ask a question
une **possibilité** possibility
la **poste** post office
poster un message post a message [9]
pouah! yuck! yech!
une **poule** hen [E4]
le **poulet** chicken **25**
pour for [6]; in order to **21**
pour que so that
pour qui? for whom? [8], **R3**
le **pourcentage** percentage
pourquoi why **R3**[8]
* **pouvoir** to be able, can, may **27**
pratique practical
pratiquer to participate in
des **précisions** *f.* details
préféré favorite
préférer to prefer **18;** to like (in general)
je préfère I prefer [5], **R3**
tu préférerais? would you prefer?
premier (première) first **16**
le premier de l'an New Year's Day
le premier étage second floor
le premier mai Labor Day *(in France)*
c'est le premier juin it's June first [4B]
* **prendre** to take, to have *(food)* [I], **26**
prendre + du, de la *(partitive)* to have (some) **26**
prendre le petit déjeuner to have breakfast **25**
un **prénom** first name
préparer to prepare; to prepare for **21**
près nearby [13]
près d'ici nearby, near here
tout près very close
une **présentation** appearance
la présentation extérieure outward appearance
des **présentations** *f.* introductions
pressé in a hurry
prêt ready
un **prêt** loan
prêter à to lend to, to loan **27, 28**
prête-moi... lend me... [3C]
principalement mainly
le **printemps** spring [4C], **AX**
au printemps in the spring [4C]
pris (*p.p. of* **prendre**) took **26**

un **prix** price
quel est le prix ...? what's the price ...? **17**
un **problème** problem
prochain next **21, 23**
le week-end prochain next weekend **21**
un **produit** product
un **prof, une prof** teacher *(informal)* [2A, 9], **AX**
un **professeur** teacher [9]
professionnel (professionnelle) professional
un **programme** program
un **projet** plan
une **promenade** walk
faire une promenade à pied to go for a walk [8], **14**
faire une promenade à vélo to go for a ride (by bike) **14**
faire une promenade en voiture to go for a drive (by car) **14**
* **promettre** to promise
une **promo** special sale
proposer to suggest
propre own
un **propriétaire, une propriétaire** landlord/landlady, owner
la **Provence** Provence *(province in southern France)*
pu (*p.p. of* **pouvoir**) could, was able to **27**
n'a pas pu was not able to
public: un parc public city park
un jardin public public garden
la **publicité** commercials, advertising, publicity
une **puce** flea
un marché aux puces flea market
puis then, also
puisque since
un **pull** sweater, pullover **17**
les **Pyrénées** (the) Pyrenees *(mountains between France and Spain)*

Q

qu' (*see* **que**)
une **qualité** quality
quand when [8], **R3**
c'est quand, ton anniversaire? when is your birthday? [4B], **AX**
une **quantité** quantity **25**
quarante forty [1C], **AX**
un **quart** one quarter
... heure(s) et quart quarter past ... [4A], **AX**
... heure(s) moins le quart quarter of ... [4A], **AX**
un **quartier** district, neighborhood [13]
un joli quartier a nice neighborhood [13]
quatorze fourteen [1B], **AX**
quatre four [1A], **AX**
quatre-vingt-dix ninety [2B], **AX**
quatre-vingts eighty [2B], **AX**
quatrième fourth **16**
que that, which
que veut dire...? what does ... mean? [I]
qu'est-ce que (qu') what *(phrase used to introduce a question)* [8]
qu'est-ce que c'est? what is it? what's that? [9]
qu'est-ce que tu penses de...? what do you think of ...? **17**
qu'est-ce que tu veux? what do you want? [3A]
qu'est-ce qu'il y a? what is there? [9], **R2;** what's the matter?
qu'est-ce qui ne va pas? what's wrong?
un **Québécois, une Québécoise** person from Quebec
québécois from Quebec
quel (quelle) what, which, what a **18**
quel (quelle)...! what a...!
quel âge a ta mère/ton père? how old is your mother/your father? [2C]
quel âge a-t-il/elle? how old is he/she? [9]
quel âge as-tu? how old are you? [2C]
quel est le prix...? what is the price ...? **17**
quel jour est-ce? what day is it? [4B], **AX**
quel temps fait-il? what's (how's) the weather? [4C]
quelle est la date? what's the date? [4B], **AX**
quelle est ton adresse? what's your address? [13]
quelle heure est-il? what time is it? [4A], **AX**
à quelle heure? at what time? [4A], **AX**
à quelle heure est...? at what time is ...? [4A], **AX**
de quelle couleur...? what color is ...? [12], **AX**
quelqu'un someone **24**
quelque chose something **24**
quelques some, a few [9]
une **question** question
une **queue** tail
qui who, whom [8]
qui est-ce? who's that (this)? [2A, 9]
qui se ressemble... birds of a feather ...
à qui? to whom? [8]
avec qui? with who(m)? [8]
c'est qui? who's that? *(casual speech)*
de qui? about who(m)? [8]
pour qui? for who(m)? [8]
qui? whom? **R3**
quinze fifteen [1B], **AX**
quoi? what? [9]
quotidien (quotidienne) daily
la vie quotidienne daily life

R

raconter to tell about
une **radio** radio [9], **AX**
écouter la radio to listen to the radio [5]
raisin: le jus de raisin grape juice [3B]
une **raison** reason **avoir raison** to be right **22**
ranger to pick up **21**
rapidement rapidly
un **rapport** relationship
une **raquette** racket [9], **AX**
une raquette de tennis tennis racket **15**
rarement rarely, seldom [7]
un **rayon** department *(in a store)*
réalisé made, directed
récemment recently
une **recette** recipe
recherche: un avis de recherche missing person's bulletin

un **récital** (*pl.* **récitals**) (musical) recital
reconstituer to reconstruct
un **réfrigérateur** refrigerator
refuser to refuse
regarder to look at, watch [I, 7]
regarde ça look at that [9]
regarder la télé to watch TV [5], **AX**
un **régime** diet
être au régime to be on a diet
régional (*m.pl.* **régionaux**) regional
regretter to be sorry
je regrette, mais... I'm sorry, but ... [5]
régulier (régulière) regular
une **reine** queen
rencontrer to meet **21**
une **rencontre** meeting, encounter
un **rendez-vous** date, appointment **14**
j'ai un rendez-vous à... I have a date, appointment at ... [4A]
rendre visite à to visit, come to visit **20, 28**
la **rentrée** first day back at school in fall
rentrer to go back, come back **22;** to return, go back, come back **14**
réparer to fix, repair **21**
un **repas** meal **25**
* **repeindre** to repaint
répéter to repeat [I]
répondre (à) to answer, respond (to) [I], **28**
répondez-lui (moi) answer him (me)
répondre que oui to answer yes
une **réponse** answer
un **reportage** documentary
représenter to represent
réservé reserved
une **résolution** resolution
un **restaurant** restaurant [13]
au restaurant to (at) the restaurant [6]
dîner au restaurant to have dinner at a restaurant [5]
un restaurant trois étoiles three star restaurant
rester to stay **14, 24**
retard: un jour de retard one day behind
en retard late
retourner to return; to turn over
réussir to succeed **19**
réussir à un examen to pass an exam **19**
* **revenir** to come back **15**
revoir: au revoir! good-bye! [1C]
le **rez-de-chaussée** ground floor
un **rhinocéros** rhinoceros [E4]
riche rich **20**
rien (de) nothing **24**
rien n'est parfait nothing is perfect
ne... rien nothing **24**
une **rive** (river) bank
une **rivière** river, stream
le **riz** rice **25**
une **robe** dress **17**
le **roller** in-line skating **21**
faire du roller to go in-line skating **21**
des rollers in-line skates **21**
romain Roman
le **rosbif** roast beef **25**
rose pink [12], **AX**
rosse nasty *(colloq.)*
une **rôtie** toast *(Canadian)*
rôtir to roast
une **roue** wheel
rouge red [E1, 12]
rougir to turn red
rouler to roll
roux (rousse) red-head
une **rue** street [13]
dans la rue (Victor Hugo) on (Victor Hugo) street [13]
russe Russian

S

sa his, her **16**
un **sac** book bag, bag [I]; bag, handbag [9], **AX**
sais (*see* **savoir**)
je **sais** I know [I, 9], **28**
je ne sais pas I don't know [I, 9]
tu sais you know **28**
une **saison** season [4C]
toute saison all year round (any season)
une **salade** salad [3A], **25;** lettuce **25**
un **salaire** salary
une **salle** hall, large room
une salle à manger dining room [13]
une salle de bains bathroom [13]
une salle de séjour informal living room
un **salon** formal living room [13]
salut hi!, good-bye! [1C]
une **salutation** greeting
samedi Saturday [4B], **23**
samedi soir Saturday night
à samedi! see you Saturday! [4B]
le samedi on Saturdays [10]
une **sandale** sandal **17**
un **sandwich** sandwich [3A], **AX**
sans without
des **saucisses** *f.* sausages
le **saucisson** salami **25**
* **savoir** to know *(information)*
je **sais** I know [I, 9], **28**
je ne sais pas I don't know [I, 9]
tu sais you know **28**
un **saxo (saxophone)** saxophone **15**
une **scène** scene, stage
les **sciences** *f.* **économiques** economics
les **sciences** *f.* **naturelles** natural science
un **scooter** motor scooter [9], **AX**
second second
seize sixteen [1B]
un **séjour** stay; informal living room
le **sel** salt **25**
selon according to
selon toi in your opinion
une **semaine** week [4B], **21**
cette semaine this week **23**
la semaine dernière last week **23**
la semaine prochaine next week **23**
par semaine per week, a week
semblable similar
le **Sénégal** Senegal *(French-speaking country in Africa)*
sensationnel (sensationnelle) sensational
séparer to separate
sept seven [1A], **AX**
septembre *m.* September [4B], **AX**
septième seventh **16**
une **série** series
sérieux (sérieuse) serious
un **serveur, une serveuse** waiter, waitress
servi served
une **serviette** napkin **25**
ses his, her **16**

seul alone, only; by oneself **21**
seulement only, just
un **short** shorts **17**
si if, whether
si! so, yes! *(to a negative question)* [10]
un **signal** (*pl.* **signaux**) signal
un **signe** sign
un signe orthographique spelling mark
un **singe** monkey [E4]
situé situated
six six [1A], **AX**
sixième sixth **16**
le **skate** skateboarding **21**
un **skate** skateboard **21**
faire du skate to go skateboarding **21**
le **ski** skiing
le ski nautique water-skiing **21**
faire du ski to ski **21**
faire du ski nautique to go water-skiing **21**
skier to ski
snob snobbish
le **snowboard** snowboarding **21**
faire du snowboard to go snowboarding **21**
un snowboard snowboard **21**
la **Société Nationale des Chemins de Fer (SNCF)** *French railroad system*
une **société** society
un **soda** soda [3B]
une **soeur** sister [2C], **16**
la **soie** silk
la **soif** thirst
avoir soif to be thirsty **22**
j'ai soif I'm thirsty [3B]
tu as soif? are you thirsty? [3B]
un **soir** evening **21**
ce soir this evening, tonight **23**
demain soir tomorrow night (evening) **21, 23**
du soir in the evening, P.M. [4A]
hier soir last night **23**
le soir in the evening
une soirée (whole) evening; (evening) party
soixante sixty [1C, 2A], **AX**
soixante-dix seventy [2A], **AX**
un **soldat** soldier
un **solde** (clearance) sale en solde on sale
la **sole** sole *(fish)* **25**

le **soleil** sun
les lunettes *f.* **de soleil** sunglasses **17**
sommes (*see* **être**)
nous sommes... it is, today is ... *(date)*
son (sa; ses) his, her **16**
un **sondage** poll
une **sorte** sort, type, kind
* **sortir** to leave, come out
un **souhait** wish
la **soupe** soup **25**
une **souris** mouse (computer)
sous under [9], **R2**
le **sous-sol** basement
souvent often [7]
soyez (*see* **être**): soyez
les **spaghetti** *m.* spaghetti **25**
spécialement especially
spécialisé specialized
une **spécialité** specialty
le **sport** sports **15, 21**
faire du sport to play sports **21**
des vêtements *m.* **de sport** sports clothing **17**
une voiture de sport sports car **15**
sportif (sportive) athletic [11]
un **stade** stadium [13]
un **stage** sports training camp; internship
une **station-service** gas station
un **steak** steak [3A]
un steak-frites steak and French fries [3A]
un **stylo** pen [I, 9]
le **sucre** sugar **25**
le **sud** south
suggérer to suggest
suis (*see* **être**)
je suis + *nationality* I'm ... [1B]
je suis de... I'm from... [1B]
suisse Swiss [11], **AX**
la **Suisse** Switzerland
suivant following
suivi followed
un **sujet** subject, topic
super terrific [7]; great [12], **17**
un **supermarché** supermarket [13]
supersonique supersonic
supérieur superior
supplémentaire supplementary, extra
sur on [9], **R2; about**

sûr sure, certain
bien sûr! of course! [6]
oui, bien sûr... yes, of course ...! [5]
tu es sûr(e)? are you sure? **16**
sûrement surely
la **surface: une grande surface** big store, self-service store
surfer to go snowboarding
surfer sur l'Internet (sur le Net) to surf the Internet
surtout especially
un **survêtement** jogging or track suit **17**
un **sweat** sweatshirt **17**
une **sweaterie** shop specializing in sweatshirts and sportswear
sympa nice, pleasant *(colloq.)*
sympathique nice, pleasant [11], **AX**
une **synagogue** Jewish temple or synagogue
un **synthétiseur** electronic keyboard, synthesizer

T

t' (*see* **te**)
ta your [2C], **16**
une **table** table [I, 9]
mettre la table to set the table **25**
un **tableau** (*pl.* **tableaux**) chalkboard [I]
une **tablette** tablet (computer) [9]
Tahiti Tahiti *(French island in the South Pacific)*
une **taille** size
de taille moyenne of medium height or size
un **tailleur** woman's suit
se **taire: tais-toi!** be quiet!
une **tante** aunt [2C], **16**
la **tarte** pie **25**
une **tasse** cup **25**
un **taxi** taxi
en taxi by taxi **14**
te (to) you **27**
un **tee-shirt** T-shirt **17**
la **télé** TV [9], **AX**
à la télé on TV
regarder la télé TV [5]
télécharger to download
un **téléphone** telephone [9], **AX**

téléphoner (à) to call, phone [5], [7], **28, AX**
télévisé: des jeux *m.* **télévisés** TV game shows
un **temple** Protestant church
le **temps** time; weather
combien de temps? how long?
de temps en temps from time to time
quel temps fait-il? what's (how's) the weather? [4C]
tout le temps all the time
le **tennis** tennis **15**
jouer au tennis to play tennis [5]
des tennis *m.* tennis shoes, sneakers **17**
un **terrain de sport** (playing) field
une **terrasse** outdoor section of a café, terrace
la **terre** earth
une pomme de terre potato **25**
terrifiant terrifying
tes your **16**
la **tête** head [E2]
un **texto** text message [9]
le **thé** tea [3B]
un thé glacé iced tea **25**
un **théâtre** theater [13]
le **thon** tuna **25**
tiens! look!, hey! [2A, 10]
un **tigre** tiger [E4]
timide timid, shy [11], **AX**
le **tissu** fabric
un **titre** title
toi you **15**
avec toi with you [5]
et toi? and you? [1A]
les **toilettes** *f.* bathroom, toilet [13]
un **toit** roof
une **tomate** tomato **25**
le jus de tomate tomato juice [3B]
un **tombeau** tomb
ton (ta; tes) your [2C], **16 c'est quand, ton anniversaire?** when's your birthday? [4B]
tort: avoir tort to be wrong **22**
une **tortue** turtle [E4]
un bifteck de tortue turtle steak
toujours always [7]
je n'aime pas toujours... I don't always like ... [5]
un **tour** turn
à votre tour it's your turn

la **Touraine** Touraine *(province in central France)*
tourner to turn [13]
la **Toussaint** All Saints' Day *(November 1)*
tout (toute; tous, toutes) all, every, the whole
tous les jours every day
tout ça all that
tout le monde everyone
tout le temps all the time
toutes sortes all sorts, kinds
tout completely, very
tout droit straight [13]
tout de suite right away
tout près very close
tout all, everything
pas du tout not at all **15**
un **train** train **21**
tranquille quiet
laisse-moi tranquille! leave me alone! **28**
un **travail** (*pl.* **travaux**) job
travailler to work [5, 7], **AX**
une **traversée** crossing
treize thirteen [1B], **AX**
trente thirty [1C], **AX**
un **tréma** diaeresis
très very [11]
très bien very well [7]
ça va très bien things are going very well [1C]
ça va très mal things are going very badly [1C]
trois three [1A], **AX**
troisième third **16;** *9th grade in France*
trop too, too much **17**
trouver to find, to think of **17**
comment trouves-tu...? what do you think of ...? how do you find ...? **17**
s'y trouve is there
tu you [6]
la **Tunisie** Tunisia *(country in North Africa)*

U

un, une one [1A]; a, an [2A], [10]
unique only
uniquement only
une **université** university, college
l' **usage** *m.* use

un **ustensile** utensil
utile useful
utiliser to use
en utilisant (by) using
utilisez... use ...

va (*see* **aller**)
va-t'en! go away! **14**
ça va? how are you? how's everything? [1C]
ça va! everything's fine (going well); fine, I'm OK [1C]
on va dans un café? shall we go to a café?
on y va let's go
les **vacances** *f.* vacation
bonnes vacances! have a nice vacation!
en vacances on vacation [6]
les grandes vacances summer vacation **21**
une **vache** cow
vais (*see* **aller**): **je vais** I'm going **14**
la **vaisselle** dishes
faire la vaisselle to do the dishes
valable valid
une **valise** suitcase
vanille: une glace à la vanille vanilla ice cream
varié varied
les **variétés** *f.* variety show
vas (see **aller**)
comment vas-tu? how are you? [1C]
vas-y! come on!, go ahead!, do it! **14**
le **veau** veal **25**
une **vedette** star
un **vélo** bicycle [9], **AX**
à vélo by bicycle **14**
faire une promenade à vélo to go for a bicycle ride **14**
un vélo tout terrain (un VTT) mountain bike
un **vendeur, une vendeuse** salesperson
vendre to sell **20**
vendredi *m.* Friday [4B], **AX**
vendu (*p.p. of* **vendre**) sold **23**
* **venir** to come **15**
le **vent** wind

une **vente** sale
le **ventre** stomach [E2]
venu (*p.p. of* **venir**) came, come **24**
vérifier to check
la **vérité** truth
un **verre** glass **25**
verser to pour
vert green [E1, 12], **AX**
 les • haricots *m.* **verts** green beans **25**
une **veste** jacket **17**
des **vêtements** *m.* clothing **17**
 des vêtements de sport sports clothing **17**
veut (*see* **vouloir**): **que veut dire...?** what does ... mean? [I]
veux (*see* **vouloir**)
 est-ce que tu veux...? do you want ...? [5], **R3**
 je ne veux pas... I don't want ... [5], **R3**
 je veux... I want ... [5], **26, R3**
 je veux bien... I'd love to, I do, I want to ... [5], **26**
 qu'est-ce que tu veux? what do you want? [3A]
 tu veux...? do you want ...? [3A]
la **viande** meat **25**
la **vie** life
 la vie quotidienne daily life
viens (*see* **venir**)
 viens... come ... [I]
 oui, je viens yes, I'm coming along with you
vieux (vieil, vieille; *m.pl.* **vieux)** old **19**
 le Vieux Carré *the French Quarter in New Orleans*
le **Viêt-nam** Vietnam *(country in Southeast Asia)*
vietnamien (vietnamienne) Vietnamese
une **vigne** vineyard
un **village** town, village [13]
 un petit village small town [13]
une **ville** city
 en ville in town, [6]
 une grande ville big city, town [13]
le **vin** wine
vingt twenty [1B, 1C], **AX**
violet (violette) purple, violet [E1]
un **violon** violin **15**
une **visite** visit
 rendre visite à to visit *(a person)* **20, 28**
visiter to visit *(places)* **23, 20**
vite! fast!, quick!
vive: vive les vacances! three cheers for vacation!
* **vivre** to live
le **vocabulaire** vocabulary
voici... here is, this is..., here come(s) ... [2A]
 voici + du, de la *(partitive)* here's some **26**
 voici mon père/ma mère here's my father/my mother [2C]
voilà... there is ..., there come(s) ... [2A]
 voilà + du, de la *(partitive)* there's some **26**
la **voile** sailing **21**
 faire de la voile to sail **21**
 la planche à voile windsurfing **21**
* **voir** to see **21, 23**
 voir un film to see a movie **21**
un **voisin, une voisine** neighbor [9], **AX**
une **voiture** car [9], **AX**
 une voiture de sport sports car **15**
 en voiture by car **14**
 faire une promenade en voiture to go for a drive by car **14**
une **voix** voice
le **volley (volleyball)** volleyball **15**
un **volontaire, une volontaire** volunteer
 comme volontaire as a volunteer
vos your **16**
votre (*pl.* **vos**) your **16**
voudrais (*see* **vouloir**): **je voudrais** I'd like [3A, 3B, 5], **26**
* **vouloir** to want **26**
vouloir + du, de la *(partitive)* to want some (of something) **26**
vouloir dire to mean **26**
voulu (*p.p. of* **vouloir**) wanted **26**
vous you [6]; (to) you **27**
 vous désirez? what would you like? may I help you? [3B], **17**
 s'il vous plaît please [3B]
un **voyage** trip
 bon voyage! have a nice trip!
 faire un voyage to take a trip [8]
voyager to travel [5, 7], **AX**
vrai true, right, real [12]
vraiment really **15**
le **VTT** mountain biking **21**
 faire du VTT to go mountain biking **21**
 un VTT mountain bike **21**
vu (*p.p. of* **voir**) saw, seen **23**
une **vue** view
 un point de vue point of view

les **WC** *m.* toilet
un **week-end** weekend **22, 23**
 bon week-end! have a nice weekend!
 ce week-end this weekend **21, 23**
 le week-end on weekends
 le week-end dernier last weekend **23**
 le week-end prochain next weekend **21, 23**

y there
 il y a there is, there are [9]
 est-ce qu'il y a...? is there ...?, are there ...? [9]
 qu'est-ce qu'il y a? what is there? [9]
 allons-y! let's go! **14**
 vas-y! come on!, go ahead!, do it! **14**
le **yaourt** yogurt **25**
des **yeux** *m.* (*sg.* **oeil**) eyes [E2]

un **zèbre** zebra
zéro zero [1A], **AX**
zut! darn! [1C]

ENGLISH-FRENCH VOCABULARY

The English-French vocabulary contains only active vocabulary.

The numbers following an entry indicate the lesson in which the word or phrase is activated. (**I** stands for the list of classroom expressions at the end of the first **Images** section in Book 1A; **E** stands for **Entracte**, and **AX** stands for **Appendix**.)

Nouns: If the article of a noun does not indicate gender, the noun is followed by *m. (masculine)* or *f. (feminine)*. If the plural *(pl.)* is irregular, it is given in parentheses.

Verbs: Verbs are listed in the infinitive form. An asterisk (*) in front of an active verb means that it is irregular. (For forms, see the verb charts in Appendix 4C.)

Words beginning with an **h** are preceded by a bullet (•) if the **h** is aspirate; that is, if the word is treated as if it begins with a consonant sound.

a, an un, une [2A], [10]
- **a few** quelques **25**
- **a little (bit)** un peu [7]
- **a lot** beaucoup [7]

able: to be able (to) *pouvoir **27**
about de **15**
- **about whom?** de qui? [8], **AX**

accessories des accessoires *m.* **17**
acquainted: to be acquainted with *connaître **28**
- **are you acquainted with ...?** tu connais...? [2B]

address une adresse [13]
- **what's your address?** quelle est ton adresse? [13]

after après **21, 22**
- **after that** ensuite **22**
- **afterwards** après **22**

afternoon l'après-midi *m.* **21**
- **in the afternoon** de l'après-midi [4A]
- **this afternoon** cet après-midi **23**
- **tomorrow afternoon** demain après-midi **23**
- **yesterday afternoon** hier après-midi **23**

to **agree** *être d'accord [6]
airplane un avion **21**
- **by airplane** en avion **21**

all tout
- **all right** d'accord [5]
- **not at all** pas du tout **15**

alone seul **21**
- **leave me alone!** laisse-moi tranquille! **28**

also aussi [1B, 7]
always toujours [7]
- **not always** pas toujours [5]

A.M. du matin **[4A]**
am (*see* **to be**)
- **I am ...** je suis + *nationality* [1B]

American américain **2, 19, AX**
- **I'm American** je suis américain(e) [1B, 11]

amusing amusant [11]
an un, une [2A, 10]
and et [1B, 6]
- **and you?** et toi? [1A]

annoying pénible [12]
another un(e) autre
to **answer** répondre (à) **28**
any des [10]; du, de, la, de l', de **26**
- **not any** pas de [10], **26**

anybody: not anybody ne... personne **24**
anyone quelqu'un **24**
anything quelque chose **24**
- **not anything** ne... rien **24**

apartment un appartement [13]
- **apartment building** un immeuble [13]

appetizer un • hors-d'oeuvre **25**
apple une pomme
- **apple juice** le jus de pomme [3B], **25**

appointment un rendez-vous **14**
- **I have an appointment at...** j'ai un rendez-vous à... [4A]

April avril *m.* [4B], **AX**
are (*see* **to be**)
- **are there?** est-ce qu'il y a? [9]
- **are you...?** tu es + *nationality?* [1B]
- **there are** il y a [9]
- **these/those/they are** ce sont [12]

arm un bras [E2]
to **arrive** arriver **14**
- **as ... as** aussi... que **19**

to **ask** demander (à) **28**
at à [6]; chez **14**
- **at (the)** au, à la, à l', aux **14**
- **at ...'s house** chez ... **14**
- **at ... o'clock** à ... heure(s) [6], **AX**
- **at home** à la maison [6]
- **at last** enfin **22**
- **at the restaurant** au restaurant [6]
- **at what time?** à quelle heure? [4A, 8], **R3**
- **at what time is ...?** à quelle heure est ...? [4A], **AX**

athletic sportif (sportive) [11]
to **attend** assister à **21**
attention: to pay attention *faire attention [8]
August août *m.* [4B], **AX**
aunt une tante [2C], **16**
automobile une auto, une voiture [9], **AX**
autumn l'automne *m.*, **AX**
- **in (the) autumn** en automne [4C]

avenue une avenue [13]
away: go away! va-t'en! **14**

back le dos [E2]
back: to come back rentrer **14, 24;** *revenir **15**
to go back rentrer **14, 24**
in back of derrière [9]
bad mauvais [12], **AX**
I'm/everything's (very) bad ça va (très) mal [1C]
it's bad (weather) il fait mauvais [4C]
that's bad c'est mal [12]
too bad! dommage! [7]
badly mal [1C]
things are going (very) badly ça va (très) mal [1C]
bag un sac [I, 9], **AX**
banana une banane **25**
banknote un billet **20**
baseball le baseball **15**
basketball le basket (basketball) **15**
bathing suit un maillot de bain **17**
bathroom une salle de bains [13]
to **be** *être [6]
to be ... (years old) *avoir... ans [10]
to be able (to) *pouvoir **27**
to be acquainted with *connaître **28**
to be active in *faire de + *activity* **21**
to be careful *faire attention [8]
to be cold (*people*) *avoir froid **22;** (*weather*) il fait froid [4C]
to be going to (*do something*) *aller + *inf.* **14**
to be hot (*people*) *avoir chaud **22**
to be hungry *avoir faim [10], **22**
to be lucky *avoir de la chance **22**
to be present at assister à **21**
to be right *avoir raison **22**
to be supposed to *devoir **27**
to be thirsty *avoir soif [10], **22**
to be warm (*people*) *avoir chaud **22, 23**
to be wrong *avoir tort **22**
beach une plage [13]
beans: green beans les •haricots *m.* verts **25**
beautiful beau (bel, belle; *m.pl.* beaux) [9]
it's beautiful (nice) weather il fait beau [4C]
because parce que (qu') [8]
bed un lit [9], **AX**
bedroom une chambre [9, 13]
been été (*p.p. of* *être) **23**
before avant **21, 23**
behind derrière [9]
below en bas [13]
belt une ceinture **17**
best meilleur **19**
better meilleur **19**
beverage une boisson [3B], **25**
bicycle un vélo, une bicyclette [9], **AX**
by bicycle à vélo **14**
take a bicycle ride *faire une promenade à vélo **14**
big grand [9, 12]
bill (*money*) un billet **20**
birthday un anniversaire [4B]
my birthday is (March 2) mon anniversaire est le (2 mars) [4B]
when is your birthday? c'est quand, ton anniversaire? [4B]
bit: a little bit un peu [7]
black noir [E1, 12], **AX**
blond blond [9], **AX**
blouse un chemisier **17**
blue bleu [E1, 12], **AX**
boat un bateau (*pl.* bateaux) **21**
book un livre [I, 9], **AX**
boots des bottes *f.* **17**
bothersome pénible [12]
boulevard un boulevard [13]
boutique une boutique **17**
boy le garçon [2A, 2B], **AX**
bread le pain **25**
breakfast le petit déjeuner **25**
to have breakfast prendre le petit déjeuner **25**
to **bring** (*a person*) amener **18;** (*things*) apporter **27**
to bring something to someone apporter quelque chose à quelqu'un **27**
brother un frère [2C], **16, AX**
brown brun [9]; marron (*inv.*) [12]
building: apartment building un immeuble [13]
bus un bus
by bus en bus **14**
touring bus un autocar, un car **21**
but mais [5]
butter le beurre **25**
to **buy** acheter **33, 34**
to buy (some) acheter + du, de la (*partitive*) **26**
by: by airplane, plane en avion **21**
by bicycle à vélo **14**
by bus en bus **14**
by car en voiture **14**
by oneself seul(e) **21**
by subway en métro **14**
by taxi en taxi **14**
by train en train **14**

café un café [6]
at (to) the café au café [6]
cafeteria: school cafeteria la cantine de l'école **25**
cake un gâteau (*pl.* gâteaux) **25**
calculator une calculatrice [9]
to **call** téléphoner [7]
came venu (*p.p. of* *venir) **23**
camera un appareil-photo (*pl.* appareils-photo) [9], **AX**
can *pouvoir **27**
can you ...? est-ce que tu peux...? [5], **R3**
I can't je ne peux pas [5]
Canada le Canada
Canadian canadien (canadienne) [1B, 11], **AX**
he's/she's (Canadian) il/elle est (canadien/canadienne) [2B]
cannot: I cannot je ne peux pas [5]
I'm sorry, but I cannot je regrette, mais je ne peux pas [5]
cap (baseball) une casquette **17**
car une auto, une voiture [9], **AX**
by car en voiture **14**
card une carte **(playing) cards** des cartes *f.* **15**
careful: to be careful *faire attention [8]
carrot une carotte **25**
cat un chat [2C], **AX**
cell phone un portable [9], **AX**
cereal les céréales *f.* **25**
chair une chaise [I, 9], **AX**
chalk la craie [I]

piece of chalk un morceau de craie [I]
chalkboard un tableau (*pl.* tableaux) [I]
checkers les dames *f.* **15**
cheese le fromage **25**
cherry une cerise **25**
chess les échecs *m.* **15**
chicken le poulet **25**
child un (une) enfant **16**
children des enfants *m.* **16**
Chinese chinois [11], **AX**
chocolate: hot chocolate un chocolat [3B]
to **choose** choisir **19**
chose, chosen choisi (*p.p. of* choisir) **23**
Christmas Noël **21**
at Christmas à Noël **21**
church une église [13]
cinema le cinéma [6]
to the cinema au cinéma [6]
city une ville [13]
in the city en ville [6]
clarinet une clarinette **15**
class une classe [6]
in class en classe [6]
classmate un (une) camarade [9], **AX**
to **clean** nettoyer **21**
clothing des vêtements *m.* **17**
sports clothing des vêtements *m.* de sport **17**
coffee le café [3B, 13]
coin une pièce **20**
cold le froid
to be (feel) cold *avoir froid **22**
it's cold (*weather*) il fait froid [4C]
college student un étudiant, une étudiante [9], **AX**
color une couleur [12]
what color? de quelle couleur? [12]
to **come** arriver **14**; *venir **15**
come on! vas-y! **14**
here comes ... voici... [2A]
to come back rentrer **14, 24**; *revenir **15**
to come to visit rendre visite à **20, 28**
comfortable comfortable [13]
compact disc un compact (disc), un CD [9], **AX**
computer un ordinateur, un PC [9], **AX**
computer game un jeu d'ordinateur (*pl.* les jeux d'ordinateur)
concert un concert **14**
to **continue** continuer [13]
cooking la cuisine **25**
cool: it's cool (*weather*) il fait frais [4C]
cost le coût **17**
to cost coûter
how much does ... cost? combien coûte...? [3C], **17**
it costs ... il/elle coûte... [3C]
country(side) la campagne **21**
to (in) the country(side) à la campagne **21**
course: of course! bien sûr! [5]; mais oui! [6]
of course not! mais non! [6]
cousin un cousin, une cousine [2C], **16**
crepe une crêpe [3A]
croissant un croissant [3A]
cuisine la cuisine **25**
cup une tasse **25**
cute mignon (mignonne) [11], **AX**

to **dance** danser [5, 7], **AX**
dark-haired brun [9]
darn! zut! [1C]
date la date [4B], **AX**; un rendez-vous **14**
I have a date at ... j'ai un rendez-vous à... [4A]
what's the date? quelle est la date? [4B]
daughter une fille **16**
day un jour [4B], **21**
what day is it? quel jour est-ce? [4B]
whole day une journée
dear cher (chère) **17**
December décembre *m.* [4B], **AX**
department store un grand magasin **17**
desk un bureau [I, 9], **AX**
dessert le dessert **25**
to **detest** détester **25**
did fait (*p.p. of* *faire) **23**
difficult difficile [12]
dining room une salle à manger [13]
dinner le dîner **25**
to have (eat) dinner dîner **7, 25**
to have dinner at a restaurant dîner au restaurant [5]
dish (*course of a meal*) un plat **25**
to **do, to make** *faire [8], **AX**
do it! vas-y! **14**
I do je veux bien **26**
to do + *activity* *faire de + *activity* **21**
to do my homework *faire mes devoirs **21**
docking station un dock [9]
dog un chien [2C], **AX**
door une porte [I, 9], **AX**
done fait (*p.p. of* *faire) **23**
downstairs en bas [13]
downtown en ville [6]
dozen une douzaine **25**
dress une robe **17**
drink une boisson [3B], **25**
to **drink** *boire **26**
drive: to take a drive *faire une promenade en voiture **14**
drums une batterie **15**
dumb bête [11]
during pendant **21**
DVD un DVD [9]

ear une oreille [E2]
to **earn** gagner **20**
Easter Pâques *m.* **21**
at Easter à Pâques **21**
easy facile [12]
to **eat** manger [7], **AX**
I like to eat j'aime manger [5]
to eat breakfast *prendre le petit déjeuner **25**
to eat dinner dîner [7], **25**
to eat lunch déjeuner **25**
to eat (some) manger + du, de la (partitive) **26**
egg un oeuf **25**
eight •huit [1A], **AX**
eighteen dix-huit [1B], **AX**
eighth •huitième **16**
eighty quatre-vingts [2B], **AX**
elegant élégant **17**
elephant un éléphant [E4]

eleven onze [1B], [3C]
eleventh onzième **16**
English anglais(e) [1B, 11], **AX**
errand: to run errands *faire les courses **25**
evening un soir **21**
in the evening du soir [4A]
this evening ce soir **23**
tomorrow evening demain soir **21, 23**
event un événement **14**
everything tout
everything's going (very) well ça va (très) bien [1C]
everything's (going) so-so ça va comme ci, comme ça [1C]
how's everything? ça va? [1C]
exam un examen
to pass an exam réussir à un examen **19**
excuse me excusez-moi [13]
expensive cher (chère) **17**
eye un oeil (*pl.* yeux) [E2]

fall l'automne [4C], **AX**
in (the) fall en automne [4C]
false faux (fausse) [12]
family une famille [2C], **16**
far (from) loin (de) [13]
fashion la mode
in fashion (fashionable) à la mode **17**
fat: to get fat grossir **19**
father un père **16**
this is my father voici mon père [2C]
February février *m.* [4B], **AX**
to **feel like** *avoir envie de + *inf.* **20**
few: a few quelques [9]
fifteen quinze [1B], **AX**
fifth cinquième **16**
fifty cinquante [1C], **AX**
film un film **14, 21**
finally finalement **22**
to **find** trouver **17**
fine ça va [1C]
fine! d'accord [5]
everything's fine ça va bien [1C]
that's fine c'est bien [12]
to **finish** finir **19**
finished fini (*p.p. of* finir) **23**
first d'abord **22;** premier (première) **16**
it's (June) first c'est le premier (juin) [4B]
fish un poisson **25**
five cinq **[1A], AX**
to **fix** réparer **21**
flute une flûte **15**
food la nourriture **25**
foot un pied [E2]
on foot à pied **14**
for pour [6]
for whom? pour qui? [8]
fork une fourchette **25**
forty quarante [1C], **AX**
four quatre [1A], **AX**
fourteen quatorze [1B], **AX**
fourth quatrième **16**
franc (former monetary unit of France) un franc [3C]
that's (it's) ... francs ça fait... francs [3C]
France la France [6]
in France en France [6]
French français(e) [1B, 11], **AX**
how do you say ... in French? comment dit-on... en français? [I]
French fries des frites *f.* **25**
steak and French fries un steak-frites [3A]
Friday vendredi *m.* [4B], **AX**
friend un ami, une amie [2A], un copain, une copine [2A], **AX**
school friend un (une) camarade [9]
from de **22**
from (the) du, de la, de l', des **15**
from where? d'où? **15**
are you from ...? tu es de...? [1B]
I'm from ... je suis de... [1B]
front: in front of devant [9]
fruit(s) des fruits *m.* **25**
funny amusant [11]; drôle [12]

to **gain weight** grossir **19**
game un jeu (*pl.* jeux) **15;** un match **14**
to play a game (match) *faire un match [8]
to play a game jouer à + *game* **15**
garage un garage [13]
garden un jardin [13]
gentleman un monsieur (*pl.* messieurs) [2A]
to **get: to get fat** grossir **19**
to get thin maigrir **19**
girl une fille [2A], **AX**
to **give (to)** donner (à) **27, 28**
give me donne-moi, **donnez-moi** [3A, 3B]
please give me s'il te plaît donne-moi [3B]
glass un verre **25**
glasses des lunettes *f.* **17**
sunglasses des lunettes *f.* de soleil **17**
to **go** *aller **14**
go ahead! vas-y! **14**
go away! va-t'en! **14**
to go (come) back rentrer **14, 24;** *revenir **15**
to go by bicycle *aller en vélo **14**
to go by car, by train ... *aller en auto, en train... **14**
to go food shopping *faire les courses **25**
to go rock climbing *faire de l'escalade **21**
to go shopping *faire des achats **21**
to go to assister à **21**
gone allé(e) (*p.p. of* *aller) **24**
good bon (bonne) [12]
good morning (afternoon) bonjour [1A]
that's good c'est bien [12]
the weather's good (pleasant) il fait bon [4C]
good-bye! au revoir!, salut! [1C]
good-looking beau (bel, belle; *m.pl.* beaux) [9, 12], **19**
grandfather un grand-père [2C], **16**
grandmother une grand-mère [2C], **16**
grandparents les grands-parents *m.* **16**
grape juice le jus de raisin [3B]
grapefruit un pamplemousse **25**
gray gris [12], **AX**
great super [12], **17**
green vert [E1, 12], **AX**

green beans les •haricots *m.* verts **25**
guitar une guitare [9], **15**

had eu (*p.p. of* *avoir) **23**
hair les cheveux *m.* [E2], **15**
he/she has dark hair il/elle est brun(e) [9]
half: half past ... ... heure(s) et demie [4A], **AX**
half past midnight minuit et demi [4A], **AX**
half past noon midi et demi [4A], **AX**
ham le jambon **25**
hamburger un hamburger [3A]
hand une main [E2]
handbag un sac [9]
handsome beau (bel, belle; *m.pl.* beaux) [9, 12], **19**
hard difficile [12] **17**
to **hate** détester **25**
to **have** *avoir [10]; (*food*) *prendre **26**
do you have ...? est-ce que tu as...? [9]
I have j'ai [9]
I have to (must) je dois [5]
to have (some) *avoir + du, de la (*partitive*); *prendre + du, de la (*partitive*) **26**
to have a picnic *faire un pique-nique **21**
to have breakfast *prendre le petit déjeuner **25**
to have dinner dîner **25**
to have dinner at a restaurant dîner au restaurant [5]
to have to *avoir besoin de + *inf.* **20**; *devoir **27**
he il [3C, 6, 10]; lui **15**
he/she is ... il/elle est + *nationality* [2B]
head la tête [E2]
to **hear** entendre **20**
hello bonjour [1A, 1C]
to **help** aider **21, 27**
may I help you? vous désirez? [3B], **17**
her elle **15**; son, sa; ses **16**; la **28**
(to) her lui **28**
her name is ... elle s'appelle... [2B] **R1**
what's her name? comment s'appelle-t-elle? [9]
here ici [6]
here comes, here is voici [2A]
here's my mother/father voici ma mère/mon père [2C]
here's some voici + du, de la (*partitive*) **26**
this ... (over here) ce... -ci **18**
hey! dis! [12]; tiens! [2A, 10]
hey there! dis donc! [12]
hi! salut! [1C]
high school student un (une), élève [9], **AX**
him lui **15**; le **28**
(to) him lui **28**
his son, sa; ses **16**
his name is ... il s'appelle... [2B], **R1**
what's his name? comment s'appelle-t-il? [9]
home, at home à la maison [6], **AX**; chez **(moi, toi...) 15**
to go home rentrer **14, 24**
homework les devoirs *m.* **21**
homework assignment un devoir [I]
to do my homework *faire mes devoirs **21**
to **hope** espérer **18**
horse un cheval (*pl.* chevaux) [E4]
hospital un hôpital [13]
hot chaud [4C], **23**
hot chocolate un chocolat [3B]
hot dog un •hot dog [3A]
to be hot (*people*) *avoir chaud **22**
it's hot (*weather*) il fait chaud [4C]
hotel un hôtel [13]
house une maison [13]
at someone's house chez + *person* **14**
how? comment? [8]
how are you? comment allez-vous?, comment vas-tu?, ça va? [1C]
how do you find ...? comment trouves-tu...? **17**
how do you say ... in French? comment dit-on... en français? [I]
how much? combien (de)? **20**
how much does ... cost? combien coûte...? [3C], **17**
how much is that/this/it? c'est combien?, ça fait combien? [3C]
how old are you? quel âge as-tu? [2C], **R1**
how old is he/she? quel âge a-t-il/elle? [9] **R1**
how old is your father/mother? quel âge a ton père/ta mère? [2C]
how's everything? ça va? [1C]
how's the weather? quel temps fait-il? [4C]
to learn how to *apprendre à **26**
hundred cent [2B], **17, AX**
hungry avoir faim [3A]
are you hungry? tu as faim? [3A]
I'm hungry j'ai [3A]
to be hungry avoir faim [10], **22**
husband un mari **16**

I je [6], moi **15**
I don't know je ne sais pas [I, 9]
I have a date/appointment at ... j'ai un rendez-vous à... [4A]
I know je sais [I, 9], **28**
I'm fine/okay ça va [1C]
I'm (very) well/so-so/(very) bad ça va (très) bien/comme ci, comme ça/(très) mal [1C]
ice la glace [3A], **25**
ice cream une glace [3A], **25**
iced tea un thé glacé **25**
idea une idée **20**
it's (that's) a good idea c'est une bonne idée **20**
if si
in à [6], **14**; dans [9]
in (Boston) à (Boston) [6]
in class en classe [6]
in front of devant [9], **R2**
in order to pour **21**
in the afternoon de l'après-midi [4A]
in the morning/evening du matin/soir [4A]

in town en ville [6]
in (the) au, à la, à l', aux **14**
inexpensive bon marché (*inv.*) **17**
ingredient un ingrédient **25**
in-line skating le roller **21**
in-line skates des rollers **21**
to go in-line skating faire du roller **21**
instrument un instrument **15**
to play a musical instrument jouer de + *instrument* **15**
intelligent intelligent **25**
interesting intéressant [11], **AX**
to invite inviter [7]
is (*see* **to be**)
is there? est-ce qu'il y a? [9], **R2**
isn't it (so)? n'est-ce pas? [6]
there is il y a [9] **R2**
there is (some) il y a + du, de la (*partitive*) **26**
it il, elle [6], [10]; le, la **28**
it's ... c'est... [2A]
it's ... (o'clock) il est... heure(s) [4A]
it's ... euros ça fait... euros [3C]
it's fine/nice/hot/cool/cold/bad (*weather*) il fait beau/bon/chaud/frais/froid/mauvais [4C], **AX**
it's (June) first c'est le premier (juin) [4B]
it's not ce n'est pas [12]
it's raining il pleut [4C], **AX**
it's snowing il neige [4C], **AX**
what time is it? quelle heure est-il? [4A]
who is it? qui est-ce? [2A, 9]
its son, sa; ses **16**
Italian italien, italienne [11], **AX**

J

jacket un blouson, une veste **17**
jam la confiture **25**
January janvier *m.* [4B], **AX**
Japanese japonais(e) [11], **AX**
jeans: pair of jeans un jean **17**
to jog *faire du jogging **21**
jogging le jogging **21**
jogging suit un jogging, un survêtement **17**
juice le jus
apple juice le jus de pomme [3B], **25**
grape juice le jus de raisin [3B]
orange juice le jus d'orange [3B], **25**
tomato juice le jus de tomate [3B]
July juillet *m.* [4B], **AX**
June juin *m.* [4B], **AX**

K

ketchup le ketchup **25**
keyboard un clavier **15**
kilogram un kilo (de) **25**
kind gentil (gentille) [11]
kitchen une cuisine [13]
knife un couteau **25**
to know *connaître **36**
do you know ...? tu connais...? [2B]
I (don't) know je (ne) sais (pas) [I, 9], **28**
you know tu sais **28**

L

lady une dame [2A], **AX**
lamp une lampe [9]
large grand [9], [12]
last dernier (dernière) **23**
last month le mois dernier **23**
last night hier soir **23**
last Saturday samedi dernier **23**
at last enfin **22**
to learn (how to) *apprendre (à) + *inf.* **26**
left gauche
on (to) the left à gauche [13]
leg une jambe [E2]
lemon soda la limonade [3B]
to lend prêter (à) **27, 28**
lend me prête-moi [3C]
less ... than moins... que **19**
let's go! allons-y! **14**
lettuce la salade **25**
library une bibliothèque [13]
like: what does he/she look like? comment est-il/elle? [9]
what's he/she like? comment est-il/elle? [9]
to like aimer [7]
do you like? est-ce que tu aimes? [5]
I also like j'aime aussi [5]
I don't always like je n'aime pas toujours [5]
I don't like je n'aime pas [5]
I like j'aime [5]
I like ..., but I prefer ... j'aime..., mais je préfère... [5]
I'd like je voudrais [3A, 3B, 5]
what would you like? vous désirez? [3B], 17
to listen écouter [7]
to listen to CDs écouter des CD **21**
to listen to the radio écouter la radio [5], **AX**
little petit [9, 12], **17**
a little (bit) un peu [7]
to live habiter [7]
living room (*formal*) un salon [13]
to loan prêter (à) **27, 28**
long long (longue) **17**
to look (at) regarder [7], **AX**
look! tiens! [2A, 10]
look at that regarde ça [9]
I'm looking for ... je cherche... **17**
to look for chercher **17**
what does he/she look like? comment est-il/elle? [9]
to lose perdre **20**
to lose weight maigrir **19**
lot: a lot beaucoup [7]
to love: I'd love to je veux bien [5]
luck la chance **22**
to be lucky *avoir de la chance **22**
lunch le déjeuner **25**
to have (eat) lunch déjeuner **25**

M

made fait (*p.p. of* *faire) **23**
to make *faire [8]
man un homme [9]; un monsieur (*polite term*) [2A], **AX**
many beaucoup (de) [7]
how many combien de **20**
map une carte [I]
March mars *m.* [4B], **AX**
match un match [8]
to play a match *faire un match [8]
May mai *m.* [4B], **AX**

may *pouvoir **27**
maybe peut-être [6]
mayonnaise la mayonnaise **25**
me moi [1A], **27**
excuse me pardon [13], **17**
(to) me me, moi **27**
meal un repas **25**
mean méchant [11], **AX**
to mean *vouloir dire **26**
what does … mean? que veut dire…? [I]
meat la viande **25**
to meet rencontrer **21**
to meet for the first time *connaître (*in passé composé*) **28**
Mexican mexicain(e) [11], **AX**
midnight minuit *m.* [4A]
milk le lait **25**
mineral water l'eau *f.* minérale **25**
Miss Mademoiselle (Mlle) [1C]
modern moderne [13]
Monday lundi *m.* [4B], **AX**
money l'argent *m.* **21**
month un mois [4B], **19**
last month le mois dernier **23**
next month le mois prochain **23**
this month ce mois-ci **23**
moped une mob (mobylette) [9]
more … than plus… que **19**
morning le matin **21**
good morning bonjour [1A]
in the morning du matin [4A]
this morning ce matin **21**
tomorrow morning demain matin **23**
yesterday morning hier matin **23**
mother une mère [2C], **16**
this is my mother voici ma mère [2C]
motorbike une mob (mobylette) [9], **AX**
motorcycle une moto [9], **AX**
motorscooter un scooter [9], **AX**
mountain une montagne **21**
mountain bike un VTT **21**
mountain biking le VTT **21**
to do mountain biking faire du VTT **21**
to (at/in) the mountain(s) à la montagne **21**
mouth une bouche [E2]
movie un film **14, 21**
movie theater un cinéma [6]
movies le cinéma [13]
at (to) the movies au cinéma [6]
MP3 player un (lecteur) MP3 [9]
Mr. Monsieur (M.) [1C]
Mrs. Madame (Mme) [1C]
much, very much beaucoup [7]
how much? combien? **20**
how much does … cost? combien coûte…? [3C], **17**
how much is it? ça fait combien?, c'est combien? [3C]
too much trop **17**
museum un musée [13]
music la musique **15**
must *devoir **27**
I must je dois [5]
my mon, ma; mes [2C], **16**
my birthday is (March 2) mon anniversaire est le (2 mars) [4B], **AX**
my name is … je m'appelle… [1A], **R1**

name: his/her name is … il/elle s'appelle… [2B]
my name is … je m'appelle… [1A]
what's…'s name? comment s'appelle…? [2B]
what's his/her name? comment s'appelle-t-il/elle? [9]
what's your name? comment t'appelles-tu? [1A]
napkin une serviette **25**
nasty méchant [11]
nationality la nationalité [1B], **AX**
nearby près [13]
neat chouette [12]
neck le cou [E2]
to need *avoir besoin de **20**
neighbor un voisin, une voisine [9], **AX**
neighborhood un quartier [13]
a nice neighborhood un joli quartier [13]
never ne… jamais **24**
new nouveau (nouvel, nouvelle; *m.pl.* nouveaux) **19**
next prochain **21, 23**
next week la semaine prochaine **23**
nice gentil (gentille), sympathique [11], **AX**
it's nice (beautiful) weather il fait beau [4C]
night: tomorrow night demain soir [4A]
last night hier soir **23**
nine neuf [1A], **AX**
nineteen dix-neuf [1B], **AX**
ninety quatre-vingt-dix [2B], **AX**
ninth neuvième **16**
no non [1B], [6]
no … pas de [10], **26**
no? n'est-ce pas? [6]
nobody ne… personne, personne **24**
noon midi *m.* [4A]
nose le nez [E2]
not ne… pas [6]
not a, not any pas de [10], **26**
not always pas toujours [5]
not anybody ne… personne **24**
not anything ne… rien **24**
not at all pas du tout **15**
it's (that's) not ce n'est pas [12]
of course not! mais non! [6]
notebook un cahier [I, 9]
nothing ne… rien, rien **24**
November novembre *m.* [4B], **AX**
now maintenant [7], **23**

o'clock heure(s)
at … o'clock à… heures [4A]
it's … o'clock il est… heure(s) [4A]
object un objet [9], **AX**
ocean la mer **21**; l'océan *m.*
to (at) the oceanside à la mer **21**
October octobre *m.* [4B], **AX**
of de [6]
of (the) du, de la, de l', des **15**
of course not! mais non! [6]
of course! bien sûr [5]
of whom de qui [8]
often souvent [7]
oh: oh, really? ah, bon? [8]
okay d'accord [5]

I'm okay ça va [1C]
old vieux (vieil, vieille; *m.pl.* vieux) **19**
he/she is ... (years old) il/elle a... ans [2C]
how old are you? quel âge as-tu? [2C]
how old is he/she? quel âge a-t-il/elle? [9]
how old is your father/mother? quel âge a ton père/ta mère? [2C]
I'm ... (years old) j'ai... ans [2C]
to be ... (years old) *avoir ... ans [10]
omelet une omelette [3A]
on sur [9], **R2**
on foot à pied **14**
on Monday lundi [10]
on Mondays le lundi [10]
on vacation en vacances [6]
one un, une **1**; (*we, they, people*) on **20**
oneself: by oneself seul **21**
only seul **21**
open ... ouvre... (ouvrez...) [I]
opinion: in my opinion à mon avis **19**
or ou [1B, 6]
orange (*color*) orange (*inv.*) [E1, 12]
orange *(fruit)* une orange **25**
orange juice le jus d'orange [3B], **25**
order: in order to pour **21**
to **organize** organiser [7], **AX**
other autre **25**
our notre; nos **16**
out of style démodé **17**
over: over (at) ...'s house chez... **15**
over there là-bas [6]
that (one), over there ça, **là-bas** [9]
overcoat un manteau (*pl.* manteaux) **17**
to **own** *avoir [10]

P.M. du soir [4A]
pain: a pain pénible [12]
pants un pantalon **17**
pantyhose des collants *m.* **17**
paper le papier [I]
sheet of paper une feuille de papier [I]
parents les parents *m.* **16**
park un parc [13]
party (*informal*) une fête, une soirée, une boum **14**
to **pass a test (an exam)** réussir à un examen **19**
past: half past ... ... heure(s) et demie [4A]
quarter past ... ... heure(s) et quart [4A]
to **pay (for)** payer **20**
to pay attention *faire attention [8], **AX**
pear une poire **25**
peas les petits pois *m.* **25**
pen un stylo [I, 9], **AX**
pencil un crayon [I, 9], **AX**
people des gens *m.* [10], **AX; on 20**
perhaps peut-être [6]
person une personne [2A, 9]
pet un animal (*pl.* animaux) domestique [2C], **AX**
to **phone** téléphoner [7]
piano un piano **15**
to **pick up** ranger **21**
picnic un pique-nique **14**
to have a picnic *faire un pique-nique **21**
pie une tarte **25**
piece: piece of chalk un morceau de craie **[I]**
ping-pong le Ping-Pong **15**
pink rose [12], **AX**
pizza une pizza [3A]
place un endroit **14**
place setting un couvert **25**
to **place** *mettre **18**
placed mis (*p.p. of* *mettre) **23**
plain moche **17**
plane un avion **21**
by plane en avion **21**
plate une assiette **25**
to **play** jouer [7]
to play a game jouer à + *game* **15**
to play a game (match) *faire un match [8], **AX**
to play a musical instrument jouer de + *instrument* **15**
to play basketball (soccer, tennis, volleyball) jouer au basket (au foot, au tennis, au volley) [5]
pleasant sympathique [11]
it's pleasant (good) weather il fait bon [4C]
please s'il vous plaît (*formal*) **[3B]; s'il te plaît** (*informal*) [3A]
please give me ... s'il te plaît, donne-moi... [3B]
polo shirt un polo **17**
pool: swimming pool une piscine [13]
poor pauvre **20**
poorly mal [1C]
popular à la mode **17**
poster une affiche [9]
potato une pomme de terre **25**
pound une livre (de) **25**
to **prefer** préférer **18, 25**
I prefer je préfère + *inf.* [5]
I like ..., but I prefer ... j'aime..., mais je préfère... [5]
to **prepare** préparer **21**
pretty joli [9], **17, AX**
price un prix **17**
what's the price? quel est **le prix? 17**
pullover un pull **17**
pupil un (une) élève [9]
to **purchase** acheter **21**
purple violet (violette) [E1], **AX**
to **put** *mettre **18**
to put on *mettre **18**

quantity une quantité **25**
quarter un quart
quarter of ... ... heure(s) moins le quart [4A], **AX**
quarter past ... ... heure(s) et quart [4A], **AX**

R

racket une raquette [9], **AX**
radio une radio [9], **AX**
to listen to the radio écouter la radio [5]
rain: it's raining il pleut [4C], **AX**
raincoat un imper (imperméable) **17**
rarely rarement [7]
rather assez [11]

really: oh, really? ah, bon? [8]
really?! vraiment?! **15**
red rouge [E1, 12], **AX**
relatives les parents *m.* **16**
to rent louer **21**
to repair réparer **21**
to respond répondre **28**
restaurant un restaurant [13]
at (to) the restaurant au restaurant [6]
have dinner at a restaurant dîner au restaurant [5]
to return rentrer **24;** *revenir **15**
rice le riz **25**
rich riche **20**
ride: to take a bicycle ride *faire une promenade à vélo **14**
right vrai [12]; droite
right? n'est-ce pas? [6]
all right d'accord [5]
to be right *avoir raison **22**
to (on) the right à droite [13]
roast beef le rosbif **25**
rock climbing l'escalade *f.* **21**
to do rock climbing *faire de l'escalade **21**
room une chambre [9]; une salle [13]
bathroom une salle de bains [13]
dining room une salle à manger [13]
formal living room un salon [13]
to run (*referring to objects*) marcher [9]

S

sailing la voile **21**
salad une salade [3A], **25**
salami le saucisson **25**
salt le sel **25**
sandal une sandale **17**
sandwich un sandwich [3A]
Saturday samedi *m.* [4B], **23**
see you Saturday! à samedi! [4B]
last Saturday samedi dernier **23**
next Saturday samedi prochain **23**
saw vu (*p.p. of* *voir) **23**
saxophone un saxo (saxophone) **15**
say *dire **28**
say … dites…
say! dis (donc)! [12]
how do you say … in French? comment dit-on… en français? [I]
school une école [13]
school cafeteria la cantine de l'école **25**
school friend un (une) camarade [9]
sea la mer **21**
to (at) the sea à la mer **21**
season une saison [4C]
second deuxième **16**
to see *voir **21**
see you tomorrow! à demain! [4B], **21**
seen vu (*p.p. of* *voir) **23**
seldom rarement [7]
to sell vendre **20**
September septembre *m.* 4B], **AX**
to set the table *mettre la table **25**
seven sept [1A], **AX**
seventeen dix-sept [1B], **AX**
seventh septième **16**
seventy soixante-dix [2A], **AX**
she elle [6, 10], **15**
sheet of paper une feuille de papier [I]
ship un bateau (*pl.* bateaux) **21**
shirt une chemise **17**
shoe une chaussure [2A]
tennis shoes des tennis *m.* **17**
shop une boutique **17**
shopping: shopping center un centre commercial [13]
to go food shopping *faire les courses **25**
to go shopping *faire des achats **21**
shore la mer **21**
short court **17;** petit [9, 12], **17**
he/she is short il/elle est petit(e) [9]
shorts un short **21**
should *devoir **35**
to show indiquer; montrer à **27, 28**
to shut fermer [I]
shy timide [11]
silly bête [11]
to sing chanter [5, 7], **AX**
sir Monsieur (M.) [1C]
sister une soeur [2C], **16**
six six [1A], **AX**
sixteen seize [1B], **AX**
sixth sixième **16**
sixty soixante [1C], [2A], **AX**
skateboard un skate
skateboarding le skate **21**
to go skateboarding faire du skate **21**
to ski *faire du ski **21**
skiing le ski **21**
skirt une jupe **17**
small petit [9, 12], **17**
sneakers des tennis *m.* **17**
hightop sneakers des baskets *m.* **17**
snow: it's snowing il neige [4C], **AX**
snowboard un snowboard, un surf (des neiges) **21**
snowboarding le snowboard, le surf (des neiges) **21**
to go snowboarding faire du snowboard **21**
so alors [7]
so-so comme ci, comme ça [1C]
everything's (going) so-so ça va comme ci, comme ça [1C]
soccer le foot (football) **15**
sock une chaussette **17**
soda un soda [3B]
lemon soda une limonade [3B]
sold vendu (*p.p. of* vendre) **23**
sole (*fish*) la sole **25**
some des [10]; du, de la, de l' **26;** quelques [9]
somebody quelqu'un **24**
someone quelqu'un **24**
something quelque chose **24**
son un fils **16**
sorry: to be sorry regretter
I'm sorry, but (I cannot) je regrette, mais (je ne peux pas) [5]
soup la soupe **25**
spaghetti les spaghetti *m.* **25**
Spanish espagnol(e) [11], **AX**
to speak parler [7]
to speak (French, English, Spanish) parler (français, anglais, espagnol) [5]
to speak to parler à **28**
to spend (*money*) dépenser **20;** (*time*) passer **21**

spoon une cuillère **25**
sports le sport **21**
to play a sport *faire du sport **21**; jouer à + *sport* **15**
sports clothing des vêtements *m.* de sport **17**
spring le printemps [4C], **AX**
in the spring au printemps [4C]
stadium un stade [13]
to stay rester **14**
steak un steak [3A]
steak and French fries un steak-frites [3A]
stereo set une chaîne hi-fi [9], **AX**
stomach le ventre [E2]
store un magasin [13], **17**
department store un grand magasin **17**
straight tout droit [13]
strawberry une fraise **25**
street une rue [13]
student (*high school*) un (une) élève [9]; (*college*) un étudiant, une étudiante [9]
to **study** étudier [5, 7], **AX**
stupid bête [11]
style: in style à la mode **17**
out of style démodé **17**
subway le métro **14**
by subway en métro **14**
to **succeed** réussir **19**
sugar le sucre **25**
summer l'été *m.* [4C]
summer vacation les grandes vacances **21**
in the summer en été [4C]
sun le soleil **17**
Sunday dimanche *m.* [4B], **AX**
sunglasses des lunettes *f.* de soleil **17**
supermarket un supermarché [13]
supper le dîner **25**
to have (eat) supper dîner [7], **25**
sure bien sûr [5]
sure! mais oui! [6]
are you sure? tu es sûr(e)? **16**
sweater un pull **17**
sweatshirt un sweat **17**
to **swim** nager [7], **AX**
I like to swim j'aime nager [5]
swimming pool une piscine [13]
swimsuit un maillot de bain **17**
Swiss suisse [11]

table une table [I, 9], **AX**
to set the table *mettre la table **25**
tablet (computer) une tablette [9]
to **take** *prendre [I], **26**
to take along amener **18, 27**
to take a bicycle ride *faire une promenade à vélo **14**
to take a drive *faire une promenade en voiture **14**
to take a trip *faire un voyage [8], **AX**
to take a walk *faire une promenade à pied **14**
to **talk** parler [7]
to talk to parler à **28**
tall grand [9, 12]
taxi un taxi **14**
by taxi en taxi **14**
tea le thé [3B]
iced tea un thé glacé **25**
teacher un (une) prof [2A, 9]; un professeur [9]
telephone un téléphone [9], **AX**
to telephone téléphoner [7], **AX**
television la télé [9]
to watch television regarder la télé [5]
to **tell** *dire **28**
ten dix [1A, 1B], **AX**
tennis le tennis **15**
tennis racket une raquette de tennis **15**
tennis shoes des tennis *m.* **17**
to play tennis jouer au tennis [5]
tenth dixième **16**
terrific génial [12]; super [12], **17**
test un examen
to pass a test réussir à un examen **19**
text message un texto [9]
than que **19**
thank you merci [1C]
that que **17**; ce, cet, cette **18**
that is ... c'est... [9, 12]
that (one), over there ça, là-bas [9]
that's ... c'est... [2A, 9, 12]; voilà [2A]
that's ... euros ça fait... euros [3C]
that's bad c'est mal [12]
that's a good idea! c'est une bonne idée! **20**
that's good (fine) c'est bien [12]
that's not ... ce n'est pas... [12]
what's that? qu'est-ce que c'est? [9]
the le, la, l' [2B, 10]; les [10]
theater un théâtre [13]
movie theater un cinéma [13]
their leur, leurs **16**
them eux, elles **15**; les **28**
(to) them leur **28**
themselves eux-mêmes
then alors [11]; ensuite **22**
there là [6]
there is (are) il y a [9], **R2**
there is (here comes someone) voilà [2A]
there is (some) il y a + du, de la (*partitive*) **26**
there's some voilà + du, de la (*partitive*) **26**
over there là-bas [6]
that (one), over there ça, là-bas [9]; ce...-là **18**
what is there? qu'est-ce qu'il y a? [9]
these ces **18**
these are ce sont [12]
they ils, elles [6]; eux **15**; on **20**
they are ce sont [12]
thin: to get thin maigrir **19**
thing une chose
things are going (very) badly ça va (très) mal [1C]
to **think** penser **17**
to think of penser de, trouver **17**
to think that penser que **17**
what do you think of ...? comment trouves-tu...?, qu'est-ce que tu penses de...? **17**
third troisième **16**
thirsty: to be thirsty *avoir soif **22**
are you thirsty? tu as soif? [3B]
I'm thirsty j'ai soif [3B]

thirteen treize [1B], **AX**
thirty trente [1C], **AX**
3:30 trois heures et demie [4A]
this ce, cet, cette **18**
this is ... voici... [2A]
those ces **18**
those are ce sont [12]
thousand mille [2B], **17**
three trois [1A], **AX**
Thursday jeudi *m.* [4B], **AX**
tie une cravate **17**
tights des collants *m.* **17**
time: at what time is ...? à quelle heure est...? [4A]
at what time? à quelle heure? [4A]
what time is it? quelle heure est-il? [4A]
to à [6], **14;** chez **14, 15**
to (the) au, à la, à l', aux **14**
in order to pour **21**
to class en classe [6]
to someone's house chez + *person* **14**
to whom à qui [8]
today aujourd'hui [4B], **23**
today is (Wednesday) aujourd'hui, c'est (mercredi) [4B], **AX**
toilet les toilettes [13]
tomato une tomate
tomato juice le jus de tomate [3B]
tomorrow demain [4B], **AX**
tomorrow afternoon demain après-midi **23**
tomorrow is (Thursday) demain, c'est (jeudi) [4B], **AX**
tomorrow morning demain matin **23**
tomorrow night (evening) demain soir **23**
see you tomorrow! à demain! [4B], **21**
tonight ce soir **23**
too aussi [1B, 7]; trop **17**
too bad! dommage! [7]
touring bus un autocar, un car **21**
town un village [13]
in town en ville [6]
track suit un survêtement **17**
train un train **21**
by train en train **14, 21**
to **travel** voyager [5, 7], **AX**
trip: to take a trip *faire un voyage [8]
trousers un pantalon **17**
true vrai [12]
T-shirt un tee-shirt **17**
Tuesday mardi *m.* [4B], **AX**
tuna le thon **25**
to **turn** tourner [13]
to **turn on** *mettre **18**
TV la télé [9]
to **watch TV** regarder la télé [5]
twelfth douzième **16**
twelve douze [1B], **AX**
twenty vingt [1B, 1C], **AX**
two deux [1A], **AX**

ugly moche **17**
uncle un oncle [2C], **16, AX**
under sous [9]
to **understand** *comprendre **26**
I (don't) understand je (ne) comprends (pas) [I]
unfashionable démodé **17**
United States les États-Unis *m.*
upstairs en • haut [13]
us nous **15**
(to) us nous **27**

vacation les vacances *f.* **21**
on vacation en vacances [6]
summer vacation les grandes vacances **21**
veal le veau **25**
vegetable un légume **25**
very très [11]
very well très bien [7]
very much beaucoup [7]
violin un violon **15**
to **visit** (*place*) visiter [7], **20, AX**
(*people*) **rendre visite à 20, 28**
volleyball le volley (volleyball) **15**

to **wait (for)** attendre **20**
walk une promenade **14**
to take (go for) a walk *faire une promenade à pied **8, 14**
to walk *aller à pied **14;** marcher [9]
to **want** *avoir envie de **20;** *vouloir **26**
do you want ...? tu veux...? [3A]
do you want to ...? est-ce que tu veux...? [5]
I don't want ... je ne veux pas... [5]
I want ... je veux... [5], **26**
I want to je veux bien **26**
what do you want? qu'est-ce que tu veux? [3A]; vous désirez? [3B], **17**
wanted voulu (*p.p. of* *vouloir) **26**
warm chaud [4C], **23**
to be warm (*people*) *avoir chaud **22**
it's warm (*weather*) il fait chaud [4C]
was été (*p.p. of* *être) **23**
to **wash** laver **21**
to **waste** perdre **20**
watch une montre [9]
to **watch** regarder [7]
to watch TV regarder la télé [5]
water l'eau *f.* **25**
mineral water l'eau minérale **25**
to water-ski *faire du ski nautique **21**
water-skiing le ski nautique **21**
we nous [6], **15;** on **20**
to **wear** *mettre **18;** porter **17**
weather: how's (what's) the weather? quel temps fait-il? [4C]
it's ... weather il fait... [4C]
Wednesday mercredi *m.* [4B], **AX**
week une semaine [4B], **21**
last week la semaine dernière **23**
next week la semaine prochaine **23**
this week cette semaine **23**
weekend un week-end **21**
last weekend le week-end dernier **23**
next weekend le week-end prochain **21, 23**
this weekend ce week-end **23**
weight: to gain weight grossir **19**

well bien [7]
well! eh bien! **18**
well then alors [11]
everything's going (very) well ça va (très) bien [1C]
went allé (*p.p. of* *aller) **24, R2**
what comment? quoi? **17;** qu'est-ce que [8]
what color? de quelle couleur? [12], **AX**
what day is it? quel jour est-ce? [4B], **AX**
what do you think of ...? comment trouves-tu...?, qu'est-ce que tu penses de...? **17**
what do you want? qu'est-ce que tu veux? [3A]; vous désirez? [3B], **17**
what does ... mean? que veut dire...? [I]
what does he/she look like? comment est-il/elle? [9]
what is it? qu'est-ce que c'est? [9]
what is there? qu'est-ce qu'il y a? [9], **R2**
what time is it? quelle heure est-il? [4A]
what would you like? vous désirez? [3B], **17**
what's ...'s name? comment s'appelle...? [2B]
what's he/she like? comment est-il/elle? [9]
what's his/her name? comment s'appelle-t-il/elle? [9]
what's that? qu'est-ce que c'est? [9]
what's the date? quelle est la date? [4B], **AX**
what's the price? quel est le prix? **17**
what's the weather? quel temps fait-il? [4C], **AX**
what's your address? quelle est ton adresse? [13]
what's your name? comment t'appelles-tu? [1A], **R1**
at what time is ...? à quelle heure est...? [4A]
at what time? à quelle heure? [4A, 8]
when quand [8], **R3**
when is your birthday? c'est quand, ton anniversaire? [4B], **AX**
where où [6, 8], **R3**
where is ...? où est...? [6]
where is it? où est-ce? [13]
from where? d'où? [13]
whether si
which quel (quelle) **18**
white blanc (blanche) [E, 12], **AX**
who qui [8]
who's that/this? qui est-ce? [2A], [9]
whom? qui? **R3**
about whom? de qui? [8]
for whom? pour qui? [8]
of whom? de qui? [8]
to whom? à qui? [8], **R3**
with whom? avec qui? [8], **R3**
why pourquoi [8]
wife une femme **16**
to win gagner **20**
window une fenêtre [I, 9], **AX**
to windsurf *faire de la planche à voile **21**
windsurfing la planche à voile **21**
winter l'hiver *m.* [4C], **AX**
in the winter en hiver [4C]
with avec [6]
with me avec moi [5]
with you avec toi [5]
with whom? avec qui? [8], **R3**
woman une dame (*polite term*) [2A]; une femme [9], **AX**
to work travailler [5, 7], **AX;** (*referring to objects*) marcher [9], **AX**
does the radio work? est-ce que la radio marche? [9]
it (doesn't) work(s) well il/elle (ne) marche (pas) bien [9]
would: I'd like je voudrais [3A, 3B, 5]
to write *écrire **28**
wrong faux (fausse) [12]
to be wrong *avoir tort **22**

Y

year un an, une année [4B]
he/she is ... (years old) il/elle a... ans [2C]
I'm ... (years old) j'ai... ans [2C]
to be ... (years old) *avoir... ans [10]
yellow jaune [E1, 12]
yes oui [1B, 6]; (*to a negative question*) **si!** [10]
yes, of course oui, bien sûr [5]
yes, okay (all right) oui, d'accord [5]
yes, thank you oui, merci [5]
yesterday hier **23**
yesterday afternoon hier après-midi **23**
yesterday morning hier matin **23**
yogurt le yaourt **25**
you tu, vous [6], **15; on 20**
you are ... tu es + *nationality* [1B]
and you? et toi? [1A]
(to) you te, vous **27**
your ton, ta; tes [2C]; votre; vos **16**
what's your name? comment t'appelles-tu? [1A]
young jeune [9], **AX**

zero zéro [1A], **AX**

INDEX

CREDITS

Front Cover
©Patrice Coppee/Workbook Stock/Getty Images

Back Cover
Level 1a: ©David Noble/Travel Pictures
Level 1b: ©Patrice Coppee/Workbook Stock/Getty Images
Level 1: ©Travelpix Ltd/Stone/Getty Images
Level 2: ©David Sanger/The Image Bank/Getty Images
Level 3: ©Shaen Adey/Gallo Images/Getty Images

Photography
All photos by Lawrence Migdale/PIX except the following: 22 (t) ©S. Martin/ESA/Getty Images; 25 (tl, tr) ©ImageClub/Getty Images; 25 (cl) Courtesy National Archives, photo no. 19-N-1581; 25 (br) © Visions of America, LLC/Alamy; 25 (bl) ©Herbert Orth/Time Life Pictures/Getty Images; 195 (tl) ©Marc Sayag/Alamy; 195 (tcl) ©bobroy20/Fotolia; 195 (bcl) ©Jose Ignacio Soto/Fotolia; 195 (bl) ©Body Philippe/hemis.fr/Getty Images; 198 (cr) ©Corbis; 205 (t) ©leproducer/Fotolia; 212 (br) Getty Images; 217 (b) ©David R. Frazier Photolibrary, Inc./Alamy; 227 (tr) ©Comstock Images/Getty Images; 227 (br) ©PhotoDisc/Getty Images; 227 (tcl) PhotoDisc/Houghton; 227 (tcr) ©Sebastian Green/Alamy; 227 (bcl) ©Medioimages/Getty Images; 227 (bl) GK Hart/Vikki Hart/Photodisc/Getty Images; 235 (c) ©Stockbyte/Getty Images; 242 © Hergé/Moulinsart 2011; 243 © Hergé/Moulinsart 2011; 245 (tl) ©Andia/Alamy; 273 (b) ©D. Hurst/Alamy; 273 (b) ©Alfonso de Tomas/Alamy; 275 (tr) ©Jupiterimages/Getty Images; 275 (bc) ©Comstock Images/Getty Images; 275 (r) ©Sergey Galushko/Alamy; 283 (b) ©Alex Stokes/Alamy; 285 (r) ©Marie-Reine Mattera/Corbis; 288 (bl) ©Stockbyte/Getty Images; 305 (r) ©Frans Lemmens/Getty Images; 309 (t) ©Polypix/Imagestate Media Partners Limited - Impa/Alamy; 309 (br) ©Photo and Co/Stone/Getty Images; 312 (b) ©Andre Jenny/Alamy; 313 (br) ©Photo and Co/Stone/Getty Images; 315 (b) ©Mike Kemp/Tetra Images/Alamy; 321 (b) ©Wernher Krutein/Corbis; 331 (cr) ©RTimages/Fotolia; 331 (inset) ©Jeff Mitchell/FIFA/Getty Images; 341 (cr) ©Gail Mooney/Corbis; 344 ©Photononstop/Superstock; 356 (tr) ©Mitch Diamond/ImageState Media; 357 (br) ©Melissa Gaskell/Alamy; 358 (cr) ©Hipix/Alamy; 358 (tr) ©Kay Maeritz/Getty Images; 358 (bl) ©Gary Blakeley/Fotolia; 359 (t) ©Stamp Collection/Alamy; 362 (bg) ©Fotolia; 415 (cr) ©David Sanger Photography/Alamy; 416 (bg) ©anankkml/Fotolia; PA2 (cr) ©Geoff Manasse/Digital Vision/Getty Images